ADVANCE PRAISE FOR *THE TRUMP FILES*

This is Citizen Jack's book, a masterful demonstration of a personal view turned sociopolitical gold.

—**CHARLES R. AULT JR.**, Professor Emeritus, Lewis & Clark College

It must be noted that Jack Hassard is very personal in his writing tone. He does not spare his emotional sentiments on the political activities not only in his adopted state of Georgia, but the nation at large—and here, he takes no prisoners: he is very direct with his points and tells inconvenient and bitter truths that most of us wish we were as courageous enough to enunciate. It is here that, as an academic, he felt compelled to provide evidence to support them. This is where Hassard shines, because even if the reader does not agree with his political views, they are compelled to consider his evidence and arrive at better conclusions than they otherwise would have, but not before they have been baptized into an elevated awareness of how the world works. Hassard illustrates, with the pen of a maestro, why it is important for average citizens to be vigilant of governmental policies—not because it is politically advantageous to do so, but because it is our responsibility to do so.

—**CHARLES B. HUTCHISON**, PhD, The University of North Carolina at Charlotte

The Trump Files includes a real-time chronicling of events during the Trump presidency that reminds one of all the egregious actions, shattering of democratic norms, lies and misinformation, and abuse of power that took place over the course of four years. Provided is an excellent timeline of Trump and his administration's actions, statements, and activities during the Covid-19 pandemic, which resulted in hundreds of thousands of Americans losing their lives. Anti-science sentiments, intertwined with racial prejudice, politicized recommendations by the CDC to wear masks and social distance, and further polarized our country in red and blue states.

—**CAROL MAGLIO,** business owner, telecommunications pioneer, and citizen of Texas

By making his blog into a book, we can put the pieces together, event by event, amnesia attack after amnesia attack. At my section in the UN, our motto was "The devil is in the details." Hassard continues to be a fine citizen diplomat, using his skills to try to bring peace and understanding to the world. So harness your hopes and dig in. All of you should enjoy this book.

—**PAUL HILLERY,** former United Nations researcher; writer, lecturer, and editor, Mannheim, Germany

THE TRUMP FILES

THE
TRUMP
FILES

AN ACCOUNT
OF THE TRUMP
ADMINISTRATION'S
EFFECT ON
AMERICAN
DEMOCRACY,
HUMAN RIGHTS,
SCIENCE,
AND PUBLIC HEALTH

JACK HASSARD

Copyright © 2022 by Jack Hassard

All rights reserved. No part of this book may be reproduced in any form, without written permission from the publisher.

 Northington-Hearn

Published in the United States by Northington-Hearn Publishing
Marietta, Georgia, 2022
www.northington-hearn.com

Library of Congress Cataloging-in-Publication Data
Names: Jack Hassard, author. Charles R. Ault Jr., writer of foreword.
Title: The Trump Files: An Account of the Trump Administration's Effect on American Democracy, Human Rights, Science, and Public Health.
Description: Marietta, GA: Northington-Hearn Publishing (2022). Includes bibliographical references and index.

ISBN 979-8-9854857-0-7 (hardcover)
ISBN 979-8-9854857-1-4 (paperback)
ISBN 979-8-9854857-2-1 (ebook)

BIO010000 BIOGRAPHY & AUTOBIOGRAPHY / Political
BIO011000 BIOGRAPHY & AUTOBIOGRAPHY / Presidents & Heads of State
POL046000 POLITICAL SCIENCE / Commentary & Opinion

Editing and design services provided by Indigo: Editing, Design, and More, www.indigoediting.com
Developmental editing and line editing by Kristen Hall-Geisler
Proofreading by Sarah Currin and Bailey Potter
Cover and interior book design by Jenny Kimura
Ebook conversion by Vinnie Kinsella
Indexing by Kento Ikeda

Printed in the United States of America
1st Printing

For
Mary-Alice

CONTENTS

Citizen Jack — xi
Prologue — 1

PART I: TRUMPISM — 18
Chapter 1: Authoritarianism — 49
Chapter 2: Dangerousness — 60
Chapter 3: Moral Worldviews — 71

PART II: RIGHTS — 86
Chapter 4: Racial Justice — 102
Chapter 5: Free and Fair Elections — 114

PART III: SCRUTINY — 121
Chapter 6: Investigations — 128

PART IV: SCIENCE — 139
Chapter 7: Degrading the Environmental Protection Agency — 159
Chapter 8: Fires, Hurricanes, and Floods — 173
Chapter 9: Existential Threats — 191

PART V: COVID-19 — 221
Chapter 10: SARS-CoV-2 — 253
Chapter 11: Trump's COVID-19 Response — 267
Chapter 12: School in the Age of COVID-19 — 290

PART VI: DEPARTURE — 301
Chapter 13: Political Violence — 309

Epilogue	328
Further Reading	343
Acknowledgments	347
Index	355
About the Author	371

CITIZEN JACK

Scientists often characterize the Earth as interacting spheres: atmosphere, biosphere, and geosphere. By analogy, humanity creates its own spheres of interaction. The simplest example is the blogosphere—the interconnected community of internet writers and thinkers, a subset of the noosphere, the realm of mind. My interactions with the mind of Jack Hassard began through an encounter with his blog, now converted into this magnificent book, *The Trump Files: An Account of the Trump Administration's Effect on American Democracy, Human Rights, Science, and Public Health*. His vivid, real-time documentation of the nation's turbulent Trump years returns the reader to those troubling days of not-so-very-long-ago. His commentaries make time travel feel possible.

Despite the discomfort, there is great value in revisiting and revitalizing memories of the recent political craziness. It turns out, despite Jeb Bush's debate admonition to his strangely coiffured opponent, one *can* insult their way to the presidency. What began with insults ended (or paused?) with the Big Lie of election fraud. Pundits and journalists, biographers and historians, business associates and family members, politicians and psychologists: all have competed for the listener and reader attention in their efforts to deliver definitive analysis of the Trump phenomenon. Jack Hassard offers something different and refreshing and, at the same time, sobering. Between the lines you might detect the ominous voice of Will Robinson's robot uttering in deep tones, "Danger, danger, America."

He offers the reader a citizen's perspective buffered by careful synthesis of scholarly analyses. Every chapter is accessible and engaging; his portrait of Trump, detailed and complete, nuanced and stark, drawn from his experiences as a geoscientist, global environmental educator, university professor, and Georgian. This is Citizen Jack's book, a masterful demonstration of a personal view turned sociopolitical gold.

Trump knows, or thinks he knows, Russia—a place of easy credit and oligarchs interested in purchasing luxury real estate. Americans, as a consequence of Russian electoral interference and disinformation, think of Russia as sinister and threatening.

Jack Hassard knows a different Russia. His blog posts about the news of WikiLeaks, timed to defeat Hillary Clinton, prompted him to reflect on years of his collaboration with his counterparts in Russia. Diplomacy for President Trump meant "deals"—deals to build towers and sponsor pageants, all in the name of enriching the Trump brand (e.g., in 2007, Trump vodka). Jack Hassard, in contrast, practiced "citizen diplomacy," the long-term commitment to building relationships and trust, embodied in twenty years of extensive involvement in the Global Thinking Project, led in Russia by Dr. Galena Manke and Dr. Anatoly Zakhlebny.[1]

Hassard prizes his personal relationships with educators from other nations, the student exchanges they organized together, and the contributions cross-cultural understanding can make to reducing the risk of nuclear war and climate catastrophe. The contrast between Jack Hassard's perspective and Donald Trump's record in regard to these existential threats is profound. For Jack, youth and hopes for their future come first, not branding for profit.

Concern for youth stems naturally from a life as an educator. Jack recently reposted on his blog, *The Art of Teaching Science* (jackhassard.org), a fictional letter from an adolescent living in 2051. His imaginary student, Skyler F., expressed how much she valued her school-day lessons on why people's opinions are hard to change.

---

[1] Dr. Galina Manke was a biology teacher at Moscow School 710 and researcher at the Academy of Pedagogical Sciences. Anatoly Zakhlebny is chief researcher of the Federal State Institute for the Development of Educational Strategy at the Russian Academy of Education. He is a professor and doctor of pedagogical sciences, as well as chairman of the Scientific Council on Environmental Problems of the Russian Academic of Education. Zakhlebny is the author of more than two hundred publications and is editor in chief of the journal *Ecological Education*.

JACK HASSARD

Skyler's reflections gave Jack a chance to share reliable, expert climate science. Hassard has had a field day drawing attention to the gap between reliable science, depended upon for the exercise of responsible citizenship, and Trump's climate change denialism, medical science quackery, and reinforcement of anti-science bias in the nation. *The Trump Files* lays bare the Trump administration's record on censorship, politicization of grants, sidelining experts, and suppressing information at odds with its agenda.

Malfeasance in the communication of scientific knowledge merely ices the cake of Trumpian political shenanigans that alarm Jack, especially as a citizen of Georgia. Local politics are personal politics. He shares his in-depth account of the pressures on Georgian electoral officials to alter the vote count as well as his local perspective on the significance of electing two Democratic senators (Raphael Warnock and Jon Ossoff)—the outcome that tipped the US Senate. As a Georgian, these events were more than news to Jack, and his daily blogs tracked the drama.

In terms of human suffering and the consequences of disinformation, the COVID-19 pandemic stands as the most significant political story of the Trump years. As a senior citizen and retiree, not to mention scientist, Jack's antennae tuned into the unfolding interplay between undeniable events and White House spin. Reading daily blog entries, in time travel fashion, recreates the tension.

The events of January 6, 2021, maximized his blogging intensity. Soon afterward, the House impeached the president for sedition. The Big Lie (the assumption of electoral fraud) endures sans evidence, becoming a litmus test for Republican base support. Jack's year of reflection while writing *The Trump Files* only intensified their meaning and significance to him.

Jack's blog, his primary database, anchors the book, but he examines events with reports and analyses from many other well-respected sources. At crucial junctures *The Trump Files* organizes months of entries as comprehensive charts—in effect, frightening timelines to revisit.

Citizen Jack has blogged about science, climate, education, and politics since 2005. He was ready with the right tool at the right time to capture an epoch of American history that will reverberate for decades. Watching with astonishment as the Trump years unfolded, he asked why Americans have been receptive to Trump's messaging and susceptible to his dishonesty (ten to fifteen lies per day!), immorality, and narcissism. He asks readers to ponder how the citizens of the United States might restore the norms of a democratic society, beginning with securing voting rights.

In 1992 I introduced my students, future teachers, to a well-conceived textbook by Jack Hassard, *Minds on Science*, and drew upon its main ideas for a long time. In 2015 I happened upon his rhetoric treating science teaching as an art. Jack continues to hone his talents as a painter and has consistently demonstrated his capacity as a thinker. With the eye of an artist and the mind of a scholar, Jack brings to life the days and details of pandemic and insurrection, plus the threats of dishonesty and suppression we dare not forget. Parts of the manuscript read as if the events are unfolding in real time, as if reported in the 1947–1957 CBS television and radio news program *You Are There*.

Exhibit designers in museums, zoos, and aquaria present visitors with "layered text." A bold, brief level functions like a newspaper headline. Linger at the exhibit and you will notice more text—on the scale of a brief tweet. Sometimes on headphones, sometimes in writing, the final layer fills in the important details about, for example, how penguins communicate with body language. *The Trump Files* places on exhibit the six years (pre-election to post-insurrection) of Donald Trump at center stage in the nation's consciousness. The book's organization enables readers to delve layer by layer into Jack's reconstruction and analysis of these years. He treats them topically: Trumpism and authoritarianism, the pandemic and mismanagement, anti-science and misinformation, insurrection and suppression of rights, departure and prospects for the future.

Trump railed about "fake news." From one citizen's perspective, dishonesty, more than any other attribute, characterizes Trump's legacy. Try on Citizen Jack's goggles and look at the world we endured. Try not to flinch.

Charles R. Ault Jr.
Professor Emeritus, Lewis & Clark College
Author, *Beyond Science Standards*
Blog: kip-ault.com

PROLOGUE

In a dark time, the eye begins to see.
—Theodore Rothke, "In a Dark Time"

DURING A BEAUTIFUL MIDDAY CEREMONY ON JANUARY 20, 2021, I watched the inauguration of a new American president. On this day Joe Biden and Kamala Harris were sworn in as the president and vice president of the United States, respectively. But it wasn't the peaceful transfer of power from the sitting president to his successor that we normally experience. Donald Trump refused to attend Joe Biden's inauguration. Trump forgot that four years earlier he said at his 2017 inauguration that "every four years, we gather on these steps to carry out the orderly and peaceful transfer of power, and we are grateful to President Obama and First Lady Michelle Obama for their graciousness throughout this transition. They have been magnificent."[2]

Trump's solipsism prevented him from attending the ceremony that would transfer his power to President-Elect Biden. After all, he's made it clear that "only he can fix it." How could he possibly recognize Biden as the next president? He's not conceded and insists he won the election by a landslide.

Instead, he fled from Washington early in the morning on the same day, to Mar-a-Lago, a resort in Palm Beach, Florida. For four years this

---

[2] "Inaugural Address, Donald Trump," Inaugural Address | The American Presidency Project, January 20, 2017, retrieved April 1, 2022, https://www.presidency.ucsb.edu/documents/inaugural-address-14.

president held America hostage. Regrettably, he continues with his pathetic fable that he didn't lose the 2020 election, that it was stolen.

From 2015 forward, my blog told story after story about a strangely coiffed New York television personality and businessperson with no experience in government or governing, except being sued by the Department of Justice for human rights abuses by refusing to rent to Black families.[3] Derived from my stories, *The Trump Files: An Account of the Trump Administration's Effect on American Democracy, Human Rights, Science, and Public Health* tracks how Trump's presidency, a grim period in American history, affected not only the United States but the entire world.

During the four years that Trump was president, I was working in my home office in Marietta, Georgia, with a view of the woods in a protected wetlands called Mud Creek. For nearly thirty years, I've written from this office, which I share with my wife, Mary-Alice.

I base the story I tell about Donald Trump on my research and blog writing, and on conversations with colleagues and friends here in the United States, as well as in Russia, Australia, and Spain. Much of the research was dependent on what my colleague Mercedes Schneider calls "digital research."[4] I made use of scholarly journals, books, and government reports. I also utilized a vast array of media resources, especially newspapers and magazines written by acknowledged journalists and writers.

FOUR POINTS OF VIEW

I've authored this book from several personal angles. Perhaps the most significant perspective I bring to the book is my career as a science educator for nearly forty years. In 1962 I began as a high school science teacher in Weston and Lexington, Massachusetts. After attending graduate school at Boston University (while I was teaching), I received a National Science Foundation Academic Institute award to attend The

---

[3] *United States v. Fred C. Trump, Donald Trump, and Trump Management, Inc.*73-1529 (EDNY, 1975).
[4] M. K. Schneider, *A Practical Guide to Digital Research* (New York: Garn Press, 2020). Schneider has written several books on educational reform using digital research as her source of information. She is also a prolific blogger at https://deutsch29.wordpress.com/.

JACK HASSARD

Ohio State University, where I did my doctoral work in science education and geology. I began my career as a professor of science education at Georgia State University (GSU) in 1969.

The personal experience of teaching science at the high school and university levels informs my *Trump Files* analyses of science. My authoring of science and science education textbooks (e.g., *The Whole Cosmos Catalogue of Science Activities*, 1977, 1992, Goodyear; *Minds On Science*, 1992, HarperCollins; *Science as Inquiry*, 1999, 2009, Goodyear; and *The Art of Teaching Science*, 2005, 2009, Oxford & Routledge) enhances my insights into how Trump's malevolence and ignorance distorted science in the public sphere.

I also wove citizen diplomacy into the book.[5] Citizen diplomacy is the idea that individual citizens can shape relationships with foreign nations.[6] I was mentored by Francis Underhill Macy, a dedicated environmentalist, energy activist, and citizen diplomat. He led the first trip that I took to the Soviet Union with the Association for Humanistic Psychology (AHP) in 1983. The association sponsored the first of many Soviet-American exchanges during the most dramatic period of the Cold War. Relationships between the Soviet and American governments were at an all-time low, with fear of nuclear war dominating the minds of people in the Soviet Union and America. The AHP exchange was a human potential movement pioneering project that brought psychologists, medical practitioners, educators, and activists together in the Soviet Union.

Macy did groundbreaking work with hundreds of activists in Russia, Ukraine, Georgia, and Kazakhstan. He initiated scores of delegations and exchanges between Americans and their counterparts in the former Soviet Union, especially in the areas of psychology, environment, and citizen action. Indeed, in 1961, just after receiving his master's degree from Harvard in Slavic studies, he led the first-ever citizen diplomatic

---

[5] J. V. Montville, "Track Two Diplomacy: The Work of Healing History," *The Whitehead Journal of Diplomacy and International Relations*, 2006, http://blogs.shu.edu/journalofdiplomacy/files/archives/03Montville.pdf.
[6] Jack Hassard, "Citizen Diplomacy to Youth Activism: The Story of the Global Thinking Project," in M. Mueller and D. Tippins, eds., *EcoJustice: Citizen Science and Youth Activism*, Environmental Discourses in Science Education, vol I, Springer, Cham, 2015, https://doi.org/10.1007/978-3-319-11608-2_25.

mission to the USSR where Soviet citizens met Americans for the first time. A Russian speaker, scholar, and humanist, Macy was the inspiration for much of the work that would follow in educator and student exchanges and global environmental activism.

Francis Underhill Macy, standing in front of the Russian train Tolstoy on the first AHP trip to the Soviet Union in 1983.

His encouragement and teaching gave me the foundation to create an American and Soviet education exchange program centered at GSU. Together with American and Russian colleagues, we designed and implemented a global environmental science program, the Global Thinking Project (GTP).[7] This work came about through travel to Russia (formerly the Soviet Union) for twenty years and collaboration with multiple USSR research institutions and schools in Moscow, Tbilisi, St. Petersburg, Yaroslavl, Chelyabinsk, and Pushchino. American and Russian researchers, teachers, and students worked together during the Soviet eras from Brezhnev to Gorbachev and then the Russian presidencies of Yeltsin and Putin. The GTP led to collaboration with educators in other

---

[7] Jack Hassard and Julie Weisberg, *Environmental Science on the Net: The Global Thinking Project* (Chicago: Goodyear Books, 1999). Julie Weisberg and I were co-directors of the GTP. Dr. Weisberg, who holds a PhD in neurobiology and was professor of education at Agnes Scott College, most recently retired as associate dean, Georgia Gwinnett College. The GTP is a "hands across the globe" education project that provides a paradigm for students and teachers to participate in environmental study and to use new technology tools with peers around the world. During the project, students monitored and analyzed important physical and biological aspects of their environment, such as the environmental quality of their classroom and the quality of air and water in their community, as well as the study of solid waste, acid rain, tap water, and the creation of local community-based environmental topics. The skills and knowledge that students constructed were then applied as students engaged in collaborative learning projects linking classrooms globally. In our view, students were seen as citizen scientists who integrated science and societal problems and issues. In so doing, students learned that problems that are typically addressed as science problems have social, political, economic, and ethical aspects as well.

countries, especially Australia and Spain.[8] I interviewed educators from these countries, and they will appear later in the book.

By participating in firsthand experiences in Russia for more than twenty-five three-week periods over two decades, I know Russia in a different way than Donald Trump does. I worked with Russian colleagues from the ground up, and little by little relationships built upon trust grew and developed over the years—and still exist to this day.

Another perspective that I bring to the book is my sense of place. I live in Georgia, which has a diverse population of more than 10 million people spread across five distinct urban areas and many rural counties. I wasn't born here, but I've lived in the Atlanta area for over fifty years, so I consider myself a citizen of Georgia.

Near the end of the Trump era, Georgia became a focal point of the 2020 election, followed by the dual senatorial elections in January 2021 in which the Democrats prevailed to take back the US Senate. I've used my experiences as a citizen and a professor at GSU to write stories about Trump's involvement in Georgia politics and the law. You'll find blog posts and discussions of how Georgia played a significant role in the Trump administration's demise.

I have much to report about and learn from Georgia. In early January 2021, Donald Trump called Brad Raffensperger, Georgia's secretary of state, to tell him to find votes that would change the outcome of the election in Trump's favor. Beginning in 2021, Trump was under investigation for vote fraud by the district attorney in Fulton County, Georgia, because of that phone call. Georgia has also played a significant role in voter suppression, not only after Trump left office, but years earlier when hundreds of thousands of voters were purged from the roles.

Another mindset that contributed to this book is the fact that I've been a blogger at *The Art of Teaching Science* since 2005 and have written there throughout the George W. Bush, Barack Obama, and Donald Trump presidencies. During the Bush and Obama presidencies,

---

[8] Roger Cross in Australia and Ramon Barlam and Narcís Vives in Catalonia, Spain.

I wrote about the social, economic, and corporate forces that affect public education. I explored the dreadful embrace of testing, Common Core goals, and standards that impede the work of classroom teachers, especially in science. I also criticized the movement to privatize public education, which advocates using public funding to support alternatives such as charter schools and vouchers.

The core ideas of *The Trump Files* are based on four years of blogging while Trump was president. I've used the blog posts to share with you my personal and professional views of Trump and his administration.

MALIGNANT NORMALITY

Donald Trump presented the United States with what Dr. Robert Jay Lifton calls "malignant normality,"[9] which occurs when society begins to see forms of destructive and dangerous behavior as normal. Donald Trump and Trumpism render an array of malignant normality. Lifton, born in 1926, is an American psychiatrist and author who is known for his studies of psychological causes and effects of wars and political violence, and he has been one of the most outspoken critics of Donald Trump.

Science educator Charles "Kip" Ault, professor emeritus of science education at Lewis & Clark College, has suggested that Trump's malignant normality includes megalomania, willful ignorance, dishonesty, and fraud.[10] Add Ault's thinking to what Lifton says about Trump's malignant normality and a condition of extreme abnormality emerges that replaces American democracy. The circumstance of Trump's malignant normality includes extensive lying, falsification, systemic corruption, attacks on critics, disregard of intelligence agencies and findings, repudiation of climate change truths, embrace of dictators, and berating of international allies.[11]

---

[9] R. J. Lifton, *The Climate Swerve: Reflections on Mind, Hope, and Survival* (New York: The New Press, 2017). Lifton's concept of "malignant normality" emerged from of his study of Nazi doctors who over time and through perverse counseling, drinking together, and assurances and support of each other were adapted to evil.
[10] Kip Ault, personal email, August 6, 2021. Dr. Ault is the author of *Challenging Science Standards*, 2015, and *Beyond Science Standards*, 2021, Rowan & Littlefield Publishers.
[11] R. J. Lifton, *Losing Reality: On Cults, Cultism, and the Mindset of Political and Religious Zealotry* (New York: The New Press, 2019), 189.

In Lifton's view, professionals should use their knowledge to expose and bear witness to such normality. For instance, Lifton worked with Vietnam War veterans to help them deal with the painful realities of war so that they could continue their antiwar activities. He also worked in the doctors' antinuclear movement to talk about the effects of nuclear weapons. Lifton said that his task in the Hiroshima study was to record surviving people's experience after the atomic bomb was dropped on their city.[12] Over time he understood himself to be a witnessing professional.

Lifton's writing influenced the purpose of my writing—bearing witness—and indeed supplied the support and rationale to write often on my blog about Trump and his actions. In short, Lifton believes it is important that witnessing professionals decide to document what they see and observe and make their observations available to others.

Even before Trump became president, I was incensed by his views and remarks about immigrants, African Americans, climate change, the environment, healthcare, rival politicians, and the press. Blogging was a way to share my views and find research that shed further light on Trump's behavior and its effects on society.

THEMES FOR WRITING

There was much to write during the time Trump was in the White House. And it continued long after he was in office. For example, I describe how Donald Trump weakened American democracy, dishonored the nation's foundational values, and perverted the rights of people to vote. He also disparaged science and scientists, belittled the work of medical and healthcare workers, and inflicted damage on environmental protections developed over the past fifty years.

Trump's abuse of power as president—by bribing the president of Ukraine—resulted in his first impeachment. Trump lied about the pandemic, leading to hundreds of thousands of deaths. Near the end of his term, he instigated an attempted coup d'état of the United States government. The coup attempt resulted in his second impeachment

---

[12] R. J. Lifton, *Death in Life: Survivors of Hiroshima* (New York: Random House, 1991).

while president. The subsequent trial took place in February 2021, after he left office. Fifty-seven senators found Trump guilty of inciting an insurrection.

DAY OF INFAMY

The events on January 6, 2021, revealed Donald Trump acting like any dictator or tyrant. The world witnessed the actions of a dictator trying to undermine a vulnerable American democracy. Trump tried to convince others that he won the 2020 presidential election and that he had the right to strongarm members of Congress, the Justice Department, and state officials to change the vote in his favor. He promoted conspiracy theories of wide-scale election fraud, digital vote manipulation, and mail-in voting irregularities, especially in Black voter precincts.

The unprecedented attack on the nation's Capitol building, encouraged by Trump and other actors who appeared on the rally stage on January 6, may result in sedition charges against the former president and his sycophants. But more dangerously, Trump left in his wake an autocratic and orchestrated movement to suppress and restrict voting rights across the country. State voter suppression has been at the center of voting rights abuses in the United States since the nation's founding. Even after the Voting Rights Act of 1965, southern states continued to restrict and suppress Black people from voting in local and national elections.

Dr. Bandy X. Lee, an American psychiatrist who has written several books[13] about Donald Trump, reminds us that "when a coup attempt goes unpunished, it becomes a training exercise."[14] Dr. Lee is an eminent psychiatrist whose scrutiny of Trump provided me with valid and reliable assertions of Trump's unstable behavior. Although hundreds of American insurrectionists have been arrested and face myriad charges, the US Senate Republicans blocked an independent investigation of the

---

[13] Bandy X. Lee, *The Dangerous Case of Donald Trump* (New York: Thomas Dunne Books, 2019); *Profile of a Nation: Trump's Mind, America's Soul* (New York: World Mental Health Coalition, Inc., 2020). These two books provide a core of the mental health of Donald Trump that I write about.
[14] Bandy X. Lee, "When a coup attempt goes unpunished, it becomes a training exercise," Twitter, May 9, 2021, retrieved April 1, 2022, https://mobile.twitter.com/BandyXLee1/status/1391376829844500482.

January 6 riot. Republicans in Congress have, to their disgrace, even downplayed the failed coup. Trump has still not been held accountable for the coup attempt.

We face certainty that such an attack will happen again. A member of the Three Percenters, a right-wing militant group, wrote a letter in jail while being held on charges for storming the Capitol on January 6. He said that those attacking the building could have overthrown the government if they had wanted. He warns that another January 6 type of attack is possible. As of this writing, he faces twenty years in prison.[15]

RUSSIAN CONNECTIONS

Donald Trump had decades of connections with Russia before he entered the White House. Many of Trump's senior advisors also had years of experiences and contact with Russian officials. However, he and his team downplayed their relationships with Russia throughout their time in office. But Russia played a significant role in getting Trump elected in 2016 and attempted that again in 2020. In fact the Trump campaign went out of its way to connect with anyone who could "get dirt" on Hillary Clinton, even from foreign governments. Russian interference in the 2016 election was not an anomaly, and it indeed might have been caused by Hillary Clinton's political views of Russia. Perhaps the Russians felt Trump would be more agreeable to their worldview. As I will explore later, the United States has intervened in more foreign elections than the Russians.

MY CONNECTIONS WITH RUSSIA

My experience with Russia is different from Donald Trump's associations with Russia. The foundation for my experiences began in 1981 as a private citizen joining with others to make contact and develop relationships with people in the Soviet Union. My story is shared by hundreds of other Americans and Canadians who were willing to travel to the Soviet

---

[15] Joshua Kaplan and Joaquin Sapien, "In Exclusive Jailhouse Letter, Capitol Riot Defendant Explains Motives, Remains Boastful," ProPublica, May 11, 2021, retrieved May 14, 2021, https://www.propublica.org/article/in-exclusive-jailhouse-letter-capital-riot-defendant-explains-motives-remains-boastful.

Union, paying their own way, at a time when the governments of each country had little to no communication with each other.

This was the early 1980s, and it was a time of heightening fears of nuclear war. The media played a role in exacerbating the tension that already existed between the United States and the Soviet Union. But through the actions of individuals and small groups of citizens, significant lines of communication were opened between our countries. Francis Underhill Macy, who I mentioned earlier, Paul von Ward, and Anya Kucharev opened these channels based on their previous work in international relations and citizen diplomacy. Fortunately, I met them at the same time in 1983 on our way to Moscow.

Von Ward was a US diplomat for eighteen years, beginning in the Johnson administration. He later founded an international nonprofit dedicated to cross-cultural understanding and cooperation.

Anya Kucharev was one of the originators of the Esalen Soviet-American citizen diplomacy gatherings in 1980. The AHP Soviet Exchange Project built itself on the work of the Esalen program. Consequently, Kucharev's participation was crucial. She helped people build bridges with Soviets and became the "cross-cultural Sherpa" for many of us.[16] She was also a scholar and activist and wrote an important book, *Information Moscow*,[17] which was designed for visitors from the West to Moscow and other locations in the Soviet Union.

Those of us who traveled to the Soviet Union during this time were known as citizen diplomats. We chartered new territory by bringing our experiences in education, psychology, and psychiatry to find Soviet citizens in similar fields and talk with each other. That's what we did: talk. We met in small groups and as individuals and discussed topics of mutual interest.

Dr. Inna Volkova was one of the first persons that I met. She was a respected researcher at the Institute for US and Canadian Studies, a Soviet think tank. She and I talked about how our countries could improve their relationships with each other; to her, it was centered on

---

[16] B. Menzel, P. Hillery, J. Christensen, and A. F. Costa, Anya Kucharev: Global Peacemaker (Heidelberg: Baier DigitalDruck, 2021).
[17] Anya Kucharev, *Information Moscow, Western Edition, 1987–1988* (San Francisco: US Information Moscow, 1987).

the simple idea of talking and collaborating with each other. Just as Kucharev said, Volkova was ready for in-depth discussions on a range of subjects. She studied and wrote on Eastern religious movements in the United States and was also studying Buddhism and Zen. From this early conversation with her, I realized that we and the Soviets had a lot in common and would be able to move forward and plan activities and events in the coming years.

A week earlier, the Soviets had shot down Korean Air Lines Flight 007, and here I was, talking about that tragedy with Dr. Volkova. I made notes of our conversation in my journal, which I kept for each trip that I made to the USSR/Russia. In my journal I wrote that Inna believed "we, the Soviets, are responsible, I am responsible." But tensions were high between the United States and the USSR, so when a Korean flight strayed over Soviet territory, the Soviets suspected it was a provocation to test its military preparedness. Both sides blamed the other for the plane's downing. Reagan suspended all Soviet passenger air service to the United States. We were supposed to fly from Washington to Moscow on a Soviet flight, but Marylou Foley, our Washington, DC, travel agent who specialized in Soviet travel, had to reroute us through Helsinki.

Traveling as citizens to the Soviet Union was the point of citizen diplomacy. Track I diplomacy (government officials to government officials) was at an all-time low between our countries. This was the perfect time to implement Track II, or citizen diplomacy. After meetings with two Soviet institutions, we met with Arthur A. Hartman, the US ambassador to the USSR. Hartman also realized the importance of citizen-to-citizen communication. Consequently he made it possible for all embassy staff to have a weekday off so that they could go out, away from their compound, and mingle with ordinary Soviet citizens.

On another trip I met Dr. Alexander Orlov, who was a psychologist at the Institute for General and Educational Psychology. At the time, he was head of the institute's Teacher Education Laboratory in Moscow, where I met him and his team members. He and I became close friends and colleagues over the years. Orlov was steeped in humanistic psychology and education. He helped me navigate the world of Soviet education and became an advisor on future projects. Orlov encouraged his lab associates to explore human potential and ways of improving teacher education research. He translated and made possible the publication of American psychologist Carl Rogers's book *Freedom to Learn*. He is currently a professor of social science at the National Research University Higher School of Economics.

The relationships I had with Inna Volkova and Alexander Orlov were typical of the kinds that formed because of the citizen diplomacy work of hundreds of Americans and Soviets. Soviets were active and interested in forming relationships and building on these in the years ahead.

As citizen diplomats, we traveled regularly to the Soviet Union. Often we saw and worked with each other twice a year. As we kept coming back to the USSR, our relationships deepened and resulted in planning and collaboration. By 1987 our citizen diplomacy work resulted in a collaboration between the USSR Academy of Pedagogical Sciences and GSU. This collaboration resulted in the development and implementation of the GTP. The Academy of Pedagogical Science is responsible for the administration of seventeen education research institutes spread across Russia. It is comparable to the US Department of Education's Regional Education Laboratories, which are located across ten regions of the country. The Academy of Pedagogical Sciences later was renamed the Russian Academy of Education. The initial contractual agreement was signed by Vasily Vasilovich Davydov,[18] head of the Academy of Pedagogical Science and the dean of the College of Education at GSU. The agreement, which was originally outlined in a popular restaurant in Atlanta,[19] led to the development of research projects between American and Soviet researchers and teachers. This in turn eventually led to the creation of the GTP.

---

[18] Dr. Davydov and I met on several occasions. He was one of the most respected educators and psychologists in Russia. He is widely known for his work on psychology of instruction and in particular his work on activity theory. I had the pleasure of driving him around Atlanta to show him the sights and enable him to take pictures to show to his family when he returned to Moscow.

[19] Dr. Yuvanali Koulutkin and Dr. Yulia Siroyezhina of the Leningrad Institute of Adult Education and Research joined me for coffee in Decatur, Georgia, in December 1988. We wrote an initial draft of an agreement for collaborative research between the Academy of Pedagogical Sciences and GSU. They were members of the first Soviet delegation to visit Atlanta that culminated with a conference at GSU for local teachers and educators.

Initial meeting among American and Soviet educators and researchers at the Research Institute of Adult Education of the USSR Academy of Pedagogical Sciences in Leningrad, 1987.

Participants included twelve American teachers, administrators, and professors from Georgia and fifteen Soviet researchers from the Institute of Adult Education and Research. This meeting led to a formal research agreement between the Academy and GSU to implement research and writing projects that led to the formation of the GTP and years of official exchanges among researchers, teachers, and students. Two years later, because of this meeting, we established one of the first telecommunications networks between American and Russian schools. Six of the Soviets sitting in the room in the photo above would be the first group of Soviets to travel to Atlanta and help foster our plans for the future.

The GTP brought hundreds of citizens from Georgia and Russia together, impacting not only these participants but also the families of these students, teachers, and researchers and resulting in many lasting relationships. Mathew Searels, a former student of the GTP from a rural part of Georgia, recently shared with me some of his impressions about his 1998 trip to Russia. I asked him how the exchange with Russia had impacted him.[20]

He replied, "The ways the project impacted me are immense, uncountable, and there are many I likely haven't realized. I reflect on

---

[20] Mathew Searels (vice president, CN Utility Consulting; former participant in the GTP American–Russian Exchange Program; former student, Lafayette Middle School, Lafayette, Georgia [1998]), LinkedIn interview with the author, August 13, 2021.

the experience frequently (weekly at minimum)." And then he added, "Every time I hear the news or the public discussing their perception of global affairs, I recall how warm and inviting my Russian family is. I recall how excited the entire community was to meet me and how proud they were to have an American visiting. I was treated like a king."

But what I realized from talking with him was that the teenagers we brought together experienced a vision that we could not have expected. He added this: "I am fascinated with ecosystem dynamics, and I attribute the GTP as the catalyst that ignited the scientific exploration and fueled my unquenchable thirst for knowledge and discovery. It helped shape my viewpoint of the world as a system that does not have purely mutually exclusive parts, but our individual decisions have far-reaching impacts."[21]

Trump's Russian Connections

Donald Trump, on the other hand, has not traveled very often to Russia. And when he did, he didn't seem interested in meeting ordinary Russian citizens. Trump's purpose in traveling to Russia was very different from mine and the other citizen diplomats and people that we brought together. Trump's first trip to Russia was in 1987 to propose the building of a Trump Tower in Moscow. He made another trip in 1997 to talk about building luxury hotels, followed by a 2007 trip to promote Trump Vodka. His final trip to Russia was in 2013 to host the Miss Universe Pageant in Moscow. Trump never worked his way up from knowing Soviet and Russian citizens; he was only ever there to make a deal. He already had made deals selling hundreds of his New York luxury condominiums to Soviets; now he was there to cash in on other transactions.

Trump went out of his way to try to meet up with Russian leaders. For example, in 1988 Trump claimed that Soviet President Mikhail Gorbachev and his wife would tour the Trump Tower while in New York for meetings at the United Nations and with US President Ronald Reagan and Vice President George H. W. Bush. As a joke on Trump, a

---

[21] Searels interview.

Gorbachev impersonator showed up at Trump Tower and talked with him for a few minutes on Fifth Avenue.

While we were planning and coordinating meetings among American and Soviet teachers and educators across Russia, Trump tried to stage Soviet boxing matches and a "Tour de Trump" cycling event; neither ever happened. During these years, while the GTP was expanding across Russia and other countries, several of Donald Trump's properties went bankrupt, including the Trump Taj Mahal and Trump Hotels & Casino Resorts. He was getting further into debt and looking for financial institutions that would lend him the funds he needed.

Before Trump became president, he went out of his way to meet President Vladimir Putin of Russia, but these efforts went nowhere. His first contact occurred when Putin called to congratulate Trump as the winner of the 2016 presidential election. Little did Trump know that Putin directed Russian intelligence officers to hack Hillary Clinton's campaign computers and coordinate with WikiLeaks to harm her campaign and to do what he could to help elect him president of the United States.

ORGANIZATION OF *THE TRUMP FILES*

This book is a record of what Donald Trump did as president as captured by my blog posts, which provide a live play-by-play of the era. The blog posts are presented in thirteen chapters. Within each chapter, they are listed chronologically and dated so that you can relate them to your own experience during this time. They are presented as a chronicle of my observations of Trump and his sycophants as they attempted to govern the country.

You will find ahead discussions how Trump's "America First" policy led to human rights violations in the United States and how his denial of truth and science led to worsening the SARS-CoV-2 pandemic, which became the leading cause of death in America. His administration created a botched program to deliver vaccines to millions of citizens.

The book is divided into six parts, and each part tells a story about the Trump era's immeasurable damage to American society and a democratic form of government. I've drawn upon the research and writing of journalists and scholars from around the world to enhance and expand upon my posts.

Part I, Trumpism, sets the stage with the story of how extreme polarization of American society made it possible for Trump's "America First" policy to gain the White House. The story explores how an authoritarian president led America's democracy into danger.

Part II, Rights, is a story of immigration violence, equity, and voting rights. I show how the Republican Party is suppressing the rights of Americans to have free and fair elections, the cornerstones of liberal democracy.

Part III, Scrutiny, is a story of Donald Trump's chronic violation of his oath of office. He was impeached twice, and he led a campaign to obstruct the Mueller investigation of Russian interference in the 2016 election. This is a story of corruption as seen by one citizen from Georgia.

Part IV, Science, is a science educator's story of how Trump's administration dismantled and diminished science in all areas of government at the peril of the Earth's air, water, land, climate, and—most importantly—citizens. The scientific and medical research communities were undermined not only by Donald Trump but also by hundreds of his appointees, including cabinet members carrying out orders to create disorder in the scientific community.

Part V, COVID-19, is the tragedy of Donald Trump's failure as a leader during the SARS-CoV-2 pandemic and the impact on millions of Americans, including more than 700,000 American deaths in the first year and a half of the pandemic. The story explains how viruses come about, how they can be mitigated, and what happens if people are not told the truth about infectious diseases.

Part VI, Departure, is the final chapter of Trump's presidency. It describes how Trump promoted the Big Lie conspiracy that the 2020 election was stolen from him, even though he lost the electoral college vote 306–232 and the popular vote by 7 million. It's a story of how Trump instigated political violence by sending right-wing mobs to seditiously attack the nation's Capitol, which led to his second impeachment for causing an insurrection. He departed on January 20, 2021.

Posts that were previously published on my blog have been edited for clarity and consistency in this book. In addition, I have added Author's Updates with new information that has come to light since the original publication of these posts.

The Trump Files is the product of my dissent and resistance to Trump's presidency. In *A Field Guide to Climate Anxiety*,[22] Sarah Jaquette Ray calls upon citizens globally to cultivate resiliency. In her words, being resilient "is finding yourself alive the day after, with some fight left. Resilience means trying to keep it going here, there, anywhere, everywhere."[23] I also learned from Ray that resistance (for example, to Trump and Trumpism) means you fight not because you think you can win. You fight because you must.

---

[22] Sarah Jaquette Ray, *A Field Guide to Climate Anxiety* (Oakland: University of California Press, 2020).
[23] Ray, *Field Guide*, 140.

PART I: TRUMPISM

> When day comes, we ask ourselves, where can we find light in this never-ending shade?
> —Amanda Gorman, "The Hill We Climb"

INTRODUCTION

AFTER THE ELECTION I SAT WITH FRIENDS ON A BENCH OUTSIDE a hotel on a warm Ocala, Florida, day on Thanksgiving 2016. We talked about the dismay we felt knowing in a few months that Donald Trump would become president of the United States. How did this happen, we asked each other? What were we thinking? When Trump has gone, how does America carry on?

But as you will find out, I've asked the wrong questions here. The question that I should pose here is, what happened to America to make it ready for a Trump presidency?

Here in Part I of this book, I describe how the tidal wave of Trumpism, along with its political ideologies, emotions, and feeling, brought America into the heart of an unsuccessful coup. An American crisis, brewing for years, came to the surface in the 2016 and 2020 election campaigns. Even though Trump lost the second campaign and is out of office, his legacy of corruption, conspiracy, and lying is still with us. After his defeat in the 2020 election, Trumpism has become the core of the Republican Party. Maybe it should be renamed the Party of Trump.

The rise of Trumpism needs to be understood and not ignored. In this book I will explore Trumpism and show how it appeared but more importantly how it affected government, science, foreign and domestic policy, human health, and the dignity of fellow humans.

What were the conditions that opened the doors for Donald Trump?

EXTREME POLARIZATION

According to the Pew Research Center, Republicans and Democrats have moved further apart in their attitudes toward many social issues such as voting, race, gender, guns, the Capitol rioters, and education.[24] During the Trump years, Republicans and Democrats were split even further. Trump's approval rating when he left office showed the widest gap between the two parties in many decades. Extreme polarization resulted in people feeling uncomfortable even talking about Trump. Divisions were not uncommon even among members of the same family, as was the case in my own family.

In 1994 when the Pew Research Center began asking Americans ten "values questions" on subjects including the role of government, environmental protection, and national security, the average partisan divide between Republicans and Democrats was 15 percent.[25] At the end of one year of Trump's presidency, the gap on the same questions had increased to 36 percent. Another finding was attitudes about higher education. Republicans who said college and universities were having a negative effect on the way things were going in the country rose from 37 percent in 2015 to 58 percent in 2017. Trust in the press also changed with Trump in office. Republicans expressed widespread distrust of the press, whereas Democrats expressed more trust of the same news outlets that Republicans were asked about.

Although America is polarized into Republican (red) states and Democratic (blue) states, it's not as simple as using the political terms Republican and Democrat, or red and blue, to understand American polarization.

---

[24] "Political Attitudes and Values," Pew Research Center, June 2021, https://www.pewresearch.org/topics/political-attitudes-and-values/.
[25] Michael Dimock and John Gramlich, "How America Changed During Trump's Presidency," Pew Research Center, January 29, 2021, accessed June 3, 2021, https://www.pewresearch.org/2021/01/29/how-america-changed-during-donald-trumps-presidency/.

FOUR NARRATIVES—TWO COUNTRIES

George Packer[26] explains how the United States has fractured into four parts: "free and real" America on one side, and "smart and just" America on the other side. Parker's analysis gives us the insight to understand how America elected a demagogue by the name of Donald Trump. An understanding of the four parts is a key to understanding why so many people voted for Trump regardless of his 30,000 lies, his gross bigotry, and his anger directed at anyone who disagreed with him. His voters didn't care about this.

I'll briefly touch of the four narratives that Parker identified that I think will provide some insight as to why Trump was supported by millions of Americans, even beyond his presidency. I found this analysis very interesting, especially when I asked the question, where do I fit in? As you read my brief review of Parker's ideas, you might ask yourself the same question.

Here is how Parker begins his analysis of the narratives that define America's values:

> The 1970s ended postwar, bipartisan, middle-class America, and with it the two stable narratives of getting ahead and the fair shake. In their place, four rival narratives have emerged, four accounts of America's *moral identity*. They have roots in history, but they are shaped by new ways of thinking and living. They reflect schisms on both sides of the divide that has made us two countries, extending and deepening the lines of fracture. Over the past four decades, the four narratives have taken turns exercising influence. They overlap, morph into one another, attract and repel one another. None can be understood apart from the others, because all four emerge from the same whole.[27]

---

[26] George Packer, *Last Best Hope: America in Crisis and Renewal* (New York: Farrar, Straus & Giroux, 2021).
[27] Packer, *Last Best Hope*, 69–70.

Free America.[28] This is Parker's first narrative, which he says has been the most politically powerful of the four. Free America is the narrative that combines libertarian ideas with consumer capitalism. We might call this the conservative movement that was jumpstarted by Ronald Reagan in the 1980s. It was made up of traditionalists including Protestants, orthodox Catholics, southern agrarians, would-be aristocrats, and alienated individualists. This was the main strand of conservatism.

Free America was the underlying theme on right-wing radio talk shows that hit the airways in the 1980s hosted by the likes of Rush Limbaugh, Neal Boortz, Sean Hannity, and many more.[29] Right-wing radio dominated the airways (with about 80 million listeners per day) and was especially popular with people living in red states. I've listened to some of these shows over the past thirty years, especially Neal Boortz, whose show originated in Atlanta. Although I found it painful to listen to some of these shows (not so much with Boortz), not to do so meant I wouldn't understand what drives them and what they talk about. In my opinion, Limbaugh was the "voice" of free America. Most of the others followed his lead.

Free America became the dogma of the Republican Party. Americans were duped by Reagan and Gingrich and continue to be with Mitch McConnell and Kevin McCarthy. The Koch brothers poured millions into propaganda machines and campaigns for elected office on behalf of corporate power brokers and fossil fuel companies.

Parker says that real freedom means growing up and acquiring the ability to participate fully in political and economic life.

Smart America.[30] A new class of Americans emerged from what is known as the knowledge economy. These were people with college degrees who became salaried professionals in a myriad of professions, including information technology, computer engineering, scientific research, design, management consulting, civil service, financial analysis,

---

[28] Packer, *Last Best Hope*, 70–85.
[29] Jeffrey M. Berry and Sarah Sobieraj, "Understanding the Rise of Talk Radio," *PS: Political Science and Politics* 44, no. 4 (2011): 762–767, retrieved August 20, 2021, http://www.jstor.org/stable/41319965.
[30] Berry and Sobieraj, "Rise of Talk Radio," 85–101.

law, journalism, the arts, and higher education. I've studied and worked in the halls of smart America at the high school and university levels. And I've carried my university identity into retirement with the label of emeritus professor.

Real America.[31] Real America, according to Parker, goes back a long way. It says that "the authentic heart of democracy beats hardest in common people who work with their hands[32] goes back to the eighteenth century."[33] In the early nineteenth century, populist democracy was in vogue, identifying farmers, mechanics, and laborers as the real Americans. A key point here is that popular democracy conveyed an anti-intellectual bias to politics, and it's not faded. And one other fact: real America has always been white. There were exceptions, especially within labor movements in the early twentieth century. But any coming together was soon brought to a halt by the pressure of white supremacy.

Real America is also religious, evangelical, and fundamentalist Christian. Real America is patriotic and has a strong national character. It is hostile to humanitarianism and international engagement. According to Parker, the narrative of real America is white Christian nationalism.

Just America.[34] In 2014, the character of America changed, according to Parker. Even though the civil rights movement brought civil rights and voting rights laws and the country elected Barack Obama, the first Black American president, there was something else happening on the streets of American cities and towns.

Parker says that Just America emerged as a national narrative in 2014 in Ferguson, Missouri, when police killed a Black eighteen-year-old

---

[31] Berry and Sobieraj, "Rise of Talk Radio," 101–118.
[32] I grew up in a "real American" family home in a town on the outskirts of Boston. My father worked in the Boston shipyards as a carpenter during WWII, was a loyal union member and shop steward for many years in Dedham Bakery Company, and later worked as an engineer in the New England Boyd Teflon Coating Company. My father was an expert carpenter who worked with his hands to build his own garage and added a bedroom to our home. My mother and father raised five of us in a small home near the edge of Jennings Pond in Natick, Massachusetts. However, our family values included the importance of education and the acceptance of people from different cultures, occupations, and beliefs.
[33] George Packer, "How America Fractured into Four Parts," *The Atlantic*, July/August 2021 Issue, retrieved April 2, 2022, https://www.theatlantic.com/magazine/archive/2021/07/george-packer-four-americas/619012/.
[34] Berry and Sobieraj, "Rise of Talk Radio," 118–139.

and left him on the street for hours. The murder of Black Americans continued, but many of these murders were captured on video and then posted on social media.

Just America emerged from the civil rights movement of the 1950s and 1960s. It was based on the moral views of Dr. Martin Luther King Jr. and many other civil rights activists. In the present age, Black Lives Matter is moral ground upon which the civil rights movement has coalesced.[35]

CRITICAL RACE THEORY

In recent years, there have been several documents and documentaries published that present a past that a lot of people want to forget or change. Beginning in 1619, a year before Pilgrims dropped anchor in Plymouth, enslaved African people arrived on the shores of Jamestown on the ship *White Lion*. Urged by Nikole Hannah-Jones, an American investigative journalist,[36] the *New York Times* has documented this in The 1619 Project[37] and in the new origin story in Hannah-Jones's book of the same name.[38] The project aims to reframe the country's history, understanding it with the beginning of American slavery and exploring the consequences and contributions of Black Americans at the center of the story of America.

Donald Trump retaliated against The 1619 Project by promoting a "patriotic education" curriculum titled the 1776 Project.[39] According to many historians, Trump's 1776 Commission report "warps the history of racism and slavery."[40] In fact, Trump had the audacity to release the report on Martin Luther King Jr. Day in 2021, just a few days before he was exiled to Florida. The 1776 Project rejects the claim that the true

---

[35] Aldon Morris (2021, February 3). "From civil rights to black lives matter," *Scientific American*, February 3, 2021, Retrieved May 9, 2022, from https://www.scientificamerican.com/article/from-civil-rights-to-black-lives-matter1/.
[36] It's worth noting that her alma mater, the University of North Carolina, offered her a professorship in 2021, but without tenure. After weeks of protest by faculty and students, the UNC trustees voted to offer her tenure. Hannah-Jones turned the job down.
[37] *The 1619 Project, New York Times*, August 14, 2019, https://www.nytimes.com/interactive/2019/08/14/magazine/1619-america-slavery.html.
[38] Nikole Hannah-Jones et al., eds., *The 1619 Project: A New Origin Story* (New York: One World, 2021).
[39] Derrick Clifton, "How the Trump Administration's '1776 Report' Warps the History of Racism and Slavery," NBCNews.com, January 20, 2021, retrieved November 19, 2021, https://www.nbcnews.com/news/nbcblk/how-trump-administration-s-1776-report-warps-history-racism-slavery-n1254926.
[40] Clifton, "Trump Administration's '1776 Report.'"

founding of America was in 1619. It remains steadfast that America was founded by the British who landed near Cape Cod.

The 1619 Project has irked Republicans. Around the country, many school districts banned the teaching of the project and related ideas. Texas, and some other states, have passed critical race theory (CRT) bills. CRT, which started in law, spread to many other areas, such as political science, ethnic studies, Indigenous studies, and philosophy, but especially scholarship in education.[41] As a science educator for more than forty years, which spanned the period of the civil rights and CRT movements, the present hysterics about CRT is an abomination to the crucial role that public education plays in teaching racial justice.

Although CRT is not taught as a course in K–12 schooling, teachers of all subject areas have incorporated issues that are central to CRT theorists. In my own writing, I have explored tracking, high-stakes testing, standardizing curriculum, multicultural education, and charter schools.[42] Science educators have embodied CRT into a framework called culturally responsive teaching.[43] The curriculum of American public schools emphasizes teaching science, mathematics, social studies, and language arts, which builds bridges from school to communities.

CRT is not a new idea. The person that many consider the "father of CRT" is Derrick Bell (1930–2011).[44] Bell was an American lawyer, professor at Harvard University, and civil rights activist. As a scholar he wrote foundational papers and books about CRT. He was involved in several desegregation lawsuits that led to his formulation of the theory. One of the first cases was *Hudson v. Leake County School Board* (1963). The white school board voted to close the Harmony School, a Black school in the middle of Leake County, Mississippi. The school was built by Black citizens in the 1920s and was funded by the philanthropist Julius Rosenwald, who funded five thousand Black schools in the South. In

---

[41] Richard Delgado and Jean Stefancic, *Critical Race Theory: An Introduction* (New York: New York University Press, 2016).
[42] Jack Hassard, *Science Education* ebook series, Kindle edition.
[43] A. H. Mackenzie, "Why Culturally Relevant Science Teaching is Vital in Our Classrooms," *The Science Teacher* 89, no. 2 (2021): 6–8.
[44] Jelani Cobb, "The Man behind Critical Race Theory," *The New Yorker*, September 10, 2021, retrieved November 13, 2021, https://www.newyorker.com/magazine/2021/09/20/the-man-behind-critical-race-theory.

the case of the Harmony School, Winson Hudson (1916–2004), founder and vice president of the local chapter of the National Association for the Advancement of Colored People (NAACP), met with Derrick Bell, who was an attorney with the NAACP Legal Defense and Educational Fund, New York City.[45] Hudson sought Bell's assistance to help her and other Black citizens of Harmony sue the school board. The case led to the reopening and desegregation of the Harmony School. However, Bell and Hudson began to question whether they did the right thing in forcing integration. In the South, the integration of schools led to the establishment of private "segregation academies" and white flight, leaving the schools essentially segregated.[46]

Bell realized that decisions in civil rights cases were of limited value. He concluded that racism is so deeply rooted in American society and its structures that it has been able to reassert itself after limited successes in court cases. Bell began to write and argue that racism is permanent. Accordingly, his ideas became the foundation for the CRT that emerged in the 1980s.[47]

CRT is based on the thinking and writing of scholars from all cultures, historical periods stretching back to the early nineteenth century, and the present work of thousands of CRT scholars at universities around the world. Diane Ravitch provides an early example of CRT when she quoted from a Frederick Douglass speech that was given on July 4, 1852.[48]

Richard Delgado and Jean Stefancic, in their important work about CRT, insist that it "tries not only to understand our social situation but to change it." They believe that CRT can transform society for the better.[49]

There is Republican movement amongst state legislatures and school boards to outlaw CRT. Republicans or conservative activists use CRT as a catchphrase for any examination of systemic racism.

---

[45] Winson Hudson and Constance Curry, *Mississippi Harmony: Memoirs of a Freedom Fighter* (New York: Palgrave Macmillan, 2004).
[46] Cobb, "The Man behind Critical Race Theory."
[47] Cobb, "The Man behind Critical Race Theory."
[48] Frederick Douglass, "What to the Slave Is the Fourth of July?" *Frederick Douglass: Selected Speeches and Writings*, Philip S. Foner, ed. (Chicago: Lawrence Hill, 1999), 188–206, https://liberalarts.utexas.edu/coretexts/_files/resources/texts/c/1852%20Douglass%20July%204.pdf.
[49] Delgado and Stefancic, *Critical Race Theory*, 10.

These critics of CRT include many ideas that have penetrated public education such as social justice as well as culturally responsive and critical thinking. They are disingenuous in that a few years ago, they used the catchphrase "critical thinking and academic freedom" to disguise the intent of "intelligent design" being part of the science curriculum. Creationism and intelligent design made stealth appearances in some state science classrooms.[50]

CRT rattled school board members and parents who think their children will be exposed to ideas about race and social justice. They complain that teaching about CRT will make white kids feel bad if they discuss slavery, segregation, and the Ku Klux Klan. This is simply deceitful. Most middle and high school students are quite able and interested in reading about and discussing cultural issues. Some of the literature that high school students read focuses on questions about immigration, poverty, environmental justice, and racial discrimination. As a science educator, I wrote books in 1970s that included the role of women in science and how Black, Asian, and Hispanic/Latino science was integral to knowing science.[51]

Marisa Lati wrote in her *Washington Post* article that the movement to ban CRT from K–12 schools and colleges is an attempt in assuring that the history of many people of color are not taught in schools. She added that to ban CRT erases the legacy of discrimination and lived experiences of Black, Brown, and Native people.[52]

In a groundbreaking book offering a new narrative of the African role in creating the Americas, Christina Proenza-Coles pushes the history of Afro Americans back into the 1500s.[53] Indeed, she shows that there is only an illusion distinguishing American history from African American history. Like Hannah-Jones, Proenza-Coles states that Africans and their

---

[50] Jack Hassard, "Creationism and Intelligent Design Make Stealth Appearances in Louisiana and Tennessee Science Classrooms," Jackhassard.org, April 23, 2012, retrieved November 18, 2021, https://jackhassard.org/creationism-intelligent-design-stealth-appearances-louisiana-tennessee-science-classrooms/.
[51] Joseph Abruscato and Jack Hassard, *The Whole Cosmos Catalogue of Science Activities for Kids of All Ages*, 2nd ed. (Menlo Park: Good Year Books, 1977).
[52] Marisa Iati, "What Is Critical Race Theory, and Why Do Republicans Want to Ban It in Schools?" *Washington Post*, July 12, 2021, retrieved November 14, 2021, https://www.washingtonpost.com/education/2021/05/29/critical-race-theory-bans-schools/.
[53] Christina Proenza-Coles, *American Founders: How People of African Descent Established Freedom in the New World* (Montgomery: NewWorld Books, 2019).

descendants preceded the English in settling what would become the United States. Indeed, in Georgia, eighty years before Jamestown, a settlement of Maroons, descendants of Africans in the Americas, established the first settlement in the state where I now live. She also points out that Africans outnumbered Europeans four to one until 1820. Indeed Africans were on every exploratory and military campaign from "Canada to Chile."[54]

The current narrative about CRT is steeped in ignorance of American history and contemporary prejudices. Critical race theory is not taught in the public schools, but racial justice is.

INSIDE TRUMPISM

In my research on *The Trump Files*, I discovered the work of Arlie Russell Hochschild, a University of California, Berkeley sociologist. She writes that Trumpism is intimately tied to its namesake. She suggests "to understand the future of the Republican Party, we have to act like political psychiatrists."[55]

One metaphor she used stood out for me. Hochschild explains that "Trumpism is an emotional planet that orbits Trump's star. Breaking the connection between Trump and the better part of the GOP will require either that Trump disappears (an unlikely proposition) or that a larger star emerges from the Republican backbench (also unlikely)."[56] It's evident that even now, Trump leads the Republican Party.

In her book, *Strangers in Their Own Land*,[57] Hochschild writes a compelling and empathetic story about how people make sense of their lives giving rise to a gulf separating people with widely different views about politics, economics, religion, and issues such as abortion, gay marriage, gender roles, race, guns, and the Confederacy. Her book brings to light how people feel about life and the emotions that inspire their political views.

---

[54] Proenza-Coles, *American Founders*.
[55] Derek Thompson, "The Deep Story of Trumpism," *The Atlantic*, December 29, 2020, https://www.theatlantic.com/ideas/archive/2020/12/deep-story-trumpism/617498/.
[56] Thompson, "Trumpism."
[57] Arlie Russell Hochschild, *Strangers in Their Own Land: Anger and Mourning on the American Right* (New York: The New Press, 2018).

One of Hochschild's goals was to break through what she calls "empathy walls," which she views as an obstacle to deep understanding of another person, one that can make us feel indifferent or even hostile to those who hold different views. Hochschild wondered if it was possible to cross the empathy wall to know others from the inside, to see reality through their eyes, to understand the links between life, feeling, and politics. How does life feel to people on the right?[58]

Hochschild's research was important to my understanding of the people who supported and flocked to Trump. The United States has polarized groups of people who have different outlooks on politics and life rooted in their firsthand experiences and family history. I wanted to make sure I understood who the people were that seemed to live into two different realities. But more importantly I wanted to understand Trumpsters.

Most of the people she met were working class and Tea Party advocates. In her years of work she discovered the Great Paradox[59]: Why is hatred of government most intense among people who need government services? And indeed, most of these people live in red states. She says about the divide or polarization between blue and red states:[60]

> Across the country, red states are poorer and have more teen mothers, more divorce, worse health, more obesity, more trauma-related deaths, more low-birth-weight babies, and lower school enrollment. On average, people in red states die five years earlier than people in blue states.

Hochschild embedded herself in St. Charles, Louisiana. I know St. Charles, as I've driven to the city at least thirty times on my way to and from Round Top, Texas, accompanied by my wife. In addition to both being educators, we own an antiques business and travel twice a year to the Round Top Antiques Festival to sell antiques at the Marburger Farms

---

[58] Hochschild, *Strangers*.
[59] Arthur Goldhammer, "The Great Paradox," *The American Prospect*, August 31, 2016, https://prospect.org/power/great-paradox/.
[60] Hochschild, *Strangers*, 8.

Antique show. To reach St. Charles, we travel west along I-10, and as we approach the lake in St. Charles, there is a magnificent bridge that carries us across the lake. But as we drive down the bridge traveling west, the horizon is filled with oil and gas refinery storage tanks that populate the landscape in all directions.

Industrial pollution is severe in Louisiana, not to mention the pollution in the area around St. Charles, the area Hochschild studied. Large petrochemical plants have created toxic air, water, and land in many areas of Louisiana. There are five oil refineries in Lake Charles, and the oil and gas industry has built twelve other refineries in Louisiana. Only Texas has more refineries.

It is here where Hochschild realized that the Great Paradox was extreme. People are harmed by the pollution caused by energy industry corporations such as Dow Chemical and Union Carbide, neither of whom think anything of dumping wastewater into the area's waterways.

Yet she found that many of the people in her study felt a deep connection to nature and were brought up as fishmen and hunters. The people in Louisiana have a deep distrust of the federal government, even though it could help with environmental and economic issues facing them. The Great Paradox is that people who have a need for government services have a negative opinion of big government, yet when they need help, such as Medicaid, they will take the steps necessary to be eligible.

Why do people who need help from the government hate it? The emotions and feelings that guide this view are deep. It is understood as part of the Great Paradox. It was what would push the storm of Trumpism across America.

And it isn't just people in states such as Louisiana, Mississippi, and Alabama. The discontent that exists there is also found in the "flyover" or heartland states in the Midwest, such as Kansas, Iowa, Nebraska, Indiana, Missouri, and South and North Dakota.

The people she met in the red state of Louisiana were waiting for a Trump. Throughout the country, especially in red states, Trump was welcomed with open arms.

According to Hochschild, the scene was set for Trump's rise. She identified three elements that came together that favored Donald Trump. Most of the people she met talked about being on shaky economic ground. They went through periods of upheaval because of losing a job or experiencing an environmental disaster such as a hurricane or flooding. Climate change has played havoc on the Gulf Coast states. Over the years that I traveled along the coast, the evidence of flooding has only increased. One woman who was working as a hotel receptionist told us that she had just finished the repairs on her home after Hurricane Harvey in August 2017 only to be flooded again by the most recent hurricane, Barry, on July 13, 2019. Hurricane Ida devastated Louisiana in 2021. Power losses, flooding, and uprooting of thousands of people rivaled the harm caused by Hurricane Katrina in 2005.

People Hochschild met also felt culturally marginalized. They were angry that people would cut in line ahead of them. Line cutters, according to Hochschild, appear to be cutting in front of working-class whites who are in line seeking the American dream. Line cutters include government workers, as well as minority groups, Americans of color, women, immigrants, refugees, and LGBTQ people.

They also were upset that people make them feel humiliated because of their views. For many of them, they felt they were part of a demographic in decline. Hochschild says that they began to feel like a besieged minority. Trump's rallies were the perfect venue to nurse their wounds (see Blog Post 2.4 on the Trump rallies).

TRUMP'S AMERICA FIRST

To "prepare" for the presidency, Trump immersed himself in right-wing media. He watched Fox News on cable television and especially paid attention to the likes of right-wing talk radio's Rush Limbaugh, Michael Savage, and Sean Hannity. In a recent analysis of how this happened, Lawrence Rosenthal says that this about Trump's preparation:

> The substance of Trump's presidential campaign, the issues he thundered about in rallies and debates, was the direct result

of what he found in these right-wing media. What he found there was a populist revolt. This revolt was congenial to him in terms of his own politics and, even more so, in terms of his vulgar, over-the-top style. Donald Trump won the 2016 election by convincing America's right-wing populists to migrate ideologically—from the Tea Party's free-market fundamentalism to Trump's anti-immigrant, America First nationalism.[61]

Rosenthal is chair and lead researcher of the Berkeley Center for Right-Wing Studies, which was founded in 2009 at the University of California, Berkeley.

America is a liberal democracy two hundred years in the making. Donald Trump led an assault on liberal democracy in four short years. He did this by undermining the norms of democracy and surrounding himself with people who were loyal only to him to further his autocratic goals. During his presidency, Trump tried to derail the Mueller investigation of Russian interference in the 2016 election. He was impeached twice for obstruction of justice and for inciting an insurrection on the US Capitol. No president of the United States has been scrutinized as much as Donald J. Trump.

When Trump walked into the Oval Office in January 2017, he was accompanied by Steve Bannon and Stephen Miller. They carried with them a white nationalist agenda. Bannon, former executive chairperson of the right-wing Breitbart News Network, compared himself to Lenin and suggested that there was a need for war in the United States.[62] Bannon was Trump's chief strategist for seven months in 2017. He had great influence over Trump, especially in recommending cabinet members who would help deconstruct departments in the administration of the United States.

He was arrested in 2020 for defrauding people of $25 million in a scheme claiming he was soliciting donations to help fund the wall along the southern border. He was charged also with using $1 million of the funds for personal acquisitions. After a few days in jail, Bannon

---

[61] Lawrence Rosenthal, *Empire of Resentment: Populism's Toxic Embrace of Nationalism* (New York: The New Press, 2020).
[62] Anne Applebaum, *Twilight of Democracy: The Seductive Lure of Authoritarianism* (New York, Doubleday, 2020), 150.

was pardoned on January 19, 2021, by Trump. On November 12, 2021, he was indicted by a federal grand jury on two counts of contempt of Congress from his failure to comply with a subpoena issued by the Select Committee Investigating the January 6 breach.[63]

Miller, assistant to the president and senior advisor for policy, however, stayed until the end of Trump's term in office. Miller had formed an anti-immigrant bias while in high school and at Duke University. His first job was as press secretary for Michele Bachman, a Republican representative from Minnesota. Bachman blamed immigrants for bringing crime, drugs, and disease to the country.

Miller then became communications director for Jeff Sessions, senator from Alabama. His work with Sessions brought him into the inner workings of immigration law. Sessions was chair of the Senate Subcommittee on Immigration, Citizenship, and Border Safety. Sessions advocated stricter immigration controls and aggressive pushback against President Barack Obama's executive actions on immigration.

As soon as Trump announced his candidacy, Bannon recommended he hire Miller as speechwriter. Miller directed Trump to promote the America First message and stricter immigration policies in the campaign and in the presidential debates with Hillary Clinton.

After the election, Miller asked to head the Domestic Policy Council, a group in the White House. Miller made this request because the position did not require Senate approval; he didn't want to lie about policy questions if he had to appear before the Senate. This tactic also gave him the ear of Trump. It meant that he would be the chief architect of Trump's immigration policy. In fact, Miller cowrote one of Trump's first executive orders, "Protecting the Nation from Foreign Terrorist Entry into the United States"—the travel ban.[64] Miller became one of Donald Trump's America First whisperers. According to Jonathan

---

[63] United States Department of Justice, "Stephen K. Bannon Indicted for Contempt of Congress," news release no. 21-1122, November 15, 2021, retrieved January 5, 2022, https://www.justice.gov/opa/pr/stephen-k-bannon-indicted-contempt-congress. The case is being investigated by the FBI's Washington Field Office. The case is being prosecuted by the Public Corruption and Civil Rights Section of the US Attorney's Office for the District of Columbia.

[64] Sahil Kapur, "Trump Adviser Stephen Miller Reveals Aggressive Second-Term Immigration Agenda," NBCNews.com, October 30, 2020, retrieved February 5, 2021, https://www.nbcnews.com/politics/immigration/trump-adviser-stephen-miller-reveals-aggressive-second-term-immigration-agenda-n1245407.

Blitzer,[65] Miller's obsession with restricting immigration and punishing immigrants defined Trump's administration.

Also, according to Jean Guerrero,[66] author of *Hate Monger*, a biographical work of Stephen Miller, Donald Trump, and the white nationalists' agenda, it's impossible to understand the Trump era without recognizing the major influence of Stephen Miller. He was with Trump throughout the campaign and Trump's years in the White House. He and Trump became experts in messaging, so much so that millions of Americans fell in line with their conspiracies and lies.

Miller, after leaving office with Trump, continues his white supremacist views on various right-wing media outlets. As of publication, he's reportedly teaming up with Alabama congressperson Mo Brooks, who famously shouted on January 6, 2021, at the "Stop the Steal" rally, "Today is the day American patriots start taking down names and kicking ass. Are you willing to do what it takes to fight for America? Louder! Will you fight for America?"[67] Brooks has been accused in a legal suit of breaking DC laws by inciting a riot that aided violent actors who inflicted emotional distress on members of Congress. The Department of Justice refused to defend Brooks. Mo Brooks is a perfect match for Stephen Miller.

Donald Trump showed the kinds of behaviors that historians associate with demagogues. Instead of a liberal democracy, demagogues foster an illiberal, one-party state. I believe that Trump wished he was president of an illiberal, one-party state. If the insurrection that he instigated had been successful resulting in an overturned election, America would have become a one-party state.

THE RUSSIA I KNOW

From 1981 to 2002, hundreds of citizen diplomats worked to improve communications between Americans and Russians. The people involved

---

[65] Jonathan Blitzer, "How Stephen Miller Manipulates Donald Trump to Further His Immigration Obsession," *The New Yorker*, February 21, 2020, retrieved February 22, 2021, https://www.newyorker.com/magazine/2020/03/02/how-stephen-miller-manipulates-donald-trump-to-further-his-immigration-obsession.

[66] Jean Guerrero, *Hatemonger: Stephen Miller, Donald Trump, and the White Nationalist Agenda* (New York: HarperCollins, 2020).

[67] Michael Kranish, "Mo Brooks Urged a Jan. 6 Crowd to 'Fight.' Now His Actions Long before the Insurrection Face New Scrutiny," *Washington Post*, January 11, 2022, retrieved April 2, 2022, https://www.washingtonpost.com/politics/2022/01/10/mo-brooks-jan6-eric-swalwell-lawsuit-insurrection/.

in these citizen diplomacy projects witnessed the changes that occurred in the Soviet Union in the late 1980s when Mikhail Gorbachev became president of the Soviet Union. Gorbachev initiated policies of glasnost (openness of government and dissemination of information) and perestroika (reform of economics and politics) while we were beginning our collaborative work. We held international conferences at GSU in Atlanta and the Academy of Pedagogical Sciences in Moscow and St. Petersburg exploring reform in the USSR and education in each country.[68] For many years we exchanged delegations of researchers, teachers, and students, and designed a collaborative internet-based ecological program.

The Russian people whom we met were professional colleagues, husbands, wives, children, and teens who were family oriented, religious, and highly literate in science and art.

Bill and Gail Fisher,[69] parents of two American students who participated in two separate exchanges, visited their Russian counterparts on two occasions. They said that the Russians "were not ogres perhaps envisioned during the Cold War; they actually are warm and loving folks, not a lot different from us as the core, just coming from a different experience base."

The Russian people we knew were not the stereotype often portrayed in the media. They loved their country and always shared with us their rich history and literature, especially poetry and appreciation for the arts. They also knew far more about American literature than we knew about Russian literature. Most Russian students had read many American classics. On an early school visit, a student at Moscow School 710 asked me who was my favorite Russian poet.

Many Russians are naturalists, and several invited us to Siberia on different occasions. Phil Gang, one of the founders of the GTP, spent a summer in an ecology camp for teachers on Lake Baikal.

When I discuss Russia in this book, it is based on twenty years of collaboration and the building of friendships with Russian people. Many

---

[68] Jack Hassard, "The AHP Soviet Exchange Project: 1983–1990 and Beyond," *Journal of Humanistic Psychology* 30 no. 3 (1990): 6–51, https://doi.org/10.1177/0022167890303002.

[69] Used with permission of Gail and Bill Fisher, parents of students from Dunwoody High School, Dunwoody, Georgia.

of us hosted Russian colleagues in our homes over a lengthy period. We were invited to dinners, parties, school events, conferences and trips to museums, the circus, ballet and opera performances, natural history excursions, and more. Hundreds of teenagers were hosted in American and Russian homes in our project, resulting in changed beliefs about each other and lifetime friendships. Some of our students studied in Russia and then pursued careers in international relations, ecology, and environmental science. We learned much about life, learning, and teaching from our Russian colleagues, and we believe it was reciprocal.

Perhaps one of the most enchanting experiences we had was teaching in each other's classrooms. In 1986, I suggested to Vadim Zhudov,[70] the director of Moscow School 710, that on the next visit to his school in October 1987, American teachers would come prepared to teach science, mathematics, literature, and social studies to Russian students at any age level. He agreed, and that agreement set into motion a novel way to work with each other. Putting your reputation as a teacher on the line, rather than simply sitting in a class and observing others teach, was a gamechanger for our collaboration. This act built a bridge of friendship and trust and allowed us to go further in our collaboration.

The night before five Americans taught lessons in several areas of science to students in Moscow School 710, one of the codirectors of the Foreign Affairs Department of the Academy of Pedagogical Sciences told me that this was an important project in Soviet–American relations because this would be the first time Americans would teach Soviet children.[71] When Russian teachers came to Atlanta, they also taught classes in several area schools. The Soviet teachers, like their American counterparts, used a variety of approaches when they taught American students

---

[70] Vadim Zhudov headed an important school in our project. He was well known and respected in the education profession in the Soviet Union, and after we collaborated for a year or so, he introduced us to schools in Puschino, Yaroslavl, and Chelyabinsk, which we visited and invited to Atlanta over the next ten years. Dr. Jennie Springer, principal of Dunwoody High School near Atlanta, began a fruitful collaboration with Zhudov. Together they arranged the first exchange of students between American and Soviet schools. Moscow School 710 and Dunwoody High School became partner schools in the GTP and exchanged teachers and students over the next ten years.

[71] We tried a variety of approaches with Soviet children. In all of the lessons, the students were invited to take their experiments and materials home to show their parents, such as fossil crinoid stems, pendants the children made, and materials to illustrate the laws of physics. Dr. Alexi Matushkin, director of the Institute for General and Education Psychology, observed our lessons and reported to us that when students brought materials from the lessons home to share with their parents, it was well received. Matushkin said that we were the "talk of the town."

for the first time. When we visited schools in other Russian cities, our teaching experiment continued with great success and appreciation.

Trust didn't happen overnight. To get to a place of mutual collaboration, we showed up every year to meet with our Russian colleagues. During this time, I worked with people who held positions of power in various Soviet and Russian organizations. In 1987, Olga Olenynikova made arrangements with Vadim Zhudov and Victor Onushkin, director of the Institute of Adult Education and Research, Leningrad, for ten Soviet teachers and researchers to come to Atlanta for two weeks of meetings, visits to schools, and social and cultural events. There were three teachers in the group from Moscow School 710. About a week before they were to fly from Moscow to Atlanta, I was informed that the three teachers would not be on the flight manifest. I found out that Communist Party leaders did not want teachers traveling out of the country. I let them know our disappointment in and disapproval of their decision, and made it clear that to go forward, this policy would have to change. It did. A year later, the delegation of Soviets that came to Atlanta consisted of six teachers and six researchers.

The United States Information Agency (USIA) funded exchange projects to bring American and Russian citizens together with a goal of helping to democratize Russia by fostering exchanges between American and Russian youth. The GTP at GSU[72] received grants from the USIA to support hundreds of educators and students in multicultural exchanges during the 1990s. The openness that Gorbachev started resulted in solid friendships and working relationships with colleagues in six Russian cities for many years.

Although difficult, it is possible to overcome neoliberal and conservative policies and engage colleagues whose cultural and political context is much more authoritarian than we consider in the West. When ordinary people are brought together to discuss common interests and concerns, actions can appear that would be surprising even to the most progressive among us.

---

[72] Jack Hassard, "Citizen Diplomacy to Youth Activism: The Story of the Global Thinking Project," in M. P. Mueller and D. J. Tippins, (eds.,) *Ecojustice, Citizen Science, and Youth Activism: Situated Tensions for Science Education* (Switzerland: Springer, 2015), 397–425.

As you proceed through the book, I will introduce you to educators and students not only from America, but Russia, Australia, and Spain, all of whom participated in our exchange programs and the GTP. They have much to say about the importance of cross-cultural exchanges and the value of bringing people together whose upbringing and outlooks on life might be different. It's my belief that given the present state that exists between the US and Russia as a consequence of Russia's invasion of Ukraine, new ways of collaboration are necessary to stop the war, not less. The governments of Ukraine and Russia need to find ways to work together and seek guidance from other countries, as well.

VLADIMIR PUTIN'S RUSSIA

During the 1990s, Vladimir Putin rose from being a senior KGB officer to an assistant to the democratic mayor in Leningrad. In 1996, he moved to Moscow. He was appointed deputy chief of the Presidential Property Management Department of Boris Yeltsin's Russian Federation administration. Putin was responsible for foreign property of the state and organized the transfer of the former assets of the Soviet Union and Communist Party to the Russian Federation. He was promoted to deputy chief of presidential staff a few months later. While he was a member of Yeltsin's staff, on June 27, 1997, he defended his dissertation at the Saint Petersburg Mining University in St. Petersburg. On July 25, 1998, Yeltsin appointed Putin head of the Federal Security Service (FSB), the successor agency to the KGB. He held this powerful position until August 9, 1999, when he was appointed as one of three first deputy prime ministers. Later that day he was appointed acting prime minister of the Russian Federation.[73]

By the end of the year, Yeltsin resigned, and Putin then became the acting president of Russia. One of Putin's first acts as president was to pardon Yeltsin of all crimes and charges leveled against him.

---

[73] Kim Hjelmgaard and Anna Nemtsova, "A Life on the World Stage, but Scant Biographical Details: What We Know of the Life of Vladimir Putin," *USA Today*, February 19, 2022, retrieved April 10, 2022, https://www.usatoday.com/story/news/world/2022/02/19/putin-biography/6830111001/.

Based on all of this, the natural question to ask is how Putin went from a KGB officer to president of one of the most powerful countries in the world. So who is Mr. Putin? This question is explored in detail in the book *Mr. Putin: Operative in the Kremlin* by Fiona Hill and Clifford G. Gaddy.[74] The authors say he consolidated power during this period by taking control of two wars in the North Caucasus against Chechnya that spanned from August 1999 to April 2009. Chechnya, a small Muslim republic, had sought independence since the Soviet Union collapsed. Putin directed a brutal war against Chechnya to put down any attempt at separation. Grozny, Chechnya's capital city, was bombed relentlessly and destroyed. Between 25,000 and 50,000 Chechens, mostly civilians, died or went missing. By 2009, Russian loyalists in Chechnya were in control. But these wars exposed Putin's viciousness.[75]

He was elected for his first full term in 2000, and he began to crack down on the media and his political opponents. He extended his control by the forceful annexation of land in Georgia. In 2014 Russia started a protracted conflict with Ukraine in the regions of Crimea and Donbass. Russia's upper chamber of government approved military force in Ukraine, and so Russia invaded using soldiers and equipment without insignia. Within months Crimea was annexed.

The Ukraine–Russian war continues to this day. More than 10,000 troops have been killed. Civilian casualties have exceeded 13,000 killed and more than 30,000 wounded according to the United Nations High Commissioner for Human Rights.[76]

Most of the protests carried out by political opponents of Putin in Russia have been widely attended and peaceful, in the same way that Black Lives Matter protests were in many American cities after the murders of Breonna Taylor, Ahmaud Arbery, and George Floyd in 2020. Yet police in each country, with federal support of armed combative troops, often without insignia on their clothing, used excessive

---

[74] Fiona Hill and Clifford G. Gaddy, *Mr. Putin: Operative in the Kremlin* (Washington, DC: The Brookings Institution, 2013).
[75] Greg Myre, "Russia's Wars in Chechnya Offer a Grim Warning of What Could Be in Ukraine," NPR, March 12, 2022, retrieved April 10, 2022, https://www.npr.org/2022/03/12/1085861999/russias-wars-in-chechnya-offer-a-grim-warning-of-what-could-be-in-ukraine.
[76] US Department of State, *Ukraine—United States Department of State*, November 4, 2021, retrieved January 5, 2022, https://www.state.gov/reports/2020-country-reports-on-human-rights-practices/ukraine/.

force against peaceful protestors, many of whom sustained injuries and arrest.

From both the US intelligence agencies and the Mueller investigation, we know that Donald Trump's 2016 campaign for president of the United States was aided by Russian operatives after they hacked the campaign headquarters of Hillary Clinton. Then the hacked emails and other documents were passed on to WikiLeaks. Finally, the stolen material was used to create misinformation about Hillary Clinton's campaign on multiple social media platforms such as Twitter and Facebook. Lastly, a report released by the Federal Bureau of Investigation (FBI) reported that Trump was aided by the Putin government in the 2020 election, as well as in 2016.[77]

Donald Trump and Vladimir Putin are autocrats and nationalists. It's difficult not to see Trump and Putin other than through the lens of authoritarianism. Throughout Trump's term in office, the United States drifted toward authoritarian and autocratic rule. Anne Applebaum[78] shows how liberal democracy is under siege, not only in the United States but in other countries around the world. Applebaum is a Pulitzer-prize-winning American journalist and historian. She makes a crucial point when she says that dictatorial leaders do not rule alone. They rely on political allies, bureaucrats, and the media. Trump hired people like Paul Manafort, Rick Gates, Steve Bannon, and Stephen Miller, all of whom who embraced autocracy.

Trump filtered his cabinet and close advisors by removing those not loyal to him. Being loyal to the "leader" is one of the personifications of autocracy. In addition to Putin, Trump rubbed shoulders with autocratic leaders of illiberal states such as Kim Jong-un of North Korea, Andrzej Duda of Poland, and Recep Tayyip Erdoğan of Turkey.

Trump's ascendency to the presidency was a signal to illiberalism internationally and in the United States. Trump's vulgarity, mockery, and insults combined with his aversion to criticism led to resentment toward

---

[77] National Intelligence Council, "Foreign Threats to US 2020 Elections," March 10, 2021, retrieved March 26, 2021, https://www.dni.gov/files/ODNI/documents/assessments/ICA-declass-16MAR21.pdf.
[78] Anne Applebaum, Twilight of Democracy: The Seductive Lure of Authoritarianism. (New York: Doubleday, 2020).

his targets. People who were confined to the fringes of politics now found a new place in the mainstream. Trump's attacks on immigrants were welcomed by white nationalists and supremacists.[79]

In Trump's case, he fired administrators, cabinet members, and other officials to remove those people who were not loyal to him and would not be willing to carry out his conspiracies and policies. The first to go was James Comey, director of the FBI. Many others followed.

> **Author's Update:** On February 24, 2022, Vladimir Putin invaded Ukraine. Cities and towns have been bombed and leveled; millions of Ukrainians have fled their country and millions more have been displaced. Like Donald Trump, Putin lied to the Russian people, telling them that the "special military operation" in Ukraine is to protect people who have been facing genocide by the Kiev regime. He lied to the world, saying they invaded to de-militarize and de-Nazify Ukraine. Putin has threatened the world, saying that he would act against anyone tempted to interfere with him. He put his nuclear forces on high alert, using this as a provocation aimed at NATO.[80] Further discussion and analysis of the Russian invasion of Ukraine can be found on my blog at jackhassard.org.

AUTHORITARIANISM

Trump used the playbook of authoritarians, and this has had a distinct effect on American politics and democracy, even after he left office. Authoritarian playbook strategies include rigging elections, calling the press "enemies of the people," stacking the judiciary, insisting on law and order, perpetuating conspiracy theories, and lying. This authoritarian playbook will have lasting effects on American society and politics.[81]

---

[79] Rosenthal, *Empire of Resentment*.
[80] Bloomberg, *Translation of Vladimir Putin's Televised Address on Ukraine*, Bloomberg.com, retrieved March 20, 2022, https://www.bloomberg.com/news/articles/2022-02-24/full-transcript-vladimir-putin-s-televised-address-to-russia-on-ukraine-feb-24. Putin's threats have raised the alarm of many that he might use nuclear weapons.
[81] Lena Surzhko Harned and Luis Jimenez, "President Trump's Use of the Authoritarian Playbook Will Have Lasting Consequences," YubaNet.com, December 17, 2020, retrieved January 20, 2021, https://yubanet.com/opinions/lena-surzhko-harned-and-luis-jimenez-president-trumps-use-of-the-authoritarian-playbook-will-have-lasting-consequences/.

Authoritarianism is no longer a threat to the United States; it's arrived, and it is the underlying policy of the Republican Party. As author and professor of pedagogy, Henry A. Giroux has said the Republican Party no longer hides its racism and has boldly engaged in voter suppression.[82] Specifically, Republicans have made clear that they endorse the white supremacist idea that the United States should be a white nation much like they think America used to be.

At the center of the authoritarian shift by the Republicans is the Big Lie (*Magnum Mendacium*) and voter suppression in state legislatures. The Big Lie directly led to the January 6, 2021, insurrection, and by mid-February of that year, the Republican Party and state legislators had started dangerous and unprecedented restrictive voting bills in more than forty-two states.

Georgia has led the way by passing a bill on March 25, 2021, that will limit people's opportunity to vote, especially in the neighborhoods of people of color. Brian Kemp, the governor of Georgia, signed the bill in a closed-door meeting with six white legislators looking on, while Park Cannon, a Black Georgia representative knocked on the door wanting to see the governor sign the bill. She, however, was arrested by a team of police, dragged from the state house, and charged with two felonies. This is a perfect example of authoritarianism in action. If this isn't also a case of racism and suppression, then what is?

The current wave of voter suppression bills, especially the Georgia bill, is a backlash against the successful campaigns of activist groups, such as Fair Fight led by Stacey Abrams. Fair Fight helped register a million new voters in Georgia, which helped win the state for Joe Biden and elect Raphael Warnock, the first Black senator from Georgia, and Jon Ossoff, the winner of the other Georgia US Senate election.

Voter suppression bills are being circulated to state legislatures by the Koch brothers-backed American Legislative Exchange Council (ALEC).[83] Known as the "bill mill," ALEC provides copycat legislation to states that

---

[82] Henry A. Giroux, "Threat of Authoritarianism Is No Longer on the Horizon: It's Arrived in the GOP," Truthout.org, March 26, 2021, retrieved March 27, 2021, https://truthout.org/articles/threat-of-authoritarianism-is-no-longer-on-the-horizon-its-arrived-in-the-gop/.

[83] ALEC, funded by corporations in the United States and globally, secretly collaborates with Republican state legislatures to push specific laws using "model bills" that designed to affect almost every area of American life, including voting rights (https://www.exposedbycmd.org/alec/).

are members of the council. Republicans only have to fill in the blanks to make the written draft look like the bill originated and was written by said state legislators. Therefore, you will note that the bills in Republican-held legislatures look a lot alike. It's because they share ALEC-generated voter bills.[84] I spent a lot of time investigating ALEC and have seen many of their bills presented in the Georgia legislature. The legislators who file the bills act as if they came up with the idea and the language.

ALEC bills are not just about voting. They include a wide range of policy initiatives, such as bills on worker and consumer rights, tort reform and injured Americans, and privatizing schools and higher education.[85]

2020 was not the first time that ALEC circulated voter suppression bills. After Barack Obama was elected president in 2008, ALEC started circulating a host of voter suppression bills. More than thirty states were writing election laws ahead of elections in 2010, 2012, and beyond.

The new voting laws, such as those in Georgia, Florida, Texas, and other states, require voter ID. According to the Center for Media and Democracy,[86] this requirement would serve to disenfranchise many low-income, minority, elderly, and student voters, many of whom do not have driver's licenses. In many states, the offices that would supply IDs are not found near the communities that would have the greatest needs. For many of these people, taking the time to get an ID would be burdensome and might result in many people simply not voting. Wisconsin added a requirement to its voting bill that requires the ID have the current address of the voter, which would harm university students and low-income voters who might often move.

The Republican Party lost big time in fair and just elections in 2020. Republican legislators have launched an effort to limit voting and make it harder for people to cast a ballot to make sure they don't lose future elections. The bills are obviously racist and will face strong pushbacks, resistance, and lawsuits.

---

[84] "Democracy, Voter Rights, and Federal Power," ALEC Exposed, Center for Media and Democracy, retrieved May 9, 2021, https://www.alecexposed.org/wiki/Democracy,_Voter_Rights,_and_Federal_Power.
[85] The Center for Media and Democracy has done activist work to expose the bills that ALEC has developed and is passing on to legislatures across the country. ALEC Exposed is the go-to website to find the bills that might be infiltrated into your state legislature: https://www.alecexposed.org/wiki/ALEC_Exposed.
[86] ALEC Exposed website.

Controlling elections is one of the hallmarks of authoritarian governments. Donald Trump tried to "steal" the election not simply by calling foul but by using the office of the president to try and force state officials and even the Department of Justice either to change votes or simply claim he was the winner.

The current effort to change election laws throughout the country stems from Trump's failure to "steal" the election. Republicans believe the only way they can win is to restrict voting. According to the Brennan Center for Justice, there have been more than 165 restrictive bills in 42 states introduced this year, compared to 35 in the previous year.[87]

The suppression and the associated control of elections is a fundamental goal of the Republican Party. The purpose of storming the Capitol was to change the outcome of the 2020 election. It didn't work. Perhaps suppressing voters by changing election laws will change the outcome of future elections.

POLITICAL RIGHTS AND FREEDOM OF THE PRESS

According to the Freedom House's 2020 annual assessment and rankings of the political rights and civil liberties of a country, the United States' democratic institutions have suffered erosion "as reflected in partisan pressure on the electoral process, bias and dysfunction in the criminal justice system, harmful policies on immigration and asylum seekers, and growing disparities in wealth, economic opportunity, and political influence." We are not the most democratic country in the Freedom House rankings. Norway and Finland are the most democratic countries, with a score of 100/100, while the United States' score was 83/100.[88]

Over the past fourteen years, democracies are in decline, according to Freedom House. For example, in 2019, 64 countries experienced deterioration in political rights and civil liberties, compared to only 37 improving.[89] Dictators and authoritarian regimes continue to hold power over their citizens. Indeed, Donald Trump drifted toward authoritarianism

---

[87] Brennan Center for Justice, July 1, 2021, https://www.brennancenter.org/.
[88] Sarah Repucci, *A Leaderless Struggle for Democracy* (Washington, DC: Freedom House, 2020), https://freedomhouse.org/report/freedom-world/2020/leaderless-struggle-democracy.
[89] Repucci, *Leaderless Struggle*.

by removing safeguards for the most vulnerable, disregarding the rights of opposition groups and critics, and trying to steal the presidential election by invoking an insurrection on January 6, 2021.

Trump's persistent lying and his use of conspiracy theories created a new normal for truth and reliability. According to Henry Giroux, under the Trump regime, a culture of lying normalized a world where truth was not only undermined but lost its legitimacy. Truth, in Trump's world, is assigned to "fake news." In a sense, a form of illiteracy appeared during the Trump years that led to threats and violence.[90]

For example, the governor of Michigan, who was using the science of social distancing and isolation to mitigate the coronavirus, was threatened with violence when the state capitol was attacked by right-wing mobs. One of the groups of militants plotted to kidnap and kill her.[91] They were arrested and face state and federal charges. One of them was sentenced to six years in prison. In short, normalizing lying and conspiracy has led the nation into a realm of dangers.

DANGEROUSNESS

Donald Trump is a dangerous man. There is plenty of evidence to support this. The best description of him was offered by his niece, Dr. Mary Trump.[92] In interviews she described specific events and family patterns that created this damaged man. Dr. Trump reveals important ideas about her grandfather, Fred Trump, that would have had a direct impact on Donald Trump's character and led to him becoming a dangerous person.

One of the lessons that the Trump sons (Donald, Fred Jr., and Robert) and daughters (Maryanne Trump Barry and Elizabeth Trump Grau) learned at an early age was that life has only winners and losers. Donald Trump applied this principle throughout his life. When John McCain died, Trump told his staff, "We're not going to support that

---

[90] Giroux, "Threat of Authoritarianism."
[91] Jaclyn Diaz, "One of the Men Charged in the Michigan Governor Kidnap Plot Gets Six Years in Prison," NPR, August 26, 2021, retrieved October 14, 2021, https://www.npr.org/2021/08/26/1031172713/kidnap-plot-prison-michigan-governor.
[92] Mary L. Trump, *Too Much and Never Enough: How My Family Created the World's Most Dangerous Man* (New York: Simon & Schuster, 2020).

loser's funeral." He also said that John McCain was not a war hero. During a television interview, Trump said, "He's a war hero because he was captured. I like people that weren't captured." In other words, there is only one winner; everyone else is a loser.[93]

Mary Trump points out that to the Trumps, "winners versus losers" was not only about business, it was also how Fred Trump Sr. ran his family. Then she explains that the second philosophy of life according to Fred Trump Sr. was the power of positive thinking. Everything is always good. There is no room for feelings. Even if you are suffering, as his wife often did because of being in hospital with broken bones, he'd come into the room where she was recuperating and say, "Everything's great, right, toots?"[94] We must wonder why she had so many broken bones.

This is a clear path to becoming a cruel and unempathetic human being. Empathy is the ability to understand another's experience in the world as if you were that person but without ever losing the "as if" condition.[95] Donald Trump rarely, if ever, showed any signs of empathy. During the year that the COVID-19 pandemic ravaged the world, he said he would take no responsibility for the disease spreading across the country. And he also followed his father's instructions in saying always that everything is all right. "We have the coronavirus under control." "It will get warm, and the virus will disappear."[96] After getting the coronavirus disease and being hospitalized himself, he told Americans, "You shouldn't let the virus control your life. Everything will be just fine."[97]

Mary Trump explains the myth of Donald Trump's success. The projects that he developed, the Grand Hyatt and the Trump Tower,

---

[93] Trump, *Too Much and Never Enough*, 43.
[94] Gabrielle Schonder, The *Frontline* Interview: Mary Trump, *Frontline*, July 30, 2020, retrieved February 27, 2021, https://www.pbs.org/wgbh/frontline/interview/mary-trump/.
[95] Carl Ransom Rogers, *A Theory of Therapy, Personality, and Interpersonal Relationships: As Developed in the Client-Centered Framework* (New York: McGraw Hill, 1959), retrieved March 27, 2021, https://www.google.com/books/edition/A_Theory_of_Therapy_Personality_and_Inte/zslBtwAACAAJ?hl=en.
[96] Jon Greenberg, "'We Have It Totally under Control.' A Timeline of President Donald Trump's Response to the Coronavirus Pandemic," *Poynter*, March 24, 2020, retrieved April 2, 2022, https://www.poynter.org/fact-checking/2020/we-have-it-totally-under-control-a-timeline-of-president-donald-trumps-response-to-the-coronavirus-pandemic/.
[97] Donald J. Trump, "Don't Let the Coronavirus Dominate Your Life!" October 2, 2020, retrieved April 2, 2022, https://www.youtube.com/watch?v=OuhBF74ZD8E.

were financed by his father. His father's connections and money built the myth. According to Dr. Trump, the Atlantic City debacle and failure opened Fred Trump Sr.'s eyes that it was his funding, and not Donald's ability, that led to any success. He began to realize that Donald might not be good at anything. However, because he had been perpetuating the myth and financing Donald's work, Fred Trump Sr. needed to continue to support him.

The gravity of Donald Trump as president of the United States couldn't be any clearer than what happened on January 6, 2021. On that day he incited mobs of white supremacists to storm the Capitol and try an insurrection and takeover of the United State government. Trump led a failed coup. This mob of individuals was driven by Trump's Big Lie. Their actions stand for what has become of the Republican Party.

Unfortunately, the danger that was provoked on that day continues to this day in the form of Trumpism. Trump would likely plot to take control over the Republican Party, knowing that a majority of Republicans support him running for president in 2024.[98] He is carefully choosing those he will support in future elections, especially 2022. He is taking out his revenge on those Republicans who didn't support him in the last days of his term.

TRUMP'S MENTAL HEALTH

According to some healthcare professionals, it is unethical to withhold an assessment of someone when there is more than sufficient information. In her most recent book, *Profile of a Nation: Trump's Mind, America's Soul*, Dr. Bandy X. Lee says that a group of Harvard psychiatrists and other mental health professionals stated, "We know more about this president than we do about any patient we have ever treated."[99] Donald Trump may be out of office, but his "profile" is like it was when he was in the Oval Office. He is still a danger to all citizens

---

[98] Gabriela Schulte, "Poll: Just under Half of Voters Support Trump Running in 2024," *The Hill*, October 21, 2021, retrieved November 19, 2021, https://thehill.com/hilltv/what-americas-thinking/577199-poll-just-under-half-of-voters-support-trump-running-in-2024.
[99] Lee, *Profile of a Nation*, 42.

of the United States. And the longer he is out of office, the more that is revealed about just how dangerous he is.

According to Lee, Trump "follows his gut" rather than preparing, deliberating, or listening to career advisors when meeting with world leaders or talking about problems such as the COVID-19 pandemic. He usually will say, "We'll see what happens," a clear signal that he is unwilling or unable to decide how to solve a problem. When the pandemic was "breaking out," Trump claimed that it was a hoax perpetuated by Democrats. He seemed more concerned about how reports about the pandemic were affecting the stock market.

There is considerable information and firsthand accounts to develop a full picture of Trump's character, motivations, and mind. Lee supplies five accounts written by a biographer (Tony Schwartz), a national security advisor (John Bolton), a personal lawyer and fixer (Michael Cohen), a presidential journalist (Bob Woodward), and a family member (Dr. Mary Trump). Lee's assessment, which I read along with the original books written by each author, provide panoramic insights into Donald Trump's mind and behavior.

In Bob Woodward's book *Rage*, former Secretary of State Rex Tillerson and former director of national intelligence Dan Coats agreed during a phone call that there might be a time to announce publicly that Donald Trump was dangerous and unfit for office.[100] Woodward concluded that the "man is not fit for the job."[101] His book *Peril*, coauthored with Robert Costa, is even more disturbing.[102] The book explores the last days of Trump in office and reveals the corruption that erupted in the Oval Office in an attempt to overthrow the American government and its election.

Tony Schwartz, ghostwriter for *Trump: The Art of the Deal*, spent a lot of time with Trump. He explained of Trump that "lying is second nature to him."[103] And if he was called out for a lie, he would double down, repeat the lie, and become hostile.

---

[100] Lee, *Profile of a Nation*, 64–65.
[101] Bob Woodward, *Rage* (New York: Simon & Schuster, 2019), 390.
[102] Bob Woodward and Robert Costa, *Peril* (Simon & Schuster: New York, 2021).
[103] Lee, *Profile of a Nation*, 55.

Lee considered John Bolton's account of Trump the least reliable because of his motivation in releasing the book when he did and not coming forward during the impeachment hearings. Bolton saw firsthand that Trump lacks the mental ability and basic requirements to be fit for the presidency.[104]

Michael Cohen not only worked for Trump as his personal attorney but, Lee suggests, he got closer to Trump than his family. In his account, Cohen revealed that Trump was "a cheat, a liar, a fraud, a bully, a racist, a predator, a con man."[105] According to Lee, Cohen's description of Trump is consistent with what mental health professionals have witnessed. Cohen reveals that Trump did indeed "collude" with the Russians, although not at the level that Mueller and his investigators were thinking. Cohen says that Trump did try to build a Trump Tower in Moscow. It was true that Trump would welcome any kind of help from Putin, and he admired Putin because he believed the Russian leader was very wealthy.[106]

Donald Trump is authoritarian, dangerous, and solipsistic. I've included blog posts that describe Trump's narcissism and his attempt to impart authoritarian rule in the United States. You will find discussions of why I named him "The Authoritarian" and how I believed he could be resisted. He was the most dangerous president ever to take up residence in the White House. You'll find posts about how he was and still is a clear and present danger. I believe that Donald Trump is a con man, and if he were to become president again, our nation would face an existential threat more menacing than the climate crisis.

---

[104] Lee, *Profile of a Nation*, 57.
[105] Lee, *Profile of a Nation*, 59.
[106] Michael Cohen, *Disloyal: A Memoir: The True Story of the Former Personal Attorney to President Donald J. Trump* (New York: Skyhorse Publishing, 2020).

CHAPTER 1:
AUTHORITARIANISM

1.1.[107] BLOG POST, 31 JULY 2016: I ALONE CAN FIX IT

Long before I saw Rev. Dr. William J. Barber II speak, I had read many of his published papers, especially in the *Nation* magazine. Rev. Dr. Barber is president of the North Carolina NAACP and has dedicated his life to social justice. I admire him and the work he has been doing. Rev. Dr. Barber is also cochair of the Poor People's Campaign and president of the Repairers of the Breach. Rev. Dr. Barber is working with Congress to unveil a congressional resolution for a Third Reconstruction, which seeks to expand voting rights, implement immigration reform, raise minimum wage, set up a jobs program, and more. According to Rev. Dr. Barber, there is not a scarcity of resources; what there is, is a scarcity of social justice conscience.[108]

On July 29, 2016, Rev. Dr. Barber gave a speech at the Democratic National Convention (DNC) in Philadelphia. It was the fourth night of convention speeches given by Democratic luminaries. But this speech stood out from the others.

In his speech at the DNC, Rev. Dr. Barber said that there are some issues that are not left versus right or liberal versus conservative. They are right versus wrong. He said we need to embrace our deepest moral values and push for revival of the heart of our democracy when we fight to reinstate the power of the Voting Rights Act.

---

[107] Please note that throughout the book, the blog posts are numbered in sequence and dated signifying when the post was published on my blog.
[108] Amy Goodman, "Rev. Barber calls for 'Third Reconstruction' to Lift 140 Million Out of Poverty," Truthout.org, May 21, 2021, retrieved May 22, 2021, https://truthout.org/video-rev-barber-calls-for-third-reconstruction-to-lift-140-million-out-of-poverty/.

Rev. Dr. Barber said he normally wouldn't endorse a particular candidate for the presidency, but when he heard "stuff" at the Republican National Convention (RNC) that bordered on heresy—when he heard a candidate at the 2016 RNC say, "I alone can fix it"[109]—then he hoped if the opportunity came to speak at the DNC, he might consider it.

The speech he delivered is as relevant now as it was in 2016. I've listened to his speech many times, and each time I hear Rev. Dr. Barber say that the heart of democracy is on the line in the next election and beyond.

One of the ideas that resonates with me is Rev. Dr. Barber's statement that "we must shock this nation and fight for justice for all. We can't give up on the heart of democracy, not now, not ever!" I cheered when he said he believed it was a moral obligation to get about the business of defeating the Republican Party's nominee, Donald Trump.

He started off by saying, "I might not normally be here as a preaching individual, but when I hear human voices and positions are here, and I know [Hillary Clinton] is working to embrace our deepest moral values, and we should embrace her. But let me be clear that [neither] she nor any person can do it alone. The watchword of this democracy and the watchword of faith is we." A link to Rev. Dr. Barber's speech is provided in the footnotes.[110] I hope you will take the ten minutes to listen to his words and then consider what they might mean to you, your community, and the nation.

In his speech he went on to say there is a need for the kind of language that's not left or right or conservative or liberal, but moral fusion language that says:

- It is extreme and immoral to suppress the right to vote.
- It is extreme and immoral to deny Medicaid to millions of poor people, especially when denied by people who have been elected to office and receive their own insurance through that office.

---

[109] Yoni Appelbaum, "Trump's Claim: 'I Alone Can Fix It," *The Atlantic*, July 22, 2016, retrieved November 19, 2021, https://www.theatlantic.com/politics/archive/2016/07/trump-rnc-speech-alone-fix-it/492557/.
[110] Rev. Dr. William J. Barber II, "We Must Fight for the Heart of Our Democracy!" speech given at the 2016 Democratic National Convention, https://www.youtube.com/watch?v=DNcP82-trrA.

- It is extreme and immoral to raise taxes on the working poor and cut earned-income tax credits, especially to slash taxes for the wealthy.
- It is extreme and immoral to shut off people's water in Detroit.
- It is extreme and immoral to end unemployment compensation for those who have lost jobs through no fault of their own.
- It is extreme and immoral to resegregate and underfund our public schools.
- It is mean, it is immoral, it is extreme to kick hardworking people when they are down.

1.2. BLOG POST, 25 NOVEMBER 2016: WHY I NAMED HIM "THE AUTHORITARIAN"

On this blog, I refer to the next POTUS as "The Authoritarian." My choice for using this term to name him is based on the research done by George Lakoff.[111] Lakoff is the retired distinguished professor of cognitive science and linguistics at the University of California, Berkeley. He is now director of the Center for Neural Mind & Society. I read and studied much of Lakoff's work over the past decade and have found it important in my understanding of authoritarianism and a deeper understanding of how liberal and conservative political views differ. I found Lakoff's theory of moral worldviews relevant to understanding Donald Trump. In earlier blog writing, Lakoff's theory helped me answer questions about K–12 public education. I wanted to explain why authoritarianism loomed over education, making it difficult to implement many progressive reforms I valued.

Lakoff's theory explains why we can call Donald Trump an authoritarian. I know this is a bit academic, but his theory is quite practical and helpful in understanding Trump and the Americans who are moved by his views.

---

[111] George Lakoff, *Moral Politics: How Liberals and Conservatives Think* (Chicago: University of Chicago Press, 2010).

Using a conceptual metaphor of nation as family, Lakoff maps two types of families. They are the "nurturant" family and the "strict father" family. An idealized nurturant family is expressed in terms of progressive values: empathy, caring, support for each other, public resources for all. We might call these people liberals or maybe progressives. An idealized strict father family is expressed in terms of power and authority, which rests with the head of the family (the father) or the head of the nation—authoritarian values. These are conservatives.

Lakoff makes it clear that the head of the strict father family cannot be a loser, corrupt, or a betrayer of trust. Father knows best. But here is what Layoff says characterizes the president-elect:

> LOSER: To the American majority, he is a loser, a minority president. It needs to be said and repeated.
>
> CORRUPT: He is corrupting his office in a direct way by refusing to put his business interests in a blind trust. By doing so, and by insisting on his children both running the business and getting classified information, he is using the presidency to make himself incredibly wealthy. This is corruption of the highest and most blatant level.
>
> BETRAYER OF TRUST: Trump is a betrayer of trust. He is acting like a dictator—and even supporting Putin's anti-American policies.[112]

In Lakoff's analysis, the president-elect is interested only in absolute authority, money, power, and celebrity. These are not the characteristics of a president in a democratic society, but let's face it, this is what we have. Although we have had authoritarian presidents in the past, none have risen to the level of betrayal of democratic principles as has Donald

---

[112] George Lakoff, "A Minority President: Why the Polls Failed and What the Majority Can Do," Common Dreams, November 22, 2016, retrieved November 24, 2016, https://www.commondreams.org/views/2016/11/22/minority-president-trump-why-polls-failed-and-what-majority-can-do.

Trump. As Lakoff points out, we must create a powerful network of communication and call out The Authoritarian, and make sure that he knows not only that he's being watched but also that there are moral imperatives on the opposite end of his, and that they are rooted in the principles of democracy, which have had to be fought for by many people living in this country. He and his administration will present a clear and present danger.

Here are some of behaviors that are most associated with The Authoritarian:

- Autocratic
- Dictatorial
- Imperious
- Totalitarian
- Tyrannical
- Dogmatic
- Harsh
- Severe
- Unyielding
- Despotic
- Oppressive

His attitude toward the press sends chills down my spine and further undermines the free exchange of ideas. We should know what the president is up to. His ideas should be known and should be subject to criticism. We should be able to question The Authoritarian.

The problem is the next POTUS doesn't want anyone questioning what he thinks or does. If you do, he'll call you out, or worse.

1.3. BLOG POST, 30 APRIL 2017: RESISTING THE NARCISSIST IN THE WHITE HOUSE

Sometimes it's hard to believe what's happened to our country in the wake of the last presidential election. But, that said, we must face what is happening, act, and support and be a part of the opposition and protestation of the deconstruction of America and its relationship with the rest of the world.

Here are two ideas that are pertinent to understanding Trump's mental fitness, as well as those around him.

- **Narcissistic:** A person having an excessive or erotic interest in oneself and one's physical appearance; vain, self-obsessed, egotistic, arrogant, self-centered.
- **Sycophant:** Someone who is a self-seeking, servile flatterer; flattering parasite.

After thanking President Barack Obama and First Lady Michelle Obama for their gracious aid throughout the transition, he launched into a dreadful attack on democratic norms and expectations.

Early in his inaugural speech, he said, "This American carnage stops right here and stops right now."[113] This was also the speech where Trump's vision for the country is going to be "America first." The slogan was used among Americans who resisted entering WWII. It was also associated with anti-Semites during this time and tended not to be used for decades, until now. Trump also used his words to insult politicians by saying that politicians who are "all talk and no action" will no longer be accepted. This was used to refer to Representative John Lewis, and it caused dozens of Democrats to skip the inauguration.

Donald Trump painted a dark picture of the world in his inaugural speech. He continued to repeat this mantra of the presidential campaign, not only within the White House but especially when he goes on the road like he did on the hundredth day of his presidency in front of a crowd in Pennsylvania. As one Republican advisor to Ronald Reagan put it, "Last night's speech by Trump was the most divisive ever by a president."[114]

---

[113] Shane Goldmacher, "This American Carnage Stops Right Here," Politico, January 24, 2017, retrieved April 3, 2022, https://www.politico.eu/article/this-american-carnage-stops-right-here/.
[114] Mary Papenfuss, "Reagan Adviser Slams Trump Rally Speech as 'Most Divisive Ever' from a President," HuffPost.com, April 30, 2017, retrieved November 20, 2021, https://www.huffpost.com/entry/adviser-trump-divisive-speech_n_5905617fe4b02655f83e0aef.

Resistance to Trump's actions and lies were immediate and wide-ranging. Here are some of them.

INAUGURATION

The first action was no action. Few people showed up on January 20, 2017, to watch the inauguration, although the narcissist claims the media was wrong. Even when one of his own government agencies took pictures of the crowds at his and Obama's first inauguration, Trump defied the images that showed clearly how massive Obama's inauguration was—and how his was not.

However, Trump can take credit for the fact that hundreds of demonstrations were held across the United States. These were held the same day of the inauguration protesting the very nature of Trump's existence.

THE WOMEN'S MARCH

The second and most important action to confront and block Trump's world was the Women's March on January 21, 2017. The numbers worldwide are staggering: 500,000 people (about half the population of South Dakota) marched in Washington, DC. More than 2 million marched in other US cities. Worldwide, 81 countries held marches in 168 locations. Organizers reported after the marches that at least 5 million people (about twice the population of Mississippi) took part, with 673 marches held worldwide. In the United States, the only protest that rivaled the Women's March were marches held in protest of the Vietnam War.[115]

ROGUE TWITTER SITES

One of the first rogue Twitter groups to open an account was @AltBadlandsPark out of fear that the Trump administration would inflict damage to this national park's website. Would Trump's minions block or remove data that is available to all of us?

Employees at the Environmental Protection Agency (EPA) and Departments of Interior, Agriculture, and Health and Human Services

---

[115] Anemona Hartocollis and Yamiche Alcindor, "Women's March Highlights as Huge Crowds Protest Trump: 'We're Not Going Away,'" *New York Times*, January 21, 2017, https://www.nytimes.com/2017/01/21/us/womens-march.html.

had reported that notices appeared instructing them to take down certain pages and to watch what is said to the media, and that papers written by department employees should be checked before being published in any form. The muzzling of information is a huge problem for us and is not unprecedented. The George W. Bush administration was a champion of the Muzzle Award.[116]

What followed was the emergence of many rogue accounts, some of which claimed to be authored by employees of various government agencies. The sites do a service by highlighting the discontent that exists across the federal government.[117]

THE MARCH FOR SCIENCE

On Earth Day, April 22, 2017, more than 600 cities across the world held rallies and marches called the March for Science.[118] It initially was called the Scientists' March on Washington. The significance of the March for Science was a rebuttal to the Trump administration's lies, fake news obsession, and the unimaginable impact on human health and the environment.

For example, Trump has recommended the EPA budget be cut by 30 percent, which would mean that thousands of people will lose their jobs and dozens of programs that are carried out by the states would be abolished. Recently I talked with the parents of a young woman who is an environmental lawyer. She works with a nonprofit in the DC area that helps companies move towards clean energy usage. I asked the parents what their daughter thought of Trump's EPA budget cuts. Their daughter said she just couldn't talk about it and spent a lot of time crying before getting on with her important task. I told these parents that their daughter is one of many lawyers who are using their knowledge and experience to fight the good fight against Trump and his minions.

The March for Science showed that science should be nonpartisan. However, it also showed that scientists, with non-scientists, can protest

---

[116] Chris Mooney, *The Republican War on Science* (New York: Basic Books, 2005).
[117] Some of the accounts can still be accessed, such as twitter.com/ActualEPAFacts and altnps.org
[118] March for Science: https://marchforscience.org/.

together to question the Trump administration's view of science and to call out a Congress that ignores science in the face of its effect on the people.

It also showed that there is a large segment of the world's population that believes government policy should be evidence-based and accepts, for example, the scientific communities' consensus on climate change and evolution.

THE PEOPLE'S CLIMATE MARCH

On April 29, 2017, the one-hundredth day of Trump's administration, people marched in Washington, DC, and many locations in cities around the US. This was a direct protest to the Trump administration's disregard for climate science and its disregard for environmental policies designed to protect human health and the environment.[119]

The People's Climate March couldn't be any timelier, especially considering the EPA website. If you follow the link titled "Climate Change" on EPA's list of Environmental Topics, it's written, "This page is being updated." The list then says that the page is being updated to fall in line with EPA priorities under Administrator of the EPA Scott Pruitt and Trump. So right now, the climate change page is down, and they redirect you to a snapshot of the page taken on January 19, 2017, when Obama was still president.

1.4. BLOG POST, 5 MAY 2017: CURING OURSELVES OF THE ITCH FOR ABSOLUTE KNOWLEDGE AND POWER

> I beseech you, in the bowels of Christ: Think it possible you may be mistaken.
>
> —Oliver Cromwell

It's difficult to think in terms of tolerance in the age in which America elected a president who doesn't give one hint of being tolerant. What

---

[119] Nicholas Fandos, "Climate March Draws Thousands of Protesters Alarmed by Trump's Environmental Agenda," *New York Times*, April 29, 2017, retrieved January 20, 2021, https://www.nytimes.com/2017/04/29/us/politics/peoples-climate-march-trump.html.

he does do is encourage violence, not only in his campaign rallies, but now, after being elected, he's back on the road holding the same rallies and encouraging hate, bigotry, and racism. With access to the most powerful military in the world, he ordered the launch of fifty-nine Tomahawk missiles, unleashing violence with the push of a button. Even Wilbur Ross, Trump's commerce secretary, said at the Milken Institute Global Conference that the Syria missile strike was "after-dinner entertainment." The guests found his comment humorous and burst into laughter.[120]

What we have here among the people who Trump has assembled in the White House and in his administration are a lot of people who believe in certainty. They believe they have the right answers, never thinking for a moment that they might be wrong, or that in the interests of a civil society, they might compromise. As Oliver Cromwell said, in the quote at the top of this post, "Think it possible you may be mistaken."

Yet people were killed in the Syria bombing, and Americans at a conference, dressed to the nines, laughed at the bombing and found it humorous. What were they thinking?

And today, the House of Representative barely passed a bill (voting 217–213) that replaces the Affordable Care Act, which would mean that more than 20 million people (about the population of New York) could lose their health coverage. This bill also reduces Medicaid payments to the states, which would mean either not as many people would be supported or the support would be less. In addition to the poor, Medicaid also is a lifeline for people with disabilities. To remove or lessen support would be devastating to people in need of it.[121] All major medical groups opposed the bill.

In the Senate, however, John McCain cast the deciding vote, 51–49, against the legislation aimed at dismantling the Affordable Care Act. To

---

[120] Michael R. Gordon, Helene Cooper, and Michael D. Shear, "Dozens of US Missiles Hit Air Base in Syria," *New York Times*, April 6, 2017, retrieved January 20, 2021, https://www.nytimes.com/2017/04/06/world/middleeast/us-said-to-weigh-military-responses-to-syrian-chemical-attack.html.

[121] David Morgan Yasmeen Abutaleb, "US House Passes Republican Health Bill, a Step toward Obamacare Repeal," *Scientific American*, May 4, 2017, retrieved January 20, 2021, https://www.scientificamerican.com/article/u-s-house-passes-republican-health-bill-a-step-toward-obamacare-repeal/.

say the least, Republican Senate leader Mitch McConnell was shocked and had to announce that the billed failed.[122]

I could go on and describe other actions by this administration that show how little they think of people and the effects of their actions on the well-being of citizens. Instead, they are more interested in protecting the interests of businesses and think tanks, and less interested in science. Consequently, we find that the EPA's purpose to protect the environment and human health is being trampled on by ignorance. Scott Pruitt, the EPA administrator and the president's chief denier of climate science, wants to destroy the EPA by reducing its budget by 30 percent, which will lead to unhealthy and unsafe environments (think the Flint River fiasco, which is being repeated across the country).

These are examples of an attack on citizens not only in the US but in other countries as well. Tomahawk missiles, climate science denial, and ignorance are all signs of intolerance and certainty.

Since January 20, the bigotry, racism, and hate crimes have increased enormously.

---

[122] Susan Davis and Domenico Montanaro, "McCain Votes No, Dealing Potential Death Blow to Republican Health Care Efforts," NPR, July 28, 2017, retrieved January 20, 2021, https://www.npr.org/2017/07/27/539907467/senate-careens-toward-high-drama-midnight-health-care-vote.

CHAPTER 2:
DANGEROUSNESS

2.1. BLOG POST, 10 NOVEMBER 2016: HOW COULD WE?
Like many of you, I've spent the day after mourning for our country and the people who have been abused and threatened by the man who was elected over one of the bravest women that we could have had for our president.

- How could we?
- How could we choose the bully?
- How could we enable the press to rarely call him out and hold him accountable for stiffing the American people about his taxes, fraud, sexual assault charges, racist beliefs and actions, his outrageous attitude toward women, and his endless lies?
- How could we allow the far right into the White House through cabinet appointees? It will be a rogue's gallery of has-been politicians and corporate raiders.
- How could we turn our backs on children and families?
- How could we pick a person who thinks climate change is a hoax and will look to remove the environmental protections that have been put in place since *Silent Spring*?
- How could we enable the privatizers of public education to have a voice at 1600 Pennsylvania Avenue?
- How could we not overcome the racism and bigotry that drove his campaign and turned his rallies into assemblies without hoods?

- How could we open the door to the White House to a man who has assaulted countless scores of women, insulted and threatened people who have religious beliefs different from many of us, insulted Mexicans who seek a better life, and riled up the worst in Americans by threatening to build a wall along the Mexican/American border?
- How could we?

Author's Update: According to the *APA Dictionary of Psychology*, "dangerousness" is the state in which individuals become likely to do harm to themselves or to others representing a threat to their own or other people's safety.[123]

Trump's dangerousness becomes visible when we acknowledge that Trump and Trumpism are an assault on reality.[124] Trump has created a community of zealous believers, which you can witness anytime you view a video of one of his rallies. He appointed people to his cabinet positions who were opposed to the actual work of those agencies.

Robert Jay Lifton describes Trump's extreme grandiosity as the perfect remedy for those souls who attend his rallies and voted for him. His dangerousness also appears when his falsehoods morph into government policy, as it did when he sent troops to the border or troops to Portland and other cities around the country. Trump lacks any form of ideology, but according to Lifton, he does have a narrative. His narrative appeared when he announced his run for the presidency and then was repeated at every one of his hundreds of rallies during the 2016 and 2020 elections. His narrative is dangerous and solipsistic. Lifton describes Trump's narrative as:

> America has been great in the past but has been in the wrong hands and allowed to become weak and misused

---

[123] *APA Dictionary of Psychology*, American Psychological Association, s.v. "dangerousness," retrieved January 5, 2022, https://dictionary.apa.org/dangerousness.
[124] Lifton, *Losing Reality*, 155.

by foreign forces, especially allies, who cheat and take advantage of us. He, Trump, and only he, has both the strength and negotiating skills to "make America great again."[125]

2.2. BLOG POST, 14 DECEMBER 2016: A CLEAR AND PRESENT DANGER

There is little doubt that the incoming Republican administration presents a clear and present danger to all citizens in the US and the rest of the world. Never has such an inexperienced, corrupt, and autocratic administration been given the reins to American democracy. This lapse is coupled with a Congress that is in denial of research-based policies for science, health, the environment, and education.

First, we have one of worst presidents-elect in history. He did not secure the votes of the majority. He lost the election by more than 3 million votes, and there is some suspicion that the votes tallied in Wisconsin, Michigan, and Pennsylvania may be contested. If the results in these three states swing to Clinton, she would win the election. Jill Stein, the Green Party presidential candidate, has raised more than $2 million to fund this and has requested recounts in these three states. Wisconsin has indicated it will begin a recount now. The Clinton campaign has joined in the effort.

The Authoritarian is calling foul and is reeling. The words and actions that Trump used and put on display during the primary and presidential campaign describe his beliefs and understandings, which resonated with many but were repulsive to many more. He said Mexicans are criminals, rapists, and drug dealers. He called a judge Mexican because his surname is Hispanic and claimed he would be biased against him in his university fraud case. The judge was born and raised in Indiana.

Degrading women (mocking Carly Fiorina's appearance by saying "look at that face"; saying that Megan Kelly "had blood coming out of her

---

[125] Lifton, *Losing Reality*.

whatever") and using phrases such "lying Ted Cruz," "crooked Hillary," or "little Marco," are part of his lexicon, which he will carry to the White House, perhaps in a disguised form.

He thinks of people as either winners or losers and is quick to give his opinion. In one interview he was asked about Senator John McCain's ordeal as a prisoner of war for seven years. He said, "He was a war hero because he was captured. I like people who weren't captured."

Most incendiary are his racist plans to round up "bad hombres" and create a registry for Muslims, and one of his allies even brought up the disgraced idea of internment camps!

The Authoritarian is also inept when it comes to literature, history, and science. In a tweet in 2012, he said, "The concept of global warming was created by and for the Chinese to make US manufacturing non-competitive."

In addition to his racism, sexism, misogyny, sexual assaults, and corruption, there are other concerns ranging from national security and education to climate change.

NATIONAL SECURITY

The *Washington Post* has reported that Trump has only had two intelligence briefings, turning these away daily. It's reported that he is taking part in fewer briefings than earlier presidents-elect. During the election campaign, he claimed to know more about ISIS and how to defeat it than US Army generals. He also said he wanted to be unpredictable and not say what he is thinking. Many experts on national security are deeply concerned about his lack of preparation and knowledge about security.[126]

EDUCATION

He had little to no respect for public education, and of course he picked as secretary of education a person holding similar beliefs, Betsy DeVos, a billionaire philanthropist from Michigan with zero experience with

---

[126] G. Miller and A. Entous, "Trump Turning Away Intelligence Briefers Since Election Win," *Washington Post*, November 23, 2016, https://www.washingtonpost.com/world/national-security/trump-turning-away-intelligence-briefers-since-election-win/2016/11/23/5cc643c4-b1ae-11e6-be1c-8cec35b1ad25_story.html.

public schools and a predominant advocate for vouchers and charter schools. His choice of DeVos is an injustice for public education. For thirty years or more, Republicans have been dismantling public education one voucher or charter school at a time. And DeVos has been central in this attempt. It's no surprise this person of privilege would be given this post. Add another billionaire to the cabinet. The *New York Times* journalist Kate Zernike said this about DeVos:

> But Ms. DeVos's efforts to expand educational opportunity in her home state of Michigan and across the country have focused little on existing public schools, and entirely on establishing newer, more entrepreneurial models to compete with traditional schools for students and money. Her donations and advocacy go entirely toward groups seeking to move students and money away from what The Authoritarian calls "failing government schools."[127]

The Network for Public Education is calling on US senators to turn her down for cabinet secretary. The Network for Public Education[128] said this about her nomination:

> DeVos believes that the market solves all problems, and she and her husband's foundation spent 1.5 million dollars to persuade the Michigan legislature to kill a bill to regulate charter schools in the state. Thanks to her efforts, 80% of the charters in Michigan operate for profit, without accountability or transparency. Send a clear message to the Senate that Betsy DeVos should not be confirmed as US Secretary of Education. Her hostility towards public schools disqualifies her.

---

[127] Kate Zernike, "Betsy Devos, Trump's Education Pick, Has Steered Money from Public Schools," *New York Times*, November 24, 2016, retrieved November 20, 2021, https://www.nytimes.com/2016/11/23/us/politics/betsy-devos-trumps-education-pick-has-steered-money-from-public-schools.html.
[128] Network For Public Education, retrieved January 6, 2022, https://networkforpubliceducation.org/.

CLIMATE CHANGE

Trump thinks climate change is a political issue, and he falls in line with many lawmakers who are in denial of climate change science. Climate change is an existential threat. The hottest temperatures recorded since record-keeping began have occurred in the past ten years, yet Donald Trump says more research is needed. And more than half the Republicans in Congress deny climate change and the related scientific research that overwhelmingly asserts the realness of climate change. And not because of natural rhythms but because humans have been so good at burning fossil fuels.

Denying climate change is the tip of the iceberg (no pun intended). To deny science in this case leads to a populace that is steeped in ignorance and is sliding off a flat Earth. Ironically, science teachers in our public schools teach the science of climate change in earth science courses. It's part of the curriculum. So the children and teenagers of climate deniers come home each day with ideas that are counter to their parents'.

> **Author's Update:** Chapters 8 and 9 are devoted to extreme weather events and the existential threat of climate change, respectively.

2.3. BLOG POST, 16 AUGUST 2017: WHAT IS ALT-RIGHT?

If there is an alternative right (alt-right), then there must be an alternative left (alt-left)—at least according to Donald Trump, who came down from his gold-plated apartment in New York and said so. He even challenged a reporter who covers the White House to define the term because he has no idea what the term means. Does he know what the term alt-right is? No, but if he were to listen to any of the reporters at this press briefing, he would have learned this about the term alt-right:

- Alt-right was a term coined by a white nationalist, Richard Spencer, to describe the white nationalist movement.
- Alt-right is a movement based on an ideology of white nationalism and anti-Semitism.

- The goal of the alt-right is to destroy the left.
- Alt-right is anti-immigrant, anti-feminist, and against gay and transgender rights.
- Alt-right wants its own homeland within the United States.

ALT-RIGHT AT CHARLOTTESVILLE

At the "Unite the Right" rally in Charlottesville, Virginia, (August 11–12, 2017), the alt-right, which organized the protest about taking down a Confederate statue, outnumbered any of those Americans who were protesting the alt-right's presence in the city. One reporter from NPR, who was on the ground among the protestors, described the "many sides" quite differently than the president. She said that for every American flag at the protest, there were a hundred Nazi flags.[129]

All the alt-right agitators were armed with helmets, clubs, guns, and sprays, and many were in military-style costumes. Those protesting the Nazis and other alt-right groups were the ones not shouting Nazi slogans, such as "blood and soil," and were not an armed camp or group. Many were clergy, and normally the clergy protest peacefully. Although some of those with the clergy had clubs and guns, they were so outnumbered, the NPR reporter made it clear that there were two distinct groups: one armed to the teeth and the other in normal street clothes.[130]

THERE IS NO ALT-LEFT

According to political scientists, there is not an equivalent "alt-left" group. It doesn't exist. However, you might ask: What would be the opposite of a white nationalist group? What are we talking about here? You mean there is a similarity of morality between the ideologies of neo-Nazi white nationalism and those who oppose them?

I don't think so. The alt-right is a fascist collection of people who have faith in autocrats, tyrants, and authoritarians, and they accept a totalitarian way of life.

---

[129] Dave Davies, "In the Wake of Charlottesville, Journalist Begins 'Documenting Hate' in America," *Fresh Air*, NPR, August 2, 2018, https://www.npr.org/2018/08/02/634890750/in-the-wake-of-charlottesville-journalist-begins-documenting-hate-in-america.
[130] Davies, "Wake of Charlottesville."

But the outrageous idea here is that the president of the United States has publicly defended them and called those who oppose these fascists "alt-left," as if there is an equivalency. And throughout his only term in office, Trump supported and asked for help from the alt-right.

> **Author's Update:** When the nation's Capitol was stormed by a white mob on January 6, 2021, there were people who claimed it was alt-left members who infiltrated the Trump protestors. According to FBI reports, the insurrectionists were members of known right-wing groups.[131] Eleven members of the Oath Keepers, a right-wing group, were charged with sedition conspiracy in January 2022.[132]

2.4. BLOG POST, 10 JULY 2021: THE TRUMP RALLIES

Trump took advantage of the discontent that existed in people who lived in red states and would attend his rallies. During the 2016 campaign for president, Trump held 323 rallies, 186 during the primary and 137 during the general election. Most rallies were held in red states, drawing more than 1.4 million people (about half the population of Nevada). All the attendees were white, except for a few protestors and Black security guards or vendors.

In my search for information about the Trump rallies, I found the research of Caroline Teisen Mohan,[133] entitled "Donald Trump Did a 'Very Good' Job: A Rhetorical Analysis of Candidate Trump's Campaign Speeches."

According to Mohan, at these rallies Trump ramps up the crowds of people using "Gingrich-izing" public broadcasting, which is to turn name-calling into a strategic political tool. Indeed, as pointed out by Mohan, Newt Gingrich's strategy is the basis for many politicians'

---

[131] Daniel Funke, "FBI Investigation of Capitol Riot Focuses on Far-Right Groups," Politifact, January 20, 2021, https://www.politifact.com/article/2021/jan/20/fbi-investigation-capitol-riot-focuses-far-right-g/.

[132] United States Department of Justice, "Leader of Oath Keepers and 10 Other Individuals Indicted in Federal Court for Seditious Conspiracy and Other Offenses Related to U.S. Capitol Breach," Justice News, January 13, 2022, retrieved April 15, 2022, https://www.justice.gov/opa/pr/leader-oath-keepers-and-10-other-individuals-indicted-federal-court-seditious-conspiracy-and.

[133] Caroline Mohan, "Donald Trump Did a "Very Good" Job: A Rhetorical Analysis of Candidate Trump's Campaign Speeches," *Senior Honors Projects*, 2010–2019 (bachelor's thesis, James Madison University, 2019), 632, https://commons.lib.jmu.edu/honors201019/632.

communication playbooks. She found that Trump used Gingrich-style word association and inflammatory, reality-skewing speech. That is, Donald Trump used his speeches to take advantage of people who were vulnerable or who had little understanding of the political sphere. In Mohan's study, she described the word combinations and symbols to cause confusion, fear, and resulting anger to win the White House.[134]

Trump was an emotions candidate, according to Arlie Russell Hochschild,[135] the University of California, Berkeley sociologist whose book takes us inside the world of Trump followers. Trump uses phrases and name-calling to elicit emotional responses from his fans and then praises them. He treats them like children or adults who need parenting. This approach is right out of the authoritarian playbook described by George Lakoff,[136] retired distinguished professor of cognitive science and linguistics at the University of California, Berkley. In the conservative/authoritarian worldview, the metaphor that determines how Trump behaves is a family that needs a homeland, citizens as siblings, the government as parent, and so forth.

Trump has been successful at playing the role of the strict father, who is the only one capable of solving problems (only he isn't). He claims, "I alone can fix it." This insistence leads Trump to tell his audience that they must place their trust in him, not anyone else, including God.

Trump demonized his opponents. At his rallies, he used pronouns such as "we" and "us" and "I" to create a bond or collective among the attendees. Mohan cites John A. Powell, professor of law at the University of California, Berkeley who uses the term "othering" to explain how language is used to establish an "out-group" of those who don't share his ideas. At the rallies he used expressions that led to forms of prejudice using words such as "they" and "them."

Here are some phrases from some of his rallies that provide the audience with ways to connect with Trump, and vice versa:

---

[134] Mohan, "Trump Did a 'Very Good' Job," 11.
[135] Hochschild, *Strangers in Their Own Land*.
[136] Lakoff, *Moral Politics*.

- "We're not going to let other countries rip us off!"
- "We're going to build a high wall and Mexico's going to pay for it!"
- "We're going to build up our military!"
- "We're going to knock the hell out of ISIS!"
- "Get that guy out. Get him out."
- "Why is this taking so long? I can't believe it's taking this long."
- "I've been greedy. I'm a businessperson…take, take, take. Now I'm going to be greedy for the United States." (wild cheers)
- "I'd like to punch him in the face."
- "In the good old days, they'd have ripped him out of that seat so fast."

In Mohan's research, she pointed to a piece published in *The Atlantic* by Charles Duhigg.[137] His article "The Real Roots of American Rage" explores how anger became the dominant emotion in American politics. Trump was an expert performer. He integrated rage and retribution to bash political opponents and those who voted for his second impeachment.

I have been to a few political rallies, but none were even close to being as dangerous as the ones that I saw broadcast on FOX or CNN. They were dangerous to the cities that hosted the rallies and to people who encountered Trump's attendees. Trump's campaign rallies increased assaults by 2.3 times in host cities.[138] Interestingly, the authors found no corresponding link between assaults and rallies for Hillary Clinton's rallies. A Stanford study[139] linked Trump rallies to 30,000 COVID-19 cases and over 700 deaths. The study was based on an analysis of twenty-one rallies from June to September 2020. Even though most of the rallies

---

[137] Charles Duhigg, "The Real Roots of American Rage," *The Atlantic*, July 15, 2019, retrieved May 17, 2021, https://www.theatlantic.com/magazine/archive/2019/01/charles-duhigg-american-anger/576424/.
[138] Niraj Chokshi, "Assaults Increased When Cities Hosted Trump Rallies, Study Finds," *New York Times*, March 16, 2018, https://www.nytimes.com/2018/03/16/.
[139] Douglas Bernheim, et.al., "The Effects of Large Group Meetings on the Spread of COVID-19: The Case of Trump Rallies," SIEPR, October 30, 2020, Stanford: Stanford University, Department of Economics.

investigated in this study were outside (eighteen out of twenty-one), people still got sick attending these.[140] You may remember that Herman Cain, a 2016 presidential candidate, was infected with COVID-19 after attending the June 20, 2020, Tulsa rally and later died. Herman Cain was also a conservative radio talk show host in Atlanta. Cain's death is the result of Trump's deliberate ignorance of the science that advocated social distancing and wearing masks.

On June 26, 2021, Trump launched a series of rallies beginning in Ohio. He targeted congressional members who voted against him in the second impeachment trial with a series of "revenge" rallies. The first was held in the district of Ohio Representative Anthony Gonzalez, who voted to impeach Trump. The rallies are despicable rants against elected congressional officials who, regardless of political party, were willing to vote according to their personal conscience based on the evidence presented in House and the Senate, rather than along political party lines.

These revenge rallies are dangerous signposts for American democracy of how authoritarianism and repression have taken over the Republican Party. Trump is naming who should run against the congressional members he considers his enemies. In their book *After Trump*,[141] Bob Bauer and Jack Goldsmith, each of whom served in prominent levels of the executive branch for Barack Obama and George W. Bush, respectively, explore the need for a reconstruction of the presidency after Trump's term. They recall that Trump said he can do anything he wants as president. Now that he is not president, Trump believes that he still can do what he wants, and in so doing disregards the norms upon which the US democracy is built.

---

[140] "Study: Trump Campaign Rallies Likely Led to Over 700 COVID-related Deaths," Axios, October 31, 2020, https://www.axios.com/study-trump-campaign-rallies-coronavirus-700-deaths-14914ee5-3aa2-458b-a478-366fc8189ab9.html.
[141] Bob Bauer and Jack Goldsmith, *After Trump: Reconstructing the Presidency* (Washington, DC: Lawfare Press, 2020).

CHAPTER 3:
MORAL WORLDVIEWS

3.1. BLOG POST, 5 JUNE 2017: TRUMP'S MORAL WORLDVIEW

Politics,[142] according to some scientists, is about moral values. Indeed, conservatives and liberals not only have different goals or values, but they also have different modes of thought. Liberal or progressive modes of thought are connected to the ideals of American democracy as seen in the nation's founding documents. Yet conservatives have characterized defenders of traditional American ideals such as civil liberties, the welcoming of immigrants, and public education as extremists.

Trump's moral worldview is based on Lakoff's "strict father" metaphor for a worldview that appears in an authoritarian family with a strict father as the head. From early childhood on, Trump learned and practiced in a reward-and-punishment family environment how to conceptualize the world as a fight against evil and to always fight ruthlessly against the enemy. For Trump, there are no limits to truth, because in the end it's his goal to always come out on top, to do the deal, to win, to use retribution, and to never apologize or empathize with others or their views.

Trump does have a moral worldview. We will explore the moral worldview of Donald Trump using the research of George Lakoff.[143] We start with two of Trump's favorite conspiracy theories:

---

[142] **Author's Update:** I've added two paragraphs to the original post to add context.
[143] Lakoff, *Moral Politics*.

- Global warming is a hoax perpetrated by the Chinese to serve their economic interests.
- President Barack Obama was not born in the United States.

We've heard Donald Trump repeat these false statements for a decade. Trump's worldview allows these beliefs to hold true (for him). Even with contravening evidence that the Chinese didn't invent the idea of global warming or that President Obama was born in Hawaii, which is part of the United States, Trump still believes in his two ideas. He holds on to these ideas because his brain resists new ideas. He infuriates many around him with his lies and penchant for conspiracy theories to "back up" his ideas.

Although many people deal with the world in a comparable way, no Oval Office occupant comes close to living in the world of denial, distortion of facts, and fantasies that Trump believes. Some would say he is the archetypical science denier. I am not just speaking about climate change, but all the policy decisions that rely on logic, science research, and wisdom. These are missing from Trump's brain.

So this question should not surprise you: Why would he reject the facts that have been agreed upon by scientists and citizens in all but two counties (three now that the US pulled out of the Paris Agreement on climate change)? He is boxed in to the racist and isolationist concept of "America First," as are many of his cabinet appointees. Sometimes when I hear them speak, I am amazed how they can join the selfish and unrealistic policy that underscores the "America First" notion.

Yesterday, Nikki Haley, former governor of South Carolina, was talking as an expert on climate science explaining why global climate change was not an American issue and that getting out of the Paris Agreement was to protect the American people. Haley is not a scientist, although as governor of South Carolina, she should have been aware of how climate change was affecting the coast of her own state. Flooding along the Atlantic coast has increased as the temperature of the Earth has increased.

For a decade Trump picked up and promoted the "birther" falsehood, even when photos and documents proved Obama to be a citizen of the US. Obama showed a video clip of his birth at the 2011 White House Correspondents' Dinner, tongue in cheek.

Trump flew around the US in his airplane, landing in places like New Hampshire, announcing once again that he knows that President Obama is an illegal immigrant and was not born in this country and he shouldn't be the president. His "birther" notion was racist and appealed to a sizable part of the electorate, and Trump, for more than ten years, fanned this racist conspiracy theory. Even when he was forced to say that Obama was born in America, he blamed the idea on Hillary Clinton—which is not true. But it's another clear example of how Trump works by twisting and turning, and as he walks away with a smirk on his face, he's giving you the finger.

Trump is like a wounded tiger. He knows he lost the popular vote to Hillary Clinton. More people voted for her than for him, and he is not happy.

In Trump's world, people are either winners or losers, good or bad, virtuous or evil. So now he's in the loser category. In fact, not as many people showed up at his inauguration as for Obama's first one, a fact he fought even to the present day by creating a crack committee to investigate election fraud. Trump insisted that 3 million illegal immigrants voted fraudulently in the election, and that's the reason why he lost the popular vote. The committee later disbanded because of lack of fraud.

The election fraud conspiracy is no different from any other of Trump's conspiracies: Obama wiretapped the Trump Tower phones; immigrants from Mexico are rapists, drug dealers, and criminals; the sale of German-made cars is bad for America. It goes on and on.

> **Author's Update:** The United States officially rejoined the Paris Agreement on January 20, 2021.

MORAL WORLDVIEWS

Traditional American moral values are progressive.[144] If you look at pro-

---

[144] Lakoff, *Moral Politics*.

gressive policies, whether in government, schooling, or business, they are based on empathy, together with responsibility and strength to act on empathy. In this light, it isn't about caring. It's about taking responsibility, then acting powerfully and courageously. Lakoff points out that ethics of care shape government and requires two roles: protection and empowerment.

Lakoff says that protection is "more than just the army, police, and fire department. It means social security, disease control and public health, safe food, disaster relief, health care, consumer and worker protection, environmental protection."[145]

Conservative thought has a different moral thought than progressive thought. In the conservative mind, morality begins with obedience to an authority. The authority functions to protect people from evil in the world. In this view, obedience is enforced by punishment. Lakoff says that loyalty is needed to keep the hierarchy of the conservative view, or "obedience is freedom." Do you recall that Donald Trump asked James Comey for his loyalty? Comey said he could only be loyal to his oath to defend the Constitution. And now, even with Trump out of the White House, Republicans are lining up to show fealty to him for fear of retaliation.

METAPHORS FOR MORALITY

George Lakoff has explored how liberals and conservatives think. He says that conservatives and liberals support opposite policies because they have contradictory moral worldviews. He puts it this way:

> Conservatives and progressives typically support opposite policies because they have opposite moral worldviews—opposite notions of right and wrong. Moral worldviews are important to people, part of their self-identity. People tend to think of themselves as good and moral, not considering that there could be an opposite view of what is moral.[146]

---

[145] Lakoff, *Moral Politics*, 47.
[146] Lakoff, *Moral Politics*, 2.

Lakoff uses a conceptual system to explain differences in moral thinking using a metaphorical conception of the nation as a family. He projects two metaphors:

1. The strict father—the conservative worldview
2. The nurturant parent—the liberal or progressive worldview

STRICT FATHER

The strict father metaphor results in moral strength, which requires one to stand up to evil and have self-discipline to engage evil. The strict father metaphor sees the world in terms of a war of good against the forces of evil that must be fought ruthlessly. For the strict father, moral strength is of the highest order. Moral weakness, according to the conservative worldview, will lead to welfare, teenage sex, and illegal drugs. According to the strict father morality, we all start morally weak, and we need a strong parent to discipline us so we won't become immoral.

The strict father subsumes moral authority, retribution, moral order, moral boundaries, moral essence, moral purity, and self-defense. Reward, punishment, and competition are integral to the strict father model.

NURTURANT PARENT

The essence of the nurturant parent is caring, being cared for, caring about, and deriving meaning from mutual interaction and care. Open, two-way communication is key to the nurturant parent metaphor. Protection is a form of caring. Children are respected, nurtured, and communicated with from birth on. Empathy, happiness, and learning to take care of themselves are integral. Morality is empathic. We learn to experience what it is like to be in someone else's shoes. I feel for you.

MORAL VIEW OF DONALD TRUMP

For Trump, those who show empathy toward others are weak and should not be in leadership positions. Instead of showing some form of caring toward the British people over the past two weeks after they endured three terror attacks, he picked a fight with the mayor of London and said that the Justice Department should have given the original order to ban Muslims to the Supreme Court.

His tweets expose his moral worldview. The archetype of the strict father morality, Trump shocks with tweets, such as "James Comey better hope that there are no 'tapes' of our conversations before he starts leaking to the press"[147] or "pathetic excuse by London Mayor Sadiq Khan who had to think fast on this 'no reason to be alarmed' statement."[148]

Trump's moral view is narcissistic, and because he thinks he is the most important person in the world, he undermines himself by subverting his colleagues and staff. We've never before seen the lying that characterizes press conferences conducted by his staff or himself. His moral view has diffused into the minds of his cabinet members, and we see them trying to explain actions taken, such as dropping us out of the Paris Agreement or initiating the Muslim travel ban.

Trump does have morals, but they are based on a worldview that sees a dangerous world, one that requires him to fight this evil. He won't change and see that there are alternative ways of seeing the world. Even when provided with scientific research on climate change, he resorts to hitting the messenger and ignoring what was presented. It appears also that he prefers not to seek professional advice within the American government, but instead prefers to watch Fox News in order to form policy.

The way to "fight" Trump is through collaboration and protests that are based on a different worldview. This worldview is described by Lakoff as the nurturant parent morality.

The essence of collaboration and protests is caring and deriving meaning through mutual interaction. I was in England when the Ariana Grande memorial concert in Manchester was held. The memorial concert is the example that we are looking for. I was moved listening

---

[147] Jordyn Phelps, "Trump Says Comey 'Better Hope' There Are No 'Tapes' of Their Conversations, White House Won't Say If There Are Recordings," ABC News, May 12, 2017, retrieved November 20, 2021, https://abcnews.go.com/Politics/trump-warns-comey-hope-tapes-conversations/story?id=47368560.
[148] Maya Rhodan, "Donald Trump Attacks London Mayor Sadiq Khan on Twitter," Time, June 5, 2017, retrieved November 20, 2021, https://time.com/4805285/donald-trump-twitter-london-attack/.

to ordinary citizens that came out, a day after the attacks in London, to bear witness to the caring and love of the people in Manchester. Empathy for others, compassion, and resolve are the characteristics that will always elude Donald Trump.

We mustn't bend to his level. As Michelle Obama said, "When they go low, we go high."

3.2. BLOG POST, 12 JULY 2017: WHY DOES POTUS MAKE THE OFFICE OF PRESIDENT A LAUGHINGSTOCK?

I received a letter from a friend and colleague, Dr. Roger Cross, who lives in Australia. Back in the day, we were colleagues in the field of science education research and worked together on many projects, including the GTP.

We've kept up with each other over the years via email. Last night I received the following letter from him in which he asked why the president of the United States is making a laughingstock of the office.

> Hello Jack,
> Trust all is well with you both and you are enjoying life.
> I'm wondering (as are many Australians) whether we shouldn't transfer our allegiance to China (the Chinese president would never behave like Trump does in public!) as your president seems intent on damaging America's good name. Why does he make the Office of President a laughingstock? I wish I knew what is going on.
> Anyway—we potter along in the deep countryside of South Australia, so I suppose it doesn't really matter.
>
> Best wishes mate.
> Roger

I responded to Roger with this letter.

> Hi Roger,
> I don't have a simple answer to the Trump debacle.

Right now, chaos reigns in the White House. Trump is acting like a wounded (self- and family-inflicted) tiger. He's made no public appearances since returning from the G20. He's outraged at his staff. He's irked that the Russian "thing" stays front and center of his presidency.

Why is he acting like this now? If he looks back at the G20 he realizes (in private) that he's been isolated and he fell for Putin hook, line, and sinker. Even his own party is slowly disavowing themselves.

But the actions of his son may have been what broke the camel's back. It was just revealed that Donald Jr. received an invite to meet with a Russian government lawyer. She said she had information that could incriminate Hillary. Trump Jr. said that was good. He loved it. They met in Trump Tower, one floor under Trump's office. Also attending was Jared Kushner, Trump's son-in-law, and Paul Manafort, Trump's campaign manager at the time. Trump Jr. released emails admitting there was a meeting. He did so because the New York Times was set to release them.

If this meeting did happen, it could be the smoking gun in the Russian investigation. A special prosecutor was appointed about two months ago to investigate connections or collusion between the Trump campaign staff and Russia. All along Trump and associates have denied any connection with Russia. But many have been caught cheating—even the US attorney general lied in his senate hearing about Russian meetings. He had several meetings.

So this meeting that Trump Jr. had with the Russian attorney is big. It's another concrete example of how Trump's associates (now family) have indeed been involved and met with Russians, and their meetings were directly tied to the campaign for the presidency. Trump Jr. has denied any involvement with Russia, and now, in July, it turns out that he not only met with a Russian official but relished the idea because there was dirt on Hillary Clinton.

America is divided. Those who voted for Trump still support him, although some are leaving his ranks. Those that didn't, like us, are outraged. Families are divided. It's hard for me, Roger, to understand how people can see any good in this man. He's a serial liar. A serial denier. He's gotten away with this his entire life. Unfortunately for him, a democracy is not a business. He will eventually be had, removed from office via the Twenty-Fifth Amendment, impeached, resign, or be defeated in the next election.

His administration is on course to do damage to the environment, energy infrastructure, education, transportation, and mostly morality.

I liked what the Pope had to say about America and Russia. To the Pope it's dangerous for these two nations to collaborate on anything because they have a distorted view of the world. They (we) have no interest in the serious problems facing the world today—the poor, immigration, and migrant workers.

There is much more to this.

Best regards,
Jack

3.3. BLOG POST, 29 AUGUST 2019: IS DONALD TRUMP A TYRANT?

In France, at the 2019 G7 summit, is Donald Trump beginning to realize he's not number one on the world stage? I noticed he was off balance and stone-faced in public and spoke with little to no authority. He knows that he's been outmaneuvered by the president of France, Emmanuel Macron, when he learned the foreign minister of Iran was secretly invited to the G7 summit by President Macron. When Trump spoke in public, he resorted to his lies.

Brian Stelter of CNN raised the issue that all in the media have avoided with Trump: What is going on with him? Is he unfit to carry out the responsibilities of the office of the president? Why doesn't he tell the truth? Why is his reality so different from most Americans? Why does he deny, in so many instances, his involvement in events that have happened and there is evidence to undermine his statements? Could it be that behind President Trump's behavior is some form of mental illness?

In the book *The Dangerous Case of Donald Trump*, Jeffrey D. Sachs writes in the foreword to the new edition:

> Donald Trump is a profound danger to Americans and to the rest of the world. He will remain a profound danger until he is no longer president, since the dangers clearly result from Trump's serious mental impairments that are untreated and are impervious to treatment. The authors of this volume deserve our nation's gratitude and, most important, our deep attention and political response.[149]

IS HE A TYRANT?

As soon as Trump was in office, he filed paperwork for the 2020 presidential race. And he planned a series of campaign-like rallies to feed his supporters the narcissistic vitamins that they need as much as he does. Indeed, Trump and his followers feed on each other.

Trump has been called a narcissist by many authors and journalists. But Trump is not simply a narcissist. He may be a tyrant. In discussing tyrants past or present, Elizabeth Mika explains that "each one of them promises to bring back law and order, create better economic conditions for the people, and restore the nation's glory."[150]

BECOMING A TYRANT

For a tyrant to appear in a society, three conditions are needed: the tyrant, his supporters (the people), and the society at large that supplies a ripe ground for the collusion between them. According to Mika, political scientists call this the toxic triangle. She also says that the force to bind

---

[149] Lee, *The Dangerous Case of Donald Trump*, 4.
[150] Elizabeth Mika, "Who Goes Trump? Tyranny as Triumph of Narcissism," in Bandy X. Lee, *The Dangerous Case of Donald Trump: 27 Psychiatrists and Mental Health Experts Assess a President* (New York: St. Martin's Press, 2017), 289–308.

all three is narcissism. The tyranny of Hitler and Stalin can easily be forgotten, and there lies a danger to humanity.[151] According to Henry Giroux, forgetting results partly from miseducation. It also comes from denial.[152]

It's for others to decide if Trump is a tyrant. But there is an agreement among most that Hitler, Stalin, and Mussolini were tyrants. Perhaps if we remember what they were like, we can begin to look at the behavior of the current president of the United States in an unusual way.

Mika supplies details about tyrants that need to be examined. Many in the American press, especially the main broadcast networks (ABC, NBC, FOX, and CBS) have not pursued the truth about Trump, but instead only describe his behavior as if his actions are normal. They aren't normal.

For instance, Mika suggests that in the 1930s, many German moderates "underestimated" Hitler and as a result didn't take him seriously. I believe we are doing the same with Trump. Consider this quote from Mika's chapter:

> Hitler was seen by many as a bombastic but harmless buffoon, while many others, including members of clergy, intellectual elites, and the wealthy were nevertheless mesmerized by his grand visions of Germany's future glory, and eagerly supported his agenda.[153]

TRUMP'S TYRANT FRIENDS

Mika also suggests that tyrants tend to identify with other tyrants. Why is it that Trump continues to indulge his relationships with Putin and Kim Jong-un? When Trump talks about these two, he flatters them, while he derides former members of his own administration, members who were held in some esteem, such as Pentagon head Jim Mattis. He believes Putin over his own intelligence agencies and claims that the recent North Korean missile launches are okay, when in fact these launches are provocations.

---

[151] Mika, "Who Goes Trump?"
[152] Giroux, "Threat of Authoritarianism Is No Longer on the Horizon."
[153] Mika, "Who Goes Trump?" 301.

Hatemongering has become an integral part of Trump's persona. He has launched attacks on a wide range of people, but especially if their skin color or native language is different from his. Hatemongering was also a fundamental part of Hitler's war on Jewish people and others that were different from him. This comparison is not to be dismissed as overreaching at all.

TRUMP'S AUDIENCES

Finally, in this post, I'd point out that those who attend the Trump rallies are integral to Trump's behavior. His audience feeds him with physical manifestations of their support, such as their chants, shouting, and dress. At the same time, Trump cheers these people on by lying to them about the nature of our society. His rallies are full of rage and hate, and he constantly wreaks havoc on any of the press that dare attend these events. For the members of the press, they are taking well-documented chances by attending these rallies.

3.4. BLOG POST, 16 JUNE 2020: WHEN TRUMP SENDS YOU RUNNING FOR COVER

It seems like every day is a day when Trump sends you running for cover. It's an affirmation of the danger that this man has brought to everyone. He hasn't made America great again. He and his sycophants have marched to a drummer eroding the principles of the American democracy. And in the age of COVID-19, his inactions have led to more people dying in the United States than any other country on earth. More than 2.1 million Americans have been infected and more than 109,900 people have died from the virus.

The Tulsa rally is one example when Trump sends you running for cover. There are many others. But I want to start with the Tulsa rally.

THE TULSA RALLY

In Trump's world, the coronavirus is not an obstacle to risk the health of people who will have their temperatures checked and sign a release that they will not sue Trump if they die from the virus. You're kidding, you say. No, I'm not. Trump will storm into Tulsa to give a speech to 20,000 people who will crowd into the BOK (Bank of Oklahoma) Center.

However, Tulsa health officials and the *Tulsa World* newspaper "don't know why he chose Tulsa, but we can't see any way that his visit will be good for the city."[154] Not only is the rally a dangerous event, but both Trump and Pence have lied about the pandemic challenge that faces Tulsa. The city's healthcare system will have to deal with any effects of the rally, where people will be spitting and rolling over each other. The pandemic has killed more than 109,900 people in the United States at this time.

Still Trump and Pence want to put about 20,000 more at risk. If you are planning to go to the rally, many of us suggest that you reconsider for the sake of your family and friends.

Equally offensive is that Trump originally planned the rally for June 19, which is Juneteenth, which marks the end of slavery in Texas on June 19, 1866. Its original celebration marked the first anniversary of the day that African Americans in Galveston, Texas, first learned of the Emancipation Proclamation, more than two years after it was initially issued. It's a holiday and is commemorated annually throughout the United States, including where I live in Marietta, Georgia. I don't believe it was a coincidence to have the rally on Juneteenth. But Trump was forced to postpone it by one day because of the global protests against police violence and racism. Furthermore, Tulsa is where at least 300 people, mostly Black, died in 1921.[155] Republican Oklahoma Governor Kevin Stitt had invited Trump to visit the site of the Tulsa race massacre, which decimated Black Wall Street, as it was known. However, Monroe Nichols, the US congressional representative for this part of the state, doesn't want Trump to step one foot on the site. He didn't.

---

[154] "Tulsa World Editorial: This Is the Wrong Time and Tulsa Is the Wrong Place for the Trump Rally," Tulsa World, June 15, 2020, retrieved January 6, 2022, https://tulsaworld.com/opinion/editorials/tulsa-world-editorial-this-is-the-wrong-time-and-tulsa-is-the-wrong-place-for/article_26388374-1747-5120-bc01-24b81c1b0c78.html.

[155] Hannibal B. Johnson, *Black Wall Street: From Riot to Renaissance in Tulsa's Historic Greenwood District* (Fort Worth: Eakin Press, 2007.)

Author's Update: The Tulsa conference was a bust. The million or so people who had signed up to go didn't materialize. A prank was pulled, inflating attendance expectations for the Tulsa rally. TikTok users and K-pop (Korean pop music) fans registered hundreds of thousands of tickets for the rally. A young woman put a note on a social media platform telling people to sign up for the Tulsa rally but telling them not to go. They didn't. Only 6,200 people showed up.

CLEAR AND PRESENT DANGER

Trump and his administration's behavior, if permitted to continue, will bring harm to Americans. Although there are only 258 days (about eight and a half months) left in his administration, he continues to endanger the country now by his lack of leadership and knowledge about the pandemic. He has been totally inept in leading the US during this pandemic. He was late in recognizing the pandemic. Instead he used this time to spread lies about the virus. Now, he wants to forget that the virus exists and sacrifice American lives. He is only interested in himself and getting re-elected.

RUN FOR COVER

Here are some examples of actions, speeches, or lies when Trump makes you run for cover. I've only listed twelve examples. Just a couple of days ago, Professor David Markowitz had an article published in *Forbes* about Trump's lying.[156] In 2020, he averaged 23.3 lies per day, slightly more than he lied in 2019.

- Riding down the golden escalator at Trump Tower on June 16, 2015, announcing his candidacy for president.
- Signing an executive order banning foreign nationalists from seven Muslim countries from visiting the US.
- Blocking Congress from obtaining documents about the census citizenship question and trying to bar the full Mueller report from being given to Congress.

---

[156] David Markowitz, "Trump Is Lying More than Ever: Just Look at the Data," *Forbes*, May 5, 2020, retrieved February 24, 2021, https://www.forbes.com/sites/davidmarkowitz/2020/05/05/trump-is-lying-more-than-ever-just-look-at-the-data/.

- Throwing paper towels into a crowd of people at a relief center in San Juan, Puerto Rico, after the island had been devastated by Hurricane Maria.
- Suggesting people inject bleach into the body to kill the coronavirus.
- Attacking journalists and the press.
- Assaulting and attacking the intelligence community, especially when he said he couldn't see any reason that Putin's Russia would have anything to do with the 2016 election.
- Spreading misinformation about the coronavirus by saying such things like it's no different from the flu or it will just go away when it gets warm.
- Attacking four Muslim women members of Congress.

Trump is putting America at risk by continuing his reckless behavior and the effects of his ignorance and narcissism. I have no idea if he will be re-elected. To prevent this disaster from happening, we need to be smart, dedicated, and willing to join together, especially with the young activists who are leading the national protests against police brutality and racism through Black Lives Matter, which may be the largest movement in American history.[157] We also need to help the fight against voter suppression by supporting Stacey Abrams's Fair Fight group in its efforts to unearth and eradicate voter suppression.

---

[157] Larry Buchanan, Quoctrung Bui, and Jugal K. Patel, "Black Lives Matter May Be the Largest Movement in US History," *New York Times*, July 3, 2020, retrieved March 19, 2021, https://www.nytimes.com/interactive/2020/07/03/us/george-floyd-protests-crowd-size.html.

PART II: RIGHTS

> Never, ever be afraid to make some noise and get in good trouble, necessary trouble.
> —John Lewis

INTRODUCTION

ON FRIDAY, JANUARY 27, 2017, DONALD TRUMP SIGNED EXECUTIVE Order 13769, "Protecting the Nation from Foreign Terrorist Entry into the United States." This was otherwise known as the "Muslim ban" and was one of the earliest "America First" populist political policies of the Trump administration. According to a *Los Angeles Times* report, the executive order was developed primarily by Stephen Miller and Steve Bannon without any consultation with the US Department of Justice's Office of Legal Counsel.[158] In typical fashion, the White House denied this report and added that they had received input from the Department of Homeland Security and State Department officials. This was not true.

This executive order was the first of many anti-immigrant policy changes in the Trump administration. Continuing forward, the Trump administration followed a pattern of bigotry and human rights violations until he left office.

RACIAL EQUITY

Charles Blow, journalist for the *New York Times* and author, observed

---

[158] Brian Bennett, "Travel Ban Is the Clearest Sign Yet of Trump Advisors' Intent to Reshape the Country," *Los Angeles Times*, January 30, 2017, retrieved November 20, 2021, https://www.latimes.com/politics/la-na-pol-trump-immigration-20170129-story.html.

that nearly half the people who voted in the 2020 election cast their ballots for Donald Trump, an "unrepentant racist who ran for reelection under the racially coded 'law and order' mantra, encouraged police brutality, defended Confederate monuments, and attacked the Black Lives Matter movement."[159] He also notes that most white people voted for Trump. Trump also got the largest non-white vote of any Republican since 1960. Although Joe Biden won the presidency—thanks to the support of Black voters, especially in key swing states—the Republicans held strong in down-ballot elections around the country.

But something disparate happened in the state of Georgia. According to Blow, a coalition of voters—led by Black voters—turned Georgia blue for the first time in decades. Biden won the presidential election in Georgia, but only after the state counted the ballots three times. The results were the same each time. Possibly committing an elections interference crime, Donald Trump called the Georgia governor, secretary of state, and other officials asking them to find votes to change the outcome of the election in his favor. They turned him down.

In double runoff elections for US Senate, Democrats took both seats, with Raphael Warnock and Jon Ossoff beating out their Republican opponents. How did this happen? And how did Joe Biden win the presidential election in Georgia?

Stacey Abrams and large numbers of activists are the answer. Stacey Abrams ran for governor of Georgia in 2018, gaining more than 2 million votes, but she lost by 50,000 votes. During the runup to the election, I received many phone calls and text messages from Stacey Abrams's Fair Fight organization making sure I was indeed voting. I've been a longtime supporter of Abrams, so whenever they called, they got the answer they were looking for.

The New Georgia Project (NGP) was founded by Abrams in 2014 to register and engage Georgians civically. The NGP registered 800,000 voters (about half the population of Nebraska) in Georgia. The state

---

[159] Charles M. Blow, *The Devil You Know* (New York: HarperCollins, 2021), 4.

was flipped blue due to the efforts of NGP and Fair Fight. Charles Blow says this about the election in Georgia:

> Georgia became the model for how Black people can potentially experience true power in this country and alter the political landscape.[160]

Georgia's landscape turned from red to blue, giving hope to new possibilities. However, a backlash has emerged among white Republican lawmakers not only in Georgia, but in every state where Republicans hold majorities in the legislature. Georgia Republicans lost three key elections in 2020, and in March 2021 they changed election laws to make voting more difficult for Black and poor people. Thirty percent of the electorate in Georgia is Black. The Republicans have gone out their way to hinder and block the ability of Black Georgians to vote.

IMMIGRATION VIOLENCE

The Trump administration stomped on the idea of racial equity. Trump's border wall became the symbol of his anti-immigrant, racist policy along the southern border of the United States. Building the border wall was a disaster. Only 600 miles of the 2,000-mile border has fencing. Journalists for *USA Today* make the case that there isn't a wall between the US and Mexico. For example, Texas, which accounts for half the border, has almost no fencing. Even with billions of dollars spent, the major distance along the border is not fenced. And much of the border land is remote and new roads would have to be constructed to build the wall. *The Wall*,[161] a USA Today Network special report and winner of the Pulitzer Prize in 2018, uses video technology, stories, podcasts, and virtual reality to analyze the border wall. It provides visually stunning images and video as well interviews with people along both sides of the border.

---

[160] Blow, *The Devil You Know*, 7.
[161] Anne Ryman, ed., "The Wall: An In-Depth Examination of Donald Trump's Border Wall," *USA Today*, 2018, retrieved January 27, 2021, https://www.usatoday.com/border-wall/.

What is astounding about the *USA Today* report is that journalists explored every foot of the 2,000-mile border. The US government has spent more than $2 billion (about $6 per person in the US) over at least ten years building extraordinarily little fencing. And the journalists point out that where fencing exists, it's full of gaps. Indeed, 1,350 miles (about half the width of the United States) of the border is open land.

Trump has used the wall as a messianic promise to his followers.[162] At his rallies, the wall was one of the chants and narratives used between Trump and his followers. The chant "Build that wall" was promoted at every Trump rally and always ended with Trump asking, "Who's going to pay for the wall?" "Mexico!" the audience of Trump cultists would respond. Trump used the wall to manufacture crises at the border by claiming that caravans of criminal immigrants were invading our country and needed to be stopped in their tracks. Trump even sent US troops to the border. And governors of some southern states have followed suit and sent National Guard troops as well.

The United Nations High Commissioner for Refugees (UNHCR) stated in the *Women on the Run* report that most of the women escaping El Salvador, Guatemala, Honduras, and Mexico established eligibility for asylum or protection under the Convention against Torture. Women from these countries shared their stories with the UNHCR as the basis for this report. Seeking asylum is a lawfully protected act. The women interviewed made it clear that the violence they suffered is an ongoing threat to thousands of women in Central America.[163]

The Trump administration did horrific injustices to thousands of people fleeing terror in Central America. Attorney General Jeff Sessions announced on April 6, 2018, a "Zero Tolerance Policy for Criminal Illegal Entry" along the southwest border. The intent of this policy was to ramp up criminal prosecution of people entering the United States illegally. Soon after the policy was implemented, immigrant parents traveling with their children were criminally prosecuted and separated from their children.

---

[162] Lifton, *Losing Reality*, 154.
[163] United Nations High Commissioner for Refugees, "Women on the Run: First-Hand Accounts of Refugees Fleeing El Salvador, Guatemala, Honduras, and Mexico," 2015, retrieved January 27, 2021, https://www.unhcr.org/5630f24c6.html.

More than 3,000 children were separated from their parents.[164] The policy was deemed cruel by world leaders, religious groups, and lawmakers. Two months later, the order to separate families was halted; however, the zero-tolerance policy continued. To this day, hundreds of children separated by the Trump administration are still not reunited with their parents, many of whom were returned to their home country. The zero-tolerance policy was rescinded by the Biden administration.

However, the border is a continuing problem. Even with a new administration, thousands of people from Central America are migrating to the United States to flee from terror and severe and violent weather caused by climate change.

The border has become a new military-industrial complex. Todd Miller, reporting on the southern border, calls it the "border-industrial complex."[165] Over the past twelve years, Miller says, Customs and Border Protection (CBP) and Immigration and Customs Enforcement (ICE) gave out 105,000 contracts worth more than $55 billion to private contractors. Most of the contracts went to companies creating high-tech border fortifications for sophisticated camera systems to advance biometric and data-processing technologies. As war efforts in Afghanistan and Iraq began to wane, big security and defense companies turned their eyes toward the border.

Border contracts are a boon to companies such as General Dynamics, Lockheed Martin, Northrop Grumman, and Raytheon. More than $30 million was contributed to members of the House Appropriations Committee and the House Homeland Security Committee by these and other companies. When Trump came into office, the border-industrial complex was a $20 billion enterprise with 20,000 border patrol agents and over 650 miles of built walls. More than 200 immigration detention centers were spread across the country. According to Miller, the 450 miles of border wall that Trump

---

[164] Miriam Jordan, "Family Separation May Have Hit Thousands More Migrant Children Than Reported," *New York Times*, January 17, 2019, retrieved November 20, 2021, https://www.nytimes.com/2019/01/17/us/family-separation-trump-administration-migrants.html.

[165] Todd Miller, "The Greater the Disaster, the Greater the Profits," *Portside*, March 24, 2021, retrieved April 5, 2021, https://portside.org/2021-03-24/greater-disaster-greater-profits.

built were replacements for smaller existing barriers. The monstrous wall sections that Trump built were a mockery to the environment and the culture along the border.[166]

Hate and extremism, especially toward immigrants and people of color, have been fueled by Trump's "own toxic hate" according to Jeffrey D. Sachs. Sachs describes Trump's toxic hate this way:

> Trump is stoking mass violence in America. Hate crimes and deaths from mass shootings are soaring. And when they occur, as with the horrific attack on the synagogue in Pittsburgh, Trump's response is always more violence, calling for more guns, not fewer, and for the death penalty, while denying any role of his own toxic hate-filled speech. Herein is another sign of Trump's pathology, an utter inability to face the consequences of his own actions.[167]

Human rights violations during the Trump era have been the focus of mass protests and the organization of peaceful marches to resist his actions. However, Amnesty International has shown that the Trump administration has launched discriminatory attacks against the most vulnerable populations in the United States. The report outlines a "broadly dismal human rights record, both at home and abroad, deteriorating further in 2020."[168]

A RIOT IS THE LANGUAGE OF THE UNHEARD

In 1967 Dr. Martin Luther King Jr. gave a lecture at Stanford University that he titled "The Other America."[169] During this period, Dr. King[170]

---

[166] Miller, "The Greater the Disaster."
[167] Lee, *The Dangerous Case of Donald Trump*, 4.
[168] "United States of America Human Rights 2020," Amnesty International USA, retrieved April 15, 2022, https://www.amnestyusa.org/countries/usa/.
[169] Martin Luther King, "The Other America," speech delivered to Riverside Church in New York City, April 4, 1967, retrieved September 12, 2021, https://www.crmvet.org/docs/otheram.htm.
[170] When I was thirteen years old, I often visited a neighbor who was attending a local university studying theology. One day he told me about a fellow student from Atlanta who spoke about racial injustice that was prevalent in the South. This fellow student of my neighbor was Martin Luther King Jr. They were both attending Boston University (BU); in 1955 they each received a PhD in theology. Eleven years later I would earn my master's degree from BU. In 1969, I moved to Atlanta to begin my career as a science teacher educator.

spent a lot of time speaking out against the Vietnam War. But in this lecture, he chose to speak about racial justice and racial equality. The country had experienced summer riots in Watts and Harlem the previous two years. King made it clear that riots are socially destructive and self-defeating. He said he was "convinced that nonviolence is the most potent weapon available for people in their struggle for freedom and justice."

But he also condemned the conditions that might cause people to feel that they must engage in riotous activities. Dr. King said:

> I think America must see that riots do not develop out of thin air. Certain conditions continue to exist in our society which must be condemned as vigorously as we condemn riots. But in the final analysis, a riot is the language of the unheard.[171]

Dr. King was adamant that if America postpones justice, "we stand in the position of having these recurrences of violence and riots repeatedly. Social justice and progress are the absolute guarantors of riot prevention."[172]

On May 25, 2020, when George Floyd was murdered by Minneapolis police officer Derek Chauvin, who forced his knee into Floyd's neck for nine minutes and twenty-nine seconds, the United States erupted with protests in all major cities. Chauvin was found guilty on three counts of murder.

Instead of riots in the summer of 2020, there were protests. George Floyd protests marked an important advancement in which people of all over the world said enough is enough. Local protests in Minneapolis-Saint Paul grew nationwide to encompass over 2,000 cities and towns in sixty countries. According to some reports, between 15 million and 26 million people (about the population of Texas) participated in these demonstrations.

According to the *Washington Post*, 93 percent of individual protests were peaceful and nondestructive. And more than 7,000 demonstrations

---

[171] King, "The Other America."
[172] King, "The Other America."

involved no injuries and no property damage. It's also true that the demonstrations caused more than $1 billion in damage.[173]

PROTEST-RELATED ACTIVITY AS CRIMINAL BEHAVIOR

The mass protests that followed the murder of George Floyd led to the conviction of the police officer who murdered him. Many doubt that there would have been a conviction of guilt if these protests did not happen, or if Darnella Frazier, a teenaged girl, had not used her phone to record the murder. She was awarded an honorary Pulitzer Prize for her courage. It is rare that a police officer is even charged when a Black person is shot and killed, let alone found guilty.

Autocratic leaders such as Vladimir Putin, Alexander Lukashenko (Belarus), and Donald Trump target dissenters, often resulting in arrests, injuries, and death.

However, targeting dissenters and protestors in the United States is not new. The FBI has a long history of treating political dissent as terrorism.[174] Those surveilled include Black activists, Muslim Americans, Palestinian solidarity and peace activists, environmentalists, protestors at Trump rallies and the RNC, and many others. Perhaps one group that is targeted most are immigrants. In fact, the first targeting of political dissent by the FBI was over one hundred years ago, cracking down on immigrants who were politically active. In 2020, ICE conducted raids across the country, from Boston to San Francisco, on a single day and hoped to round up more than 2,000 undocumented immigrants.

During the 1930s J. Edgar Hoover expanded the FBI's role to research "subversives."[175] In the late 1940s, the FBI began to investigate the civil rights movement.[176] Starting in 1955, the FBI began surveilling Dr. Martin Luther King Jr. because of his involvement in the

---

[173] T. Craig, "'The United States Is in Crisis': Report Tracks Thousands of Summer Protests, Most Nonviolent," *Washington Post*, September 4, 2020, retrieved May 25, 2021, https://www.washingtonpost.com/national/the-united-states-is-in-crisis-report-tracks-thousands-of-summer-protests-most-nonviolent/2020/09/03/b43c359a-edec-11ea-99a1-71343d03bc29_story.html.

[174] Alice Speri, "The FBI's Long History of Treating Political Dissent as Terrorism," *The Intercept*, October 22, 2019, https://theintercept.com/2019/10/22/terrorism-fbi-political-dissent/.

[175] "Federal Bureau of Investigation (FBI)," The Martin Luther King, Jr., Research and Education Institute, May 21, 2018, retrieved April 3, 2022, https://kinginstitute.stanford.edu/encyclopedia/federal-bureau-investigation-fbi.

[176] "Federal Bureau of Investigation (FBI)," The Martin Luther King, Jr., Research and Education Institute, May 21, 2018, retrieved September 13, 2021, https://kinginstitute.stanford.edu/encyclopedia/federal-bureau-investigation-fbi.

Montgomery bus boycott[177] and his outspokenness against the Vietnam War. King's home and offices at the Southern Christian Leadership Conference (SCLC) were wiretapped. The attempt to discredit Dr. King and the SCLC continued even after the Civil Rights Act of 1964 was passed.

After the 9/11 attacks, Congress passed the Patriot Act,[178] which made it easier for the government to spy on ordinary Americans. This law expanded the government's authority to monitor phone and email records and track the activity of all Americans. Edward Snowden revealed the US intelligence establishment was secretly building a system that would enable the collection of everything we phoned, texted, or emailed.[179]

Now, something dangerous is happening because of the Black Lives Matter protests of 2020. In the state of Florida, the governor signed into law a bill that increased the penalties for acts of vandalism and adjusted the threshold for declaring a riot downward. Other bills reduce penalties for drivers who strike protestors if the driver feels at risk. This is hard to believe. The effort is naturally targeting the Black Lives Matter movement. Furthermore, the *New York Times* reports that lawmakers in more than thirty states have introduced "anti-protest bills." These bills are also dubbed "anti-riot" bills. More than 350 bills were proposed in the 2021 legislative session.[180] For many Republicans, changing laws to prevent the right to protest is directly targeting any Americans that disagree with their autocratic policies.

Russia has had anti-protesting bills for years. Russians have not shied away, however, from protesting. When politician Alexei Navalny was arrested after his return to Moscow in 2021, the largest protests in Russian history were seen across the country. Anastasia Edel reports that

---

[177] "Montgomery Bus Boycott," The Martin Luther King, Jr., Research and Education Institute, May 30, 2019, retrieved September 13, 2021, https://kinginstitute.stanford.edu/encyclopedia/montgomery-bus-boycott.
[178] "Surveillance under the Patriot Act," American Civil Liberties Union, retrieved September 13, 2021, https://www.aclu.org/issues/national-security/privacy-and-surveillance/surveillance-under-patriot-act.
[179] Edward Snowden, *Permanent Record: How One Man Exposed the Truth about Government Spying and Digital Security* (New York: Henry Holt and Company, 2021).
[180] P. Bump, "It's Not Just Voting: Legislators Have Introduced 100 State Bills Targeting Protesting," *Washington Post*, May 13, 2021, retrieved May 14, 2021, https://www.washingtonpost.com/politics/2021/05/13/its-not-just-voting-legislators-have-introduced-100-state-bills-targeting-protesting/.

some 200,000 people across 125 cities and towns took to the streets. They chanted "Выпустить его" (let him out).[181]

Russians are not afraid to protest, even in the face of military opposition. In August 1991, more than 200,000 Moscow residents protested for three days staring into the barrels of tank guns. They were protesting the KGB and military strongmen who had led a failed coup (putsch) against the last days of the Gorbachev era.

I was in Prague attending an international conference on telecomputing at the time. There were at least twenty Russian technology entrepreneurs in attendance. Throughout the conference, they were on the phones to find out about their families and businesses and wondered what the outcome would be. Barbara Tinker, at the Concord Consortium in Massachusetts,[182] faxed us newspaper articles that were published in the US, providing us with the only source of information we had about the coup in Moscow. I later learned that she also faxed information to Russian colleagues in Moscow and St. Petersburg. Fortunately, the limited democracy that had emerged held against the coup instigators.

Americans will continue to protest. Throughout the twentieth century, protests led to women and Black Americans and other people of color gaining the right to vote. Protests occurred during the Vietnam War on college campuses and on the streets of major cities. During the time Trump was president, protests began when he was elected and continued throughout his presidency. Of course, Trump himself led one riotous protest, an attempted coup of the United States Congress and the attempted murder of Vice President Pence, Speaker Pelosi, and others.

VOTING RIGHTS

Voting rights are on trial in the United States because of Donald Trump's "Big Lie" of voter fraud, which never occurred anywhere in the

---

[181] Anastasia Edel, "The Berlin Patient," *Foreign Policy*, April 25, 2021, retrieved April 29, 2021, https://foreignpolicy.com/2021/04/25/navalny-protest-dissent-russia-putin/.
[182] Barbara Tinker was a founding member and project manager at Concord Consortium in Concord, Massachusetts.

THE TRUMP FILES

United States. Even though the 2020 election was "the most secure in American history," since then, democracy has been under attack. The Big Lie undermined the confidence people have in the voting process. Republican state legislators have launched an attack on voting rights in America. There is a direct attack being made especially against Black voters around the country, not just in the South. And voter repression is not new.

After Barack Obama won the presidential election in 2008 by more than 8 million votes, conservatives launched widespread voter suppression laws in as many states they controlled. In her book *White Rage*, Carol Anderson explains how conservatives designed a multitude of ways to keep the people they don't want to vote away from the ballot box.[183] And it didn't begin when Obama won the election. Voter suppression had been going on for a long time. The goal of suppression has been to "intimidate and harass key populations to keep them away from the polls."[184]

Anderson is the Charles Howard Candler professor of African American Studies at Emory University. In *White Rage*, she exposes the subtle and more sophisticated disfranchisement methods, especially those used by William Rehnquist while he was practicing law in Arizona in the early 1960s. Rehnquist's sycophants sent "do not forward" mail to residents in Democratic precincts. Returned cards to the state were falsely interpreted to mean the addressee was no longer there and was then removed from the rolls. On election day, the voter removed from the rolls needed to prove they could read and interpret parts of the Constitution.[185] And, yes, this is the same Rehnquist who was appointed to the Supreme Court and became Chief Justice from 1986 to 2005.

According to the Brennan Center for Justice, there were hundreds of bills introduced during the 2021 legislative session in many states that would restrict voting. The intent is to suppress, subvert, and

---

[183] Carol Anderson, *White Rage: The Unspoken Truth of Our Racial Divide* (New York: Bloomsbury, 2016).
[184] Anderson, *White Rage*, 142.
[185] Anderson, *White Rage*.

disenfranchise voters. Figure 1 shows how this played out in 2021. The map identifies states that enacted bills in state legislatures that will either restrict or expand voting. Note that a few states enacted restrictive as well as expansive laws. Restricting or expanding the citizens' right to vote is split among the states.

As you read ahead, you will find out that the state I live in passed the earliest and one of the most restrictive bills. This bill makes it more difficult for to citizens to vote and also opens the door for the state legislature to suspend county election officials and assume the power to head elections around the state.

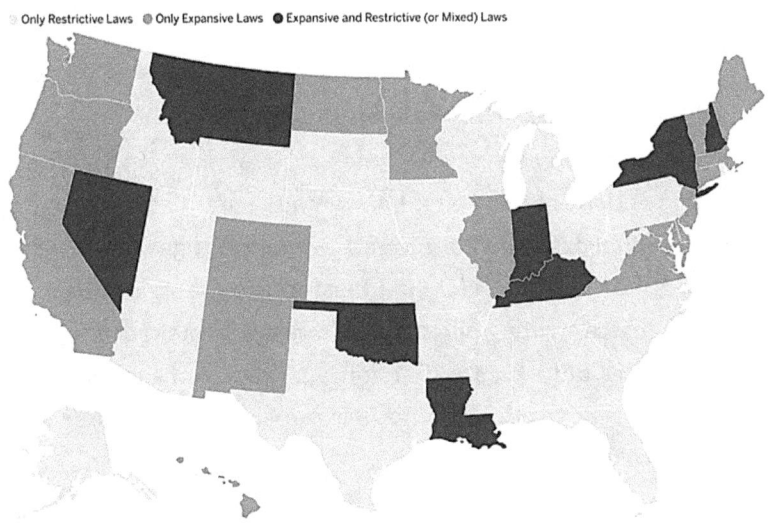

Figure 1. Voting legislation enacted in state legislatures in 2021. Data based on Brennan Center for Justice.

There were two voting bills in the Congress that failed to pass in the Senate. The first bill was the Freedom to Vote Act,[186] which would expand early voting and require that every state have at least two weeks of early voting, as well as permit no-excuse mail-in voting for every eligible voter. The bill also called for Election Day to be a public holiday. To protect individual voters, the bill would require that states have a

---

[186] C. Torres-Spelliscy et al., Brennan Center for Justice, *The Freedom to Vote Act*, December 6, 2021, retrieved January 14, 2022, https://www.brennancenter.org/our-work/research-reports/freedom-vote-act.

wide range of forms of identification to validate voters. The bill also restricted states from changing election laws and eliminated partisan gerrymandering in order to work toward neutral standards for creating vote maps. Voter registration would become automatic and include same-day voter registration.

The second bill was the John R. Lewis Voting Rights Advancement Act.[187] It was designed to strengthen the basic voting rights law and restore voting to the core protections that were in the 1965 Voting Rights Act. The recent act would put a stop to the voting rights violations that spread across the country in which state legislatures discriminated against many groups of people by lessening their ability to vote.

THE GEORGIA ELECTION LAW CASE

Georgia is a model case for new voter suppression laws that began in 2021. As a resident of this state, I have made sure that my opinions are known to Republicans and have urged Democrats fight these autocrats. Senator Raphael Warnock (D-GA) blasted the Georgia legislature for passing the massive voting bill that would restrict voter access. Warnock said, "I think it's unfortunate that some politicians have looked at the results and, rather than changing their message, they're busy trying to change the rules."[188]

Georgia Republican legislators are perpetuating Trump's Big Lie and using it as the rationale to claim there was widespread voter fraud. There was no fraud in the 2020 election. Rather than competing to earn votes, Georgia Republicans favor changing the rules to make it harder for the people who voted against them to get to the voting booth. Georgia legislators audaciously established a Special Committee on Election Integrity underscoring their action against a fair and just election system in the state. This committee missed the

---

[187] W. R. Weiser, "Why the Senate Must Pass the John Lewis Voting Rights Act," Brennan Center for Justice, January 13, 2022, retrieved January 14, 2022, https://www.brennancenter.org/our-work/analysis-opinion/why-senate-must-pass-john-lewis-voting-rights-act.

[188] Daniella Diaz, "Warnock Slams GOP-Controlled Georgia Legislature for Bill That Would Restrict Voter Access," CNN, March 21, 2021, retrieved November 21, 2021, https://www.cnn.com/2021/03/21/politics/raphael-warnock-georgia-voting-rights/index.html.

mark. The integrity of voting in Georgia has been questioned and investigated for decades. The 1965 Voting Rights Act changed the rules of voting not only in Georgia, but throughout the South. Instead of making voting more accessible to citizens, this committee made it more difficult for Georgians to vote.

I've studied this new bill, and it would restrict voting by reducing the number of ballot drop boxes and requiring voter ID for absentee ballots. It's a disturbing piece of legislation. Although the bill expands the number of days for early voting, the new law requires a personal ID on both in-person and mail-in voting. Some critics claim that this disproportionally affects voters of color.

The new law also regulates drop boxes and reduces the time for the use of mail-in voting. In past elections, drop boxes were available 24/7, but now they will be located inside the county clerk's office. And only one drop box per 100,000 voters is allowed. There are 7,234,431 registered voters in the state, which means there would be seventy-two drop boxes across a large state, or one drop box per 825 square miles. There are 345 square miles in Cobb County, where I live. Would that mean that Cobb and another county nearby would share one drop box? Also, it would be unlawful to provide water or food while voters stand in line. This cruel policy negatively impacts low-income voters who stand in line with their children so that they can take advantage of food services at voting sites.

But more egregious is that the bill enables the Georgia state election board to intervene in county- and precinct-level elections by suspending county or municipal superintendents based on performance or violation of election laws. This is rather ironic because the president of the United States interfered in the 2020 election, which is a violation of Georgia's election laws.

The law also removes the secretary of state from the election board. This is a direct attack on Brad Raffensperger, Georgia's secretary of state who stood up to Donald Trump in the phone call on January 2, 2021. I believe that this is a powerful weapon that Republicans will use in the next and future elections. They will be able to appoint their own people to direct the work at local precincts, essentially making it possible to take over elections.

In a powerful article for *Mother Jones*, Ari Berman writes that Republicans are paving the way to steal future elections. In his piece, Berman warns us that if we ignore the consequences of Trump's Big Lie and sit on the sidelines, Republicans across the country will pull off another coup by making it more difficult for people to vote and easier for them to take over the election process. Here's how he puts it:

> And make no mistake, if Republicans prevail in rigging the 2022 election, they'll be even more emboldened in 2024, especially if Trump is on the ballot. The lies of a stolen election propagated by Trump—and exploited by Republican lawmakers who know better—are now being used to lay the groundwork to sabotage elections for real. "Their endgame?" President Joe Biden asked rhetorically during a major speech in Atlanta on January 11. "To turn the will of the voters into a mere suggestion—something states can respect or ignore." This isn't just about the normal ebb and flow of partisan politics; it's a test of whether a party that is deadly serious about ending American democracy as we know it will regain control of ostensibly democratic institutions.[189]

The current effort by Republicans to deny and limit voting is a direct attack on liberal democracy. The John Lewis Voting Rights Act, if it passed, would thwart this attempt and eliminate the barriers to voting that is contained in voting bills in most state legislatures.

---

[189] A. Berman, "The Coming Coup: How Republicans Are Laying the Groundwork to Steal Future Elections," *Mother Jones*, January 13, 2022, retrieved January 14, 2022, https://www.motherjones.com/politics/2022/01/how-republicans-are-taking-over-election-system-big-lie/.

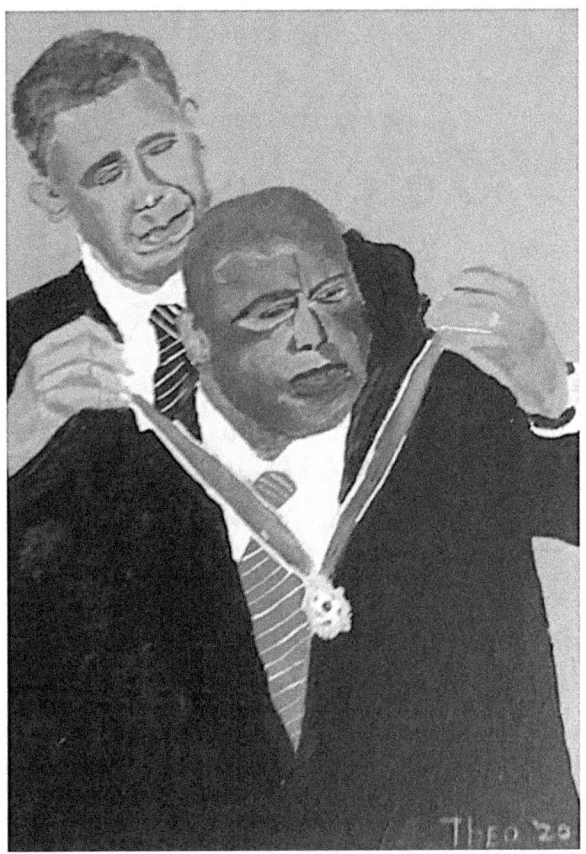

President Obama presenting the Presidential Medal of Freedom to John Lewis on February 16, 2011, who made "meritorious contributions to the security of national interests of the United States, world peace, cultural and other significant public endeavors."[190] John Lewis spent his life advocating for voting rights for all Americans. He led the "Bloody Sunday" march from Selma to Montgomery for Black voting rights in 1965. He led a peaceful march across the Edmund Pettus Bridge, but they were attacked by police on horseback. Lewis was clubbed and almost killed. My painting is based on a photo by Medill DC, CC 2.0.

---

[190] Yolande M. Minor, "Cascade's John Lewis Receives Medal of Freedom," Cascade, GA Patch, February 16, 2011, retrieved April 15, 2022, https://patch.com/georgia/cascade/cascades-john-lewis-receives-medal-of-freedom.

CHAPTER 4:
RACIAL JUSTICE

> Peaceful relations between nations require understanding and mutual respect between individuals.
> —President Dwight D. Eisenhower, 1956

4.1. BLOG POST, 1 FEBRUARY 2017: SOFT POWER AND CITIZEN DIPLOMACY: THE MUSLIM BAN

Soft power and citizen diplomacy can be traced to 1956, when President Dwight D. Eisenhower created the People-to-People Student Ambassador Program, which aimed to build a massive program of communications between Americans and citizens of other lands, distinct from government contacts. Government contact diplomacy is track one diplomacy, whereas people-to-people contact is track two diplomacy or citizen diplomacy. It's obvious that President Eisenhower would be opposed to the Trump administration's ban on citizens from Iraq, Iran, Syria, Yemen, Sudan, Somalia, and Libya entering the US.

In a *Chronicle of Higher Education* article, Keith David Watenpaugh wrote, "Why Trump's Executive Order Is Wrongheaded and Reckless."[191] Professor Watenpaugh is a historian of the Middle East and professor of human rights studies at the University of California, Davis. In the article he said:

---

[191] Keith David Watenpaugh, "Why Trump's Executive Order Is Wrongheaded and Reckless," *Chronicle of Higher Education*, July 23, 2020, retrieved January 25, 2021, https://www.chronicle.com/article/Why-Trump-s-Executive-Order/239042.

The closing of America to the world, begun by this order, is, among other things, an abandonment of the enormous capacity of American soft power embodied in exchange programs, study abroad, and efforts to rescue scholars and students—all of which promote human rights, collective security, and global commerce.

I agree with Professor Watenpaugh's assessment of Trump's wrongheaded executive order and agree with former acting Attorney General Sally Yates, who informed Trump that in her legal opinion, she was not convinced that the executive order is lawful.

Watenpaugh has recently been working with colleagues through the Institute of International Education's Scholar Rescue Fund to welcome dissidents from Iran so that they could improve their own understanding of the human rights problems that citizens in Iran face. These people-to-people contacts (what Watenpaugh calls "soft power") have been wiped out by the Trump immigration ban.

CITIZEN DIPLOMACY

For twenty years we fostered more than forty people-to-people exchanges among North American and Soviet (later Russian) middle and high school students and teachers, school administrators, professors, scholars, researchers, and activists. Even with the downing of Korean Air Lines Flight 007 in September 1983, our two countries did not ban travel to each other's country (although President Reagan did ban Aeroflot flights to the United States). In fact, our AHP group was booked on an Aeroflot flight from Washington, DC, to Moscow. Our travel agent had to scramble to find seats on a Finn Air flight to Helsinki. We took a Russian train from Helsinki direct to Moscow and were bused to our first meeting at the Institute of Psychology, affiliated with the Academy of Sciences. Although there was coldness and resentment in the room about the airline tragedy, we talked with each other and indeed planned future activities with the scholars in the institute. Our citizen diplomacy project was off to a start.

THE TRUMP FILES

WHAT IF I WERE BANNED FROM TRAVELING TO THE USSR?

If we or the Soviets were banned from each other's country, none of what happened in the next twenty years would have been possible. The hundreds of American and Russian students, teachers, administrators, researchers, and activists never would have had the opportunity to collaborate with each other or take part in the GTP, which emerged from the first people-to-people exchanges. Lack of collaboration leads to distrust, anger, and fear, and Watenpaugh is correct in saying that the "enormous capacity of American soft power in exchanges" will dwindle away under the ban imposed by Trump administration. I'm left disturbed by the actions of a small group of Trump's men who haven't a clue where they are in anyone's universe except their own.

> **Author's Update:** Trump's sycophants might consider the words of Sergey Tolstikov, a Russian teacher at Moscow 710 and one of the founders of the GTP who was involved in the GTP from 1987. Tolstikov made several trips to Georgia and worked with us when we traveled to Moscow as host at his school and translator in meetings and on field trips. He was instrumental in helping Russian and American students use an email dictionary that enabled American students to write phonetically in English so that Russian students could read it. He retired from Moscow School 710 and started a Russian translation business and now lives on the outskirts of Moscow. He said this in an email interview about the value of direct face-to-face contact between Americans and Russians:
>
>> Direct face-to-face contact, interactions at different levels, numerous discussions and collaboration, little by little created the atmosphere of understanding and mutual respect and often lead to strong friendship. Seeing American and Russian kids working together on different serious ecological projects was a heartwarming and moving experiences for me and, I am sure, for other Russian educators. GTP participation created

huge positive emotional and intellectual impact on all the participants, and as a teacher I witnessed it thousands of times.[192]

4.2. BLOG POST, 28 JUNE 2018: MOST CHILDREN AND WOMEN FLEEING CENTRAL AMERICA ARE ELIGIBLE FOR ASYLUM PROTECTION

According to the UNHCR analysis of the screenings conducted by US asylum officers, over 80 percent of women from El Salvador, Guatemala, Honduras, and Mexico who were screened on arrival at the US border "were found to have a significant possibility of establishing eligibility for asylum or protection under the Convention against Torture."[193] Why aren't they being granted asylum?

These women and their children have traveled more than 2,300 miles. If you could drive the journey, it would take at least thirty-three hours, but most of these people flee on foot and may or may not have any transportation to their destination: the border of the United States. If they do, it's via train, which is still dangerous. What we fail to realize is that these people need to get into Mexico and do so through one of a few border towns.

Most of what we have heard from the Trump administration about the people trying to seek asylum is untrue. They are not members of the MS-13 gang. In fact, according to the fact sheet published by the Washington Office on Latin America, the MS-13 gang membership makes up less than 1 percent of all criminally active gang members in the United States and Puerto Rico, and there is no sign that the number of MS-13 members in the United States has increased in the past few years.[194]

If you listen to President Trump and Attorney General Jeff Sessions, you'd think the country is being overrun by the MS-13 gang. If you want to learn about gangs and groups that play havoc in the US, then look no further than the Southern Poverty Law Center (SPLC). There

---

[192] Sergey Tolstikov (retired English teacher, Moscow School 710, and journal editor), email interview with the author, September 13, 2020.
[193] United Nations High Commissioner for Refugees, "Women on the Run."
[194] Sarah Kinosian, *Seven Facts about MS-13 Gang and How to Combat the Gang* (Washington DC: WOLA, 2017).

are over 950 "hate groups"[195] tracked by the SPLC, and most of them are populated with white American citizens, not immigrants. Indeed, the SPLC is one of the organizations in the country that fights for immigrant justice.

FAMILY SEPARATION

The people fleeing the violence in Central America are not trying to sneak across the US border. They are actively seeking out US Border Protection Services and applying for asylum.

The current US "border crisis" was manufactured by the Trump administration once Sessions announced his zero-tolerance policy (family separation policy). To me it's not surprising that Sessions made this announcement. In 1986, Coretta Scott King wrote a letter to the US Senate when the Senate was considering Sessions for a federal judgeship in Alabama. Sessions, acting as a US attorney, committed fraud in a voting rights case in which he charged three Black Alabama citizens for using absentee ballots and encouraging other Black voters to do the same (which had been used by whites for a long time).[196]

Sessions directed the FBI to punish elderly Black citizens who had used absentee ballots (legally). Ms. King said that after the ordeal, many of these citizens said they would not vote again. Many years later, Senator Elizabeth Warren tried to read Ms. King's letter in the Senate in 2017 when Sessions was being considered for the attorney general position. She never got to complete the speech. She was stopped by Mitch McConnell citing Senate Rule 19, which forbids members from imputing to a colleague "any conduct or motive unworthy or unbecoming a Senator."[197] Sessions was confirmed, and he is back at it, but this time he is going after Central American children and women who are seeking asylum in our country.

---

[195] "Hatewatch," Southern Poverty Law Center, retrieved June 27, 2018, https://www.splcenter.org/hatewatch.
[196] *Coretta Scott King's 1986 Statement and Testimony on Jeff Sessions's US District Court nomination in Alabama,* DocumentCloud, retrieved April 3, 2022, https://www.documentcloud.org/documents/3259988-Scott-King-1986-Letter-and-Testimony-Signed.html.
[197] Bill Chappell, "Read Coretta Scott King's Letter that Got Sen. Elizabeth Warren Silenced," NPR, February 8, 2017, retrieved April 3, 2022, https://www.npr.org/sections/thetwo-way/2017/02/08/514085145/read-coretta-scott-kings-letter-that-got-sen-elizabeth-warren-silenced.

The travesty at the border has intensified. Children are being separated from their parents and sent off to detention centers across the country. ProPublica has identified ninety-seven facilities spread across the US housing these children. As of today, very few of the more than 2,000 children sent to one of these facilities has been reunited with their parents. The crisis created by Trump and Sessions is immoral and it alone ought to be grounds to impeach them both.

4.3. BLOG POST, 21 JULY 2019: THE DARK CLOUD OF HATE THAT RODE THE ESCALATOR THREE YEARS AGO

When Trump came down the escalator into the basement of the Trump Tower to give his speech announcing he was running for president, he was accompanied by the darkest of clouds, even darker than the clouds when the Krakatoa volcano erupted in 1883. All hell broke loose in 1883, as it did in 2015. A cold chill emerged from the Trump Tower basement, and it's gotten worse over the last three years.

This cold chill—or what we should call the Trump Effect, a fallout of hate that has resulted in the harassment or attacks against immigrants, people seeking asylum, Latinos, Muslim Americans, African Americans, and others—appears to have no bounds. This chill has its roots on this day in 2015, and started with these words:

> When Mexico sends its people, they're not sending their best. They're not sending you. They're not sending you. They're sending people that have lots of problems, and they're bringing those problems with us. They're bringing drugs. They're bringing crime. They're rapists. And some, I assume, are good people.
>
> But I speak to border guards, and they tell us what we're getting. And it only makes common sense. It only makes common sense. They're sending us not the right people.[198]

---

[198] Adam Gabbatt, "Golden Escalator Ride: The Surreal Day Trump Kicked Off His Bid for President," *The Guardian*, June 14, 2019, retrieved November 21, 2021, https://www.theguardian.com/us-news/2019/jun/13/donald-trump-presidential-campaign-speech-eyewitness-memories.

THE TRUMP FILES

TRUMP'S LONG HISTORY OF RACISM AND OUTLANDISH BEHAVIOR

Trump has been a racist throughout his adult life. In the current media cycle, people are looking for that instance that will expose Trump as a racist. He's always been this way, long before he moved to DC.

His twisted logic is full of lies and outright racist talk in closed meetings and in public, especially before the press. Jeffrey Goldberg, editor in chief of *The Atlantic*, has assembled "50 Moments That Define an Improbable Presidency," a catalog of incidents (much like the list of incidents of obstruction set out in the Mueller report against Trump) that are outlandish.[199] Although these are not all necessarily racist, they provide a wide range of this man's outrageous behavior.

Remember, for example, that during a January 11, 2018, Oval Office meeting with US senators, Trump unleashed his "shithole nations" comment. He referred to African countries as "shithole" nations—asking why the US can't have more immigrants from Norway instead—and complained that, after seeing America, immigrants from Nigeria would never "go back to their huts."[200]

All the Republican senators in the meeting said he never used the word "shithole," but Senator Dick Durbin (D-IL) said he did. Former Georgia Senator David Perdue denied Trump used the term. I wasn't surprised that Perdue would lie about Trump as he's been one of his chief advocates in the Senate.

Trump's racial views have been well documented.[201] He has a history of speech and actions that define his own racial views and fuel racial tensions in the US, as he is doing right now with his despicable attacks on Representative Ilhan Omar (D-MN), as well as three other House Representatives: Alexandria Ocasio-Cortez of New York, Rashida Tlaib of Michigan, and Ayanna S. Pressley of Massachusetts. Everything that

---

[199] Jeffery Goldberg, ed., "50 Moments That Define the Trump Presidency," *The Atlantic*, 2019, retrieved February 25, 2021, https://www.theatlantic.com/unthinkable/.
[200] Alan Fram, "Trump: Why Allow Immigrants from 'Shithole Countries'?" AP News, January 12, 2018, retrieved April 3, 2022, https://apnews.com/article/immigration-north-america-donald-trump-ap-top-news-international-news-fdda2ff0b877416c8ae1c1a77a3cc425.
[201] German Lopez, "Donald Trump's Long History of Racism, from the 1970s to 2020," Vox.com, July 25, 2016, retrieved November 21, 2021, https://www.vox.com/2016/7/25/12270880/donald-trump-racist-racism-history.

Trump has said about Representative Omar is false, and these accusations fueled a brutal rally in North Carolina in which white Trump supporters chanted, "Send her back."[202]

Trump's tweets have fueled this attack, and finally the House of Representatives voted to condemn his remarks as racist. But only four Republicans in the House agreed with the motion.

That dark cloud of hate is visible every time we see or read about Trump. The media has a responsibility here to stop rebroadcasting his comments and instead refute his comments. The media can very easily use split-screen technology to call out Trump's hate speech. When he says that Representative Omar hates this country, they need to provide evidence that she does not. All they have to do is play a clip of her recent arrival home in Minnesota. She was received with open arms.

4.4. BLOG POST, 31 MAY 2020: AMERICA IS BURNING BY DIANE RAVITCH[203]

These are the worst of times.

Police brutality in Minneapolis murdered a Black man who allegedly used a fake $20 bill. Petty crimes are adjudicated in a court of law. Police do not have the authority or right to use lethal force when confronting an unarmed person. After a long string of similar incidents where Black people were unjustly murdered, the killing of George Floyd ignited protests across the nation. Some of the protests turned violent, and fires were burning in widely scattered cities in the midst of confrontations between police and protestors.

Racism is America's deepest, most intractable sin.

The explosion of protest is unlikely to lead to any productive change until the racists in the White House are ousted and replaced by people who are determined to fight racism. We currently have a government

---

[202] Michael Lavietes, "Trump Relished Rally Chant, Ocasio-Cortez Tells Constituents in Queens," Reuters, July 21, 2019, retrieved April 3, 2022, https://www.reuters.com/article/us-usa-trump-democrats/trump-relished-rally-chant-ocasio-cortez-tells-constituents-in-queens-idUSKCN1UG00D.

[203] Diane Ravitch, "America Is Burning," May 31, 2020, retrieved December 15, 2021, https://dianeravitch.net/2020/05/31/america-is-burning/. Used with permission of Diane Ravitch.

of old white men who have used their words and deeds to stoke the fires that are now burning.

Trump has no credibility to calm the situation or to offer solace or to promise meaningful change. He has spent many years expressing the anger of racists, repeatedly claiming that President Obama was not born in the United States, demanding the death penalty for the Central Park Five (who were ultimately found innocent), pretending never to have heard of David Duke when Duke offered his endorsement of Trump, referring to the white nationalists who marched in Charlottesville as "very fine people," appealing again and again to the gun-toting, violent people who thronged to his rallies and praising them. No need to point out that Trump has stoked the fires that are now burning. We have all seen it with our own eyes. He is like a boy who plays with matches and eventually burns down his own house.

Last night on CNN, the Rev. Dr. William J. Barber II referred to the protests as an expression of "national mourning." The protestors are reacting, he said, not only to the death of George Floyd, but to poverty, joblessness, unequal treatment, hunger, injustice—to systematic racism and inequity that have been ignored for too long. For too long, our nation has been on a trajectory that creates and enriches billionaires while millions of people of all races, but especially Black Americans, are expected to live a life of want and need and hopelessness without complaint.

Last night, the Martin Luther King Jr. Center released the text of a speech that Dr. King gave in 1967 in which he said that "a riot is the language of the unheard." He said, prophetically, "And as long as America postpones justice, we stand in the position of having these recurrences of violence and riots over and over again. Social justice and progress are the absolute guarantors of riot prevention."[204]

Franklin Delano Roosevelt laid out an "economic bill of rights" in 1944, which has since been forgotten as a small number of extraordinarily

---

[204] Joshua Bote, "'A Riot Is the Language of the Unheard': MLK's Powerful Quote Resonates amid George Floyd Protests," USA Today, May 29, 2020, retrieved April 3, 2022, https://www.usatoday.com/story/news/nation/2020/05/29/minneapolis-protest-martin-luther-king-quote-riot-george-floyd/5282486002/.

wealthy people rig the system to intensify economic inequality, abetted by willing allies like Mitch McConnell. Even a huge multi-trillion-dollar bill to relieve those suffering from the effects of the coronavirus turned out to be a package of goodies for big corporations.

Trump did not create racism, but he has used it and exploited it for his political benefit. He has ignored it, belittled its consequences, and courted the support of racists. He has made plain his contempt for his predecessor, our nation's first Black president. When Obama was elected president, many commentators declared that America was finally a post-racial society. With a man of African descent in the presidency, with a racially integrated Cabinet, with a Black man leading the Justice Department, the stain of racism would at last be abolished.

The commentators were wrong. Racism is thriving. It will destroy our nation until we assure equal justice to every citizen; until we guarantee that everyone has the same rights and privileges; until we provide every man, woman, and child with decent health care, housing, education, and a decent standard of living.

We can't eliminate racism entirely, but we can remove its adherents from the seats of power, and we can stigmatize it. We can choose leaders who fight for freedom, justice, and a decent standard of living for all people. Unless we do so, our tattered democracy will not survive. We can't let that happen. We must be willing and able to pursue genuine change, a social democracy in which every one of us is protected equally by the law and has the right to life, liberty, and the pursuit of happiness.

4.5. BLOG POST, 23 JULY 2020: STORMTROOPERS IN AMERICAN CITIES

The president of the United States is sending stormtroopers into American cities. Without any invitation from or consent of the governor of Oregon or the mayor of Portland, hundreds of camouflaged armed troops have used force against legal protestors. The protestors are not breaking the law by protesting police brutality and the unequal treatment of people of color. These stormtroopers are not there to help local law enforcement, but instead to use aggressive force against protestors.

As a result, Trump announced today that he is sending his stormtroopers to Chicago after a shooting that wounded fourteen people, again without any local consent.

Trump is using this tactic to manipulate the right of American citizens to protest on the streets, outside or inside buildings. It is a First Amendment "right of the people peaceably to assemble, and to petition the government for a redress of grievances."[205] However, Trump's administration is claiming that "lawlessness" exists in these cities. He's ready to attack the "lawless" with armed stormtroopers. Many are outraged. We all should be outraged.

STORMTROOPERS IN PORTLAND

The *Oregonian* published a report today, the fifty-fifth day of protests. It's titled "Portland Protests Continue Tuesday as Federal Officers Use Gas, Force on Hundreds Gathered Downtown."[206] According to the authors, more than 1,000 people filled the city's core for the second straight night to rally against police violence and systemic racism. They reported that there was repeated force and violence by federal officers. Officers were often seen shooting munitions, stun grenades, and gas containers at the protestors.

USING PARAMILITARY—TRUMP'S BROWNSHIRTS

Donald Trump is using paramilitary stormtroopers to scare the shit out of Americans living in America's cities, especially those that have Democratic governors or mayors. The red state cities are safe. But blue and purple states are in for it. In 1921 Adolf Hitler and Ernst Röhm used stormtroopers, a paramilitary wing of the Nazi Party, to help Hitler

---

[205] Congressional Research Service, Constitution of the United States of America: Analysis and Interpretation, S. Doc. No. 112-9 (2012).
[206] Noelle Crombie and Ryan Nguyen, "Portland Protests Continue Tuesday as Federal Officers Use Gas, Force on Hundreds Gathered Downtown," OregonLive.com, July 22, 2020, retrieved February 25, 2021, https://www.oregonlive.com/weather/2020/07/portland-protests-continue-for-55th-day-tuesday-live-updates.html.

rise and keep power in the 1920s and 1930s. Their uniforms were brown-colored shirts, mainly because they were cheap. They were called Sturmabteilung (SA), assault division.[207] They were used to disrupt the meetings of opposing parties, fighting against protestors (Red Front Fighters League of the Communist Party of Germany, Romani people, trade unionists, and especially Jewish people). Eventually these paramilitary troops were called "Brownshirts," from the color of their uniforms. Mussolini's troops were called "Blackshirts" for the same reasoning.

Donald Trump and Chad Wolf, acting secretary of Homeland Security, are using paramilitary officers in Portland and have threatened to use them in other American cities. Although they aren't Brownshirts or Blackshirts, they are disguised to deceive an "enemy" with their military camouflage. For some time, these stormtroopers used no visible identification, but now I noticed that they have "SCF" on their shirts. SCF is the Surge Capacity Force of Homeland Security, which was established after Hurricane Katrina. They are supposed to help people. Trump is instead using them to terrorize citizens in American cities who are peacefully protesting.

---

[207] Graham Land, "The Brownshirts: The Role of the Sturmabteilung (SA) in Nazi Germany," History Hit, January 13, 2021, https://www.historyhit.com/hitlers-bullyboys-the-role-of-the-sa-in-nazi-germany/.

CHAPTER 5:
FREE AND FAIR ELECTIONS

5.1. BLOG POST, 17 AUGUST 2020: MOST US CITIZENS CAN VOTE BY MAIL

Most of us living in the United States can vote by mail. There will be no need to stand in line for hours. There will be no fear of COVID-19 because you can receive your ballot by mail and then drive to a drop-off location. A friend can do the same for you. If you want to use the US Postal Service (USPS), then make sure that your ballot is time stamped before 7:00 p.m. on November 3, 2020.

However, one of the underlying fears, beyond the coronavirus, is voter suppression. In Georgia, where I have lived for more than fifty years, voter suppression in the last election (2018) possibly led to Stacey Abrams losing to Brian Kemp. Kemp was Georgia's secretary of state at the time. Kemp refused to step down from his position and managed the election in which he was on the ticket for governor. He was accused of conflict of interest by overseeing an election in which he was a candidate. He refused to go.

There were also accusations that Kemp, as secretary of state, made it difficult for some people to vote, especially Black people, the poor, and students. According to an article in the *Atlanta Journal and Constitution*, precinct closures around Georgia made it difficult for a lot of people to vote. The journal article estimated that between 55,000 and 85,000 voters were affected. Stacey Abrams lost the election by 55,000 votes.[208]

---

[208] Mark Niesse and Greg Bluestein, "The Right to Vote Becomes a Heated Battle in Georgia Governor's Race," *Atlanta Journal-Constitution*, October 21, 2018, https://www.ajc.com/news/state--regional-govt--politics/the-right-vote-becomes-heated-battle-georgia-governor-race/Mga2D1WMOvolspCJYU6YoK/.

Even today, some counties in Georgia have either moved or closed polling stations. These conditions make voting exceedingly difficult for many people, especially if people simply can't take hours off work to cast a vote. In some cases, people who had only to travel a mile or so to vote now must travel more than ten miles. Because of this situation, Black voters were 20 percent more likely to miss elections because of long distances. This statistic is also happening in other states.

VOTING BY MAIL IS ESSENTIAL BUSINESS

In the upcoming election, it is imperative that we as the people pay attention and learn as much as we can about the voting options open to us.

Voting by mail will overrule those officials who have a personal stake in making voting difficult. But it doesn't have to be that way, and it is possibly quite easy for us to fight back against the "suppressionists."

The *Washington Post* published an article stating that more than 84 percent of Americans can vote by mail.[209] I was surprised by this statistic, but by no means was I disappointed. America has 234 million voters. Only 52 million need an excuse beyond COVID-19 fears to vote by mail. That means that more than 180 million people can vote by mail. No wonder Trump is trying to undermine people's confidence in voting by mail. He has also done an end run around the USPS by naming a corrupt friend as head of the postal service and refuses to provide additional funds that the post office says it needs for the November election.

5.2. BLOG POST, 21 AUGUST 2020:
TRUTH ABOUT MAIL-IN VOTING

Mail-in voting was the subject of my most recent post. I received a flurry of comments on that post, which I also posted on Facebook.

Most comments on my Facebook page were positive. But some people are really upset about absentee and mail-in voting. One

---

[209] K. Rabinowitz and B. Mayes, "Vote by Mail: Which States Allow Absentee Voting," *Washington Post*, September 25, 2020, https://www.washingtonpost.com/graphics/2020/politics/vote-by-mail-states/.

person questioned me because I was a professor, and I was born in Massachusetts. I suppose he believed I was a liberal professor and would hold ideas in favor of mail-in voting. Another person said I should take these ideas and put them where the "sun don't shine." And then another person said that voting by mail has fraud written all over it. People had strong opinions on mail-in voting. Their opinions are important. I've used them to develop the ideas in this post.

Let's start by reviewing the history of voting in our country, with some emphasis on mail-in voting. Finally, we'll consider other factors that affect voting.

The Constitution grants states the power to set voting policy. Most states originally limited voting to property-owning or tax-paying white males. They were who could vote in the first presidential election in 1789. However, four northern states allowed free Black males to vote. Women could vote in New Jersey until 1807.

The first absentee ballots were issued by Union and Confederate troops on the battlefields during the Civil War.[210] So as far back as the early 1860s, it was possible to vote by "mail." Legal challenges and public skepticism didn't prevent voting from afar from happening. Now, in 2020, with voting by mail sure to rise because of the COVID-19 pandemic, Trump and his sycophants are claiming mail-in ballots would be fraudulent. We know this is a false claim. Trump still holds this view, which was one of the bases for his Big Lie.

From the late nineteenth and early twentieth centuries, Jim Crow laws were used to enforce racial segregation and disenfranchise and remove political and economic gains made by Black people during the period of Reconstruction (1865–1877). In 1920 the Nineteenth Amendment was ratified, giving women the right to vote. It explicitly states: "The right of citizens of the United States to vote shall not be denied or abridged by the United States or by any State on account of sex." African American woman were crucial to the suffragist movement.

---

[210] Nina Strochlic, "How Mail-in Voting Began on Civil War Battlefields," *National Geographic*, February 20, 2021, retrieved February 25, 2021, https://www.nationalgeographic.com/history/article/how-mail-in-voting-began-on-civil-war-battlefields.

During this time they not only sought the right to vote, but also fought for the civil rights of African Americans.

Most Southern states did not ratify the amendment until between 1951 and 1984. Three million women south of the Mason–Dixon line remained disfranchised after the passage of the amendment. In Southern states fear, intimidation, poll taxes, literacy tests, and violence were used to suppress the vote of African American women.

In 1965, the Voting Rights Act was passed to enforce the Fifteenth Amendment. The act secured the right to vote for racial minorities throughout the country, especially in the South. Voting is now enforced federally. Thank you, Martin Luther King Jr., John Lewis, and the other civil rights activists of the 1950s and 1960s. However, in 2013, the Supreme Court struck down a key part of the Voting Rights Act, freeing nine states (mostly in the South) to change their election laws without advance approval from the federal government.

Voting and voting rights have a history going back to the formation of the United States. Although voting in person has been the mode of voting in the US, the points listed above provide information that absentee and mail-in voting have been part of voting protocols in America. Voter fraud is rare, and even rarer with mail-in voting.

THE 2020 ELECTION

Voter interest is extremely high in the 2020 election. As a result, President Trump has announced if he loses the election, it will be because it was rigged. To him there is no way he can lose without a rigged and fraudulent election. And the culprit is mail-in voting. Trump rails and whines about this every day. It's part of his plan to discredit the general election. There is also another aspect of Trump's fraud claims. All the cases that were filed by Trump claiming fraud were in counties with large populations of African Americans. In counties that had similarly large populations but were majority white, lawsuits were not filed.

On the other side of this coin is the fear that Trump has done everything in his power to convince Americans that fraud is only a stamp away. He has torn into any state (except Florida, where he uses an absentee ballot) that allows vote by mail. Trump knows that most states have provisions that make it possible for people to vote by mail. He conveniently ignores the fact that at least three states have *only* vote by mail. Two hundred and forty million people are registered to vote in the US. Over 180 million American voters could vote by mail in November. As a result, the data from past elections would suggest that about one-third of these folks would either vote early or vote by mail. About 30 million would choose to vote by mail.

THE PANDEMIC'S EFFECT

The pandemic has changed the formula and has slowed the process of voting. The six-foot social distancing policy has made going through polling stations slower. Also, older citizens (such as me) are more susceptible to the coronavirus, which makes finding workers for the polling stations harder. The pandemic has created the situation where more people will choose to vote by mail.

Donald Trump *melted down* over the idea of more folks voting by mail. He has made it clear that if he loses, he will call the election a fraud. He has railed against mail-in voting and messaged that it will result in millions and millions of rigged votes. I believe that his constant tweets and comments in public about mail-in voting will affect people's confidence in the 2020 election results.

5.3. BLOG POST, 4 JANUARY 2021: TRUMP THREATENS GEORGIA SECRETARY OF STATE

After eighteen phone call attempts, Donald Trump finally reached Brad Raffensperger, Georgia's secretary of state. Trump's phone call was recorded[211] by Raffensperger, who later released the complete phone call.[212] The phone call is full of an absurd collection of Trumpist lies about the election in Georgia.

---

[211] "Trump Berates Georgia Secretary of State, Urges Him to 'Find' Votes," audio of a phone call, *Washington Post*, January 3, 2021, https://www.youtube.com/watch?v=o3hrN0cP58Y&feature=youtu.be.
[212] P. Firozi and A. Gardner, "Full Transcript and Audio of the Call between Trump and Raffensperger," *Washington Post*, January 5, 2021, https://www.washingtonpost.com/politics/trump-raffensperger-call-transcript-georgia-vote/2021/01/03/2768e0cc-4ddd-11eb-83e3-322644d82356_story.html.

- Trump told Raffensperger that there are thousands of votes that were not counted.
- Trump claimed that more than 5,000 people who weren't on the rolls voted. He told the secretary of state that there were more than 18,000 vacant address votes—and some of them only had post office box numbers.
- Trump said that Georgia had nearly 5,000 out-of-state voters.
- Trump said there are photographs of ballot drop boxes that were picked up. Trump claims they weren't delivered for three days.
- Trump said that he thinks that 5,000 dead people voted.

The phone call continued for an hour. Nearly every sentence is a lie or fabrication. Raffensperger corrected the president and said he found only two dead people had voted. Trump said, "When you add it up, there are at least 300,000 fake ballots." None of the previous assertions by Trump were true. They were all fabricated by Trump and White House sycophants.

I'll stop there with what Trump's call revealed. Not only was the phone call disgusting, but there is also ample evidence in the call that Trump was trying to influence the outcome of the Georgia election, and that is a crime.

Trump has done this before. In December, he called Brian Kemp, Georgia's governor, and asked him to reconvene the Georgia legislature to have them change the outcome of the election in Trump's favor. Kemp turned him down

Trump told Kemp and Raffensperger to resign. Also, Senators David Perdue (R-GA) and Kelly Loeffler (R-GA) agreed that Raffensperger should resign. Loeffler was appointed by the governor to fill out the Senate term, so she couldn't diss Kemp. Please note that Loeffler and Perdue lost their elections in Georgia's dual senate races to Raphael Warnock and Jon Ossoff, respectively.

Author's Update: The Fulton County, Georgia, district attorney has started a criminal investigation into former President Donald Trump's attempts to overturn the Georgia election results, including the Raffensperger phone call. Fani T. Willis, the district attorney, wrote in a letter that the investigation will examine violations of the law, including the solicitation of election fraud, the making of false statements to state and local governmental bodies, conspiracy, racketeering, violation of oath of office, and any involvement in violence or threats related to the election's administration.

The Trump–Raffensperger phone call was another attempt by Trump to overturn Georgia's presidential election, which was won by Joe Biden by 11,780 votes. Georgia's election was counted three times, and the results were the same. Joe Biden beat Donald Trump. Trump told Raffensperger to find at least 11,781 votes. Raffensperger politely told Trump that he has the wrong data, and he lost the election. Trump threatened Raffensperger and called him a child for not knowing what the correct election results were. Trump is in Dalton, Georgia, as I write this update for a last-ditch rally for Perdue and Loeffler, the two Republicans that are being challenged by Jon Ossoff and Raphael Warnock, respectively. The election is tomorrow, but already more than 3 million Georgians have voted.

PART III: SCRUTINY

> I do solemnly swear (or affirm) that I will faithfully execute the office of President of the United States, and will to the best of my ability, preserve, protect, and defend the Constitution of the United States.
> —US Constitution

INTRODUCTION

DONALD J. TRUMP VIOLATED HIS OATH OF OFFICE MANY TIMES throughout his term. He was under scrutiny even before he was elected president. During his first year in office, a special prosecutor, Robert S. Mueller, was named to investigate if any coordination between the Trump campaign and Russia existed with the intent of interfering in the 2016 election. In 2019 Trump was impeached for abuse of power by bribing the president of Ukraine to investigate the actions of Joe Biden and his son Hunter Biden in exchange for $400 million in military aid. On January 6, 2021, Trump incited a mob that stormed the US Capitol with the intent of overthrowing the 2020 election by "taking the country back." Finally, he was impeached a second time for inciting the insurrection and seditious acts.

Trump was scrutinized more than any president in American history. Coming under scrutiny was an ongoing characteristic of his presidency. He solicited foreign interferences in the electoral system, obstructed investigations into his actions—especially interfering with the Mueller investigation—permitted his self-serving behavior to extend to his business interests, and empowered cabinet appointees and family members to abuse their position in office.

Foreign interference, political retaliation, and conspiracy theory ideology underscore Trump's actions across the Mueller investigation and his two impeachments. Trump's actions were corrupt, and he surrounded himself with people who were willing to support his malfeasance.

At a news conference in July 2016, Donald Trump voiced his pleasure with the beginnings of Russian interference in his first election when he said, "Russia, if you're listening, I hope you're able to find the thirty thousand emails that are missing." He was referring to Hillary Clinton's emails that she had purged from her personal computer, which she said were communications on a private server. Just prior to this news conference, WikiLeaks had released Democratic Party emails that the FBI said were stolen by Russian government hackers.

Dov H. Levin, assistant professor of international relations, University of Hong Kong, wrote *Meddling in the Ballot Box*,[213] which is focused on partisan electoral interventions, as happened in the 2016 election for president. His book details how electoral interventions play an important role in world politics, especially between great powers. Levin explains and documents that meddling in another country's election has been prominent for decades. The Russians meddled in the 2016 and 2020 elections. The United States has meddled in elections as well. According to Levin, 117 partisan electoral interventions have been done by the United States and USSR/Russia between 1947 and 2000.[214] The United States intervened in eighty-one elections, while USSR/Russia intervened in thirty-six elections. Levin says that the United States and USSR/Russia interventions represented meddling in 11.3 percent of the 937 elections held during this period around the world. Another point I want to make here is that Levin reports that there were fifty-three significant military interventions by either the United States or the USSR/Russia, and the United States conducted fifty-nine covert foreign-imposed regime changes via coups d'états or arming or aiding of dissident groups.[215]

---

[213] Dov H. Levin, *Meddling in the Ballot Box: The Causes and Effects of Partisan Electoral Interventions* (New York: Oxford University Press, 2020).
[214] Levin, *Meddling*, 152.
[215] Levin, *Meddling*, 153.

Donald Trump signaled that he would welcome interference in American politics by another country. At Trump Tower in New York, one of his sons, Donald Jr., joined other Trump advisors in a meeting with two Russians who claimed to have derogatory information on Hillary Clinton. In the world of foreign power interventions in another country's elections, having helping hands in that country is essential for a successful intervention.[216]

Even before the election, the FBI opened an investigation called "Crossfire Hurricane,"[217] a counterintelligence inquiry of Russia's hacking efforts. A federal judge approved secret monitoring of several Trump campaign officials and their contacts and relationships with Russia.

Meanwhile, before Donald Trump was inaugurated, he was being investigated. James Comey, the director of the FBI, was leading an investigation into whether the Trump campaign had coordinated with Russia to interfere in the 2016 election. Then, early in Trump's term, the FBI was investigating Michael Flynn, Trump's national security advisor. Trump tried to intervene by asking Comey to let the investigation go: "He's a good guy." Trump also wanted Comey to say that Trump was not under suspicion for misconduct with Russia during the campaign. Comey didn't grant either. Trump also asked Comey for his total and complete loyalty.[218]

The constant scrutiny of Donald Trump was caused by his own rage, according to a *Washington Post* report.[219] In his anger, he fired James Comey, hoping that would cause the Russia investigation to go away. It didn't. Instead, Trump angered Rod J. Rosenstein, who oversaw the Justice Department's coordination with the FBI's Russia investigation. Trump claimed that it was Rosenstein that urged that he fire Comey. Attorney General Jeff Sessions had recused himself from the Russian investigation because of prior connections with Russia, but he failed to

---

[216] Levin, *Meddling*, 223–224.
[217] Matt Apuzzo, Adam Goldman, and Nicholas Fandos, "Code Name Crossfire Hurricane: The Secret Origins of the Trump Investigation," *New York Times*, May 16, 2018, https://www.nytimes.com/2018/05/16/us/politics/crossfire-hurricane-trump-russia-fbi-investigation.html.
[218] Michael S. Schmidt, "In a Private Dinner, Trump Demanded Loyalty. Comey Demurred," *New York Times*, May 12, 2017, https://www.nytimes.com/2017/05/11/us/politics/trump-comey-firing.html.
[219] R. Helderman, and M. Zapotosky, "'If You Took It All in in One Day, It Would Kill You': What Mueller's Investigation Has Already Revealed," *Washington Post*, March 23, 2019, retrieved February 28, 2021, https://www.washingtonpost.com/world/national-security/if-you-took-it-all-in-in-one-day-it-would-kill-you-what-muellers-investigation-has-already-revealed/2019/03/22/cb143340-41ee-11e9-922c-64d6b7840b82_story.html.

mention that he had at least one meeting with Russia's ambassador to the United States.

THE MUELLER INVESTIGATION

Because Sessions recused himself[220] from any Russian investigation, Rosenstein was in charge. Acting alone, Rosenstein appointed Mueller, the former FBI director, to lead an independent investigation of Russian interference in the 2016 election. A single-page order from Rosenstein dated on May 17, 2017, established the special council.

For two years, Mueller's investigation consumed the attention of the country. Mueller had a wide range of options and investigated anyone that had a connection with Trump, with the Trump campaign, and with Russia. Mueller had a staff of seventeen lawyers and forty FBI agents. It was a big operation. It was also the source of newspaper reports and television headlines over the period of its existence. For many of us, we thought that the investigation would shed light on the relationship between Russia and the Trump campaign. Although the investigation did cast a shadow on both the Russians and Trump's circle of confidants, it was not a fulfilling result.

The special council's final report was submitted to Attorney General William Barr two years later on March 22, 2019. Unfortunately, Barr put a spin on it that favored Trump. His television appearance offered a highly redacted summary of Mueller's release. Instead of reporting the facts of the report, Barr offered his own interpretation of the special council's thesis. I read Mueller's text, and quite a different account is described than the one Barr preferred. Journalists Rosalind S. Helderman and Matt Zapotosky also paint a different picture of its finding. Barr gave his pitch before anyone (except the White House) saw or read the report. These journalists analyzed it and offered more revealing conclusions. Early in their introduction, the journalists took Barr to task and called it:

---

[220] Trump was repeatedly furious with Sessions for his recusal, and this led Trump to fire him.

...a stunning account of how Russia worked to help the Trump campaign and how Trump's associates were willing to accept Russian assistance and it presented an explosive and detailed narrative of how Trump sought to shut down the investigation, as he was worried about its impact.[221]

Links between the Trump campaign and the Russian government were uncovered. Indeed, Russian computer operatives acted illegally and "in sweeping and systematic fashion." Mueller charged twenty-six Russian nationals with a conspiracy to hack Democratic computers with the goal of influencing the 2016 election in favor of Trump. Mueller didn't find any collusion between Trump's campaign and Russia. However, Mueller did find that many of Trump associates did have connections with Russians.

The second part of the report addresses Trump's obstruction of justice. Nearly two hundred pages detail the ways Trump tried to disable Mueller's investigation.

The Mueller investigators concluded that Trump did indeed obstruct justice in four of the episodes. Mueller didn't act on this finding and charge Trump with a crime because he accepted the Justice Department policy that a sitting president cannot be charged. So he didn't. However, Mueller also said this: "The investigation does not conclude that the president committed a crime; however, it also does not exonerate him."[222]

To some journalists, the Mueller investigation failed. It failed because it didn't conclude that Trump obstructed justice when the report outlines how he tried to stop the investigation. Mueller gave Donald Trump a pass. Mueller did not investigate Trump's history and financial past. Nor did he pursue the question of Trump's affinity for Putin. And why didn't Mueller request a grand jury subpoena for Trump's testimony?[223]

When the report came out, it was widely misinterpreted, especially by Trump and his associates. As far as Russian collaboration, Trump

---

[221] Helderman and Zapotosky, "Mueller's Investigation."
[222] *The Mueller Report: The Washington Post* (New York: Scribner, 2019), Kindle Edition, 12–13.
[223] Jeffrey Toobin, "Why the Mueller Investigation Failed," *The New Yorker*, June 29, 2020, retrieved February 9, 2021, https://www.newyorker.com/magazine/2020/07/06/why-the-mueller-investigation-failed.

claimed, "No collusion—total exoneration." Neither of these was true. Mueller had concluded that "while the investigation identified numerous links between individuals with ties to the Russian government and individuals associated with the Trump campaign, the evidence was not sufficient to support criminal charges." Some have interpreted this as pointing to insufficient evidence rather than innocence.[224]

Mueller, but especially many of his attorneys, were furious with the way Barr handled the announcement of the report. On March 27, Mueller responded with his own letter that, according to some, would have been more effective if it had been leaked or released to the public faster than it was. It didn't become public for a month.[225] The Mueller team had written introductions and executive summaries of all parts of the report, but Barr wasn't interested in releasing them. On April 18, Barr released the report and tried to make comments. Those in attendance were only interested in diving into the reports to find out what really was published.

Jeffrey Toobin wrote that Barr's written and oral comments undermined and diluted the Mueller report to such a degree that common knowledge was that there was no collusion and Trump did nothing wrong. But as Toobin points out, the special prosecution was formed because the Russian government had engaged in a systematic attempt to help Donald Trump win the election. The Mueller report shows very clearly and provides evidence that the Russian government hacked the Democratic National Committee's computers and then released the email and other documents to WikiLeaks. Barr failed to mention these findings in his public discussions of the investigation. Trump got away scot-free.[226]

PRESIDENTIAL ABUSE OF POWER: THE FIRST IMPEACHMENT

On July 25, 2019, Donald Trump had a phone call with Volodymyr Zelenskyy, president of Ukraine. Trump asked Zelenskyy to interfere in

---

[224] Toobin, "Why the Mueller Investigation Failed."
[225] Jeffrey Toobin, *True Crimes and Misdemeanors* (New York: Knopf Doubleday Publishing Group, 2020), Kindle Edition, 308.
[226] Toobin, "Why the Mueller Investigation Failed."

the 2020 American election. Trump also abused his power by blackmailing the Ukrainian president by withholding millions of dollars in military aid.

The phone call, like all the president's calls, was monitored normally by at least two members of the National Security Council (NSC). Typically, prior to the call, NSC members discuss the upcoming call with the president. NSC members also stay with the president during the call, and record of it is also stored on government computers. Those who listened in will use their notes and the computer record to draft a single report of the call. According to various sources, more than ten people listened to the Trump–Zelenskyy call.[227]

Trump was accused of an abuse of presidential power by proposing to withhold $400 million in military aid unless the Ukrainian government investigated (dug up dirt on) Joe Biden and his son Hunter Biden. The allegations that Trump and others made about the Bidens were already discredited. Debunking these claims didn't stop Trump from dispatching his personal attorney, Rudolph W. (Rudy) Giuliani, and Attorney General William Barr to Ukraine to investigate the Bidens.

Nearly a year later, Donald Trump was impeached a second time for his role in inciting political violence at the US Capitol building. In Part VI, I'll explore this in full detail.

---

[227] Tara McKelvey, "Who Listens in on a President's Phone Call?" BBC News, September 27, 2019, retrieved April 4, 2022, https://www.bbc.com/news/world-us-canada-49858318.

CHAPTER 6:
INVESTIGATIONS

6.1. BLOG POST, 18 APRIL 2019: RUSSIAN MEDIA AND HACKING CAMPAIGN FAVORED THE TRUMP CAMPAIGN

Active social media measures were used to influence the 2016 presidential campaign in favor of a positive outcome for the Trump campaign.

Two Russian organizations conspired to affect the election outcome through social media operations—active measures. The Internet Research Agency (IRA), a Russian organization funded by Russian billionaire Yevgeniy Viktoraovich Prigozhin, was established to sow discord in the US political system. IRA employees posted derogatory information that supported Trump and disparaged Clinton. The IRA bought political advertisements on social media in the names of US persons or entities. No coordination with the Trump campaign was found; however, what is the US attorney general doing to protect the US political system against the same kind of interference in the next and future elections? What are you doing, Mr. Barr?

Barr should understand that the IRA organization swept onto Twitter and Facebook and hoodwinked thousands of American voters who read their tweets and Facebook posts, which were detrimental to the Clinton campaign, and retweeted or reposted them on Facebook. The facts here are impressive. According to the Mueller report, IRA-controlled Facebook accounts made 80,000 posts between January 2015 and August 2017. Mueller estimates that 126 million persons were reached through these accounts.

Over on the IRA-controlled Twitter accounts, Mueller estimated that about 1.4 million people (about half the population of Nevada) were in contact through these IRA accounts.

6.2. BLOG POST, 20 APRIL 2019: IS THE TRUMP PRESIDENCY VALID CONSIDERING THE SPECIAL COUNSEL'S REPORT ON ELECTION INTERFERENCE IN 2016?

Donald Trump was impeached for high crimes and misdemeanors in December 2019, becoming the third president in history to be impeached.

In our collective memories, the United States has not experienced an election as it did in the 2016 presidential election in which Donald Trump was elected and Hillary Clinton was defeated. Trump attained 304 electoral votes, while Clinton got 227 electoral votes. However, in the popular vote, Clinton got 65,853,514, while Trump received 62,984,828, a difference of 2,868,686 votes in favor of Hillary Clinton. It's not the first time that a president was elected without carrying the popular vote; George W. Bush was defeated by Al Gore in the popular vote by 540,520 votes, while Bush managed to get 5 more electoral votes (271–266).

To our knowledge, the 2000 election was never investigated by a special counsel, although the actual electoral votes were determined by the Supreme Court in favor of Bush based on technical issues associated with paper ballots that were difficult to "read."[228]

JANUARY 6, 2017: CIA, FBI, AND NATIONAL SECURITY AGENCY BRIEFING

On this day the US intelligence community briefed Donald Trump, by then president-elect, and President Obama that, with high confidence, it had concluded that Russia had intervened in the presidential election through a variety of means (now detailed in the Mueller report) to assist Trump's candidacy and to harm Clinton's.

---

[228] Ena Alvarado, David A. Graham, Cullen Murphy, and Amy Weiss-Meyer, "The Bush-Gore Recount Is an Omen for 2020," *The Atlantic*, August 19, 2020, retrieved April 4, 2022, https://www.theatlantic.com/politics/archive/2020/08/bush-gore-florida-recount-oral-history/614404/.

By early February, three congressional committees announced they would be conducting inquiries into Russian interference. I can only imagine what was going through Trump's head when he listened to the report.

MARCH 2017: COMEY ANNOUNCES COUNTERINTELLIGENCE MISSION

FBI Director James Comey announced that as part of its counterintelligence mission, the bureau would be launching an investigation into the Russian government's efforts to interfere in the 2016 presidential election and to investigate the nature of any links between individuals associated with the Trump campaign and the Russian government. Furthermore, the FBI began to explore whether there was any coordination between the campaign and Russia's efforts.

MAY 9, 2017: YOU'RE FIRED!

James Comey is fired by President Trump. Comey finds out he's fired on TV while he's on the West Coast talking FBI policy with FBI agents in Los Angeles. With Comey gone, Trump hoped the Russian investigation would go away. It didn't.

MAY 17, 2017: NOT SO FAST, DONALD!

On this day, acting Attorney General Rod Rosenstein appointed Robert Mueller as special counsel and authorized him to conduct the investigation that James Comey had started.

For two years, President Trump has carried out a campaign to slander and even put an end to the Mueller investigation. When he found out that Rosenstein had appointed Robert Mueller as special counsel, he said: "This is the end of my presidency. I'm fucked."[229]

According to the Mueller report, Trump engaged in efforts to curtail the special counsel's investigation and prevent the disclosure

---

[229] Emma Newburger, "Donald Trump on Mueller's Appointment: 'This Is the End of My Presidency. I'm F----d,'" CNBC, April 22, 2019, retrieved February 12, 2022, https://www.cnbc.com/2019/04/18/donald-trump-on-muellers-appointment-this-is-the-end-of-my-presidency-im-f----d.html.

of evidence to it, including through public and private contacts with potential witnesses.

IS THE TRUMP PRESIDENCY VALID?

After living through the past two years of the Trump presidency; after reading numerous reports, papers, and interviews; and after reading the special counsel's report, it's difficult to conclude that the presidency of Donald Trump is anything but invalid.

Although Mueller's report says there was not "sufficient evidence" to charge a crime, the Mueller team did charge a few people in Trump's orbit with high crimes, especially lying to prosecutors. The report concluded that these lies interfered with their investigation of Russian election interference.

Richard Pinedo, Michael Flynn, George Papadopoulos, Paul Manafort, Alex van der Zwaan, Roger Stone, Rick Gates, and Michael Cohen were charged, found guilty, and sent to jail for various sentences.

As I will discuss in future posts, there is ample evidence to show how Trump and his associates did what they could to use the Russian interference in the 2016 election to their benefit and to denigrate Hillary Clinton.

Mueller charged thirteen Russian nationals, twelve Russian military intel officers, and Konstantin Kilimnik (a Manafort associate and Ukrainian aide). Mueller, unfortunately, did not go far enough in drawing conclusions about the Trump Organization's coziness with Russia and Russian government officials. Although individual Americans were not identified as conspiring with Russia, they did unknowingly pass on to their followers on Twitter and Facebook just what the Russian trolls were feeding them. And champions at passing on these negative ads and articles on Twitter and Facebook were the adult members of the Trump family and Trump campaign officials.

Although Trump has been in office for two years legally, there is no question in my mind that he got there with direct help from an adversary government and that we should judge his presidency as invalid. More Americans than not voted against him in 2016.

6.3. BLOG POST, 29 MAY 2019: OBSTRUCTION—TIME TO IMPEACH

> If we had confidence after a thorough investigation of the facts that the President clearly did not commit obstruction of justice, we would so state.
>
> Accordingly, while this report does not conclude that the President committed a crime, it also does not exonerate him.
>
> —The Mueller Report, 2019

As Robert Mueller stated today before the nation, he stands by his report and has nothing further to say. You may disagree with his position on continuing any further conversations, especially with Congress. But you can't disagree with his statements about Trump as cited above. If Trump didn't commit obstruction, Mueller would have said so. He didn't. And Mueller stated clearly that his team did not exonerate him. The case is not over.

THE OBSTRUCTION INVESTIGATION

What did the special prosecutor conclude about Trump's obstruction of justice investigation, as detailed in Part II of the 2019 Mueller report? Part II of the report is 182 pages long. The factual results of the Trump's obstruction investigation take up 144 of those pages. Eleven key events were investigated by Mueller.

Mueller's team spent two years investigating a myriad of ways Donald Trump attempted to interfere with the ongoing investigation of Russian interference into the 2016 presidential election. Mueller concluded that the Russian government did interfere in this election and used cyber techniques to steal information from Hillary Clinton's campaign, distribute much of it through WikiLeaks, and use the information as the basis for social media articles that favored Donald Trump's campaign over Hillary Clinton's. The use of Facebook, Twitter, and other media outlets was compelling and merciless in denigrating the Clinton campaign.

Mueller concluded that two Russians organizations interfered in the presidential election and indicted more than a dozen Russian government officials and military officers. If Trump were to accept this part of the Mueller report, he would be acknowledging that his presidency is a sham.

OBSTRUCTION EVENTS

There are eleven events that the Mueller team investigated. Each is potentially an obstruction of justice event. There is enough detail in the Mueller report to demand that the Congress of the United States begin the impeachment process against the sitting president. Here are the events:

- The campaign's response about Russian support for Trump.
- The president's conduct concerning the investigation of Michael Flynn.
- The president's reaction to public confirmation of the FBI's Russia investigation.
- Events leading up to and surrounding the termination of FBI Director Comey.
- The president's efforts to remove the special counsel.
- The president's efforts to curtail the special counsel investigation.
- The president's efforts to prevent disclosure of emails about the June 9, 2016, meeting between Russians and senior campaign officials.
- The president's further efforts to have the attorney general take over the investigation.
- The president's conduct towards Flynn, Manafort, and (name redacted).
- The president's conduct involving Michael Cohen.

Each of these events is reported in detail. There is enough evidence in the Mueller report to provide the Congress with a basis to begin the impeachment process in the House of Representatives. In my view, the Democrats need to act and fulfill their constitutional duty to oversee the executive branch and to make determinations about improper conduct and potential criminal activity.

Doing nothing is not an option.

6.4. BLOG POST, 10 JUNE 2021: A WHISTLEBLOWER'S CHRONICLE OF TRUMP'S PHONE CALL TO UKRAINE

On July 25, 2019, Donald Trump had a phone call with Volodymyr Zelenskyy, president of Ukraine. Trump asked Zelenskyy to interfere in the 2020 American election by investigating the actions of Joe Biden and his son Hunter Biden. Trump also abused his power in bribing the Ukrainian president by withholding millions of dollars in military aid if he didn't probe the Bidens.

The phone call led to the first impeachment of President Donald Trump. Because members of the NSC "listen in" to all presidential calls with foreign government executives, what was said was known to at least ten people. The phone call played an important role in the Russian–Ukrainian war.

The Russian–Ukrainian war began in 2014 between Russian forces (together with pro-Russian separatist forces) and Ukraine. In 2014, pro-Russian Ukraine President Viktor Yanukovych was removed from power by protests and a revolution in the country. At the time of Trump's phone call with Zelenskyy, the war in Eastern Ukraine and Crimea was in its third year of combat. Trump at this time was more concerned about his potential opponents in the 2020 election than the fact that Ukraine was in need of military aid. Indeed, Trump was accused of an abuse of presidential power in blackmailing a foreign president by withholding $400 million in military aid unless his government "investigated" (dug up dirt) on Joe Biden and his son Hunter Biden.

A day after the phone call, two Army lieutenant colonels on the NSC, twins Alexander and Yevgeny Vindman, went to the top lawyer at the NSC, John A. Eisenberg, concerned about the phone call.[230] Lt. Col. Alexander

---

[230] Alexander Vindman, *Here, Right Matters: An American Story* (New York: HarperCollins, 2021).

S. Vindman was the top Ukraine expert on the council. Eisenberg and one of his aides, Michael Ellis, decided to put Vindman's information into the White House's most secret server to keep it safe or to keep it away from prying eyes. A few days later, Eisenberg told Vindman not to talk about the call to anyone. The White House blocked Eisenberg from testifying at the House impeachment hearings in December 2019. Courageously, Vindman[231] did testify and was later fired by the vindictive Trump from his position in the White House.

The Vindman brothers spoke to a young CIA analyst who was already on alert about Trump's intertwining of foreign policy with personal political desires. The analyst was an expert on Ukraine, and his job was to track the effects of any action between the United States and Ukraine. The analyst also had an eye on Rudy Giuliani, who was carrying out a stealth political operation to stir up potential investigations into the Bidens. When the analyst learned about the Trump–Zelenskyy phone call, he was on high alert.

Alexander S. Vindman said that he only talked to two people, both with full clearance and both apparently included in the need-to-know group. He still to this day does not know if one of the two he spoke to about the call is the whistleblower.[232] The whistleblower, on the other hand, heard about Trump's phone call from other members of the White House Intelligence group. One of those could have been Vindman. Vindman said he does not know if he was the source. Vindman would soon learn that a silent campaign to undermine his credibility was underway because he had spoken out about Trump's phone call to Ukraine's president.

Michael Schmidt wrote about this analyst's duty to report and do something about what he believed occurred during the phone call. The following discussion is based on his research.[233] I believe this story is important to reveal the depths that this person had to go to expose wrongdoing by Donald Trump.

---

[231] The Pritzker Military Foundations appointed Alexander Vindman as its first Pritzker Military Fellow, based at Lawfare (lawfare.com). Vindman will join the staff at Lawfare for a two-year fellowship allowing him to write a book and complete a dissertation for a PhD.
[232] Vindman, *Here, Right Matters*, 161.
[233] Schmidt, M. S. (2020). *Donald Trump v. the United States: Inside the struggle to stop a president.* Random House, 379–389.

Passing on what was found would not be a simple matter of calling the boss and filing a report. It didn't work that way at all. The analyst first met with a CIA lawyer, who agreed that something needed to be done. The analyst met with the CIA's general council. The general council communicated the information to the White House, which indicated that it would not be taking this complaint seriously.

This impasse presented a serious dilemma for the analyst. Only a few people knew about the nature of the phone call, and the analyst knew about Giuliani's campaign to pressure Ukrainian officials to investigate the Bidens. The analyst was also concerned that Ukraine needed the financial aid in its fight with Russian-backed separatists. The analyst then contacted a friend who now worked as a staff member of the chair of the House Permanent Select Committee on Intelligence, Representative Adam Schiff (D-CA). The analyst was told that for anything to happen, the analyst would have to file a whistleblower complaint. This would mean finding a lawyer to guide him through the process. A lawyer was needed that understood whistleblower complaints.

He found one and they met at a coffee shop near the Capitol. The lawyer made sure that the analyst didn't tell him anything classified or privileged. At this time, the analyst only revealed that he had not witnessed the incident, but several people told him about it. The lawyer told him that he would refer him to Andrew Bakaj, a lawyer who had worked at the CIA early in his career. He reported wrongdoing in his office as a whistleblower but was forced out of his job and left the government. Now his work specializes in helping whistleblowers and others needing similar help.

He believed that the analyst stumbled across wrongdoing and now wanted to do the right thing. Bakaj advised him to write a whistleblower complaint without any advice or help from anyone else. He wrote the complaint, and after discussing it with Bakaj, he sent it on a secure government computer to Michael Atkinson, the inspector general of the Intelligence Community on August 3, 2019. A few days later, he found out that the director of national intelligence, a Trump appointee, was not going to forward the complaint to the Congress. Atkinson was not happy.

At this point Andrew Bakaj decided to hand-deliver a letter to the office of Senator Richard Burr (R-NC), chairperson of the Senate Intelligence Committee, and Representative Adam Schiff (D-CA), chairperson of the House Permanent Select Committee on Intelligence. Burr's office staff didn't seem interested in talking with him, but when he went to Schiff's office, he was invited in and sat with three of the committee's lawyers. While the lawyers were talking about the whistleblower's complaint, they learned that a letter was just received from Inspector General Atkinson claiming he was being prevented from passing on a "credible" and "urgent" complaint.

The analyst filed the complaint on August 12, but it was not released until September 26. The whistleblower's letter begins by identifying what the president did and who was involved with him. He wrote in his complaint:

> I am reporting an "urgent concern" in accordance with the procedures outlined in 50 U.S.C. §3033(k)(5)(A). This letter is UNCLASSIFIED when separated from the attachment. In the course of my official duties, I have received information from multiple US Government officials that the President of the United States is using the power of his office to solicit interference from a foreign country in the 2020 US election. This interference includes, among other things, pressuring a foreign country to investigate one of the President's main domestic political rivals. The President's personal lawyer, Mr. Rudolph Giuliani, is a central figure in this effort. Attorney General Barr appears to be involved as well.[234]

The letter (cited below) written by the whistleblower is an important document that eventually led the House of Representatives to file impeachment charges against Donald Trump and then deliver them to the Senate for a trial.

---

[234] Whistleblower Complaint (Unclassified), *USA Today*, August 12, 2019, retrieved April 5, 2021, https://www.usatoday.com/documents/6430388-20190812-Whistleblower-Complaint-Unclass/.

Trump claimed that he made a perfect call to the president of Ukraine. There was nothing done improperly or wrong in the phone call, according to Trump.[235] The whistleblower claimed that Trump wanted the Ukrainian president to:

> ...initiate an investigation into the activities of former Vice President Joseph Biden and his son, Hunter Biden; assist in purportedly uncovering that allegations of Russian interference in the 2016 US presidential election originated in Ukraine, with a specific request that the Ukrainian leader locate and turn over servers used by the Democratic National Committee (DNC) and examined by the US cyber security firm CrowdStrike, which initially reported that Russian hackers had penetrated the DNC's networks in 2016; and meet or speak with two people the President named explicitly as his personal envoys on these matters, Mr. Giuliani and Attorney General Barr, to whom the president referred multiple times in tandem.[236]

For the next few months, and during the impeachment hearings in the House, the White House refused to cooperate with the Congress and instead went out of its way to threaten and conceal documents related to the phone call. The impeachment process continued in the US Senate with members of the House prosecuting the case against Donald Trump. During and after the impeachment hearing, Trump took his revenge on anyone who testified against him. People were fired, including the Vindman brothers, and some others were forced to retire.

---

[235] Eugene Kiely, Lori Robertson, and D'Angelo Gore, "Trump's Inaccurate Claims about His 'Perfect' Call," FactCheck.org, November 20, 2019, retrieved April 4, 2022, https://www.factcheck.org/2019/10/trumps-inaccurate-claims-about-his-perfect-call/.
[236] Whistleblower Complaint.

PART IV: SCIENCE

> We must be scholars and activists. It is simply not enough to be scientists—that is, to measure and calculate—but rather we must be willing to dedicate ourselves to causes—to be activists who are willing to commit to environmental and humanitarian issues.
> —Jennie Springer, PhD[237]

INTRODUCTION

FOR FORTY YEARS I'VE BEEN A SCIENCE EDUCATOR; AUTHOR of books on science and science teaching; and co-developer of an international project between American and Russian researchers, teachers, and students who investigated serious global ecological problems, which expanded to include Australia, the Czech Republic, Spain, and other countries. I will show in this part of the book how Donald Trump and his administration impeded the ideals that science teachers and scientists across the world bring to their students about the nature of science and how it can serve humanity.

For decades, there has been a conservative agenda to push back against not only research findings in science and medicine but also the content of science that is acceptable in public schools. Political appointees holding administrative responsibility in science, medicine, and health agencies have been accused of halting, disrupting,

---

[237] Former principal, Dunwoody High School, and associate superintendent of instruction, DeKalb County Schools, Georgia. Dr. Springer was a pioneering administrator/educator in the GTP fostering exchanges among students at Dunwoody High School and Moscow School 710. Dr. Springer did her doctoral dissertation on the philosophy of global thinking.

and preventing the work of scientists and science educators. It's not new.

The Trump administration added a new level of assault to an already substantial phenomenon: the censoring, interference, and undermining of scientists, science educators, and their research. For years Republican-led state legislatures and federal agencies have imposed their will on issues they don't like, such as environmental, health, and safety regulation; the teaching of evolution and climate science; stem cell research; and legalized abortion.

Donald Trump's administration damaged science. During Trump's presidency, the EPA rolled back more than one hundred environmental regulations.[238] The health of the nation was put in a crisis with hundreds of thousands of Americans dying of COVID-19. Extreme weather events were met with ignorance and mockery for the people affected. And most alarming was Trump's decision to withdraw from the Paris Agreement, furthering the isolationist mentality of the president and the people who support him. Furthermore, conspiracy theories replaced scientific theories and evidence-based thinking, leading to a colossal assault on truth. In the closing months of Trump's presidency, James Reilly,[239] United States Geological Survey (USGS) director, ordered USGS scientists to report climate models that only focused on the next ten years. Many climate scientists objected and said that making predictions to the farthest reaches of data are what matter most for policy.

Censoring science is not new. However, the distortion of truth was ramped up significantly by the Trump administration. The perpetuation of conspiracy theories provoked violence and acts of domestic terrorism, culminating in the January 6 attack on the Congress of the United States.

As affirmation to the way the Trump presidency caused harm through its denial of science and health experts' advice, especially during the

---

[238] Nadja Popovich, Livia Albeck-Ripka, and Kendra Pierre-Louis, "The Trump Administration Rolled Back More Than 100 Environmental Rules. Here's the Full List," *New York Times*, October 16, 2020, https://www.nytimes.com/interactive/2020/climate/trump-environment-rollbacks-list.html.

[239] Adam Federman, "The Trump Team Has a Plan to Not Fight Climate Change," *Wired*, September 15, 2020, retrieved February 07, 2021, https://www.wired.com/story/the-trump-team-has-a-plan-to-not-fight-climate-change/.

COVID-19 pandemic, two major publications, *Scientific American* and the *New England Journal of Medicine*, which normally remain politically neutral, told their readers that they could not support Donald Trump in the 2020 election. Instead they recommended not voting for Trump.

GOVERNMENT SCIENCE

Scientists were not employed by the federal government until after WWII. Even after the war, most government work in science was done by scientists who were contracted to research specialized subjects. Science in the US government started with the formation of the US Office of Scientific Research and Development (OSRD) in 1941.

Vannevar Bush directed the OSRD from the start with almost unlimited access to funding and resources. He was appointed the head of the OSRD in 1941 by President Franklin Roosevelt. Bush had previously been vice president of the Massachusetts Institute of Technology (MIT) and dean of the MIT School of Engineering. He was also an inventor, and he founded the company that later became the Raytheon Company in 1922. He was also president of the Carnegie Institution of Washington in 1938. The OSRD headed up military projects during the war in such areas as bombs, guided missiles, radar, and medical treatments. The OSRD also headed the secret mission known as the Manhattan Project, which developed the first atomic weapons. Vannevar Bush in essence was the first presidential science advisor.

Bush published one of his most influential reports just after the war. *Science, the Endless Frontier* called for an expansion of government support for science.[240] The paper was a response to President Roosevelt's request to learn about how the experiences of science and scientists during the war could be used in peacetime, though it was presented to President Harry Truman in July 1945. The report was the result of input from appointed committees of prominent scientists.

One of the key ideas was that "never before has there been a national policy to assure scientific progress." Bush's report called on

---

[240] Vannevar Bush, *Science, the Endless Frontier* (Princeton: Princeton University Press, 2021).

the government to promote and support scientific research—especially basic research—and for there to be a new independent national agency funded to oversee "all research, military and civilian, biological, medical and physical, basic and applied, theoretical and experimental." It took years of congressional squabbling, but finally the National Science Foundation (NSF) was established by Congress in 1950.

Bush's most famous and basic idea was that "scientific progress is essential," and without it "no amount of achievement in other directions can ensure our health, prosperity, and security."[241] Bush also insisted that scientists should be the ones to choose what scientific projects to undertake. Bush wanted autonomy for scientists. A compromise was reached with Congress that the NSF would be overseen by a board of distinguished scientists.

Financial support for science since the NSF and other agencies of science research were developed has been an important part of the federal government. Billions of dollars cumulatively have been spent resulting in remarkable achievements in many fields of science, from astrophysics to biology and medicine and the geosciences. One of the goals of the NSF was to improve science in higher education and provide for advanced training in the current practice of science and science education. Many scientists and high school science and mathematics teachers benefited from year-long and summer institutes.[242]

At the beginning of the Trump presidency, thousands of scientists and engineers were employed by the federal government.[243] These include independent agencies such as the NSF, the National Aeronautics and Space Administration (NASA), the EPA, the National Institutes of Health (NIH), and Intelligence Advanced Research Projects Activity (IARPA). Also included are departments that have science research and development as a fundamental aspect of their purpose: the Department of

---

[241] Bush, *Science*, 9.

[242] I was one of those science teachers who benefited from NSF institutes. I attended an NSF Summer Institute in PSSC Physics at the Illinois Institute of Technology in 1963 and an NSF Academic Year Institute for mathematics and science teachers at The Ohio State University, 1966–1967. The AYI Institute led me to earn a PhD in science education and geology in 1969. I received my first grant in 1970 from the NSF.

[243] Data is based on a National Science Board, Science & Engineering Indicators, 2016. According to the report there were 23,557,000 scientists and engineers employed in the United States, which was 4.9% of total employment.

Agriculture (USDA); the Department of Defense; the Departments of the Air Force, Army, and Navy; the Department of Energy; the Department of Homeland Security; the Department of Health and Human Services; the USGS; and key committees in the legislative branch, including the House Committee on Science, Space, and Technology and the Senate Committee on Commerce, Science, and Transportation.

SCIENCE IN THE BUSH AND OBAMA ADMINISTRATIONS

George W. Bush was considered the anti-science president by several scientists, researchers, and journalists, as well as science educators such as myself. He opposed many areas of research, including global warming, stem cell research, and sex education. The state of science under the Bush administration was the subject of investigation by Chris Mooney, who reported that on February 19, 2004, the Center for Science & Democracy Union of Concerned Scientists (UCS) held a phone-in conference that confronted how science was being handled in Bush's administration.[244] The UCS announced the publication of a paper, "Scientific Integrity in Policymaking: An Investigation into the Bush Administration's Misuse of Science."[245] One of the main findings reported was that high-ranking Bush administration political appointees across several federal agencies were suppressing and distorting scientific research, especially in written reports.

It was also reported that the government's science advisory system was being manipulated to make sure the system didn't run counter to the administration's political agenda. The report also claimed that there was evidence that scientists were being censored in what they could say and or write. While Bush was president, Mooney explored the collusion of special business interests with the anti-intellectualism (anti-science) of the religious right and Republican legislators to uncover the impact on science policy and scientific research.[246] The Republicans had control of Congress for fourteen of the sixteen years preceding

---
[244] Mooney, *The Republican War on Science*.
[245] Union of Concerned Scientists, "Scientific Integrity in Policy Making: An Investigation into the Bush Administration's Misuse of Science," July 13, 2008, https://www.ucsusa.org/resources/scientific-integrity-policy-making-0.
[246] Union of Concerned Scientists, "Scientific Integrity."

Trump. This had a significant impact on halting advances in science, especially climate science.

The way science was perceived in the Obama administration was a stark contrast to the Bush administration. Each year, Obama became personally involved in school science by hosting six White House Science Fairs. Although I am not in favor of science competitions, I was thrilled that Obama would talk with high school students about their science projects. Instead of competitions, I advocate conferences and symposia where individuals and teams of students share the results of their investigations, inquiries, and research. These White House Science Fairs were televised, and millions of people watched a president converse with young people about science. How refreshing is that?

Obama attempted to restore science, and to do this he appointed key scientists to top positions in his government, including Nobel Prize-winning physicist Steven Chu, the Department of Energy, Kathleen Sebelius, the Department of Health and Human Services, and Lisa P. Jackson, the Environmental Protection Agency. Obama also upgraded the role of the Office of Science and Technology Policy (OSTP) after it had been downgraded by Bush.

Obama appointed physicist John Holdren, professor of environmental science and policy at Harvard's Kennedy School of Government, as director of OSTP. He is senior advisor to the president at the Woods Hole Research Center, a pre-eminent scientific think tank focused on global climate change, and he was involved with Obama when key science-related decisions were on the table. Obama called him "one of the most passionate and persistent voices of our time about the growing threat of climate change."[247]

Holdren headed Obama's team of advisors that laid the groundwork for eventual negotiating of a climate accord that became the Paris Agreement, which was nonbinding. Obama knew he would not be able to secure the approval of Congress; instead, he left the door open to a

---

[247] Carolyn Y. Johnson and Bena Venkataraman, *From Harvard: A Climatic Selection*, Boston.com, December 21, 2008, retrieved February 11, 2022, http://archive.boston.com/news/nation/articles/2008/12/21/from_harvard_a_climatic_selection/.

future president pulling out of the agreement. Of course, Trump yanked the United States out of the Paris Agreement in 2018, and Joe Biden signed an executive order to rejoin in January 2021.

SCIENCE IN THE AGE OF TRUMP

Science in the Trump era was diminished at the peril of the health and well-being for not only people and other living things, but Earth itself, including its air, water, land, and other natural resources.

Attacks on Science

Science was attacked hundreds of times during the Trump years, and the effects were detrimental not only to science, but to the very nature of democracy. One of the best analyses that I found was a report issued by the UCS, whose researchers identified seven types of attacks on science.[248] I examined their data and counted the number of attacks in each category. Leading the list is halting, editing, or suppressing scientific research studies. To give you an idea of how Trump's administration damaged government science, I've included a few examples for each type of attack. As you can tell from Table 1, the UCS research on the attacks on science by Trump is staggering.

Type of Attack	Number of Attacks	Examples of How Science Was Attacked
Anti-science rules/regulations/orders	46	White House posts climate science denialist misinformation. EPA suspends air pollution rules during the pandemic. CDC scientists are sidelined in decision to seal the US border.
Censorship	32	White House installs political operatives at the CDC. Email showing attempted manipulation of CDC COVID-19 study is buried. CDC scientists are pressured to downplay the risks of schools reopening during the pandemic.
Politicization of grants	12	Trump political appointees interfere in scientific grants process. Trump administration illegally withholds funding from key energy research program. EPA grants and scientific studies are reviewed by political appointees.

---

[248] Union of Concerned Scientists, "Attacks on Science," January 20, 2017, updated November 2, 2021, retrieved October 11, 2021, https://www.ucsusa.org/resources/attacks-on-science.

Type of Attack	Number of Attacks	Examples of How Science Was Attacked
Restrictions on conference attendance	6	Department of Energy scientists are barred from attending the nuclear power conference. CDC cancels the climate change conference. USGS scientists are required to justify attendance at scientific conferences.
Rolling back data collection or data accessibility	16	OSHA fails to record COVID-19 cases for all employees. Trump administration takes away hospitalization data from the CDC. EPA blocks NASA from monitoring air pollution after Hurricane Harvey.
Sidelining science advisory committees	10	US Navy quietly shuts down its task force on climate change. Trump rids federal agencies of scientific expertise. Arms control panel is dismissed.
Studies halted, edited, or suppressed	49	Trump administration prevents the publication of climate research. Administration undermines scientific report on endangered species in California. White House blocks FDA's vaccine guidance document.

Table 1. Examples of the types of attacks on science by the Trump administration as reported by the Union of Concerned Scientists.

Another way to look at how Trump and his sycophants worked to dismantle the crucial work that scientists do is to examine a timeline of their damage. The chart in Table 2 is an overview of some effects that Trump and his administrators had on the nature of science in the federal government. The chronology is plainly suggestive of how Trump shockingly damaged science. The chronology also highlights Trump's ignorance of science and the danger he posed to the American public, especially when he recommended injecting the body with bleach. This ignorance is still extremely difficult for me to believe, but I've seen the video. The chronology starts with the travel ban in January 2017.

2017	January	Travel ban prohibits people from several Muslim countries from entering the US.
	March	White House recommends reducing all departmental budgets except the Pentagon's. Congress ignored the White House.
	June	Trump announces he will pull the US out of the Paris Agreement on climate change.

	October	EPA and other science departments bar key scientists from serving on advisory committees. Gretchen T. Goldman of the UCS says this would make the government stupid.
2018	March	FEMA expels climate change from its strategic plan.
	April	EPA under Scott Pruitt proposes the "transparency rule," which would ban studies used in decision-making that didn't include personal medical data and other such data.
	May	Withdraws from Iran nuclear deal. NASA's carbon monitoring system loses its funding as part of the administration's rejection of the Paris Agreement.
	July	Trump nominates meteorologist Kelvin Droegemeier as science advisor, who doesn't take over until January 2019, two years into the Trump presidency.
	August	EPA managers change rules evaluating chemicals that would favor industry-funded research.
2019	April	Department of Defense cancels its relationship with JASON, an independent group of scientists who provide technical advice.
	September	"Sharpiegate." Trump alters hurricane maps and criticizes National Weather Service forecasters.
	November	Trump pulls the US out of the Paris Agreement.
2020	February	Misinformation begins on the nature of COVID-19. Says the virus will be mild and like the flu. Trump tells Bob Woodward in secret that he is playing down the seriousness of the virus.
	April	Blames the WHO and China for spread of COVID-19. Vows to freeze funding to the WHO. Refuses to use outside researchers' recommendations for strengthening air pollution standards. Calls for voluntary use of facial coverings but says they are not for him. Recommends hitting the body with ultraviolet light to kill the virus. Suggests injecting bleach into the body to "clean" out the virus.
	May	US withdraws from the WHO. Trump announces Operation Warp Speed to produce vaccines for COVID-19.
	July	Trump sidelines the CDC from collecting COVID-19 data. CDC communication is taken over by the White House and starts to make erroneous recommendations about how to mitigate the virus.
	August	CDC revises guidance saying people without symptoms do not need to be tested; 40 percent of infected people are asymptomatic.

	September	Confusion at CDC about testing because political appointees published documents without scientific review.
	October	A House Coronavirus Crisis Committee report reveals that Trump politically interfered with scientists in forty-seven separate incidents starting from February 20, 2020.[249] The Trump family gets COVID-19, as well as many people who work in the White House. Trump spreads the virus to others. Trump is hospitalized with the virus and uses it to pose as Mussolini when he returns to the White House to announce, "Don't let the virus control you—look at me."
	November	Trump says he will fire Dr. Anthony Fauci if he is elected in November. Earlier in the year, he blocked Fauci from testifying at a House committee meeting.

Table 2. Chronology of Trump's effect on science.

WHO'S IN CHARGE OF SCIENCE?

The Trump administration oversaw science in the federal government for four years. It's an ominous task for an administration such as Trump's, which was not equipped to deal with the problems before it. It's worth looking at who was appointed to lead some of the departments and agencies responsible for science in the federal government. I've looked at the people who oversee the departments whose work is science related. The heads of some science departments (EPA, USDA, Department of the Interior) opposed the actual work of these departments, and while they were in charge, they chose to dismantle and diminish the work of scientists and their research.

According to one report, the Trump administration has attacked science more than 150 times, a figure based on an assessment made in June 2020. During the first eighteen months of the Trump administration, 1,600 workers left the EPA, while fewer than 400 were hired.[250]

This discussion will reveal the names of some of President Trump's

---

[249] Select Subcommittee on the Coronavirus Crisis, *The Trump Administration's Pattern of Political Interference in the Nation's Coronavirus Response*, October 2, 2020, https://coronavirus.house.gov/sites/democrats.coronavirus.house.gov/files/10.2.20%20Political%20Interference%20Report%20%281%29.pdf.

[250] Anita Desikan, "150 Attacks on Science and Counting: Trump Administration's Anti-Science Actions Hurt People and Communities Nationwide," *The Equation*, Union of Concerned Scientists, June 7, 2021, https://blog.ucsusa.org/anita-desikan/150-attacks-on-science-and-counting/.

sycophants who headed important departments in the federal government. Let's start with the Office of Science and Technology Policy.

Office of Science and Technology Policy (OSTP)

Unbelievably, for two years, Trump left the Office of Science and Technology Policy vacant.[251] OSTP was established in 1976 by President Gerald Ford with the broad mandate to advise the presidents on the effects of science and technology on domestic and international affairs. We refer to this position as the Science Advisor to the President. From January 20, 2017, until January 2019, empty desks were all one could find in the OSTP's large office space in the Executive Office Building in Washington. No one was advising the president on matters of science and technology during this time. No one was in charge.

Finally, in 2019, Trump named Kelvin Droegemeier, a meteorologist with a good reputation in the science community, as director of OSTP. He left a very high-profile position at the University of Oklahoma to work with Trump. However, in his work as science advisor, he failed to mitigate some of the controversial policies enacted in those years, including the chaotic approach to the COVID-19 pandemic, withdrawing from the Paris Agreement, rolling back many environmental regulations, restricting immigration, and agreeing to deep cuts in the budgets of most federal research agencies.[252]

Environmental Protection Agency (EPA)

The EPA is the department charged with tackling the most pressing environmental and health challenges that the nation faces. Naming a head to lead the EPA is a major decision for a president to make. So who did Trump appoint as head of the EPA? Would the appointee fulfill the job responsibilities required as head of EPA? Let's take a look.

Scott Pruitt was Trump's choice to be the administrator of the EPA. Pruitt is a lawyer, former lobbyist, and the former attorney general

---

[251] Trump also failed to fill many top-level science positions. This created vulnerabilities that shouldn't have existed.
[252] J. Mervis, "'Very Disappointed.' Trump's Science Adviser Has Left US Researchers Wanting More," *Science*, October 20, 2020, retrieved February 7, 2021, https://www.sciencemag.org/news/2020/10/very-disappointed-trump-s-science-adviser-has-left-us-researchers-wanting-more.

of Oklahoma. He was confirmed by the Senate by a vote of 52–46. When he was Oklahoma's attorney general, he sued the EPA at least fourteen times, and in that role, he opposed abortion, same-sex marriage, the Affordable Care Act, and environmental regulations. He received $250,000 from the fossil fuel industry during his campaign in Oklahoma, even though he ran unopposed.

Pruitt and his successor, Andrew Wheeler, were critiqued by a group of former EPA employees in a report they published in 2020. The report was published as a website called Save EPA (saveepaalums.info). When Biden and Harris came into office in January, the need to save the EPA lessened, and so the group went back into retirement, but it has kept the website open as a resource.

Pruitt was not well received by scientists (I know that is an understatement) in the EPA, and within a year he had more than fourteen separate investigations into his spending habits,[253] conflicts of interest, extreme secrecy, and management practices. He even built a $43,000 soundproof telephone booth in his office, which violated spending laws. He set the EPA on a course to roll back rules designed to protect the nation's environment. Although Congress passes the laws, it is accepted that individual agencies, like the EPA, determine specific actions and rules that must be taken to ensure that the laws are followed. Pruitt did more harm to the EPA than any previous administrator. Finally he resigned on July 5, 2018.

Pruitt's replacement was Andrew Wheeler, an attorney who worked for a law firm that represented a large coal magnate who lobbied against the Obama administration's environmental regulations. He also was chief council to Oklahoma Senator James Inhofe, a climate skeptic and advocate for the fossil fuel energy industry.

Wheeler was a critic of greenhouse gas emissions. He pushed a so-called transparency rule that seriously limited research used by the EPA to make important environmental and health decisions. The rule prohibited the EPA from using studies that do not make raw data publicly

---

[253] Juliet Eilperin and Brady Dennis, "EPA Whistleblower Details Scott Pruitt's Spending and Travel Excesses," ChicagoTribune.com, August 22, 2019, retrieved April 4, 2022, https://www.chicagotribune.com/nation-world/ct-epa-whistleblower-scott-pruitt-excesses-20180412-story.html.

available. As a result, more than sixty scientific and medical groups criticized and opposed the rule because, among other problems, researchers did not make personal and confidential information available.

Also under Wheeler, the EPA decided not to fine companies for violating environmental regulations during the pandemic. The EPA declined to ease environmental standards for fine soot pollution (particulate matter) and weakened mercury regulation and cleanup. He declined to accept the scientific consensus on climate change, using the phrase, "What's not completely understood is what the impact is."[254]

Department of the Interior

I watched on television as Ryan Zinke rode his horse, Tonto, along the streets of Washington, DC, to his office on C Street. Then he instructed an employee to raise a flag on top of the Department of the Interior's building as a sign that he was in. This was to be done whenever he sat at his desk. He also set up an arcade game for employees called "Big Buck Hunter," which had plastic rifles that players aim at animated deer. This, said Zinke, was a way of highlighting sportsmen's contribution to conservation. The unfortunate horse took an arrogant man to the Department of the Interior.

Zinke was appointed secretary of the interior in 2017 and served until January 2019. During that time, he opened large areas off both coasts to offshore drilling. He also overturned a moratorium on new leases for coal mines on public lands. He recommended reducing the areas of several national monuments, including Bears Ears and Gold Butte. He also moved to scrap Obama-era fracking rules.[255] He was under investigation by the Department of the Interior's Office of Inspector General for ethical and financial irregularities, and he resigned soon after the investigation was launched. Zinke was replaced by David Bernhardt, an oil and fossil fuel lobbyist and Washington insider.

---

[254] Rebecca Hersher and Colin Dwyer, "Get to Know Andrew Wheeler, Ex-Coal Lobbyist with Inside Track to Lead EPA," NPR, July 6, 2018, retrieved April 4, 2022, https://www.npr.org/2018/07/06/626525274/get-to-know-andrew-wheeler-ex-coal-lobbyist-with-inside-track-to-lead-epa.

[255] Elizabeth Kolbert, "The Damage Done by Trump's Department of the Interior," *The New Yorker*, July 9, 2019, retrieved February 8, 2021, https://www.newyorker.com/magazine/2018/01/22/the-damage-done-by-trumps-department-of-the-interior.

The Department of the Interior is responsible for the management and conservation of most federal lands and natural resources, as well as the administration of programs relating to Native Americans, Alaska Natives, Native Hawaiians, and historic preservation. The department was created in 1849 and has never been administered by a Native American. That is, until Deb Haaland, US Representative from New Mexico and member of the Pueblo of Laguna, was nominated by Joe Biden and confirmed by the Senate. She is the first Native American secretary of the interior as well as the first Native American cabinet secretary in US history.

Centers for Disease Control and Prevention (CDC)

Robert Redfield replaced Brenda Fitzgerald, Trump's first director of the CDC. Fitzgerald was forced to resign after it was learned that she bought shares in a tobacco company right after being appointed. It's hard to believe how Trump went out of his way to hire people like Fitzgerald, Zinke, Wheeler, and Pruitt, but he did.

Redfield is a career scientist with a controversial past. Senator Patty Murray, the ranking member of the Senate Committee on Health, Education, Labor, and Pensions, wrote a letter to the White House questioning some of Redfield's HIV-related policies and a controversy over a clinical trial of an experimental HIV vaccine. A consumer advocacy group said that what one wants in a director of the CDC is a scientist of impeccable scientific integrity.[256]

As you read ahead, you'll see that the CDC came under scrutiny for its failed COVID-19 test and the mixed messages that emerged from the agency. This was caused by White House interference in the day-to-day activities of the agency.

In April 2020, former Trump campaign official Michael Caputo was named the CDC's spokesperson. Caputo and his team altered reports, such as morbidity and mortality weekly reports, to be consistent with Trump's public comments about the coronavirus. Caputo also blocked the

---

[256] Ed Yong, "Trump's Pick for CDC Director Is Experienced but Controversial," *The Atlantic*, March 23, 2018, retrieved March 18, 2021, https://www.theatlantic.com/science/archive/2018/03/trumps-pick-for-cdc-director-is-experienced-but-controversial/556202/.

publication of research, such as the report on the benefits of hydroxychloroquine, which stated that treatment does not outweigh the risks. Trump promoted the drug and claimed he used it. Caputo made accusations against Redfield and top CDC scientists, claiming they were using research to "hurt" Trump. Caputo had the audacity to say that his team was making sure that evidence and science-based data drove the pandemic policy and "not ulterior deep state motives in the bowels of the CDC."[257]

As of this writing, the CDC is now directed by Rochelle Walensky, MD, MPH. She was appointed by President Biden. Her reporting is just the opposite of the kind of communication that the Trump administration authorized.

Department of Agriculture (USDA)

The following story caught my attention. I'm using it as a case study to describe what happened to many scientists in the USDA under the watch of Sunny Perdue (former governor of Georgia).

Dr. Randi Johnson[258] is a twenty-eight-year veteran of the USDA, where she most recently led its program on climate change. She is one of 550 USDA scientists who were told that their offices and departments were being moved from Washington, DC, to Kansas City. She did not want to move west. And she did not want to quit her job.

She had spearheaded the climate change program at the USDA and worked with forest scientists to help them find funding for their projects. She had earned a PhD in forest genetics and a master's in forest soils. After years working in Brazil and New Zealand, she became a leading scientist at USDA. Her family was in Virginia, and her daughter had recently given birth to Johnson's first grandchild. Moving to Kansas City was worrisome for Randi because she was a sixty-two-year-old transgender woman. She lost her wife a few years before to breast cancer as well as a son who overdosed

---

[257] Daniel Cassady, "Trump-Appointed CDC Officials Reportedly Meddled with Coronavirus Reports," *Forbes*, September 12, 2020, retrieved March 18, 2021, https://www.forbes.com/sites/danielcassady/2020/09/12/trump-appointed-cdc-officials-reportedly-meddled-with-coronavirus-reports/?sh=5d53fa293fb0.

[258] Hannah Natanson, "The USDA Relocation to Kansas City Is Ripping Apart the Lives of Its Employees. Here Are Some of Their Stories," September 8, 2019, *Washington Post*, September 8, 2019, retrieved February 11, 2022, https://www.washingtonpost.com/local/social-issues/the-usda-relocation-to-kansas-city-is-ripping-apart-the-lives-of-its-employees-here-are-some-of-their-stories/2019/09/07/9108a3b0-c935-11e9-a1fe-ca46e8d573c0_story.html.

on opioids, and she was involved in her neighborhood and church. She searched for jobs in the DC area but was unsuccessful. She decided to retire, but because she was getting out earlier (age sixty-two rather than sixty-seven), her income would be reduced by $18,000 per year.

Randi wasn't the only person blindsided by Secretary Sonny Perdue's decision to retaliate because House Democrats had released independent research that didn't match the Trump administration's talking points on climate change; the Supplemental Nutrition Assistance Program, which provides nutrition benefits to needy families; and other food and agricultural issues.

The announcement to relocate was made in June 2019. Employees would have to move by September. Two-thirds of the employees decided to quit rather than move 1,057 miles. Initially employees who chose not to move were offered a buyout payment of $25,000. But because so many Agriculture Department scientists chose not to relocate, Perdue lowered the payout to $10,000. If employees accepted the buyout, they could not return to federal employment for five years.

Perdue's decision to move so many scientists was to weaken and dismantle the USDA. According to the UCS and the American Federation of Government Employees, the move not only was a blatant attack on science but also resulted in a dangerous loss of top research scientists.

Perdue spent four years coddling Trump and was accused of breaking the law in North Carolina, in which he told people at a farm conference that they should vote for Donald Trump in the November election. This is a violation of the Hatch Act, which prohibits a government official from campaigning on the government's dime. The White House responded by saying that no one outside the Beltway cares a flip about the Hatch Act.[259]

ROLLING BACK ENVIRONMENTAL RULES

The mega-rule that the Trump administration broke was reversing the United States' efforts to curb climate change by cutting the country

---

[259] **Author's Update:** Sonny Perdue was appointed chancellor of the University System of Georgia, to the fury of many professors at the state's 26 colleges and universities. See Ross Williams, "Critics Fume as Sonny Perdue Closes in on Georgia's University Chancellor Job," *Georgia Recorder*, February 16, 2022, retrieved April 4, 2022, https://georgiarecorder.com/2022/02/16/critics-fume-as-sonny-perdue-closes-in-on-georgias-university-chancellor-job/.

off from the international agreement that greenhouse gases need to be reduced. Trump cut the country off from the Paris Agreement. The Trump administration charged ahead in denying climate change by refusing to listen to governors, mayors, and local officials who were dealing with the effects of global warming by being up against megafires, hurricanes, floods, and droughts.

The Trump administration also rolled back more than a hundred environmental rules. In a *New York Times* analysis based on research from Harvard Law School, Columbia Law School, and other sources, many environmental rules were shown to have been reversed, revoked, or rolled back.[260] The rules are specific and focus on the management of distinct resources such as forests, minerals, or fisheries, as well as environmental pollution control rules. The Trump administration established a pattern of undermining and rewriting the laws that protect the environment.

The chart below identifies rule reversals that were completed or were in progress, the bulk of which affected the EPA but also the USGS and the Department of Energy. The administrators of each of these departments claimed that previous administrations overstepped their authority to impose unnecessary regulations that hurt businesses. Naturally, environmental groups and legal authorities opposed these rollbacks.

Rules	Complete	In Progress	Total
Air pollution and emissions	28	2	30
Drilling and extraction	12	7	19
Infrastructure and planning	14	0	14
Animals	15	1	16
Water pollution	8	1	9
Toxic substances and safety	9	1	10
Other	12	2	14
All	98	14	112

Table 3. Trump administration rollbacks and reversals 2017–2021.[261]

---

[260] Popovich et al., "The Trump Administration Rolled Back More Than 100 Environmental Rules."
[261] Popovich et al., "The Trump Administration Rolled Back More Than 100 Environmental Rules."

In 2021, Joe Biden's EPA administrator, Michael Regan, launched a program to evaluate and potentially rescind the Trump rollbacks. One of the important rules that Regan rescinded was the way the agency calculates the cost and benefits of air pollution rules. According to Gretchen Goldman of the UCS, Trump's EPA "fudged the numbers" to make it easier to dismiss or change public health regulations.[262]

The Biden administration has committed to reducing greenhouse gases by more than 50 percent by 2030 based on 2004 levels. Trump rejected climate science and, with his complicit EPA administrators, did little to reduce greenhouse gas emissions. For the next four years, the United States has a chance to reduce greenhouse gases and put more emphasis on air, water, and land regulations.

TRANSPARENCY

In another attempt to interfere with the integrity of scientific research, EPA Administrator Wheeler introduced a rule in 2019 that would require scientists to supply the EPA with raw data for studies if the findings were to be taken into consideration in crafting environmental regulations. Wheeler called this rule "Strengthening Transparency in Regulatory Science." By providing the raw data, Wheeler claimed the EPA can independently reanalyze and revalidate scientific data and models.

The rule meant that information would be revealed about people who had not consented to disclosing confidential data, personal information (location, travel habits, age, gender), and state of health. The scientific research community united in condemning the rule; however, two weeks before Biden took office, the rule went into effect. On February 1, 2021, a federal judge vacated the Trump administration rule limiting which studies can be used by the EPA. Three groups—the Environmental Defense Fund, the Montana Environmental Information Center, and Citizens for Clean Energy—sued in a federal court in Montana.[263]

---

[262] Gretchen Goldman, "There is a crucial but politically inconvenient fact for the Trump administration: Particulate matter kills. That's why they needed to find a way to fudge the math to justify unraveling life-saving protections. I wrote about it here with @_aploy: https://t.co/dqvizrzjed," Twitter, April 16, 2020, retrieved April 4, 2022, https://twitter.com/GretchenTG/status/1250791543360929793.

[263] J. Eilperin, "Judge Throws Out Trump Rule Limiting What Science EPA Can Use," *Washington Post*, February 1, 2021, retrieved February 8, 2021, https://www.washingtonpost.com/climate-environment/2021/02/01/trump-secret-science/.

This case highlights the wider actions of the Trump administration on the environment, including withdrawing from the Paris Agreement, weakening fuel efficiency standards, or cutting back on environmental research.

Undoubtedly, the Trump administration worked actively to dismantle science-based health and safety protections, sideline scientific evidence, and inflict harm on the progress on scientific integrity. Several reports have been published that document the attacks on science and medicine. In "The State of Science in the Trump Era," the authors concluded that a pervasive pattern of sidelining science existed in critical decision-making, compromising our nation's ability to meet current and future public health and environmental challenges.[264]

Fortunately, scientists and their allies pushed back, as well as Congress. For example, the first Trump budget recommendation included huge cuts in science departments and agencies. The Trump administration wanted the EPA budget cut by 30 percent, which would have decimated the agency. In the end, Congress passed a slight increase in EPA's budget. However, scientists were muzzled in some departments and needed to seek permission to speak to the press, publish articles, and attend conferences. In other departments and agencies, rules were changed that effected the integrity of science research.

Science in the age of Trump did not fare well; nor did citizens of the United States. The people that Trump appointed to White House positions and the appointees of many of the departments responsible for science created workplace environments that caused many scientists to leave. Trump also interfered directly in the work of scientists, as discussed in some of the blog posts in the chapters ahead.

The CDC, EPA, and other departments and agencies in the federal government were undermined by the Trump administration. Agencies and departments were reduced in size, and morale among scientists and staff dropped to exceptionally low levels. Several

---

[264] Jacob Carter et al., *The State of Science in the Trump Era: Damage Done, Lessons Learned, and a Path to Progress*, Center for Science & Democracy, Union of Concerned Scientists, January 2019, retrieved February 3, 2021, https://www.ucsusa.org/sites/default/files/attach/2019/01/ucs-trump-2yrs-report.pdf.

top scientists resigned. When the Biden transition team began to size up the effect of the Trump administration on science, they were shocked by the damage that had been done. Fortunately, Biden has appointed a powerful team of experienced administrators and scientists to bring order and professionalism back to science at the federal level.

CHAPTER 7:
DEGRADING THE ENVIRONMENTAL PROTECTION AGENCY

7.1. BLOG POST, 24 FEBRUARY 2017: EPA: FROM OBAMA'S PROTECTION TO TRUMP'S DESTRUCTION

Donald Trump has inflicted enormous harm on the American public by appointing administrators who have done nothing but roll back Obama-era policies that were designed to protect the nation's air, water, and land.

Using the Wayback Machine,[265] we can keep watch on some aspects of the EPA website now that Trump and his pick for secretary of the EPA, Scott Pruitt, are in charge. Trump wants to cut the EPA, and Pruitt, who has ties to the coal, oil, and gas industries and was a champion litigator against the EPA while he was attorney general for Oklahoma, is no friend of Earth's environment, other than helping those who take from the Earth whatever they want.

On January 24, 2017, one of the first things the Trump administration did was to demand that the EPA take down all its climate change pages. Then they were told to hold off, then told to remove them, and then told to put them back. As of this writing, the climate change page is not on the website. But the fact that the White House ordered the page to be taken down set into motion a lot of resistance. On November 13,

---
[265] The Wayback Machine (http://archive.org/) is a digital archive of the World Wide Web. The archive allows you to go back in time to see how websites looked in the past.

2020, I checked the EPA website and could not find anything when I searched for "climate change."

There has been a vigorous attempt to keep climate data safe, and people and groups have worked feverishly to download and keep all the climate data found on various government sites, including those of the EPA, NASA, the National Oceanic and Atmospheric Administration (NOAA), and the USGS.

Terri Hansen, in a Truthout article, reports that even concerned citizens lent a helping hand. Hansen tells us that John Rosa, a graduate student at Eastern Michigan University, started downloading as many copies of pages as practically possible—more than 28,000 files.[266]

There are also pages on Twitter you can visit that claim to be run by employees of EPA who mask their identity. These sites are called "rogue" sites, such as Rogue EPA Staff (@rougueepastaff). You can also find these rogue sites: @rogueNASA, @AltNatParkSer, @ActualEPAFacts, and @Alt_NASA. It's possible that these rogue sites could be hacked, and that hackers could embed files that could cause chaos on your own computers. For more on this you might consult this Kalev Leetaru's article in Forbes.[267]

However, a word of caution. We don't know who runs these sites. In some cases, all it says is "Operated by a US citizen that is not affiliated with any federal agency." I've managed websites since 1993, first at GSU, where we developed the website for the GTP.

The main site that I manage now is jackhassard.org, and it has been hacked several times, most recently in 2015. It was a serious hack, and in the end, I had to purchase the services of a web security firm.

The 2016 hacking of the Democratic National Committee's web servers, as well as Hillary Clinton's and John Podesta's accounts, was carried out by Russian hackers. They were able to make use of files they stole, pass them on to WikiLeaks, and then create stories critical of the Clinton

---

[266] Teri Hansen, "The Student-Built Website That Keeps Government Climate Data Safe," Truthout, February 24, 2017, https://truthout.org/articles/the-student-built-website-that-keeps-government-climate-data-safe/.
[267] Kalev Leetaru, "What The 'Rogue' EPA, NPS and NASA Twitter Accounts Teach Us About the Future of Social," Forbes, January 26, 2017, www.forbes.com/sites/kalevleetaru/2017/01/25/what-the-rogue-epa-nps-and-nasa-twitter-accounts-teach-us-about-the-future-of-social/?sh=4acd12d45a74.

campaign. The FBI, looking into files associated with Hillary Clinton, didn't help when the director opened his mouth a few days before the election. FBI Director James Comey may have cost Clinton the election.

Even with these concerns, these rogue sites give access points for Americans to join the resistance to Trump's destructive path of denying science and making it easier for the commercialization of public resources.

On Earth Day, 2017 the March for Science (#marchforscience) will take place in cities and towns across the United States and around the world. Millions of people will participate in these marches.

7.2. BLOG POST, 4 MARCH 2017: FROM ORDER TO CHAOS: THE ATTACK ON THE EPA

The EPA was established in 1970 under Richard Nixon's administration. Now in 2017, it is likely that at least 25 percent of the agency will be dismantled by the Trump administration. This is a crime against the well-being of all living things and their environment by the White House.

Even before the current administration took over the White House, Trump's transition team sent clear messages that the EPA was in trouble. The so-called transition team wanted names of EPA employees who worked on, drafted papers about, and did research in the fields related to climate science.

They were not doing this to give out awards! They did it to put the EPA on notice that "we are out to get you."

And so today reports are out that the EPA's budget and staff of scientists, engineers, and technical staff will be reduced by 25 percent. The EPA has more than 15,000 employees and an annual budget of $8,139,887,000. It has twenty-seven laboratories across the country, which is divided into ten regional administrations. If the EPA is cut by 25 percent, 3,750 people will be fired, and the budget will be reduced by at least $2 billion.[268]

This will devastate environmental protection activity in the states. Air and especially water pollution will increase, impacting the most

---

[268] "White House Said to Propose 25 Percent Cut in EPA Budget Plan," Bloomberg Law, March 1, 2017, retrieved April 15, 2022, https://news.bloomberglaw.com/environment-and-energy/white-house-said-to-propose-25-percent-cut-in-epa-budget-plan.

important resources for human and all other living things in the environment.

If you think the Flint, Michigan, drinking water debacle was bad, you haven't seen anything yet.

Fortunately, Congress's budget funded the EPA at the current budget level. But the real damage was done within the EPA itself. The agency rolled back more than fifty of Obama's environmental rulings, and therefore put much of the environment at risk.

> **Author's Update:** I think it is important that to point out what the attack on the EPA was. Here is a list of the major areas effected within the EPA and Department of the Interior. According to a *Washington Post* report, Trump worked to scale back or abolish more than 200 environmental protections in his one term.[269] They completed more than 125 of them. According to the reports, most of the rollbacks affect air pollution and greenhouse gas emissions.
>
> - Air pollution and greenhouse gases: The Trump administration enacted at least sixty-four policies weakening or overturning regulations aimed at curbing air pollution and greenhouse gas emissions fueling global warming.
> - Chemical safety: From plastic water bottles to farmworker pesticide exposure to chemical dangers for infants and children, the Trump administration favored industry over consumer health.
> - Drilling and extraction: The sixty-one rollbacks Trump enacted on drilling, mining, and logging ranged from weakened oil worker safety on offshore platforms to extracting fossil fuels from public lands.
> - Infrastructure permitting Center: The Trump administration circumvented environmental rules to speed

---

[269] B. Dennis, J. Eilperin, and J. Muyskens, "Trump Rolled Back More Than 125 Environmental Safeguards. Here's How," *Washington Post*, October 30, 2020, https://www.washingtonpost.com/graphics/2020/climate-environment/trump-climate-environment-protections/.

approval of major projects such as a four-lane highway that could crush desert tortoises in the Red Cliffs National Conservation Area and adopting changes that will curb public input in the development of highways, powerplants, and incinerators near communities.
- Water pollution: Trump eased restrictions on how companies store coal ash, weakened rules on dumping toxic waste from power plants into waterways, and altered which wetlands and streams require federal oversight.
- Wildlife: One of the hallmarks of former Department of the Interior Secretary David Bernhardt's legacy has been the narrowing of safeguards for endangered wildlife.

7.3. BLOG POST, 6 APRIL 2018: THE DEGRADATION OF THE EPA AND THE THREAT TO SCIENTIFIC REASONING

Although the EPA received an appropriation equal to its 2018 budget, the White House wanted to cut its budget by one-quarter, which would mean the dismantling of thousands of positions and programs that are important for environmental protection.

DEREGULATION FLOOD

The EPA has suffered since the new administrator, Scott Pruitt, arrived and began to roll back many of the regulations that had been established over a period of decades. These are part of a war on environmental protections instigated by the White House. The Environmental Integrity Project reported that a *New York Times* article identified a list of more than sixty environmental actions that are in the crosshairs of the administration, with twenty-nine already overturned, twenty-four rollbacks in progress, and nine in limbo.[270]

One that stands out for me is cancellation of Obama-era flood standards. This was done in August, before the onslaught of hurricanes that hit and devastated the Caribbean, Texas, Louisiana, North Carolina,

---

[270] Popovich et al., "The Trump Administration Rolled Back More Than 100 Environmental Rules."

and Florida. Much of the flooding of homes in Texas by Hurricane Harvey happened in areas that should have been rezoned and others that needed further protection.

But the White House and Administrator Pruitt seemed to be in bed with industry and trade groups that have itched to roll back environmental protections.

Although rumor suggested Pruitt was on the way out at EPA (he did resign), it won't change the outrageous attitude and policies of the administration that continue to wreak havoc not only on the EPA, but also other agencies at the federal level whose fundamental work is scientific research, as well as health and medicine.

WHERE ARE THE SCIENTISTS AND ADVISORS?

Another problem contributing to the danger growing in Washington is the administration's incompetence at appointing women and men to important science positions in the government. As I mentioned earlier, Trump hasn't even named a presidential science advisor. According to a report in *Catalyst*, the magazine of the UCS, the Trump administration has not kept pace with previous presidents in appointing people to science positions. At the end of the first year, Trump had only filled 20 percent of science positions in government, while Presidents Obama and Bush had appointed 62 percent and 50 percent, respectively.[271]

FUNDING SCIENCE

Although Congress rescued the budgets of most science organizations in the federal government, it did so in an environment in which the White House proposed cuts to science that were outrageous.

To give you an idea of how Trump and his White House cronies wanted to decimate the federal government, I prepared the following chart based on the White House's proposed budget and what Congress distributed for each department. Note that Congress ignored Trump's requests and instead funded most departments at higher levels.

---

[271] "UCS Finds Many Science Advisory Committees Now Sit Idle," *Catalyst* 18 (Winter 2018): 6, https://www.ucsusa.org/sites/default/files/attach/2018/03/Catalyst-Winter-2018.pdf.

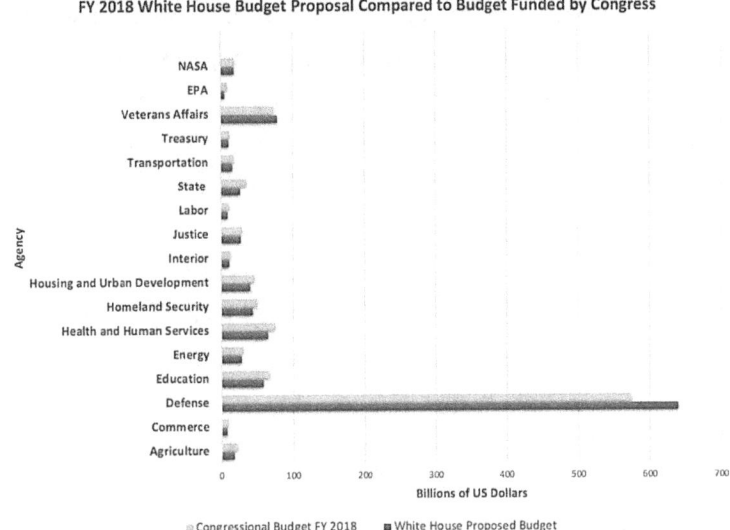

Figure 2. Comparison of White House proposed budget (dark) and congressional allocations (light).

However, there is a concerted effort by the White House to interfere with and create instability in the world of research. Trump's cabinet choices represent the most mindless group of people assembled by a president in my memory.

MARCH FOR SCIENCE—THE GLIMMER OF HOPE

Last year more than 1 million people around the world participated in the largest science-related event in history. Researchers at George Mason University surveyed hundreds of participants, and survey results were published by the Center for Climate Science Communication.[272] Key findings of the survey included:

- A majority (61%) felt that, in their country, conditions for scientists are headed in the wrong direction. Respondents in the United States assigned most blame for this to Republicans in Congress (93% said they deserve "all" or "a lot" of the blame) and Donald Trump (90% said "all" or "a lot").

---

[272] T. Myers et al., March for Science 2017: A Survey of Participants and Followers (Fairfax, VA: George Mason University Center for Climate Change Communication, 2018).

- The most common concerns expressed by participants in the United States were that the current Congress and administration would make harmful reductions in the use of scientific evidence in government decision-making (91%), cuts in government funding for research (90%), and reductions in access to government data for scientific research (81%).
- Participants expressed many goals that they held for the March for Science. The two most cited goals were "increasing evidence-based input policy-making" (89% selected this as a goal, and 38% selected it as their most important goal) and "sustaining public funding of science" (88% and 20%, respectively).
- Despite these aspirations, only about half of participants thought the march would be at least moderately effective at increasing evidence-based input policy-making (46%) and at sustaining public funding for science (52%).

On April 14, 2018, the second March for Science will be held around the world. More than two hundred events have been planned.

The assault on science and reasoning will only be changed by public protests like this one, as well as what citizens do in the ballot boxes in the 2018 and 2020 elections and future state, local, and federal elections.

There is some light in the tunnel of darkness that has assumed control in Washington.

7.4. BLOG POST, 23 JUNE 2021: THE EFFECTS OF DISBANDING SCIENTIFIC EXPERT PANELS

The EPA is responsible for monitoring air pollutants, including carbon monoxide, lead, nitrogen dioxide, ozone, sulfur dioxide, and particulate matter. Whenever Trump was asked about climate change, he would always pivot to saying we have the cleanest air and water on earth. He failed to mention that the air has been the hottest as it has in years and there is no sign of temperatures decreasing. Yet the two administrators of the EPA eroded the agency's fundamental role of protecting the environment by cutting back and undoing the regulations that had been put in place over the past three decades. In a relatively brief period, they corrupted the EPA's ability to protect the air, water, and land. The story that follows is one example of how they polluted their own agency.

This is a tale about why an independent review panel was reconvened to inform the EPA of their review of the National Ambient Air Quality Standards for particulate matter. It's an amazing story.

Gretchen Goldman, PhD in environmental engineering, Georgia Institute of Technology, is research director of the Center for Science & Democracy. She organized an unprecedented meeting in Arlington, Virginia, for two days in October 2019.[273]

Goldman and her colleagues said that the meeting should have been convened by the EPA, but she was compensating for the EPA administrator's abdication of responsibility to use science to make decisions about air quality and the protection of public health.

The problem was this: Andrew Wheeler and his predecessor, Scott Pruitt, made a habit of disbanding scientific panels of experts. In this case, Wheeler had disbanded the particulate matter expert panel and replaced it with political appointees, with the chair being an industry consultant. Goldman and some of her associates decided to reconvene the panel that was dismissed by Wheeler to review the scientific research related to particulate matter.

As Goldman pointed out, particulate matter is a pollutant mixture that kills thousands of susceptible people each year in the United States. She convened twenty particulate matter experts for two days to review the research. The panel was chaired by Chris Frey, a veteran scientist who was a member of previous EPA particulate matter panels. The group of experts produced a 183-page report[274] detailing their science advice and sent it to EPA Administrator Andrew Wheeler.

---

[273] G. Goldman et al., "We Put Science Back into EPA Air Pollution Standards, but...," April 15, 2020, retrieved February 8, 2021, https://blogs.scientificamerican.com/observations/we-put-science-back-into-epa-air-pollution-standards-but/.
[274] "Advice from the Independent Particulate Matter Review Panel (formerly EPA CASAC Particulate Matter Review Panel) on EPA's Policy Assessment for the Review of the National Ambient Air Quality Standards for Particulate Matter," September 2019, https://ucs-documents.s3.amazonaws.com/science-and-democracy/IPMRP-FINAL-LETTER-ON-DRAFT-PA-191022.pdf.

The expert panel's conclusion was that the current standard for exposure to fine particles was inadequate to protect the public health and therefore the standard needed to be strengthened. The scientists who authored the report said that the current standards are not scientifically justified and are specious. The panel recommended lowering the standard to between 8 micrograms of solid particles per cubic meter of air ($\mu g/m^3$) and 10$\mu g/m^3$, down from the current standard of 12 $\mu g/m^3$.

The report was sent to Administrator Wheeler to use in the EPA's particulate matter deliberations, but the panel was split, and in the end the EPA administrator decided to keep the particulate matter standards unchanged.[275]

And to add to the seriousness of not reviewing scientific research on any air pollutant, let alone particulate matter, a report was recently published indicating that global mortality from outdoor fine particle pollution generated by fossil fuel combustion was much higher than the researchers thought.[276] These researchers found that air pollution caused by the burning of fossil fuels such as coal and oil was responsible for 8.7 million deaths globally in 2018, which represented one in five people who died that year. The researchers studied particulate matter known as PM2.5, particulates that are less than 2.5 micrometers in diameter. We call these particles "fine particles." Because the particulates are tiny, when breathed in, they can lodge in the lungs and contribute to a range of health problems.

7.5. BLOG POST, 4 OCTOBER 2020: HOW RUTH BADER GINSBURG MADE THE EARTH A BETTER PLACE

> **Author's Update:** This blog post describes some of the work of Ruth Bader Ginsburg (RBG). I include her in my book as a rebuke to Donald Trump and Mitch McConnell, champions of hypocrisy and deceit. RBG was a champion of the rule of law and one of the most revered Supreme Court justices in our age.

---

[275] "Advice from the Independent Particulate Matter Review Panel."
[276] Karn Vohra et al., "Global Mortality from Outdoor Fine Particle Pollution Generated by Fossil Fuel Combustion: Results from GEOS-Chem," *Environmental Research* 195 (April 2021), retrieved February 10, 2021, https://doi.org/10.1016/j.envres.2021.110754.

She asked her granddaughter to convey to others that her last dying wish was that she would not be replaced on the Supreme Court until after the 2020 election. That did not happen. Instead, Mitch McConnell called Donald Trump the day that Justice Ginsburg died and told Trump to prepare of list of replacements for her on the Supreme Court. McConnell's action was not only hypocritical, but it was also dishonest. In the spring of 2016, he refused to put forward Merrick Garland, who was President Obama's nomination to replace Supreme Court Justice Antonin Scalia, who had died in February 2016. Garland's nomination was never put forward by McConnell, the first time that this happened since the Civil War. But within a month of Justice Ginsburg's death, the Republican-led senate confirmed a replacement for her.

Ruth Bader Ginsburg, Associate Justice of the Supreme Court being interviewed in 2016 by European University Institute (EUI) journalist Olivia Arigho-Stiles, licensed CC BY-SA 2.0 by EUI.

RBG had a profound effect on the world. Not only was she a Supreme Court justice, but she had attained the status of a rock star. Like John Lewis, Justice Ginsburg influenced our thinking about justice for all people. Each of these giants of American society believed in the rights for all people, regardless of race or gender. As a result, they did something about it.

Justice Ginsburg was appointed as a federal judge by President Jimmy Carter in 1980 and to the Supreme Court in 1993 by President Bill Clinton. She was involved in hundreds of cases and wrote the opinion—both for the majority and dissenting—in many of them. Her caseload is impressive.

What might surprise you is that she had a lot to say about the environment. She was involved in some landmark cases affecting the Clean Air and Clean Water Acts. Environmental science and the law are integral aspects of understanding how the government has the responsibility of protecting citizens from harmful effects of air, water, and solid waste pollution.

RBG'S CASELOAD 1993-2020

RBG wrote opinions for twenty-seven years on the Supreme Court. She authored 226 majority opinions and ninety-four dissenting opinions, among other writings.[277]

Yes, I counted the cases and made a chart of her judicial work, shown in Figure 3.

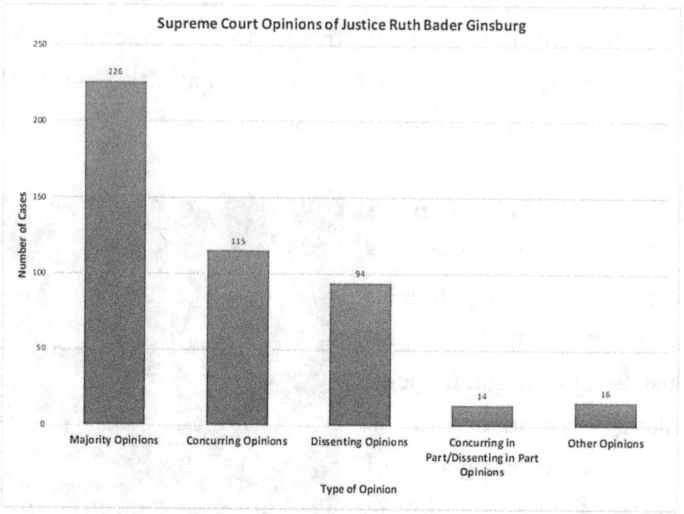

Figure 3. Supreme Court opinions by Justice Ruth Bader Ginsburg.

For example, when Ginsburg dissented in *Bush v. Gore*, she simply wrote, "I dissent." Later, in a speech at the University of Melbourne Law School, she said this about the decision: "Whatever final judgment awaits *Bush v. Gore* in the annals of history," public confidence in the whole federal judiciary (not just the Supreme Court) would be sustained "at a level never beyond repair"—a judicious way of saying that, in time, the drop in confidence could be fixed.[278]

---

[277] Emma Sarran Webster and Caitlin Wolper, "8 Essential Ruth Bader Ginsburg Supreme Court Rulings to Know About," *Teen Vogue*, September 19, 2020, www.teenvogue.com/story/ruth-bader-ginsburg-supreme-court-rulings-to-know-about.
[278] Kaytie Norman, "Read Ruth Bader Ginsburg's Fiery Speech Following *Bush v. Gore*," Early Bird Books, September 19, 2020, retrieved October 3, 2020, https://earlybirdbooks.com/ruth-bader-ginsburg-speech-bush-v-gore.

Other important cases included *Obergefell v. Hodges*, which gave same-sex couples the right to marry in all fifty states. In *Shelby County v. Holder*, which "gutted" the 1965 Voting Rights Act, Ginsburg voiced dissent. As a result of this last case, it has become more difficult for a lot of people to vote in several states, especially in the South.

RBG'S ENVIRONMENTAL RECORD

RBG authored many significant environmental opinions that had serious effects on the EPA's edict to protect America's environment. I've selected five environmental cases of hers that legal experts consider important clean air and water cases. In the discussion that follows, I've identified the lead question guiding the case, the decision the court rendered, and RBG's involvement in the case. All of the information for these five cases is based on Oyez, a free law project from Cornell's Legal Information Institute, Justia, and Chicago-Kent College of Law.[279]

Friends of the Earth v. Laidlaw, 2000

The question in this case was: Does an environmental group's citizen suit for civil penalties under the Clean Water Act become moot when the defendant, after commencement of the litigation, has come into compliance with its National Pollutant Discharge Elimination System permit? The court's decision was yes by a vote of 7–2. RBG wrote the majority opinion. She said that the rights of private citizens to bring lawsuits in federal court directly against industry in violation of important environmental laws like the Clean Water Act should be upheld.

Solid Waste Agency of Northern Cook County v. Army Corps of Engineers, 2001

The case focused on this question: May the Clean Water Act be extended to interstate waterways? The court ruled no by a 5–4 decision. Ruth Bader Ginsburg joined the dissent. She expressed support for an expansive definition of jurisdictional waters under the Clean Water Act. In this

---

[279] Oyez website, 2020, www.oyez.org/.

case, the Solid Waste Agency selected an abandoned sand and gravel pit as a solid waste disposal site. Adjacent bodies of water were affected.

Alaska Department of Conservation v. EPA, 2004

Does the EPA have the authority to overrule a state agency's decision that a company is using the "best available controlling technology" to prevent pollution? Ginsburg wrote the majority opinion (5–4 decision) and agreed that the EPA should insist that the state of Alaska do more to limit air pollution.

Rapanos v. United States, 2006

Does the phrase "waters of the United States" in the Clean Water Act include a wetland that occasionally empties into a navigable waterway? The case was unanswered. RBG joined dissent and argued that the US Army Corp of Engineers regulations should be upheld. All wetlands adjacent to tributaries of waterways should be protected to eliminate pollution of waterways. Rapanos sought to fill three wetland areas on his property to build a shopping center.

Massachusetts v. EPA, 2007

May the EPA decline to issue emission standards for motor vehicles based on policy in the Clean Air Act? Does the act give the EPA authority to regulate CO_2 and other greenhouse gases? In a 5–4 decision, RBG joined the majority, which was authored by John Paul Stevens. The court made clear that if the EPA continues its inaction on carbon regulation, it must base its decision on whether greenhouse gases contribute to climate change. The court rejected the EPA's argument that the Clean Air Act was not meant to refer to carbon emissions. The states could sue the EPA over damage caused by air pollutants in its territory.

This was considered a landmark decision in that now the EPA had to regulate greenhouse gases. The Supreme Court also made it clear that the Earth's increasing temperatures were directly related to the burning of fossil fuels.

CHAPTER 8:
FIRES, HURRICANES, AND FLOODS

8.1. BLOG POST, 2 SEPTEMBER 2017: NO MORE TIME TO HIDE: HARVEY AND GLOBAL CLIMATE CHANGE

The Trump administration will tell you now is not the time to talk about climate change because they are focusing on helping people. However, now is the time to talk about climate change because the future is grim for people in flood zones—and areas that never were labeled flood zones. And if a flood happens in areas that normally don't flood, officials will say, well, it's in a one-in-one-thousand-year floodplain, and there is less than 1 percent annual chance of a flood. The problem is that these numbers disregard how the climate of the Earth has changed since the advent of global warming. The flood zoning is out of date, and this works to the advantage of developers and insurance companies.

The sheer size of Hurricane Harvey is directly connected to global climate change, and the longer we deny this situation, the less able we will be to be in a place to make policy decisions that could lead to less flooding, the most egregious result of land-grabbing driven by greed, and the construction of neighborhoods in areas that never should have been built on in the first place.

We no longer have time to hide from the facts that exist about climate change. The evidence is all around us that the Earth's environments are changing in dangerous ways, including temperature change, increased air pollution, polar ice melting, glacial retreat, sea level rise, species extinction, changes in the migration patterns of animals, effects of water changes, and effects of extreme temperatures on plants, fires, and flooding.

FLOODING

Of all of these, flooding events (and fires) have enormous effects on people, their families, and entire communities. In an investigation reported in ProPublica, communities in Houston have been repeatedly flooded, but because of the government policy of making flood insurance available, people are encouraged to continue living in these flood-prone areas. In fact, in the ProPublica article, one extreme case, a specific property, received eighteen flood insurance payouts totaling $1.8 million, which is fifteen times the market value of the property.[280] In many cases, homeowners are required to rebuild the house at a higher elevation. Still, it's flooded again.

The flooding caused by Hurricane Harvey was horrific. According to the report I found on the *New York Times*, about 40 percent of the buildings that were flooded were in areas that were considered "of minimal flood hazard."[281]

Reservoirs built in the 1940s to control the flow of water along two rivers held during the storm, but engineers had to release water to prevent the earthen banks from breeching. All the flooding in this area was outside of the flood zone. Release of the water from the reservoirs contributed to the flooding of huge areas near the dams, which are now subdivisions of homes.

However, when the dams were built, the land around the reservoirs was grassland. Grassland decreases runoff because much of the water from rain is absorbed directly into the soil. In fact, the engineers constructed meadows and recreation areas near the dams if ever water had to be released. But politicians and home construction developers convinced the people who buy homes that development in these areas would be safe. They claimed that there hadn't been any floods of notice

---

[280] Al Shaw and Lisa Song, "How Harvey Hurt Houston, in 10 Maps," ProPublica, January 3, 2018, retrieved May 21, 2021, https://projects.propublica.org/graphics/harvey-maps.
[281] Ford Fessenden et al., "Water Damage from Hurricane Harvey Extended Far Beyond Flood Zones," *New York Times*, September 2, 2017, retrieved February 11, 2022, https://www.nytimes.com/interactive/2017/09/01/us/houston-damaged-buildings-in-fema-flood-zones.html.

in years. So for decades, development led to construction that covered over the grasslands with concrete and homes, increasing runoff and setting up a potential disaster, as happened during Hurricane Harvey.

Hurricanes in Texas have been common for centuries, but at the same time the population was rising, Earth was increasingly getting hotter and hotter, resulting in increasing the temperature of ocean waters (the source of energy for hurricanes) and increasing the melting of ice, including glaciers and especially the polar areas. This resulted in greater of amounts of water for evaporation and precipitation.

Superstorms of the magnitude of Harvey in 2017 and Sandy in 2012 will become the norm. In fact, when I wrote this blog post in September 2017, Hurricane Irma with winds of around 100 mph was in the Atlantic on a track that would bring it to the Caribbean and the US. When it blew through the Leeward Islands, it was a Category 5 storm, the first of the year. Irma made landfall in the Florida Keys with 130 mph winds and moved into Florida with the same high winds, causing enormous damage to the state.

We can't hide. We need to act and insist that local and state governments work to influence the federal government, which we know is officially living in the state of climate change denial, and get it to act to curb global warming.

> **Author's Update:** I edited this post on August 31, 2021, the day after Hurricane Ida drove itself into New Orleans and the Gulf Coast as a Category 4 storm. The flooding in Louisiana, combined with loss of power, devastated millions of people. The storm continued toward Pennsylvania, New York, and New England, bringing torrential rain and massive flooding. Ida ravished Louisiana and left millions of people, mostly Black, without shelter or power for more than a month during a pandemic.

8.2. BLOG POST, 7 AUGUST 2020: SHOCK AND AWE: THE ANTHROPOCENE IN THE AGE OF TRUMP

The Anthropocene is a proposed geological period that marks the effects of human activity on the planet Earth. According to one concept, the Anthropocene means relating to or denoting the current geological age, viewed as the period during which human activity has been the dominant influence on climate and the environment.

In a recent book, *The Shock of the Anthropocene: The Earth, History, and Us*,[282] the authors explore the environmental crises, but also a new geological period caused by human activity over the past two centuries.

The Trump administration should be feared in the context of the environmental crisis, global warming, and climate change. Although the current crisis predates the Trump era, his policies and plans for the environment, energy, and transportation will create the shock-and-awe military doctrine that has destroyed many places on the Earth. Unfortunately, Trump and his associates are science denialists and have promised to cut back on much of the progress that has been made in the last decade.[283]

Yet we must admit that the "progress" cited above is meager given the disregard of scientific evidence that the Earth is changing in accelerating ways, including temperature change, increased air pollution, polar ice melting, glacial retreat, sea level rise, species extinction, changes in the migration patterns of animals, and the effects of water changes and extreme temperatures on plants.

Planetary conditions have not improved even with the emphasis by the Obama administration on energy alternatives and environmental protection.

Blame can be placed on many actors for the damage that has been done to the Earth. Energy consumption, especially in advanced capitalist societies (such as the US and Britain), has increased at exponential rates since the 1800s, which was the time atmospheric chemist Paul Crutzen identifies as the beginning of the Anthropocene.[284]

Christophe Bonneuil and Jean-Baptiste Fressoz name ninety companies that have been responsible for 63 percent of global CO_2 and

---

[282] Christophe Bonneuil and Jean-Baptiste Fressoz, *The Shock of the Anthropocene: The Earth, History, and Us* (New York: Verso, 2017).

[283] Sean B. Carroll, "The Denialist Playbook," *Scientific American*, November 8, 2020, www.scientificamerican.com/article/the-denialist-playbook/.

[284] Harrison Smith, "Paul J. Crutzen, Nobel Laureate Who Studied Ozone and Named New 'Anthropocene' Era, Dies at 87," *Washington Post*, January 30, 2021, www.washingtonpost.com/local/obituaries/paul-crutzen-dead/2021/01/29/97e9c200-6244-11eb-afbe-9a11a127d146_story.html.

methane emissions.[285] Yet, as they point out, books are written about the "ecological crisis" but do not mention one of these companies. Chevron, ExxonMobil, and BP are among the biggest contributors to this crisis. Little mention is made of capitalism, war, or even the United States.

Trump has said he's going to bring back coal. Coal has never left our energy shopping list. Coal, which is less efficient than oil or gas, is still what we consume at great rates, and in fact, it was at a peak in 2014. Imagine. There is not much Trump can do on this front.

COUNTRIES

What should be made an issue is the shock and awe that is created by these ninety companies and the military-industrial complex led by the United States, which spends about $755 billion (2020) on its military machine and continues to wage war, especially in the Middle East. It takes nine countries, in order of spending, to equal the amount spent on the military by the United States.

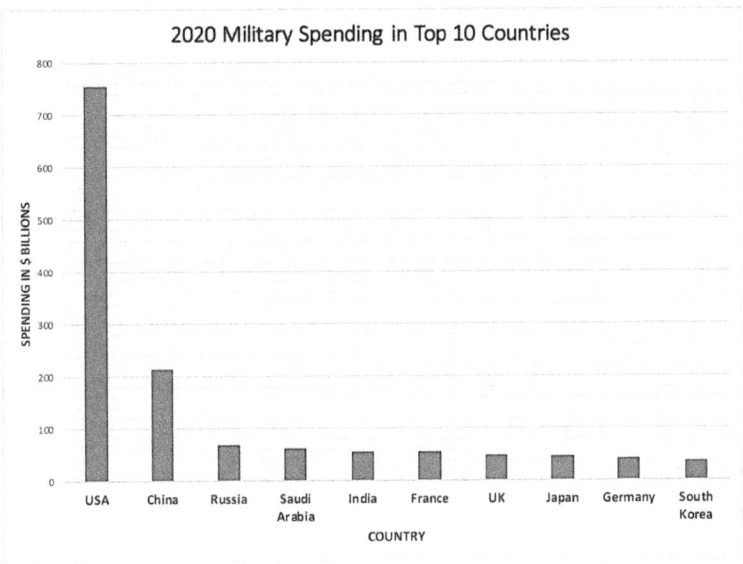

Figure 4. Military spending globally in the top ten countries.

---

[285] Bonneuil and Fressoz, *The Shock of the Anthropocene.*

COMPANIES

If you want to call out companies that are contributing to the environmental crisis based on their fossil fuel energy usage, here is a list of the top ten to get you started:

1. American Electric Power
2. Duke Energy
3. Southern Company
4. United States government (owns the Tennessee Valley Authority)
5. Berkshire Hathaway
6. Ameren Corporation
7. Luminant Generation Company
8. First Energy
9. AES Corporation
10. Excel Energy, Inc.

Why do you think we need to be active in fighting against the Trump administration? Just look to his cabinet appointees. Secretary of state—former head of ExxonMobil. EPA administrator—former attorney general of Oklahoma who sued the EPA more than fourteen times. The list goes on and on. Many, if not all, have deep connections to the companies that have caused the most damage to the Earth's environment and contributed to the rapid way in which the climate is changed.

What do you think? Shock or awe? Both?

8.3. BLOG POST, 14 AUGUST 2019: IT'S REALLY HOT! CLIMATE CHANGE, YOU THINK?

It was over one hundred degrees in Atlanta today. This was one of the hottest days in years. Schools are in session across all districts in Georgia, some of which have air conditioning systems that are old and are failing, or don't have air conditioning at all. Across the country, temperatures have soared, in some cases with little relief on the horizon. This is the new normal. We will continue to see hotter and hotter summer weather across the United States. This is the result of global warming.

In an article published in the *Washington Post*, the authors wrote that "extreme climate change has arrived in America." Their article, "2°C: Beyond the Limit," is a good assessment of the current condition of the United States' climate.[286]

As reported in the article, the United Nations Intergovernmental Panel on Climate Change predicts that an increase of global temperatures that exceeds two degrees Celsius destroys coral reefs and causes the melting of huge rafts of ice in Greenland and the Antarctic, resulting in sea level rise. The rising sea level is causing the repeated flooding of cities that I visit, including Savannah, Georgia, and Jacksonville and St. Augustine, Florida. In the future, there is the possibility that all of Florida and many of the East Coast cities will be flooded. In 2007, in *Massachusetts v. EPA*, the harm that the plaintiffs argued was flooding off New England coastal areas, which they claimed was due to sea level rise that was related to rising temperatures and increased melting of glaciers. The Supreme Court agreed with Massachusetts, which meant that the EPA must regulate greenhouse gases.

In "2°C: Beyond the Limit," the authors point out that global warming has meant increased winter temperatures as well. They point out that the average temperatures for December through February in New Jersey now exceed zero degrees Celsius, the freezing point of water. Lakes will freeze less, and snow will melt more rapidly.

Geologist and science educator Don Peck grew up in New Jersey. He said that when he was a child, the lakes were always frozen in winter, and the ice supported thriving ice companies that could deliver large blocks of ice to area consumers. He told me that "now, although there are ice companies in the area, they do not have the same level of supply of ice frozen in lakes and ponds."[287]

We can expect global warming to have significant effects on the earth. Climate scientists' models simulate climate in the future. There

---

[286] Steven Mufson et al., "Extreme Climate Change in the United States: Here Are America's Fastest-Warming Places," *Washington Post*, August 13, 2019, https://www.washingtonpost.com/graphics/2019/national/climate-environment/climate-change-america/.
[287] Personal correspondence with Don Peck, August 10, 2019.

a several models that have been developed, but in general the models project that global temperature will continue to increase but show that human decisions and behavior we choose today will determine how dramatically climate will change in the future.

The House of Representatives passed the first act on climate change in a decade. It's called the Climate Action Now Act, and it passed 231–190. Although it won't pass in the Senate, it becomes an important election issue in the 2020 presidential campaigns.

> **Author's Update:** During the summer of 2021, the Pacific Northwest and British Columbia experienced temperatures as high as 121 degrees. Death Valley reached 130 degrees. These extreme temperatures in the Pacific Northwest and British Columbia, an all-time heat record in the region, led to wildfires and many deaths. Scientists visualize the heat wave as a heat dome. In the heat dome, hot air rises vertically and then the high-pressure ridges push the hot air down toward the earth's surface. The sky is clear, and hot air is pushed toward people living on the ground.
>
> This part of the world has less air conditioning in buildings and homes, making the heat a serious health hazard. In these temperatures, farm and construction workers are unable to work. Farm workers suffer twenty times more than the rate of people who have protection from the heat. There were repeated waves of heat in the Midwest and even New England. Scientists say that these periods of extreme heat were impossible without the warming of the planet Earth.

8.4. BLOG POST, 5 SEPTEMBER 2019: TRUMP'S HURRICANE DORIAN WEATHER FORECAST DEBACLE

Early in the day on September 1, Trump met with the Federal Emergency Management Agency (FEMA) at its National Response Agency Coordinating Center in Washington. He was wearing his red hat and sitting at the head of the table, arms folded around himself. There were about a dozen people in the room, and they all listened to the National Hurricane Center's director give a detailed report and analysis based on current meteorological data about Hurricane Dorian. I'm not sure if Trump appreciated having to listen to a scientist explaining the path and forecast for Dorian. His folded arms telegraphed that nothing was getting into his brain.

Later in the day, Trump in a tweet said that the hurricane would impact South Carolina, Florida, Georgia, and Alabama. The problem here was that Dorian was not predicted to impact Alabama. Trump was informed of this at the earlier meeting with FEMA.

Even Fox News ripped Donald Trump's meteorology lesson claiming that Alabama would be hit by Hurricane Dorian. The Fox meteorologist made it clear that Alabama was never in the National Hurricane Forecast Center's official confidence cone. She pointed out that the map that Trump showed was "inaccurate, misleading, and fake."[288]

The hurricane was never predicted to approach the state of Alabama at all. And right after Trump claimed it was in Dorian's path, the governor of Alabama announced that the hurricane was not heading northwest into Alabama.

The Birmingham office of the National Weather Service immediately tweeted that Alabama would not see any impacts from Hurricane Dorian. Why did the Birmingham office release this statement? It was simply to reassure citizens in Alabama that they did not have to prepare for a hurricane when in fact the president of the United States announced they would.

The Birmingham tweet, in my view, marks the integrity of this office, which believes that its work is related to protecting life and property in the region. They were not going to let the president's fabrication rest as the truth about Hurricane Dorian.

But now we know that the decision made by the Birmingham office caused an uproar up the chain of command. At the top of the chain is Wilbur Ross, secretary of commerce. Although he was out of town, he was on the phone to acting NOAA Administrator Neil Jacobs and threatened

---

[288] Daniel Chaitin, "'Inaccurate, Misleading and Fake': Fox Meteorologist Rips Trump over Doctored Hurricane Map," *Washington Examiner*, September 5, 2019, retrieved February 11, 2022, https://www.washingtonexaminer.com/tag/donald-trump?source=%2Fnews%2Finaccurate-misleading-and-fake-fox-meteorologist-rips-trump-over-doctored-hurricane-map.

him that people would be fired if they didn't condemn the Birmingham office and make sure Trump's statement was backed by NOAA.

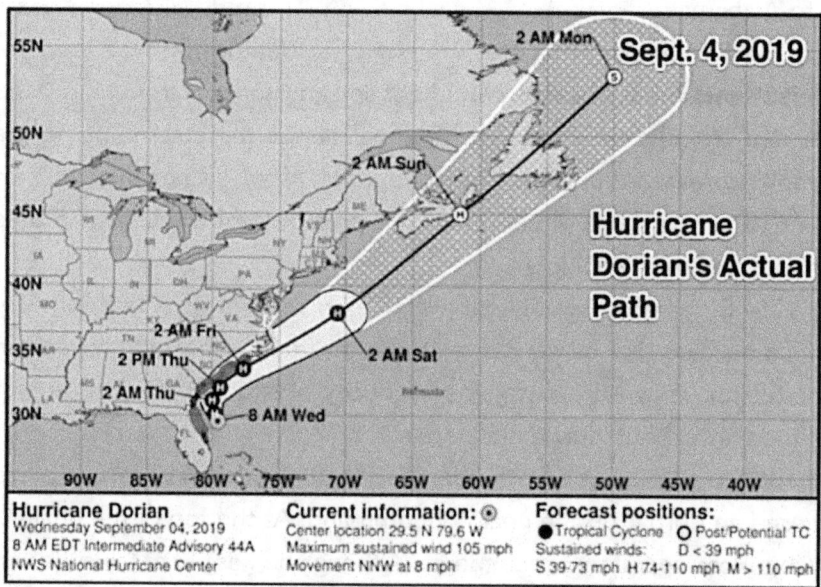

Figure 5. National Weather Service maps of Hurricane Dorian's cone on August 31, 2019, and September 4, 2019. The August 31 map shows how President Trump altered Hurricane Dorian's predicted cone to indicate the hurricane would approach Alabama. The National Weather Service did not predict Alabama in the cone's path. Source: National Weather Service, CC 2.0.

Even though Jacobs resisted at first, an unsigned statement supporting Trump's "weather forecast" was released. The statement also said that the Birmingham office was incorrect.

On September 4, Trump displayed the National Hurricane Center's August 29 map of Hurricane Dorian's projected track. The map showed an odd-shaped line that extended into Alabama, with Trump saying that this was the original map and it was clear that the hurricane was headed to Alabama. Trump fabricated the map by changing the "cone" of the hurricane's predicted path. According to the Office of Research Integrity, this is a case of misconduct by manipulation and makes the data inaccurate.

Trump did not make an honest mistake, and to make matters worse, he went into the Oval Office and shamed the scientific community, especially meteorology and climate scientists, by trying to convince the public that he was correct.

He was lying.

And he should be investigated. But of course, he wasn't. In fact, every time he had exposure on TV or when answering questions about the hurricane, he made a point to say that he was correct. Instead of being investigated, he bullied the scientific community to accept his lies and false information.

While Hurricane Dorian was destroying the Bahamas, Trump was playing golf and tweeting, uninvolved with the Category 5 storm, the worst to be heading toward the US this year.

8.5. BLOG POST, 14 SEPTEMBER 2020: WHAT'S CAUSING THE WILDFIRES IN THE WEST?

I've wondered what the main cause of wildfires raging is in the West. Are the fires linked to climate change? What role do humans play in starting fires? Are there more fires this year than in the past? Why? The toll on human and other animal and plant life is immense.

AUSTRALIAN WILDFIRES

What we see in California, Oregon, and Washington is what we saw last year in Australia. Friends of ours in Burra, South Australia, were on alert

THE TRUMP FILES

and ready to evacuate starting in October 2019. The Australian bushfires burned for nine months until all were extinguished or contained. The bushfires were devastating. Billions of animals were killed. Australian firefighters and some civilians lost their lives. Thousands of square miles of land were burned. Thousands of buildings, including homes, were destroyed. Finally, smoke from the fires circled the globe for months.

FIRES IN THE WEST

Wildfires in California are growing more dangerous. The accumulation of wood and debris in forests is fuel for fires. Housing and commercial development in areas that invade the edges of forests at higher elevations is a problem. Also, greater electricity transmission and distribution lines have caused fires, and one of the worst was in Paradise, California, in 2018. Called the Camp Fire, the towns of Paradise and nearby Concow were nearly destroyed, each losing 95 percent of their structures. Climate change is the major factor. The acreage burned in California is increasing each year. In 2000, the typical burned area was 500,000 acres. In 2018, nearly 2 million acres burned.

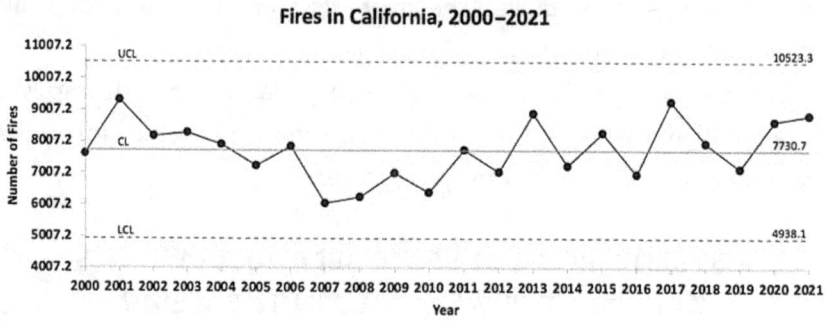

Figure 6. Process chart for the number of fires in California 2000–2021.

Figure 6 is a process chart of the number fires during the period of 2000–2021. The horizontal line in middle of the graph is the overall average of fires during this period. I'm using this type of graph as a method to judge if fires in California since 2000 are or are not within control. The tick marks on the vertical lines are the upper and lower control limits. Please note that even though the number of fires varies, it is within the control limits. We should expect the number of fires in the future to be within these control limits, unless something unusual happens.

However, according to CalFire, in 2020 there have been 7,718 fires burning 3,154,107 acres (about the area of Connecticut). Twenty people died and 5,000 structures have been destroyed. More acreage burned than in any other year. I've created a second process chart shown in Figure 7, and you can see that the fires in 2020 are outside the upper control limits—extremely outside the limits.

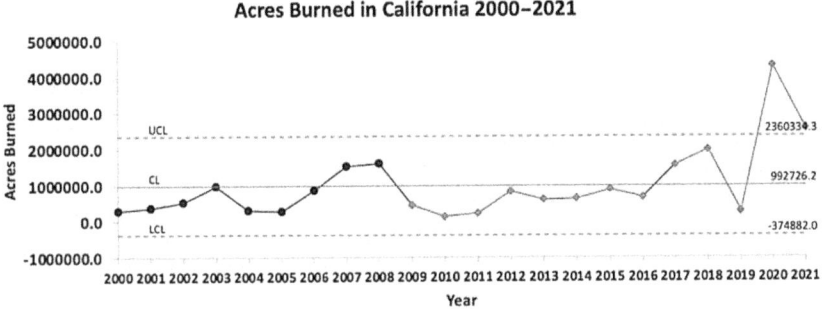

Figure 7. Control chart of acreage of land burned by California fires, 2000–2021.

CLIMATE CHANGE

Wildfires are a natural part of the landscapes in California and other western states. However, the fire season is starting earlier and lasting longer. This expansion is a climate change trend. The California Department of Forestry and Fire Protection published a report in 2019 that made recommendations for fire prevention and mitigation. Climate change, dead and dying trees, and the development of new homes in areas close to wildlands will create the perfect storm for wildfires going forward.

Climate change is a major force that has created a longer fire season. Higher temperatures have reduced the moisture levels in forests. Lower annual snow melt means dryer conditions. The conditions in California continue to cause more severe wildfires.

This year has been one of the worst on record, not only in California, but in Oregon, Washington, and Colorado as well. Look at the most recent year of fires reported in California. Note that the acreage burned for 2020 and 2021 is outside the upper control limits of acreage burned since 2000. Something significant happened in 2020. Prior to this year, the most acreage burned was 2 million acres (about the area of Connecticut). More than 5 million acres (about twice the area of Connecticut) have burned so far this year. The fire season is only half over, providing further evidence that climate change is factor in California fires. The process chart in Figure 7 shows the acreage burned from 2000–2021. Up until 2019, each point was within the limits of the process chart. In 2020 the relationship went beyond the upper limit, indicating an unusual event.

Climate change is acting as a force-multiplier that will increasingly exacerbate wildland fire issues over the coming decades. The state can expect to experience longer fire seasons, increased frequency and severity of drought, greater acreage burned, and related impacts such as widespread tree mortality and bark beetle infestation. Decades of fire suppression have disrupted natural fire cycles and added to the problem.

Unfortunately, the Republican Party has denied the science of climate change. Trump refuses to accept any part of the science and continues to claim that poor forest management (raking the forest floor) is the cause of wildfires.

Wildfires will continue to affect the western part of the United States. Data collected for forty years show the effects of climate change, forest management, and human development.

8.6. BLOG POST, 18 SEPTEMBER 2020: RAKING LEAVES WON'T PUT OUT CALIFORNIA'S FIRES

Climate change is the cause of megafires in the West. Yet Donald Trump thinks the cause was the lack of raking leaves. Science denialism has led to a colossal debacle in this country. Denying science has not only affected fires in the United States but also caused hundreds of thousands of Americans to die of COVID-19.

Raking leaves is an activity that some people dread each year. For others, it's a form of exercise. Raking leaves in the forests is also a way to manage the forests in California, but not necessarily stop fires.

I've done my share of raking leaves. I've backpacked, hiked, and explored the forests in Colorado and other locations in the West. I never realized that removing leaves would prevent the fires burning now in the American West.

For the president of the United States, raking leaves is the way to put out the fires in California and elsewhere in the West. Trump made this claim again in a meeting with California officials. To Trump it's simply a matter of clearing the forest floor. But to fire experts and scientists, his argument is not true. The total acreage of American forests is so large that it would be impossible to remove such a massive amount of debris. Summer temperatures have continued to rise. The forest floor is drier than ever. Winds are fiercer and unpredictable. Fires are burning at temperatures never witnessed. The fires are so severe that fire experts have coined a new term: megafires.

And yet, at a meeting in California, Trump dismissed anything related to climate change. I've read the minutes of the meeting and watched some video of the interaction. Here is just one part of the Trump meeting with fire officials and the governor of California. I found it painful to watch the governor and other officials talk with Trump. Deep down they can't stand the man. They know he's a liar and makes up his own facts. He believes climate change is a Chinese hoax. Yet here they are, as the West is burning, pleading with him to accept the reality of climate change. He doesn't and he won't. Yet we know climate change is the cause of megafires.

Below is a short dialogue between Wade Crowfoot, Secretary for Natural Resources of California, and President Trump. Crowfoot is an expert on natural resources and knows what's causing the worst fire season on record.

THE DIALOGUE: CLIMATE CHANGE IS THE CAUSE OF MEGAFIRES

The dialogue that follows is preposterous coming from an adult who happens to be the president of the United States.[289] Most of the students that

---

[289] Robert Mackey, "Trump Scoffs at Plea to Take Climate Change Seriously Amid Fires, Mocks Science Instead," *The Intercept*, September 15, 2020, retrieved April 4, 2022, https://theintercept.com/2020/09/14/trump-scoffs-plea-take-climate-change-seriously-amid-wildfires-mocks-science/.

I have taught would have a better sense of the predicament Californians find themselves in with the raging wildfires that are crippling the state.

After being introduced by the governor of California, Wade Crowfoot, sitting near Trump, said to him, "You may have learned that we broke a world record near Death Valley. It was over 130 degrees, and in greater LA, it reached 120 degrees. And we're seeing this warming trend make our summers warmer but also our winters warmer as well." He looks at Trump but gets no response.

Crowfoot continues: "So one area of mutual agreement and priority is vegetation management, but we want to work with you to really recognize the changing climate and what it means to our forests and work together with that science; that science is going to be key. Because if we—if we ignore that science and put our head in the sand and think it's all about vegetation management, we're not going to succeed together protecting Californians."

Trump says, "Okay. It'll start getting cooler."

Crowfoot replies, "I wish."

Trump comes back and says, "You just watch."

Crowfoot, a bit exasperated, leans forward and says, "I wish science agreed with you."

And the president announces, "Well, I don't think science knows."

Trump's responses to Crowfoot's comments highlight the president's intense science denialism. In this case he argues that it will simply get cooler. That should stop the fires. But wait. When he first started talking about the COVID-19 pandemic, he said it would get hotter, which would put a stop to the virus. That hasn't worked out, has it? So is it going get hotter or cooler?

Then Trump pulled the "science doesn't know" card on Crowfoot. During the worst fire season on record in California, the president sticks to the rules of conspiracy theorists. He furthers his disdain for information. The only way that Trump can make sense of the fires in California forests is to lay blame on those who manage the forests. Crowfoot and the governor of California know that forest management is important to mitigate against future forest fires. But it's only one part of the solution. Instead, we know that climate change is a major contributor to megafires.

THE DANGER OF SCIENCE DENIALISM

Science denialism is not new. Now these deniers have the president of the United States as one of their members. And that is dangerous.

Most Americans accept the science of climate change. Two-thirds of Americans say the federal government is not doing enough to reduce the effects of climate change, according to the Pew Research Center. Compared to more than a decade ago, more Americans say protecting the environment and dealing with global climate change should be top priorities for the president and Congress.[290]

There has been an effort in the Trump administration to roll back regulations designed to protect the environment. Yet the American people clearly disagree with these policy changes.

Science denialism is supported by the media, especially right-wing talk radio and right-wing think tanks. Misinformation around climate change and its impacts are still commonplace in some prominent mainstream media. For example, it is easy to find climate change misinformation videos on YouTube. You can easily find videos such as "What They Haven't Told You about Climate Change," or "The Truth about Climate Change," or "Actual Scientist Says: Climate Change Is a Scam!" According to a study reported in *Time* magazine, even after searching using terms such as "climate change," "global warming," and "temperature change," the "Up Next" algorithm on these YouTube searches listed many videos that pointed to misinformation about the term you searched for.

The reality of climate change is affecting most of the United States. Flooding, drought, rising shorelines, high heat indexes, and megafires are examples. It is no longer possible to ignore the factual basis that the Earth's climate is changing. It's changing because of the increase of greenhouse gases in the atmosphere, especially those caused by burning

---

[290] Cary Funk and Brian Kennedy, "How Americans See Climate Change and the Environment in 7 Charts," Pew Research Center, April 21, 2020, retrieved February 26, 2021, https://www.pewresearch.org/fact-tank/2020/04/21/how-americans-see-climate-change-and-the-environment-in-7-charts/.

fossil fuels (coal, crude oil, and natural gas). The result is an increase in the temperature of the Earth. Meanwhile, it is evident that climate change is the cause of megafires.

There is a 97 percent consensus among scientists on global warming. There are scientists who don't agree with this, but they tend to be scientists without backgrounds in climate science. There is near 100 percent agreement that climate change is real among scientists with backgrounds and expertise in climate science.

The foolishness of Trump's science denial is unacceptable. Teenagers that I've worked with in the GTP have a better understanding of the Earth. They know the Earth's atmosphere is heating up. Teenagers know that in their short lifetime, hurricanes, flooding, drought conditions, and fires are commonplace. They also have led one of the largest climate crisis protests in the world.

It's time for the politicians of this country come to terms with the reality of science. It is shocking that the man in the White House and the man at the head of the Senate possess the incompetence that they do.

Mr. President, raking the forest floor will not help put out the fires. Get your head out of the muck and step up. Better than that, run to south Florida where sea levels are rising.

> **Author's Update:** Trump may be gone from the White House, but there are many climate skeptics in the House and Senate, and they will be there for years. The blind adherence to partisan beliefs will be difficult to overcome. It will be difficult to pass laws that protect the environment and more specifically move us toward zero burning of fossil fuels. Yet surveys of the American electorate show that people believe that climate change is a danger not only to the country, but to their local communities as well. The major changes that have been made in our democracy have come from the bottom up by activists and peaceful protests. In 2018, teenagers around the world led the charge, challenging government leaders to do something now about climate change.

CHAPTER 9:
EXISTENTIAL THREATS

9.1. BLOG POST, 25 SEPTEMBER 2019: CLIMATE CHANGE YOUTH ACTIVISTS

Activists for social change come in all ages and from all countries. They protest and march for many causes that impinge on their lives. They often join with others to support each other and to bring their protests to the centers of power to demand change.

The youth of the world know that climate change is an existential threat. They also know how to challenge adult leadership to try to make changes.

We have seen climate change youth leaders march and strike from schools around the world. Hundreds of thousands of youth activists have made hundreds of media appearances. Four of these youth leaders met with two committees in the US House of Representatives. Greta Thunberg met with President Obama. She also gave a major speech at the Climate Crisis Conference at the United Nations. The four best-known youth climate change activists are:

- Vic Barrett, 20 years old, New York, member of the Alliance for Climate Education
- Benji Backer, 21 years old, Washington, president of American Conservation Coalition
- Greta Thunberg, 16 years old, Sweden, founder of Friday Strike
- Jamie Margolin, 17 years old, Washington, founder of This Is Zero Hour

It's been estimated that 4 million people marched on September 20, 2019. Streets in major cities around the world were filled with teenagers, young adults, and many others. They all were protesting the lack of progress in mitigating climate change. They want action. They want change.

CLIMATE CHANGE DENIERS

Yet lurking in the background, and then emerging on Fox News, right-wing radio, and TV talk shows and hundreds of websites and blogs, are climate change deniers. I wrote yesterday about one of these persons who lashed out at the four youth climate change leaders who met with the US House Foreign Affairs Committee.[291]

Climate change denial is an organized machine. A resource that is helpful to tease out this machine is *The Oxford Handbook of Climate Change and Society*.[292] The authors of the handbook explain how contrarian scientists, fossil fuel corporations, think tanks, and front groups have assaulted mainstream science. They've provided misinformation for decades. "Climategate" was manufactured by their finding very minor errors in an Intergovernmental Panel on Climate Change (IPCC) report and blowing it into another "gate."

For the climate change youth leaders to be successful, they need to understand climate denial. This is not very simple. Denial is complex and well-funded. It has a history much longer than the age of the climate change youth leaders.

COMPONENTS OF CLIMATE CHANGE DENIAL

The climate change denial machine is a collaboration among big corporations and foundations, conservative think tanks, front groups, and astroturf organizations. Conservative think tanks perform research and advocacy on climate science. Front groups and astroturfing are practices of masking sponsors of a message to make it appear as though it originates from grassroots participants. Media, politicians, and blogs

---

[291] Jack Hassard, "Why Should We Listen to Young Climate Change Activists?" Jackhassard.org, September 24, 2019, https://jackhassard.org/young-climate-change-activists/.
[292] John Dryzek, Richard B. Norgaard, and David Schlosberg, *The Oxford Handbook of Climate Change and Society* (New York: Oxford University Press, 2013).

reproduce, repeat, and echo misinformation and outright lies about climate change. The chart in Figure 8 shows how a top-down apparatus of organizations and individuals work together to promote an anti-intellectual, anti-science, and defiant misinformation campaign against any progress in the effort to mitigate climate change.

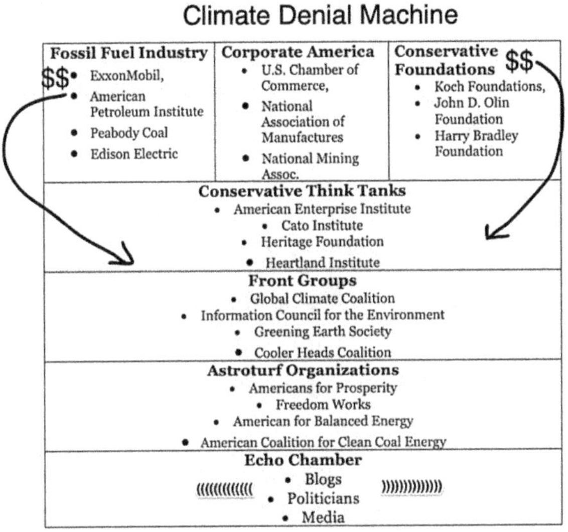

Climate Denial Machine

Fossil Fuel Industry	Corporate America	Conservative Foundations
$$ • ExxonMobil, • American Petroleum Institute • Peabody Coal • Edison Electric	• U.S. Chamber of Commerce, • National Association of Manufactures • National Mining Assoc.	$$ • Koch Foundations, • John D. Olin Foundation • Harry Bradley Foundation

Conservative Think Tanks
- American Enterprise Institute
- Cato Institute
- Heritage Foundation
- Heartland Institute

Front Groups
- Global Climate Coalition
- Information Council for the Environment
- Greening Earth Society
- Cooler Heads Coalition

Astroturf Organizations
- Americans for Prosperity
- Freedom Works
- American for Balanced Energy
- American Coalition for Clean Coal Energy

Echo Chamber
- Blogs
- Politicians
- Media

Figure 8. Components of the climate denial machine based on The Oxford Handbook of Climate Change and Society.

9.2. BLOG POST, 21 JANUARY 2020: CLIMATE GRIEF

Unfortunately, Donald Trump, president of the United States, wouldn't understand people who experience climate grief. His cavalier attitude toward any earth disaster, such as fires or hurricanes, is hopeless for those affected.

Climate grief is a reality that we don't talk about. But it's impossible not to experience climate grief from reports of natural disasters such as fires, hurricanes, tornadoes, floods, and sweltering, uninhabitable temperatures.

One of the articles I read this week was from the Health and Science weekly email I receive from the *Los Angeles Times*.[293] It was a story

---

[293] J. Rosen, "An Artist Set Out to Paint Climate Change. She Ended Up on a Journey through Grief," *Los Angeles Times*, January 11, 2020, retrieved January 19, 2020, https://www.latimes.com/la-sci-col1-climate-change-art-2019-story.html.

about an artist in Portland, Oregon. This is an artist who doesn't simply paint beautiful landscapes but has focused on landscapes that are being transformed by climate change.[294]

According to Julia Rosen,[295] Daniela Naomi Molnar ended up on a journey through grief. She, like many artists, is bearing witness to environmental changes unfolding in our time. Some have created political works that evoke outrage or guilt. Still others paint to show the beauty of the world. And many others think about how they can deal with climate stress through their art.

PAINTING ATTENTION TO CLIMATE CHANGE AND CLIMATE GRIEF

When I read the article, I was fascinated by Daniela Molnar's work, not just her painting. She says that her goal of painting newly revealed landscapes with the melting of the Eliot Glacier on Mt. Hood was to draw attention to climate change.

I taught earth science and geology as a high school teacher and college professor. I've studied glaciation of North America and have spent a lot of time in the Colorado Rockies teaching geology and simply being there. In a graduate glacial geology course at The Ohio State University, one of the field trips in the course syllabus was a flight in a beautifully decorated and cushioned DC-9 plane. The first time we were to fly, a storm blew into Columbus, cancelling the trip. I was relieved. I was nervous about flying in a DC-9. A week later, flying on a clear day, we observed and discussed landforms created by retreating glaciers. We flew over a variety of glacial depositional features including eskers, kames, moraines, and drumlins.

Later in life, when I started traveling into the West, especially Colorado, I came across a myriad of mountain glaciers, and now when I see them, I think of Daniela Molnar's work. I've also started to paint and after five years have learned to appreciate the work of artists a lot more than I did at an earlier age.

---

[294] Daniela Molnar is a visual artist, poet, wilderness guide, and professor. Molnar founded and directed the Art + Ecology program at the Pacific Northwest College of Art.
[295] Rosen, "An Artist Set Out to Paint Climate Change."

CLIMATE GRIEF

The journalist Rosen asked Molnar what her goal of painting is.[296] She said, "At first I didn't know where this was going. But as I worked and created more paintings of vanishing ice, I realized this is what it feels like to try to hold the enormous losses brought about by climate change."

Molnar created a series of new landscapes formed by the melting of mountain glaciers. She calls her climate change series *New Earth*. Through it she explores the nature of climate grief. When asked about the series, she said, "It's about how climate change is reshaping our planet and how we experience it. In my paintings I draw shapes of newly exposed ground near the glaciers. I see the new earth as a wound or new delicate skin formed over a wound."

As she continued her work, she said that she used NASA satellite images and data-based projections to find the shapes to help create her paintings. She concluded by saying that "the information swims together into composite shapes, the colors overlapping to form new colors, reflecting the fundamental interconnectedness of all life, all locales, the way that a glacier calving in Greenland causes the ocean to rise in the Marshall Islands." The idea that all things are connected is a fundamental concept in nature. One of my friends always reminded his students before taking a nature walk that "when a wildflower is picked, a star is sure to shudder."

> **Author's Update:** How does the youth of the world understand climate change? Do they experience the climate grief that is being discussed here? One way to find out is to pay attention to what teenagers and young adults are saying about the Earth's climate.
>
> Greta Thunberg is a Swedish environmental activist who is known for challenging world leaders to act on climate change mitigation. She is an example of many young activists, and her biography is a way to understand what it is that the world's youth are telling us. When I heard her talk before the House Foreign Affairs

---

[296] Rosen, "An Artist Set Out to Paint Climate Change."

Committee and the House Select Committee in Washington, DC, on September 18, 2019, she barely said anything. Instead, she said to the committee, "I don't want you to listen to me. I want you to listen to the scientists." As she said this, she pushed across the table in the committee's direction a copy of the most recent IPCC report.[297]

Yet people do listen to her. In 2018, she wrote a simple message on poster board, "School strike for climate." She then started skipping school on Fridays to strike for climate and launched "Fridays for Future," which was founded on August 20, 2018. Fridays for Future is also branded as Youth for Climate, Climate Strike, or Youth Strike for Climate. Hundreds of thousands of teenagers from around the world joined by skipping school. Soon that number reached millions of youth campaigning and marching to their drumbeat calling for action by world leaders.

I didn't have to skip school, but I did join them on the Square in Marietta, Georgia. I walked into various shops on the Square presenting a "Climate Crisis Friday" card that I had designed.[298] The message on the card was:

Figure 9. Climate Crisis Friday card.

One could argue that the youth of the world are vocalizing their grief for how climate change is not only impacting their lives now, but also their dreams for their and other's futures. But too many adults dismiss their passion and chalk it up to youthful daydreaming.

---

[297] The IPCC issues reports frequently. The IPCC prepares comprehensive assessment reports about knowledge on climate change, its causes, potential impacts, and response options. To access them, visit https://www.ipcc.ch/reports/.
[298] At the bottom of the card was a link to globalclimatestrike.net, which is a rich resource of projects and activities. I recommend visiting the site. It will be worth your time to discover the work of the world's youth.

I don't think it's a daydream! It's more of a nightmare. The psychological effects of climate change and global warming have more grave consequences for teenagers and young adults than we realize.[299]

Greta Thunberg, a Swedish environmental activist who is known for challenging world leaders to take action on climate change. She received the Rachel Carson Prize in 2019, and was Time Person of Year (2019) and has been nominated for the Nobel Peace Prize. She is author of books and videos. Source: Marked with a CC BY 2.0 license, Anthony Quintano.

Clear and present climate threat is creating havoc for all living things on the Earth and changing the very nature of the environment that we live within. The melting glaciers' landscapes that artist Daniela Molnar paints bear witness to climate change and to climate grief, as do the protests and actions of the world's youth.

When Hurricane Harvey destroyed thousands of homes and forced people to flee and seek shelter, I felt the climate grief that they must have been experiencing. Some of our friends' homes were flooded, and their neighborhoods were under siege. During the aftermath of Hurricane Harvey, I created four paintings. One of the paintings shows a family fleeing along a flooded street in Houston. The young boy's expression and body motion shows the fear he is experiencing because of this devastating storm. Fortunately his parents and older sister are by his side. In another painting a Houston police officer carries a mother and her thirteen-month-old son from the city's flooded streets.[300]

---

[299] Juanita Constible, "Let's Talk about Climate Grief and Anxiety," National Resources Defense Council, October 8, 2019, retrieved February 26, 2021, https://www.nrdc.org/experts/juanita-constible/lets-talk-about-climate-grief-and-anxiety.
[300] These paintings can be viewed at theosart.space.

9.3. BLOG POST, 25 APRIL 2021: THE CASE OF CENSORSHIP OF JAMES HANSEN, CLIMATE SCIENTIST

Climate change is an existential threat to the Earth. We've known this for a long time. In 1896 the Swedish scientist Svante Arrhenius published a report in which he said that the burning of fossil fuels will add carbon dioxide to the atmosphere, resulting in higher temperatures.

In the twenty-first century, report after report from the IPCC[301] has provided scientific information relevant to understanding human-induced climate change; its natural, political, and economic impacts; and risks and possible ways to mitigate climate change. The Sixth Assessment Report (2021)[302] indicates an increasing human footprint resulting in higher temperatures (hot extremes)[303] on every continent, heavy precipitation in some regions of each continent, and increases in agricultural and ecological drought.

The advances of understanding climate change have taken a long time and have met much resistance from politicians, government appointees, and business and industry, especially the petrochemical and fossil fuel industries. Censorship of science is a global issue[304] that has been exacerbated by the Republican administrations of Ronald Reagan, George H. W. Bush, George W. Bush, and Donald Trump, or whenever the majority leadership was held by the Republicans.

One of the first scientists who worked on global warming for more than three decades faced the same kind of treatment as other scientists whose work was condemned and ridiculed, including Rachel Carson,[305] Alice Augusta Ball,[306] Hedley Marston,[307] and Anthony

---

[301] The Intergovernmental Panel on Climate Change, IPCC, 2021, https://www.ipcc.ch/.
[302] "Sixth Assessment Report, *Climate Change 2021: The Physical Science Basis*," IPCC, 2021, https://www.ipcc.ch/assessment-report/ar6/.
[303] During the summer of 2021, the northwest region of the United States and British Columbia experienced one heat dome after another, resulting in the highest temperatures ever recorded in some of the cities in the region.
[304] Euan G. Ritchie, Don A. Driscoll, and Martine Maron, "Science Censorship Is a Global Issue," *Nature* 542 (2017): 165, https://doi.org/10.1038/542165b.
[305] Mark Stoll, "The Personal Attacks on Rachel Carson as a Woman Scientist," Environment & Society Portal, March 5, 2020, http://www.environmentandsociety.org/exhibitions/rachel-carsons-silent-spring/personal-attacks-rachel-carson-woman-scientist.
[306] Esi Edugyan, "The Silencing of Black Scientists, *Boundless*, November 8, 2019, retrieved February 1, 2021, https://unbound.com/boundless/2019/11/08/the-silencing-of-black-scientists/.
[307] Roger Cross, *Fallout: Hedley Marston and the British Bomb Tests in Australia* (Kent Town, South Australia: Wakefield Press, 2001).

Fauci.[308] The scientist I'm speaking about is James Hansen, former director of the NASA Goddard Institute for Space Studies. He is now an adjunct professor directing the Program of Climate Science, Awareness and Solutions at Columbia University's Earth Institute.

In 1988 Hansen testified before the United States Congress saying that "he was 99 percent certain the Earth was warmer then than it had ever been measured to be, there was a clear cause and effect relationship with the greenhouse effect, and lastly that due to global warming, the likelihood of freak weather was steadily increasing."[309] In his book on Hansen, Mark Bowen says it became clear that Hansen's ideas were the result of him facing headwinds from climate science deniers.

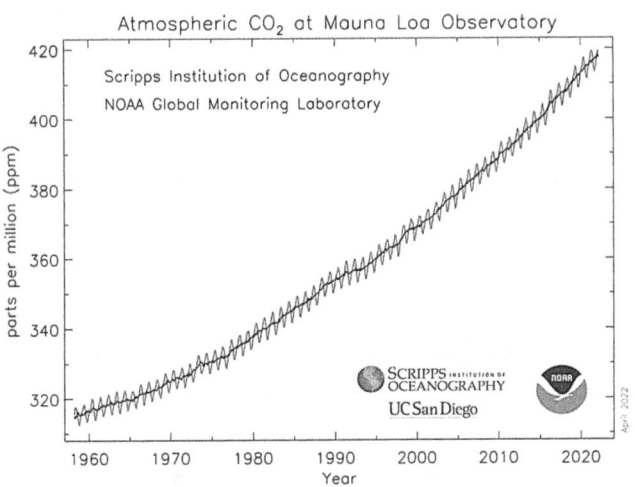

Figure 10. The Keeling curve: atmospheric CO_2 annual average amount measured at Mauna Loa Observatory 1960–2020. Credit: NOAA Global Monitoring Laboratory

I want to point out that Hansen, in 1976, published one of the earliest papers on greenhouse gases.[310] In this paper he reported that the non-carbon-dioxide gases, such as methane, nitrous oxide, and fluorinated gases, trap more heat, becoming important greenhouse

---

[308] Charlotte Klein, "Trump Health Officials Reportedly Tried to Censor Fauci's COVID Messaging," *Vanity Fair*, September 12, 2020, retrieved October 11, 2021, https://www.vanityfair.com/news/2020/09/trump-health-officials-reportedly-tried-to-censor-faucis-covid-messaging.
[309] Mark Bowen, *Censoring Science: Inside the Political Attack on Dr. James Hansen and the Truth of Global Warming* (New York: Dutton, 2008).
[310] W. C. Wang, Y. L. Yung, A. A. Lacis, T. Mo, and J. E. Hansen, "Greenhouse Effects Due to Man-Made Perturbation of Trace Gases," *Science* 194, no. 4266 (1976): 685–690, https://doi.org/10.1126/science.194.4266.685.

gases. However, it wasn't until 2007 that the EPA would start monitoring greenhouse gases.

James Hansen was convinced that he needed to share his research as widely as possible. He began by giving the Keeling talk, "Is There Still Time to Avoid 'Dangerous Anthropogenic Interference' with Global Climate?"[311] at the American Geophysical Union meeting in San Francisco. The Keeling talk is in honor of Charles David Keeling, the scientist who monitored carbon dioxide at the Mauna Loa Observatory beginning in 1958 (Figure 10).

After this and other talks, Hansen was admonished by political operatives within NASA to seek preclearance for any future media interviews, speeches, and web postings. Despite these rebukes, Hansen blew the whistle and asserted a scientist's right and responsibility to call attention to research findings and their implications for society. Hanson spoke out during George W. Bush's administration while it attempted to dissuade him from speaking freely. Finally Hansen was convinced that the United States and other countries needed to act on reducing global fossil fuel emissions now rather than later.

At the height of the censorship controversy, a top NASA administrator secretly gutted the budget for the agency's Earth scientist (Hansen) by 20 percent. Hansen would have none of it. He circulated a letter widely within the scientific community entitled "Swift Boating, Stealth Budgeting, and Unitary Executives."[312] Hansen's research on climate change conflicted with the high-level NASA administrators and the Bush White House. Hansen believes that someone within NASA changed the mission of NASA from "to understand and protect our home planet" to "to pioneer the future in space exploration, scientific discovery, and aeronautics research." To this Hansen replied that "to protect our home planet" was erased by "the slimy belly of a slug crawling in the night."

For two decades, Jim Hanson's research was subdued and

---

[311] "Censorship of Federal Climate Scientists: The Critical Case of Jim Hansen," Government Accountability Project, February 3, 2006, retrieved February 2, 2021, https://whistleblower.org/general/whistleblowers/censorship-of-federal-climate-scientists-the-critical-case-of-jim-hansen/.

[312] J. Hansen, "Swift Boating, Stealth Budgeting, and Unitary Executives," ResearchGate, November 1, 2006, retrieved August 30, 2021, https://www.researchgate.net/publication/293773830_Swift_boating_stealth_budgeting_and_unitary_executives.

undermined by three Republican administrations: Ronald Reagan, George H. W. Bush, and George W. Bush. Even when Clinton was president, the Democrats lost the Senate and House of Representatives in 1996, stalemating any progress on climate policy. This was the first time Republicans held both houses since the 1950s. It wouldn't be until Barack Obama came into power in 2009 that the Democrats could make any progress on climate and environmental science. But that lasted only two years, before the Republicans took back the House and Senate. As I explain ahead, Donald Trump's administration caused enormous harm to environmental regulations and climate change policy. We now must wonder what will happen under President Biden if his party loses control of the House or the Senate in the next election.

9.4. BLOG POST, 1 OCTOBER 2021: CLIMATE CHANGE THREAT

Kip Ault, in his book *Beyond Science Standards*, provides detailed examples of how elementary through high school students use a variety of tools to study weather and atmospheric patterns to understand the nature of climate science. The research that these students are doing is comparable to research done by EPA scientists.[313]

CLIMATE DENIAL

One of the most serious problems that we face in the context of climate change is those deniers that distort climatology to support their political and economic views. For example, some researchers have commented that climate change science has been distorted, and at the same time science is evoked as a defense. They describe how a handful of scientists obscured the truth not only about climate change, but also issues related to tobacco and vaccines. As they point out, the climate change deniers use the same playbook that big tobacco firms used to convince the public that smoking tobacco was not associated with cancer.[314]

---

[313] Charles R. Ault Jr., *Beyond Science Standards* (Lanham, MD: Rowman & Littlefield, 2021).
[314] Naomi Oreskes and Erik M. Conway, *Merchants of Doubt: How a Handful of Scientists Obscured the Truth on Issues from Tobacco Smoke to Global Warming* (New York: Bloomsbury Press, 2010).

The chief denier is Donald Trump, along with a slew of Republicans in Congress, who claim that global warming is a hoax perpetuated by the Chinese. Trump withdrew the US from the Paris Agreement, an international treaty within the United Nations Framework Convention on Climate Change. Trump and his associates claim that the accords will undermine the US economy, and at the same time, they deny that global warming is undermining and changing environments throughout the Earth.

Addressing climate change stagnated during the Trump administration. On many occasions, Trump refused to accept warnings from scientists, governors, and natural resources officials that increasing air and ocean temperatures were driving hurricanes, superstorms, and ravaging fires.

The Trump administration refused to acknowledge the facts that show how temperature rise has resulted in raising sea levels, melting glaciers, flooding coastal cities, increasing the number of Category 4 and 5 hurricanes that reach land and producing serious canopy fires, which burn to the tops of trees. Some of these wildfires are so big, they create their own weather. Wind patterns can change, but more dangerous are low pressures that are created around the fire, allowing air to rush in and create fire-induced winds. Fire tornadoes and fire clouds (pyrocumulonimbus clouds) can be formed by fire-induced winds.[315]

The EPA released a climate report in May 2021 that was hidden or delayed by the Trump administration.[316] The delay was not surprising, given the rebuke of science by Trump. The last time a climate report was released by the EPA was in 2016. The climate report, according to law, is published every four years, so visiting the EPA climate change indicators page was refreshing. EPA scientists, who had done the work three years earlier, finally had their work published and available to the American public.

During Trump's time in office, the effects of climate change were stunning yet ignored by his administration. Hurricanes, flooding, and fires caused billions of dollars in damages as well as staggering human

---

[315] Matt Simon, "California Wildfires Can Create Their Own Terrifying Weather," *Wired*, August 21, 2020, retrieved May 21, 2021, https://www.wired.com/story/california-wildfires-can-create-terrifying-weather/.

[316] "Climate Change Indicators in the United States," Environmental Protection Agency, May 3, 2021, https://www.epa.gov/climate-indicators.

loss. Much of the human suffering has disproportionally affected Black people, Indigenous people, and people of color.

Climate change is also a driving force in Central American migration. Trump treated woman and children who approached the US border inhumanely, many of whom traveled more than 2,000 miles (about twice the distance from Florida to New York City) on foot. Researchers have documented that climate displacement is especially prevalent in Guatemala, El Salvador, and Honduras, also known as the Northern Triangle. These countries have experienced climate-related impacts including food insecurity, recurring droughts, decline in agricultural production, increased vulnerability to disease, and water scarcity. Experts predict that climate change will displace up to 3.9 million people (about twice the population of New Mexico) across Mexico and Central America by 2050.[317]

CLIMATE GENERATION

Sarah Jaquette Ray, in her book *A Field Guide to Climate Anxiety*, explains that we are the "climate generation" and we live in the Anthropocene, a geological age marked by the way humans have affected the climate and environment in irreversible ways.[318] In an article published in *Scientific American*, she points out that climate anxiety is overwhelmingly a white phenomenon.[319] She says that white response to climate change is suffocating to people of color. To her, climate anxiety operates like white fragility, sucking up all the resources toward soothing the dominant group. The migrants coming to the southern border were labeled by Trump as rapists, criminals, and drug dealers. We know these characterizations are not true.

In *A Field Guide to Climate Anxiety*, Ray incorporates the idea of "resilience" as the best condition for thriving in a climate-changed world. She says this about resilience:

---

[317] "Shelter from the Storm: Policy Options to Address Climate-Induced Displacement from the Northern Triangle," Human Rights Network, April 22, 2021, retrieved April 24, 2021, https://www.humanrightsnetwork.org/climate-change-and-displaced-persons.
[318] Ray, *A Field Guide to Climate Anxiety*.
[319] Sarah Jaquette Ray, "Climate Anxiety Is an Overwhelmingly White Phenomenon," *Scientific American*, March 21, 2021, retrieved February 11, 2022, https://www.scientificamerican.com/article/the-unbearable-whiteness-of-climate-anxiety/.

Resilience must be advocated for in culturally sensitive ways, with acknowledgment that the crises of environmental change have been impacting Indigenous peoples around the globe since the age of expansion, beginning as early as the fifteenth century. Climate change is not an impending future crisis. It is an extension of ongoing extinctions, destabilization, and rapid environmental transformation. We should resist crisis narratives for the reasons I have presented in this book, but also because they perpetuate the erasure of these legacies.[320]

EMPTY WORDS

Climate grief—a feeling of despair, anxiety, or fear that causes people to feel helpless and overwhelmed—has impacted the lives of our youth. As mentioned earlier, Greta Thunberg cut school on a Friday and sat in front of the Parliament House in Stockholm. This action inspired millions of teenagers around the world to join her in an international movement to protest governments to do something about climate change. Teenagers joined her to strike from school on Fridays and to organize rallies and conferences on climate change.

However, even though governments and organizations invite teenagers to conferences and meetings, there are questions about the motivation for these gatherings. Greta Thunberg recently challenged the adults who organized a conference in Milan, Italy, in September 2021, a month before the COP26 meeting in Glasgow. The COP26 is United Nations' twenty-sixth climate change conference.

The conference in Milan, Youth4Climate: Driving Ambition and Pre-COP26, brought together four hundred youths from 197 member countries of the United Nations Framework Convention on Climate Change. The Milan person-to-person conference followed nine #Youth4ClimateLive series of interactive virtual episodes covering a wide range of climate topics in 2020 and 2021. Each episode was a discussion put on by the Italian Ministry of Ecological Transition and

---

[320] Ray, *A Field Guide to Climate Anxiety*, 140–141.

the United Nations Secretary General's Envoy on Youth.

For several years the world's youth have protested and marched to speak out and act against government's lack of action on climate change. Greta Thunberg is one of the most decisive and esteemed leaders among the youth of the world. At the conference in Milan, she ripped into adult leadership and asserted that they have done nothing but "blah, blah, blah" for the past thirty years.[321] She said the leaders of this conference cherry-pick attendees and "pretend they are listening to us, but they are not." At stake is bringing the warming of the planet under control, which means preventing a temperature increase of no more than 1.5 degrees Celsius.

According to Dr. Katja Frieler at the Potsdam Institute for Climate Impact Research in Germany, to remove the burden and lessen the grief experienced by children and youth, we need to phase out fossil fuel use. If this change is done, then planetary warming will be limited to 1.5 degrees Celsius.[322]

9.5. BLOG POST, 15 OCTOBER 2021: A LIFE DEFINED BY THE BOMB

This is a guest post written by Roger Cross, PhD, a science educator and writer from Bura, Australia. He was professor of science education at LaTrobe University, Melbourne, Australia. He is a highly regarded and respected science educator and author of many books and research papers in the field of science education. Among his books, two are about his research into the British bomb tests in Australia.

Cross's book *Fallout*[323] was the basis of the film *Silent Storm* produced by the National Film and Sound Archive of Australia. The film follows celebrated scientist Hedley Marston's attempt to blow the whistle on radioactive fallout from the British atomic tests.

---

[321] Stephen Jewkes and Giulio Piovaccari, "30 Years of 'Blah Blah Blah': Thunberg Questions Italy Climate Talks," Reuters, September 28, 2021, retrieved September 29, 2021, https://www.reuters.com/world/europe/protests-proposals-activists-face-climate-talks-test-2021-09-28/.
[322] Katja Frieler is the IPCC lead author for Key Risks Across Sectors and Regions in the 6th Assessment Report of Working Group 2. She has published more than seventy peer-reviewed articles on climate change and was named a Highly Cited Researcher in 2020.
[323] Cross, *Fallout*.

THE TRUMP FILES

Beyond Belief: The British Bomb Tests: Australia's Veterans Speak Out, coauthored by Cross and Avon Hudson, tells the stories of people who were directly involved in the British bomb testing. They also expose how government and scientists secretly supported the British, who were desperate to develop their own bomb. They report harrowing stories of how the bomb tests carried fallout around the country, affecting unsuspecting citizens as well as active service members. Many people affected by the bomb tests died of cancer and were in a sense guinea pigs for the British and Australian governments.[324]

Roger is a close friend and colleague. He and I worked together on the GTP while he was on sabbatical at GSU in the 1990s. He asked several Australian schools to join the GTP and teachers from these schools attended GTP Summer Institutes in Atlanta along with American, Czech Republic, Russian, and Spanish teachers.

> My name is Roger Cross (born 1941), and I grew up in the shadow of possible nuclear war. I remember vividly the little British government booklet informing us how to survive an atomic explosion in London. My parents took the information very seriously and believed it. We were to cover windows with newspapers and to shelter in the bath! As a teenager, I learned about the Campaign for Nuclear Disarmament (CND) and witnessed the greatest of all the rallies against nuclear weapons in Trafalgar Square, London. The philosopher and mathematician Bertrand Russell was its early chair, and many prominent figures in British life joined the movement. CND became a household slogan, but to no avail.
>
> After I moved to Adelaide, South Australia, in 1966, I was astonished to find that Australia, too, had played a part in the proliferation of nuclear weapons. The British were determined to build their own atomic bombs. When the USA and Canada

---

[324] American atomic and nuclear bomb testing was on a gigantic scale compared to what Cross and Hudson report about the British bomb testing. On each continent, atomic weapons affect millions of people who were near or in the path of nuclear fallout. In each case the Australian/British government and the American government failed to warn its citizens of the effects of testing nuclear weapons in the atmosphere and underground. Underground testing was just as dangerous as exploding bombs in the air or at the surface.

refused to allow them to explode their bombs in their countries, they turned to Australia. At that time, the early 1950s, it must be said that we Australians were sycophantic when it came to our relations with Britain. The government gave enthusiastic permission.

From 1952 to 1957, twelve atomic bombs were exploded on Australian soil, the majority at Maralinga in the far west of South Australia. I spent many years researching this terrible legacy and came to admire the only senior Australian scientist to oppose these tests. His name was Dr. Hedley Marston, and he worked for the government's scientific agency. Hedley found iodine-131 and strontium-90 contamination over large tracts of the continent. He did what he could to expose what he called the "gangster scientists" of Great Britain.

I presented a talk at a Hiroshima Day conference and met a military veteran of the British bomb tests. We wrote about the ordinary servicemen who were exposed to ionizing radiation while working at the test sites. These are chilling stories.[325]

9.6. BLOG POST, 20 OCTOBER 2021: THE NUCLEAR RISK

St. Mary's is a small town on the coast of Georgia at the border with Florida. In a graduate environmental education course, thirty students accompanied me as we boarded the Cumberland Island Ferry at St. Mary's dock to reach the barrier island of the same name. It's home to loggerhead turtles and feral horses, and very few humans. It's one of fifteen barrier islands along the Georgia coastline. Barrier islands are coastal landforms made of a type of sand dune system that are formed by wave and tidal action parallel to the coastline. They typically occur in chains, as they do along the Georgia coast.[326] Barrier islands are separated from the mainland usually by bays or rivers leading to the open ocean.

---

[325] Roger Cross and Avon Hudson, *Beyond Belief: The British Bomb Tests: Australia's Veterans Speak Out* (Kent Town, Adelaide: Wakefield Press, 2005).
[326] I have taken graduate students (mostly Atlanta-area middle and high school teachers) to four of Georgia's barrier islands including Skidaway, Sapelo, Jekyll, and Cumberland Islands.

Separating Cumberland Island and the mainland is Kings Bay, which opens to the Atlantic Ocean. It's also home to the Kings Bay Naval Submarine Base, the US Atlantic Fleet's home port for Navy fleet ballistic missile nuclear submarines armed with Trident missile nuclear weapons. A Trident is a submarine-launched ballistic missile armed with multiple nuclear bombs. Kings Bay has been in use since 1979. It's a big base with more than 16,000 acres of land, including 4,000 acres of protected wetlands.

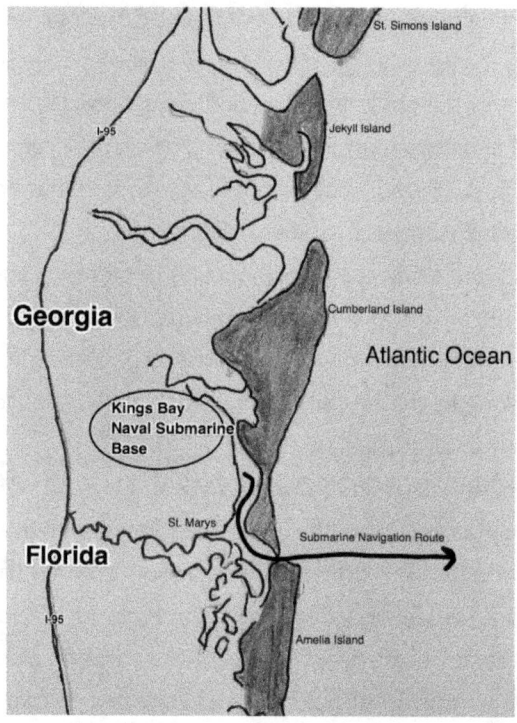

Figure 11. Map of Georgia Barrier Islands near the Kings Bay Naval Submarine Base.

On April 4, 2018, a group of seven Catholic peace activists broke into the Kings Bay Naval Submarine Base and engaged in a nuclear weapons protest. They cut through a wire barrier and left symbolic messages to convey their belief that nuclear weapons would result in omnicide—the destruction of all people. In their 2019 trial, they were found guilty on three felony counts and a misdemeanor charge. Critics of the trial believe the judge, Lisa Godbey Wood, prevented the defendants from mounting a full defense. They were not allowed to mention their religious motivations or any mention of international law or treaties restricting nuclear weapons. They were sentenced to two to five years in prison.

The US government implemented a program for the peaceful use of nuclear weapons and called it Project Plowshare (the USSR did the same thing). Exploding nuclear bombs in the atmosphere or underground and calling this "peaceful nuclear explosion" was part of a larger goal of exploiting the "peaceful" uses of the atom.

An antinuclear group began the Plowshares movement. They initially broke into the General Electric Division in King of Prussia, Pennsylvania. Re-entry vehicles for the Minuteman II missiles were made here. The Plowshares group hammered on two re-entry vehicles, poured blood on documents, and offered prayers for peace.

Ever since atomic bombs were dropped on Japan, scientists and citizens around the world began to be increasingly concerned about the destructive power of these weapons. A scientist that I met at the Unitarian Universalist Church in Atlanta (of which I was a member) worked at the Centers for Disease Control, which was located just a few miles from our church. While in a group discussion, he told us he had been a young scientist working at Los Alamos when the atom bomb was developed. He was ashamed that he worked with others to develop the bomb. People in the group gave him great comfort, but he wanted us to know that he wasn't the project's only scientist who felt this way.

The goal of antinuclear activists is to ban nuclear weapons and work toward the elimination of them. The Treaty on the Prohibition of Nuclear Weapons was adopted in 2017 and is a comprehensive treaty to attain a nuclear-free world agreed to by eighty-six nations. Although the treaty is in effect, all the nations that have nuclear weapons abstained from voting. The two nuclear weapons that were dropped on Hiroshima and Nagasaki and the worldwide testing that was done created great risk to people living in areas where testing took place, especially Australia, the United States, the Soviet Union, and the South Pacific.

TRUMP AND NUCLEAR WEAPONS

The nuclear threat is rarely discussed.[327] But it should be. These are weapons of mass destruction. I decided to examine the cost of the US spending on its nuclear program. Here is what I found. From 1940 to 1998, the United States spent $5.5 trillion on nuclear weapons and weapon-related programs.[328] Most of this money (86 percent) was spent on launch systems—B52 bombers, nuclear submarines, and missiles.

During the period of 1999–2019, the US spent on average $45 billion each year. The Congressional Budget Office is required by law to project the ten-year costs of nuclear forces every two years. For the period of 2021–2030, the Department of Defense's and the Department of Energy's combined costs would be $634 billion, or slightly more than $60 billion a year.[329] Over two-thirds of the costs would be for ballistic missiles and nuclear laboratories.

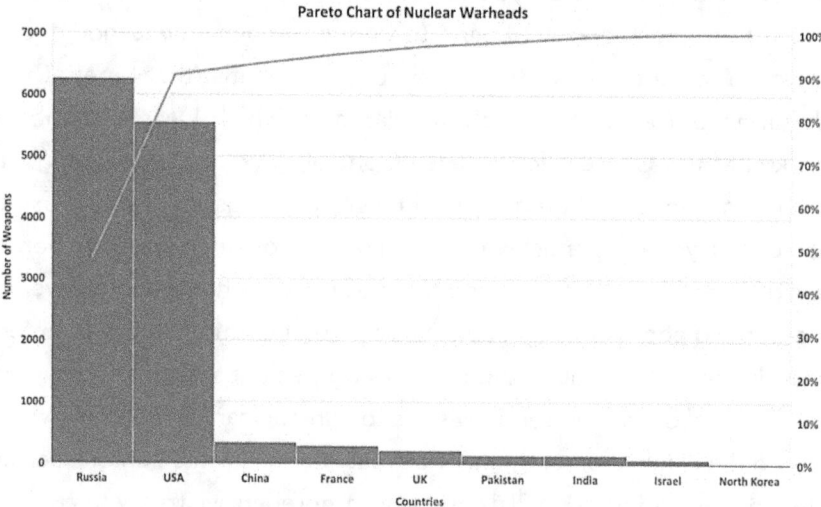

Figure 12. Pareto chart of the number and percentage of nuclear weapons by country in 2021 showing the individual values for each country and the cumulative total represented by the line.

---

[327] There are more than 13,000 nuclear weapons in the world spread unevenly among nine countries. The US and Russia account for more than 90 percent of them. There are several organizations that report on nuclear weapons. These include the Ploughshares Fund, the Federation of American Scientists, and the Bulletin of the Atomic Scientists' Nuclear Notebook.
[328] Stephen I. Schwartz, "The Hidden Costs of Our Nuclear Arsenal: Overview of Project Findings," (Presentation, Brookings Institution, Washington, DC, June 30, 1998), retrieved September 15, 2021, https://www.brookings.edu/the-hidden-costs-of-our-nuclear-arsenal-overview-of-project-findings/.
[329] Congressional Budget Office, May 2021, retrieved September 15, 2021, https://www.cbo.gov/system/files/2021-05/57130-Nuclear-Forces.pdf.

In 2016, Congress approved a nuclear weapons spending plan that will cost taxpayers $1.7 trillion between 2017 and 2046. This expenditure represents 6 percent of all national defense spending for that period. The plan calls for improved nuclear delivery systems, nuclear warheads, and supporting infrastructure. China and Russia are also investing in their nuclear capabilities, continuing the Cold War arms race.

The United States possesses 1,650 strategic nuclear warheads, while Russia has 1,700 nuclear warheads. There are seven additional countries that have nuclear arsenals: China (350 weapons), France (300 weapons), UK (225 weapons), India (150 weapons), Pakistan (150 weapons), Israel (80 weapons), and North Korea (20 weapons).

Throughout Trump's term in office, many had great concern about his mental stability and feared that he might unleash a nuclear attack on China, Iran, or North Korea. After the 2020 election, General Mark A. Milley called his counterpart in China and assured him that the US would not launch a nuclear attack on his country. If it did, Milley told General Li Zuocheng of China's People's Liberation Army that he would call to warn him. Milley called Li Zuocheng again on January 8, 2021, after the attack on Congress.

I know what I'm about say sounds bizarre, but Trump wondered: If we have so many nuclear weapons, why don't we use them? He even threatened North Korea with nuclear weapons. He said, "North Korea best not make any more threats to the United States." If they do, "They will be met with fire and fury like the world has never seen." He later met a couple of times with North Korea's Kim Jong-un and made up.

A BRIEF HISTORY OF NUCLEAR WEAPONS

In 1945 the United States dropped atomic bombs on the Japanese cities of Hiroshima and Nagasaki, killing between 129,000 and 226,000 civilians and soldiers.

The United States conducted 1,032 nuclear tests between 1945 and 1992: at the Nevada National Security Site; at sites in the Pacific Ocean; in Amchitka Island of the Alaska Peninsula; and in Colorado, Mississippi, and New Mexico. Fallout downwind contained radionuclides and gases transported thousands of miles away from the Nevada National Security Site by wind. A radionuclide is a radioactive form of an element. When a nuclear explosion occurs, about twelve different radionuclides are produced, including iodine and cobalt-60. People living in the US during these years were exposed to varying levels of radiation. The American government released very little information warning people of potential effects of nuclear fallout. Fallout of radiation moved through the food chain causing cancerous diseases.

In Area 10 of Yucca Flat at the Nevada National Security Site, a shallow (636 feet) underground nuclear test was conducted on July 6, 1962, to investigate the use of nuclear weapons for mining, cratering, and other civilian purposes such as open-pit mines, railroad and highway cuts, and dams. The program was called Project Plowshare. Plumes of radioactive fallout from this test contaminated more people in the US than any other nuclear test carried out by the US military. Radionuclides carried to the east over Nebraska, South Dakota, and Illinois and continued eastward toward the Atlantic Ocean, bringing lower levels of nucleotides. At the time, I was living in Boston, which would have been in the path of minor levels of fallout. The test released 7 percent of all radioactive fallout on the US since testing began. The government dropped the idea of using nuclear weapons for excavation; however, it continued testing devices until 1992.

In 1962 the US and the Soviet Union came close to a nuclear holocaust when the US learned that the USSR was installing medium- and intermediate-range missiles in Cuba. Although the United States held an overwhelming nuclear weapons advantage over the Soviet Union, the nuclear age became front and center of international policy and politics. The American and Soviet people did not know the truth about nuclear weapons until many years later. We were told to shield ourselves with aluminum foil and newspaper and hide in the bathtub. Weapons were being used like chess pieces as one side confronted the other. Little has been done to make the world safer from nuclear weapons. No country should have these weapons.

In 1969, President Richard Nixon ordered nuclear bombers to be put on standby for an immediate strike after North Korea shot down an

American spy plane.[330] Recent documents show that there was a plan to target twelve military targets each with a nuclear bomb. These bombs were at least twenty times as powerful of those used on Hiroshima and Nagasaki in 1945. The plan was scrapped soon after it was ordered.

However, in 1974 on the eve of Richard Nixon resigning as president, many were so concerned about his drunken state that the nuclear football that normally accompanies the president was removed from his presence during his last two hours before flying Nixon back to California after he resigned.[331]

In September 1983, while I was in Moscow in a meeting among AHP and Soviet researchers just days after Korean Air Lines Flight 007 was shot out of the skies by the Soviets, a Soviet satellite report showing incoming US nuclear missiles was received at Serpukhov-15, the secret bunker outside Moscow. Lieutenant Colonel Stanislav Petrov, the duty officer, felt the report was a false alarm. He acted on a hunch that the report, which indicated only five incoming American missiles, was wrong. If it were an attack, there would have been hundreds of missiles. He was right. And because he reported a false alarm to his superior officers, the world escaped nuclear war.[332] The false alarm was triggered by reflections from the tops of clouds. A similar episode happened in 1995 when, again, Russia thought it was under attack and nearly launched a nuclear strike.

On January 13, 2018, a ballistic missile alert was accidentally issued over television, radio, and cellphones in Hawaii. The alert stated that there was an incoming ballistic missile threat to the state and that citizens should seek shelter; the message concluded, "This is not a drill." After more than a half an hour, officials called off the alert, blaming the message on a miscommunication during a drill. However, millions of people were traumatized. Cynthia Lazaroff, founder of Women Transforming Our Nuclear Legacy and NuclearWakeUpCall, was in

---

[330] Chris McGreal, "Papers Reveal Nixon Plan for North Korea Nuclear Strike," *The Guardian*, July 7, 2010, retrieved September 17, 2021, https://www.theguardian.com/world/2010/jul/07/nixon-north-korea-nuclear-strike.
[331] Garrett M. Graff, "The Madman and the Bomb," *Politico Magazine*, August 11, 2017, retrieved September 17, 2021, https://www.politico.com/magazine/story/2017/08/11/donald-trump-nuclear-weapons-richard-nixon-215478/.
[332] Tony Long, "Sept. 26, 1983: The Man Who Saved the World by Doing...Nothing," *Wired*, September 26, 2007, https://www.wired.com/2007/09/dayintech-0926-2/.

THE TRUMP FILES

Hawaii and actually made phone calls to loved ones.[333] Cynthia is also founder of the US–Russia Exchange Initiatives, a project that began in 1983 at the same time that the AHP Soviet Exchange Program began.

Since the advent of these weapons, the US has had dozens of nuclear accidents, including the dropping of two live atomic bombs on North Carolina on January 23, 1961.[334] In fact, a commander of US nuclear forces said that the real nuclear threat to America is an accident.

9.7 BLOG POST, 1 NOVEMBER 2021: PROMOTING GLOBAL COLLABORATION IN A WORLD OF EXISTENTIAL THREATS

During the years of Trump, global collaboration was diminished to a whimper. Banning people from Muslim nations and making it difficult for people from other countries to secure visas removed the power of citizens interacting with each other in a framework of trust and acceptance.

Decades ago, in the later part of the twentieth century, there was a movement to engage students and teachers to work across the world to participate in localized and global ecological investigations. The emergence of new technologies increased the opportunities to bring people to communicate with each other. The GTP[335] was developed during this period along with other initiatives such as Global Lab[336] and the International Education and Resource Network (iEARN).[337]

The GTP was a collaboration among researchers, teachers, students, and parents from the United States and Russia, as well Australia, the Czech Republic, and Spain. The GTP emerged during a time when the internet was in its infancy and becoming a way for people to communicate with each other. Educators grasped onto the internet as a tool of collaboration.

What follows here are discussions I had with educators from Spain, the United States, and Russia. Each of the educators explains why

---

[333] Women Transforming Our Nuclear Legacy: nuclearwakeupcall.earth/women-s-project.
[334] Bill Newcott, "Remembering the Night Two Atomic Bombs Fell on North Carolina," *National Geographic: History & Culture*, January 26, 2022, retrieved February 12, 2022, https://www.nationalgeographic.com/history/article/remembering-night-two-atomic-bombs-dropped-on-north-carolina.
[335] Jack Hassard, "Teaching Students to Think Globally," *Journal of Humanistic Psychology* 37 no. 1 (1997): 24–63, https://doi.org/10.1177/00221678970371003.
[336] Global Lab was developed by TERC in Concord, Massachusetts, and was a science program used by schools around the world.
[337] iEARN is a worldwide network comprised of thousands of schools in more than 140 countries. iEARN has been an active project since 1989. https://iearn.org/.

cross-cultural collaboration is important and how they contributed to fostering international relations.

TEACHING ABOUT THE EARTH IS NOT AS IMPORTANT AS TEACHING IN OR FOR THE EARTH

Narcís Vives is an educator from Barcelona. I've known Narcís since 1992 and worked with him on several telecommunication projects. He is one of the most experienced educators using international telecommunications to link students and teachers together on common problems. Vives points out that "being an individual changemaker is not enough." He reminds us that when each and every one of us tries to individually change things for the better, "the results are poor, although better than nothing."[338]

Vives and many others have been involved in global collaboration projects for decades. He explains that "when we, teachers and students, collaborate, sharing the same vision and trying together to solve environmental or social problems, the results are great."

Vives and his colleagues in Spain and more than twenty-two Latin American countries have found that it's worth inviting teachers and students to participate in international telecommunication projects. However, he says that "projects that deal with the quality of life on our planet should be for learning with the world, not just about it." Traditional teaching has overemphasized "teaching about" ideas rather than showing students how to be involved within those ideas.

Global collaboration should begin with a strong local curriculum that helps students think locally. Vives says, "I am in favor of a local curriculum that invites students to learn about different aspects of their neighborhood: places, people, and data. Students' contributions should be meaningful and useful for the local community because when this happens, it is the whole village, neighborhood, or local community that learns."

Being open to collaborating globally is essential for dealing with the economic, social, and ecological problems that the world faces. During

---

[338] Narcís Vives (president of Itinerarium Foundation, founding member of International Education and Resources Network, honorary president of iEARN, cofounder of Clowns without Borders, director of Atlas of Diversity, and former teacher, Barcelona), email interview with the author, September 18, 2021.

the Trump administration, work across cultures was denied and exasperated by bans on Muslim citizens from traveling to the United States and the denigration of immigrants approaching the US southern border.

In our experience, students' ideas about the world grow when they are involved in global telecommunications projects. As Vives points out, successful global projects occur "when we are linked with and involved in common projects with different schools around the world." He adds that "we can share our best experiences, learn from others, and have an open dialogue about controversial issues or problems that arise. When this happens, we are creating a global network for learning and change, and we are making a meaningful contribution for the planet and its people."

YOUTH EMPOWERMENT

Ramon Barlam, professor of Social Sciences at the Institut Cal Gravat in Manresa, Spain, is a colleague and friend that I met in 1995 in Callús, a small community near Barcelona in the state of Catalonia. He is one of the world's pioneers in the use of the internet to connect students worldwide. He told me that he was lucky enough to discover the internet early on, and he "did so thinking that this tool would offer us a great chance not only to improve education but also to promote global friendship."[339] He regarded this early period as historical, and as he said, it "coincided with a project, the Global Thinking Project, and a teacher from Atlanta, Georgia."

Barlam became very involved in the GTP. He described that "at that time, I was working at L'Escola Joventut primary school in Callús, where we did a research project over the quality of the water of the Cardener River, which flows nearby. We also worked together with county institutions on the deforestation caused following the worst fires that we have suffered in Catalunya Central, those that took place in 1994. From the school we contributed to the reforestation of nearby forests as well as undertaking many other actions."

---

[339] Ramon Barlam (professor of social sciences at the Institut Cal Gravat, Manresa, teaching professional, K–College, member of LaceNet educational network and World Mobile City Project), email interview, September 17, 2021.

Barlam went on to say, "With this project and many others that followed which I took part in, we have tried to promote and foster youth empowerment to make a better world." Then he added, "Three decades later, the world has seen a distressing twist: the end of the Cold War has not led to times of stability and fair prosperity. The internet has not been able to keep the romantic spirit of its beginnings as it has succumbed to the big technological multinational greed."

In my communication with Ramon, he warns of the rise of authoritarianism by saying, "It is not only the rise of Donald Trump and Jair Bolsonaro in America and Brazil but also the resurgence of extreme right-wing political parties in Europe. In Hungary, France, and even in Germany the clamor for Hitler and radicalism resonates. In Spain the shadow of Franco, the fascist dictator, persists, and his followers walk down the streets with impunity openly hurling fascist anthems and military salutes." One is reminded of the "Unite the Right" rally in Charlottesville, which Donald Trump said had very fine people on both sides. It didn't.

In the context of where Barlam resides, he added this comment:

> We cannot forget that Spain is the country in the world, after Cambodia, with the largest number of murdered citizens for political reasons in ditches and common graves. As for Catalonia, a country which has peacefully demanded its independence, it has seen the Spanish government answer back with sheer violence against it. Watching the news programs on TV has become more and more depressing day after day.

FIGHTERS FOR THE ENVIRONMENT

The GTP designed a curriculum that would enhance collaborative environmental research and cross-cultural communication.[340] The American–Russian student and teacher exchanges made it possible for students to live and go to school with each other. Sara Crim, a

---

[340] Hassard and Weisberg, *Environmental Science on the Net*.

science educator and middle school science teacher from Walker County Schools in Georgia, participated in three student exchanges from 1995 to 1998. Crim was one of more than thirty-five American and thirty Russian teachers that participated in the GTP exchanges. Global collaboration among these educators was remarkable in that many have maintained communication with each other. By their willingness to embed themselves for weeks at a time in another culture, living in homes and teaching in a foreign nation, they helped their students become global collaborators and participants at the same time.

Crim said "to travel as a teacher from a small country school was such a rewarding experience. Each time I participated as a teacher in the GTP, my students and I were able to visit and live with Russian families in Moscow, St. Petersburg, and Chelyabinsk." In each city, she brought ten of her students, each of whom lived with a Russian family, as she did. She and her students reciprocated and hosted the Russians when they traveled to the northwest mountains of Georgia.

In an interview, she said that "during our exchanges we developed friendships and gained new families. Since finishing the project, some of my students have traveled back to Russia to visit their partners and have taken family members with them."[341]

Crim explained, "Students worked with each other at a distance and face-to-face on ecological projects such as an investigation of ground-level ozone and air pollution, an open-ended ecological study of a local stream, and other projects, including a study of the local environment, soil studies, and solid waste."

She reminded me that "from our participation in the GTP, we learned that people from entirely different cultures can work together and develop long-lasting friendships." She also told me that "we can learn to work together to solve problems that are important to our countries." She then emphasized that "problems are not so big when you can understand how a problem affects someone else in a way it doesn't affect you."

---

[341] Sara Crim (retired science teacher, Walker County Schools, Georgia, and artist, Pampa, Texas), email interview with the author, September 9, 2021.

JACK HASSARD

NEW TYPE OF THINKING

One of the leaders of the GTP in Russia was Dr. Anatoly Zakhlebny. He is an ecological researcher and educator and was instrumental in involving scientists and educators in the GTP. At the very last student conference held in Moscow, where there were one hundred American and Russian students plus thirty teachers, Zakhlebny invited twenty-five Russian scientists to mingle and talk with the students about their projects. It was not a competition, but a collaboration among students and scientists. The scientists wanted to find out what ideas students were working on and how they dealt with ecological issues.

Dr. Anatoly Zakhlebny, ecologist and chief researcher of the Federal State Institute for Development of Educational Strategy at the Russian Academy of Education and professor of pedagogical sciences provided leadership for the GTP throughout Russia. Here he is speaking to American middle and high school students and teachers from Georgia who had arrived in Moscow in October 1997 for a three-week exchange with five Russian schools in Moscow, St. Petersburg, Yaroslavl, and Chelyabinsk.

I asked Anatoly about the implementation of the GTP in Russia. He recounted, "For two decades, together with my colleagues from the Russian Academy of Education, we have tried to popularize the ideas of the Global Thinking Project among teachers in a number of Russian regions—in the Baikal region, in the Urals, in the Moscow region."[342] He conducted workshops to help teachers become acquainted with the method of integrating natural science with humanistic education.

He said that the humanistic ideas underlying the GTP were at least fifty years ahead of the mass consciousness of most people. He said, "For almost twenty-five years (after the Rio Summit 1992),[343] politicians and diplomats of many countries have mastered this type of thinking in order to reach agreement on the common goals of sustainable development." In his view, global thinking is the psychological basis for sustainable development goals. Global thinking is not unlike global citizenship or education for a global perspective.

GTP teachers and researchers viewed global collaboration as learning to see problems and issues through the eyes and minds of others. Project learning also incorporated empathy, being able to put oneself in another's shoes, and intercultural competence, which means being able to function within the norms and expectations of another culture. This is humanistic collaboration.[344]

According to Zakhlebny, "In Russia, we consider global thinking as an intellectual product of the integration of natural science knowledge about the modern scientific picture of the world and the general cultural value orientations of the individual in order to maintain established ecological quality and conditions of life of the environment."

At the end of my conversation with Anatoly, he said, "I regret that at the present stage, political relations between our countries are at a low level, and we cannot interact now on the ways of best conveying a new type of thinking about the common future on our planet to the young generation."

---

[342] Anatoly N. Zakhlebny (chief researcher of the Federal State Institute for Development of Educational Strategy at the Russian Academy of Education, professor, doctor of pedagogical sciences, and chairman of the Scientific Council on Environmental Education Problems of the Russian Academy of Education), email interview with the author, September 29, 2021.
[343] The Rio Summit 1992 was the United Nations Conference on Environment and Development held in Rio de Janeiro, Brazil.
[344] Hassard, *Teaching Students to Think Globally*.

PART V: COVID-19

> And then I see the disinfectant, where it knocks it out in a minute. One minute. And is there a way we can do something like that, by injection inside or almost a cleaning?
>
> —Donald J. Trump, April 23, 2020

INTRODUCTION

ON JANUARY 28, 2020, A MEETING WAS HELD IN THE OVAL Office. Donald Trump met with some of his national security team. He was told by National Security Advisor Robert O'Brien that the virus outbreak in China "will be the biggest national security threat you face in your presidency."[345] Another person in the room at the time said that this virus would not be anything like the 2003 SARS outbreak. SARS, or severe acute respiratory syndrome, is a viral respiratory illness caused by a coronavirus. According to Bob Woodward, O'Brien disagreed and defended his position of the virus being serious.

Indeed, Assistant National Security Advisor Matt Pottinger, who was also in the room, agreed with O'Brien. Pottinger had been in the Trump administration as a national security advisor since September 2019. He previously was a journalist and US Marine Corps officer. As a reporter, he wrote more than three dozen stories on the SARS epidemic. He spoke Mandarin Chinese and did reporting from China for seven years. He understood infectious diseases. During this meeting in the

---

[345] Woodward, *Rage*, xiii.

Oval Office, Pottinger explained to Trump that the virus in China would be as bad as the 1918 flu pandemic. He knew this outcome because he had been in touch with Chinese contacts whom he trusted and with whom he worked while he was in China.

So on January 28, Donald Trump found out that he would be facing the most serious health emergency in more than a century. Pottinger spoke out in the meeting and said to the president, "My contacts in China told me that there three factors that were accelerating the transmission of the disease. They said that contrary to some reports from the Chinese government, people were getting the disease easily from other people and it was being spread by people who didn't show any symptoms. This means a once-in-a-lifetime health emergency, a virus that's out of control."[346]

From this point on, Americans were put at risk by the failure of President Trump to heed the advice from his national security team. Instead of calling in the CDC and the National Institute of Allergy and Infectious Diseases (NIAID) for the latest research on the outbreak in China, he downplayed the disease and sidelined hundreds of scientists.

THE GREAT 1918 INFLUENZA PANDEMIC

A century ago, the world experienced the most lethal respiratory virus in human history. Early estimates were that 20 million people globally (about the population of New York) died from the disease. But recent research estimates that between 50 and 100 million people died out of a world population of 1.8 billion. Evidence shows that the influenza pandemic originated in Haskell County, Kansas, a small and remote area in the southwest corner of the state.[347] The first case was reported there. Camp Funston, a US Army training camp located on Fort Riley, southwest of Manhattan, Kansas, was visited by friends and family of the soldiers in the camp; some brought the influenza there, and it spread among the troops. Because Camp Funston was a training center, soldiers moved to other bases in the US and then to France, where WWI was

---

[346] Conversation based on Woodward, *Rage*.
[347] John M. Barry, "The Site of Origin of the 1918 Influenza Pandemic and Its Public Health Implications," *Journal of Translational Medicine*, January 20, 2004, retrieved April 5, 2022, https://www.ncbi.nlm.nih.gov/pmc/articles/PMC340389/.

raging. American soldiers traveling to France brought with them the virus that had already spread throughout the US. More than 650,000 Americans died in a matter of months.

The lessons from the 1918 flu pandemic are clear. Nonpharmaceutical methods, including keeping students out of school, banning public gatherings, and using isolation and quarantine are effective. They can mitigate the spread of a virus.

John Barry, author of *The Great Influenza: The Story of the Deadliest Plague in History*, says that truth is the most important lesson we can learn from the Great Influenza.[348] People need to tell the truth about the outbreak. Information from all levels of government needs to be based on facts and truthfulness. Anything short will result in alienation and suspicion.

The CDC has web pages about how to communicate during an outbreak or public health crisis. An important consideration for health officials is to realize that individuals will perceive the risk posed by the disease and then decide how they will deal with mitigation recommendations or orders by the government. During the coronavirus pandemic, the United States' messaging was incomplete and inconsistent, resulting in mixed messages by local and state governments. Some states were on lockdown, while other states were open for business. Florida, Georgia, and Texas lead the way in ignoring CDC guidelines. Some of my friends thought it was ironic that Georgia is on this list, given that the CDC is in Atlanta. Gatherings of hundreds of people at beaches and bars were common and resulted in what are known as super-spreader events.

School closures, limits on public gatherings, isolation, and quarantine were used during the Great Influenza in the United States. As I show Chapter 10, isolation and quarantine seem to be the most effective at preventing the disease, but mask wearing and social distancing are also important. The evidence today is that facial coverings may provide the most protection for yourself and others who might be in close contact with infected persons.

---

[348] John M. Barry, *The Great Influenza: The Story of the Deadliest Pandemic in History* (New York: Penguin Books, 2004).

However, in 1918, wearing masks was not an effective mitigation method, according to Barry.[349] Many western states enacted mask-wearing ordinances, yet people resisted wearing them. Most masks were homemade and lacked the quality that was needed to prevent exposure to the flu.

The face mask was pioneered by Dr. Wu Lien-teh, an epidemiologist who designed and used face masks after investigating a deadly disease outbreak in northeastern China in 1910.[350] Dr. Wu learned from this experience that the disease could be spread by respiratory droplets. A bacterium was responsible for the disease, which he identified as *Yersinia pestis*, known from earlier bubonic plagues. He produced a mask made from cotton and gauze with extra layers of cloth, a much-improved design over the one-layered "mouth bandage" developed by Johannes von Mikulicz in Breslau, Germany, around 1900.[351] Dr. Wu recommended that medical staff wear masks to protect themselves from disease carried by their patients. Mask wearing introduced by Dr. Wu was met with some resistance. But, as is so often the case, a colleague who refused to wear a mask died from a respiratory disease.

One of the most important things in the COVID-19 pandemic is that people need to be told the truth about the virus. The president of the United States avoided telling Americans how serious the disease was, and he obstructed the advice of science advisors on the White House Coronavirus Task Force.

THE GREAT 2019 CORONAVIRUS PANDEMIC

The first case of coronavirus is thought be an individual in the Hubei Province in China. The case dates to November 17, 2019, which, of course, is earlier than the cases that were later found in December 2019 in Wuhan, China. The Chinese considered the viral disease so serious they quarantined 11 million people (about twice the population of Arizona) in Wuhan.

---

[349] Barry, *The Great Influenza*.
[350] Sam Wong, "Dr Wu Lien-teh: Face Mask Pioneer Who Helped Defeat a Plague Epidemic," *New Scientist*, March 10, 2021, retrieved March 13, 2021, https://www.newscientist.com/article/2270735-dr-wu-lien-teh-face-mask-pioneer-who-helped-defeat-a-plague-epidemic/.
[351] Christiane Matuschek et al., "The History and Value of Face Masks," *European Journal of Medical Research*, June 23, 2020, retrieved November 27, 2021, https://www.ncbi.nlm.nih.gov/pmc/articles/PMC7309199/.

During this time the CDC and the NSC were in contact with each other about the coronavirus outbreak in Wuhan. The CDC tried to send some of its infectious disease scientists to Wuhan, but they were blocked by the Chinese government.

On January 9, the World Health Organization (WHO) announced that pneumonia-like cases in Wuhan could be a new coronavirus. Chinese scientists confirmed that a novel coronavirus had killed four and infected more than two hundred. On January 23 the WHO declared a global health emergency.

The United States had its first reported case January 20, 2020. *The New England Journal of Medicine* published a detailed study of the first case on January 31, 2020. According to the study, a thirty-five-year-old man with a four-day history of cough and fever checked into an urgent care clinic in Snohomish County, Washington, which is located north of Seattle. The man put on a mask and waited for about twenty minutes before being examined. He said he returned to Washington state on January 15 after visiting family in Wuhan, China. He indicated that he did not visit the Huanan seafood market and didn't meet persons who were ill. He came to the clinic because he had seen a health alert from the CDC about the novel coronavirus outbreak in China.[352]

They sent nasal swabs to the CDC to test for SARS-CoV-2 using overnight polymerase chain reaction testing (PCR). The PCR test is used to detect genetic material from a specific organism, such as a coronavirus. The CDC confirmed that he tested positive for the novel coronavirus. Although the patient had been discharged, he was later admitted to an airborne-isolation unit at a regional medical center for clinical observation.

ORIGIN OF SARS-COV-2

On January 23, 2020, twenty-five people had died from SARS-CoV-2. By October 15, 2021, more than 4.8 million worldwide had died from the virus.

---

[352] Michelle L. Holshue et al., "First Case of 2019 Novel Coronavirus in the United States," *New England Journal of Medicine*, May 7, 2020, retrieved February 24, 2021, https://www.nejm.org/doi/full/10.1056/NEJMoa2001191.

SARS-CoV-2 raises many questions. For example, what is its origin? Was a human infected by the virus from an animal, or was it the result of a laboratory accident?

The origin of the virus has not been determined and has sparked a controversy highlighting the "lab leak" thesis. Could a shattered container in a lab in Wuhan, China, result in a worldwide pandemic? As you will read ahead, the WHO and US Intelligence Community doesn't think it started in a lab. Most scientists, including Dr. Anthony Fauci, director of the NIAID, believe the virus began naturally jumping from animals to humans. Yet the research on the origins of SARS-CoV-2 that I uncovered does not dismiss the lab accident cause of the pandemic. In the end, what is important is how and where the virus infected humans and spread throughout the world.

A paper published in *Nature Medicine* says that despite what has been said about the lab leak theory, there is no credible evidence that SARS-CoV-2 was ever known to virologists before it emerged in 2019. The paper's author, A. L. Rasmussen, researcher at the Center for Global Health Science and Security, Georgetown University, went on to say that it appears as if SARS-CoV-2 evolved in a bat host until a spillover event into humans occurred.[353]

Rasmussen also points out that there is considerable research on the history of pathogens (viruses, bacteria, fungi, protozoa, and worms) emerging by natural means. She writes that the laboratory origin of SAR-CoV-2 has become political propaganda. Some, including Senator Tom Cotton, have suggested that the virus is a biological weapon,[354] while others have claimed that it was engineered followed by a government coverup. The US Intelligence Committee investigation in the spring of 2021 of COVID-19 dismissed each of these ideas. Misinformation published in anti-science print media blames scientists for covering up the origins of the virus. In some cases, scientists that dispute such claims are subject to harassment, violence, and sexual assault.[355] Pseudoscience

---

[353] Angela L. Rasmussen, "On the Origins of SARS-CoV-2," *Nature News*, January 13, 2021, https://www.nature.com/articles/s41591-020-01205-5.

[354] Amy Maxmen, "US COVID Origins Report: Researchers Pleased with Scientific Approach," *Nature News*, August 27, 2021, https://www.nature.com/articles/d41586-021-02366-0. The Unclassified Intelligence Community report, although inconclusive, finds that SARS-CoV-2 wasn't weaponized and was unlikely to have been engineered.

[355] Rasmussen, "On the Origins of SARS-CoV-2."

and conspiracy theories are attractive to media outlets, but they are dangerous because we need to know how and where the virus originated to help deal with future pandemics.

Another report indicated that there is near-consensus view that SARS-CoV-2 has a natural zoonotic origin.[356] However, the authors of this paper don't think we should discount a laboratory origin of COVID-19. They identify several characteristics of SARS-CoV-2 that are not easily explained by natural zoonotic origin hypothesis. And no unmistakable evidence of zoonotic transfer from a bat or intermediate species yet exists. Very few papers counter the lab theory with data analysis.[357]

In February 2020, a group of twenty-four physicians, veterinarians, epidemiologists, virologists, biologists, ecologists, and public health experts from around the world joined together to support the work being done by Chinese colleagues to find the origin of SARS-CoV-2. They also spoke out to support the idea that the virus originated in nature and not in a lab.[358]

In July 2021, the same group of scientists published another article in *The Lancet* reaffirming their original idea of a natural origin of COVID-19 based on genetic analysis of the virus and previous research on SARS-CoV and MERS-CoV.[359] Several peer-reviewed studies are cited by the scientists supporting the virus emerging from an animal to a human.[360,361,362] They also cite research that shows the lab theory of origin doesn't hold up.[363]

---

[356] Rossana Segreto et al., "Should We Discount the Laboratory Origin of COVID-19?" *Environmental Chemistry Letters* 19 (March 25, 2021): 2743–4757, https://link.springer.com/article/10.1007/s10311-021-01211-0.
[357] Segreto et al., "Laboratory Origin of COVID-19?"
[358] Charles Calisher et al., "Statement in Support of the Scientists, Public Health Professionals, and Medical Professionals of China Combatting COVID-19," *The Lancet*, February 19, 2020, https://www.thelancet.com/journals/lancet/article/PIIS0140-6736(20)30418-9/fulltext.
[359] Charles Calisher, Dennis Carroll, and Rita Colwell, "Science, Not Speculation, Is Essential to Determine How SARS-CoV-2 Reached Humans," *The Lancet*, July 5, 2021, accessed July 6, 2021, https://www.thelancet.com/journals/lancet/article/PIIS0140-6736(21)01419-7/fulltext.
[360] Diego Forni et al., "Molecular Evolution of Human Coronavirus Genomes," *Trends in Microbiology* 25, no. 1 (January 1, 2017): 35–48, https://doi.org/10.1016/j.tim.2016.09.001.
[361] H. Zhou et al., "Identification of Novel Bat Coronaviruses Sheds Light on the Evolutionary Origins of SARS-CoV-2 and Related Viruses," *Cell* 184, no. 17 (2021): 4380–4391, https://pubmed.ncbi.nlm.nih.gov/34147139/.
[362] Robert F. Garry, "Early Appearance of Two Distinct Genomic Lineages of SARS-CoV-2 in Different Wuhan Wildlife Markets Suggests SARS-CoV-2 Has a Natural Origin," Virological, May 3, 2021, https://virological.org/t/early-appearance-of-two-distinct-genomic-lineages-of-sars-cov-2-in-different-wuhan-wildlife-markets-suggests-sars-cov-2-has-a-natural-origin/691.
[363] Justin Ling, "The Lab Leak Theory Doesn't Hold Up," *Foreign Policy*, June 15, 2021, https://foreignpolicy.com/2021/06/15/lab-leak-theory-doesnt-hold-up-covid-china/.

Laboratory Incidents. Laboratory accidents or incidents have a long history stretching back to the early twentieth century. It is possible that dangerous or lethal pathogens can be accidentally released from a lab or during transport from field sites. One case involved a laboratory worker getting exposed and infected simply by a pin prick. In 2007–2008, foot-and-mouth disease was spread from a drainage pipe leak at a UK lab, even with the highest biosafety rating of BSL-4. At that time, I was traveling often to the UK to purchase antiques with my wife, and whenever I entered a farm or a large commercial field, it was necessary to walk through disinfectant pools as a safety precaution. Biosafety levels range from BSL-1 to BSL-4 based on the risk of microbes from low to high.[364] Biosafety means that safety precautions are applied that reduce the laboratory's risk of exposure to a potentially infectious microbes and to limit the contamination of the work environment.

Compromising biosafety protocols can result in infection and community spread. In 2015 a female lab worker in South Korea who was at a BSL-2 lab (a biosafety level similar to your dentist's office) was infected with dengue by a needlestick injury. In 2016, thirty staff members were exposed to a toxic bacterium in a lab in Canberra, Australia.

Initial Research Papers. One of the first papers on the origin of SARS-CoV-2 was reported by Dr. Francis Collins, director of the NIH, on the director's blog. The research Dr. Collins cites, "The Proximal Origin of SARS-CoV-2,"[365] shows that the virus arose naturally, not in a lab. It was published in *Nature Medicine*, a journal in the *Nature* portfolio of publishing. The paper was also cited in Rasmussen's "On the Origins of SARS-CoV-2" research, and it too counters the laboratory origin theory of SARS-CoV-2.

In the study published in *Nature Medicine*, two scenarios are postulated. The first is natural selection in an animal host before zoonotic transfer. Given the similarity of SARS-CoV-2 to SARS-CoV-like

---

[364] "CDC LC Quick Learn: Recognize the Four Biosafety Levels," Centers for Disease Control and Prevention, https://www.cdc.gov/training/quicklearns/biosafety/.
[365] Kristian G. Andersen et al., "The Proximal Origin of SARS-CoV-2," *Nature Medicine* 26 (2020): 450–452, https://doi.org/10.1038/s41591-020-0820-9.

coronaviruses in bats, the researchers suggest it is likely that bats serve as reservoir hosts for its progenitor.

The second scenario is natural selection in humans following zoonotic transfer. In this scenario, the virus crossed from animals to humans long before it could cause human disease. Anderson's team thinks that through gradual evolutionary changes over years or decades, the coronavirus developed the ability to spread from human to human, which could cause a serious disease.

The researchers' analysis show that SARS-CoV-2 is probably not a laboratory construct or a purposefully manipulated virus.

Finding the origin of the SARS-CoV-2 will only happen with more scientific data determined by using evidence-based approaches. Knowing the origin of the virus, whether it's a lab or not, will only advance our knowledge and surveillance of viruses that infect humans.

The 2021 WHO Study. In January 2021, a WHO international scientific and collaborative mission traveled to China and worked with scientists there for four weeks to investigate the origins of the SARS-CoV-2. The report, *WHO-Convened Global Study of Origins of SARS-CoV-2: China Part*, was published in March 2021.[366]

According to the report, it's highly unlikely that the coronavirus escaped from a lab at the Wuhan Institute of Virology. To scientists involved in the study, most say the evidence favors SARS-CoV-2 having spilled over from animals into humans. However, a few still back the idea that the virus was intentionally or accidentally leaked from a lab. When the team visited the virology lab, they found no workers at the lab with antibodies against SAR-CoV-2, which rules out the idea that someone there had been infected and then spread the virus. However, it's been reported that three workers at the lab fell sick in November 2019 and had to be hospitalized. They had COVID-19-like or seasonal symptoms.

Because of the scrutiny by the Chinese government during their time in Wuhan, some scientists went on record saying they wouldn't

---

[366] *WHO-Convened Global Study of Origins of SARS-CoV-2: China Part*, World Health Organization, March 30, 2021, https://www.who.int/publications/i/item/who-convened-global-study-of-origins-of-sars-cov-2-china-part.

trust the outcome of the investigation. The WHO-led team had little power to conduct a thorough and impartial study of the virus's origins. The Trump administration withdrew from the WHO, a decision that made it difficult to have American scientists as part of the WHO-led team to China. Although some American names were put forward, none were ever extended an invitation to join the WHO team.[367]

These journalists reported that the WHO-led team was only mandated to design and recommend scientific studies. It was not prepared to do scientific investigations and did not have laboratory forensic capabilities. This omission was unfortunate because it sheds doubt on the WHO report.

Challenges remaining include finding the animal that carried the virus from bats to humans and determining how that spillover into people occurred. To what degree can the report's findings meet the test of scientific viability?

The WHO investigation zeroed in to identify the zoonotic source of the virus and the route of introduction to the human population, including the role of intermediate hosts. The early cases of COVID-19 were associated with the Huanan market, and some other markets as well. Some cases were not associated with markets at all. The WHO research team also suggested cases might have existed before the first case in Wuhan. Investigating possible earlier events might be important.

Environmental sampling in Huanan market showed out of 923 samples in the market, 73 samples were positive. WHO researchers said this result revealed widespread contamination of surfaces with SARS-CoV-2, meaning the virus was spread by infected people, infected animals, or contaminated products. In addition, supply chains to the Huanan market included cold-chain products and animal products from twenty countries, including some samples that were reported as positive for SARS-CoV-2. The researchers also suggested evidence existed that some domesticated wildlife products sold in the market are susceptible to SARS-CoV-2.

---

[367] Jeremy Page, Betsy McKay, and Drew Hinshaw, "How the WHO's Hunt for Covid's Origins Stumbled in China," *Wall Street Journal*, March 17, 2021, retrieved May 24, 2021, https://www.wsj.com/articles/who-china-hunt-covid-origins-11616004512.

The joint international team proposed four scenarios for introduction of the virus into humans:[368]

1. Direct zoonotic transmission to humans (spillover)
2. Introduction through an intermediate host followed by spillover
3. Introduction through the (cold) food chain
4. Introduction through a laboratory incident

Using qualitative risk assessment, each pathway was investigated considering available evidence. This kind of assessment is an estimate based on qualitative data rather than quantitative data. Although quantitative data are preferred to make risk assessments, the WHO team did not have sufficient quantitative data to incorporate into their assessments.

The WHO joint team postulated the following as the likelihood of each pathway:

1. Direct zoonotic spillover is a possible to likely pathway.
2. Introduction through an intermediate host is a likely to very likely pathway.
3. Introduction through (cold) food chain products is considered a possible pathway.
4. Introduction through a laboratory incident is an extremely unlikely pathway.

It's important to note that the joint team visited nine locations, including hospitals, infectious disease centers, wholesale markets, Wuhan CDC, Wuhan Institute of Virology, and a community center in Jianxinyuan. The major finding of the joint team is that direct zoonotic spillover is a possible to likely pathway of the SARS-CoV-2.

However, scientists still do not know which animal might have carried the virus from bats to humans. The WHO report suggests that

---

[368] Page, McKay, and Hinshaw, "How the WHO's Hunt for Covid's Origins Stumbled in China."

the start of the virus outbreak might have been a month or two before mid-December 2019. Much research is needed to track down how the virus spilled over into humans.

US Intelligence Community Report. On May 26, 2021, President Biden ordered a ninety-day US Intelligence Community investigation into where the SARS-CoV-2 came from. The Intelligence Community report, which consisted of several teams of investigators, concluded that two hypotheses are plausible: natural exposure to an infected animal and a laboratory-associated incident.

The groups assessed with low confidence that the initial SARS-CoV-2 infection was most likely caused by natural exposure to an animal infected with it or a close progenitor virus—a virus that probably would be more than 99 percent like SARS-CoV-2. The low confidence emerged because of the lack of foreknowledge from the Chinese government. One group assessed with moderate confidence that the first human infection with SARS-CoV-2 most likely was the result of a laboratory-associated incident, probably involving experimentation, animal handling, or sampling by the Wuhan Institute of Virology. These analysts give weight to the inherently risky nature of work on coronaviruses. This US government report keeps the door open to a lab accident but does not have research to support its idea.

Wuhan Institute of Virology. Ever since the virus was identified in Wuhan, initial claims were that the virus leaked from the Wuhan Institute of Virology. The institute was founded in 1951 as the Wuhan Microbiology Laboratory, and over time its name changed, but the nature of its work progressed so that in 2003, it became the first BSL-4 lab in China. A BSL-4 lab is one that can contain the most dangerous biological agents using training, technology, and secure systems to prevent accidental laboratory events.

By 2018, the lab was accredited by the China National Accreditation Service for Conformity Assessment. The institute's BSL-4 allows it to investigate dangerous viruses such as SARS, influenza H5N1, Japanese encephalitis, and dengue, as well as anthrax.

The initial claims of a lab leak waned throughout 2020, but as new information surfaced in 2021, such as three employees of the institute being hospitalized with COVID-19-like symptoms in December, the lab leak gained more attention.

When Trump promoted an anti-China and anti-Asia campaign, most officials and scientists did not believe that the lab leak was a viable hypothesis. However, after the WHO's investigation of the virus was published in 2021, the hypothesis was revived. The WHO scientists were not given wide access to documents and details of the Wuhan Institute of Virology. Some of the scientists were not impressed and thought that the institute should be pressed to be more transparent with what they know about the disease. Although most of the scientific community believes the virus originated in nature, they support further work to examine the lab leak hypothesis.

The Lab Leak Idea. The Trump administration pushed the lab leak theory in the press to take the heat of their own bungling in dealing with the spread of the virus in the United States. No evidence existed then for a lab leak, and it is more unlikely now based on recent research reported in peer-reviewed journals and newsletters.

The major perpetrator of the lab leak theory is the media; it makes for good television. It also enables the media to present two sides of the origin of COVID-19, which is very similar to the media's enchantment of presenting two sides of other issues, such as evolution versus intelligent design. In a *Los Angeles Times* article, Michael Hitzik describes how CNN propped up the lab leak idea by bringing together a group of four panelists, only one of whom was a medical expert—Sanjay Gupta.[369] The lab leak side had no one with any experience in virology. The two ideas, a natural spillover and the lab leak, as equals is the unfortunate approach the media takes. There are many research studies in scientific journals about the origin of COVID-19

---

[369] M. Hiltzik, "Column: New Evidence Undermines the COVID Lab-Leak Theory—but the Press Keeps Pushing It," *Los Angeles Times*, September 28, 2021, retrieved October 11, 2021, https://www.latimes.com/business/story/2021-09-28/evidence-against-a-lab-leak-as-covid-source.

that support a natural spill from animal to human.[370,371] There are no studies that support a lab leak.

Spillover Infection Events. Pathogens such as SARS-CoV-2 are the result of spillover infection events.[372] Spillover occurs when a reservoir population (rats, bats, mosquitos) encounters a novel host population, such as humans. This is an example of zoonosis, an infectious disease caused by an agent such as a bacterium, parasite, or virus that has spilled over or jumped from an animal (normally a vertebrate) to a human.

According to many scientists around the world, a spillover occurred somewhere in China from a bat to an intermediate animal and then to a human. A SARS-CoV-2 infection can spread from human to human. The infection can spread asymptomatically. Dr. Anthony Fauci, director of the NIAID, says 40 percent of Americans with SARS-CoV-2 are asymptomatic, meaning they show no symptoms of the disease. According to the CDC, people can be infectious for ten to fourteen days. South Korean researchers estimate those infectious with symptoms were contagious for up to twenty days.

The most likely place that the spillover happened was the Huanan market. It's been reported that a third of the 168 COVID-19 cases reported in December 2019 were linked to the market. It was also discovered that many of the early cases were not only linked to the market, but the western part of the market where live animals, such as raccoon dogs, were housed. Raccoon dogs are a potential intermediate host to transmit SARS-CoV-2 to humans.[373]

The SARS-CoV-2 pandemic was not a surprise to most infectious disease scientists and journalists who specialize in studying or reporting human diseases, as well as ecological and environmental issues caused by human invasion. David Quammen's 2012 book, *Spillover: Animal*

---

[370] Smriti Mallapaty, "Closest Known Relatives of Virus behind COVID-19 Found in Laos," *Nature News*, September 27, 2021, retrieved October 11, 2021, https://www.nature.com/articles/d41586-021-02596-2.
[371] Garry, "Early Appearance of Two Distinct Genomic Lineages."
[372] Corrie Brown, "Spillover: Animal Infection and the Next Human Pandemic," review of the book by David Quammen, *Emerging Infectious Diseases* 19 no. 2 (2013): 349, https://doi.org/10.3201/eid1902.121694.
[373] Michael Le Page, "Analysis of Earliest COVID-19 Cases Points to Wuhan Market as Source," *New Scientist*, November 25, 2021, retrieved November 28, 2021, https://www.newscientist.com/article/2298195-analysis-of-earliest-covid-19-cases-points-to-wuhan-market-as-source/.

Infections and the Next Human Pandemic, reads like a fictional tale of someone's idea of how to kill off one another, either humans or other animals, on Earth.[374]

One of the important points that Quammen makes is that humanity is responsible for the large pattern of outbreaks of new zoonotic diseases. I was talking with Mike Dias, professor of biology at Kennesaw State University, on a Zoom call recently. He said as we live in closer proximity to wild animals, we should expect more zoonotic outbreaks. Think about how the Earth's population has changed over the past century. The human population was 2 billion a century ago. Now it is 7 billion. Many of us live in large and dense cities.

As Quammen says, we have penetrated and we continue to penetrate the last great forests and other wild ecosystems. This invasion has disrupted the physical structures and the ecological communities of these places.

One of the most significant spillover species is bats. Quammen described how a handful of scientists who knew little about bats but a lot about infectious diseases decided to do a review of published and unpublished research on bats. They published their paper with the title "Bats: Important Reservoir Hosts of Emerging Viruses."[375] They described the characteristics of bats and information regarding sixty-six viruses that have been isolated from bats. In 2006, they made it clear that not enough is known about bat conservation, and many questions need to be explored regarding the role of bats in disease emergence. Their paper resulted in requests for hundreds of reprints and cited thousands of times in the literature.

Bats are the major hosts for the evolution of the two previous coronaviruses, severe acute respiratory syndrome (SARS, 2002 in China) and Middle East respiratory syndrome (MERS, 2012, Saudi Arabia). The new coronavirus, SARS-CoV-2, originated in bats. Much of the early research focused on Wuhan's open-air wet markets, where customers bought

---

[374] David Quammen, *Spillover: Animal Infections and the Next Human Pandemic* (New York: W. W. Norton & Company, 2021).
[375] Charles Calisher et al., "Bats: Important Reservoir Hosts of Emerging Viruses," *Clinical Microbiology Reviews* 19, no. 3 (2006): 531–545, retrieved March 12, 2021, https://doi.org/10.1128/CMR.00017-06.

fresh meat and fish, including animals killed on the spot. Some wet markets sell wild and banned species. Crowded conditions allow viruses to spill over, spreading to and infecting other animals and humans. However, some of the people who got sick never went near the open-air market. And the first case reported in the United States was a man who had returned to the US after spending time in Wuhan and who said that he did not visit any of the markets in Wuhan.

TRUMP'S RESPONSE

Trump's history of denial and untruths about COVID-19 was disgraceful. Trump's first public denial occurred on January 21, 2020, in Davos, Switzerland, when he answered a reporter's question about the virus. Trump said, "We have it totally under control. It's one person coming in from China. We have it under control. It's going to be just fine." Trump also said he trusted the information coming out of China. He said that he has a great relationship with President Xi. "The relationship is very good."

Later in the year, Trump changed his tune about China. Trump stigmatized COVID-19 by blaming it on the Chinese and calling the virus the China virus or Chinese virus. Trump started using this racist terminology as early as March 2020. He's persisted with this racist connotation. The damage done to the Asian American community was appalling. According to various reports, Asian Americans have faced racist violence at a much higher rate since the pandemic began. Violence and hate crimes against Asian Americans took place nationwide. On March 16, 2021, a series of mass shootings occurred at three spas in the metropolitan area of Atlanta, only a few miles from where I live. Six Asian women were killed.

Donald Trump knew in early January 2020 that the coronavirus outbreak in China was serious. Parts of his government, especially the intelligence agencies, were telling him that the virus was a threat to national security. Trump ignored and denied the information that he was receiving, even when he received the President's Daily Brief.

On March 13, 2020, Trump announced a national emergency for COVID-19. His announcement came more than two months after coronavirus was identified as a serious disease by China and the WHO and was spreading across the world. By this time, more than 80,000 cases had been recorded in China and at least 600,000 cases around the world. US coronavirus cases had reached 1,678, with a death tally of 41. By the end of Trump's term in office, coronavirus cases in the United States reached 24.24 million. More than 406,000 deaths had been reported.[376]

The United States government failed its citizens not only in protecting them, but also in educating them and explaining what mitigation methods should be implemented. Trump deserves the most blame, but the NIH and at least two of its agencies should bear some responsibility as well. However, after I completed more research to investigate the relationship between the White House and the CDC, I found the relationship is not pretty.

THE CDC VERSUS THE WHITE HOUSE

The purpose of the Centers for Disease Control and Prevention is to protect the safety, health, and security of America from threats here and around the world. The CDC is in my backyard, as it's located on Clifton Road in Atlanta. Years ago when I lived in that part of Atlanta, I would drive by the agency's campus. Up until the COVID-19 pandemic, the CDC had a reputation as the world leader in disease control and prevention. However, a ProPublica investigation exposed an ugly chapter in the history of CDC. In fact, the authors of the report said this:

> When the next history of the CDC is written, 2020 will emerge as perhaps the darkest chapter in its 74 years, rivaled only by its involvement in the infamous Tuskegee experiment, in which federal doctors withheld medicine from poor Black men with syphilis, then tracked their descent into blindness, insanity, and death.[377]

---

[376] Will Stone, "On Trump's Last Full Day, Nation Records 400,000 Covid Deaths," *Kaiser Health News*, January 20, 2021, retrieved April 5, 2022, https://khn.org/news/nation-records-400000-covid-deaths-on-last-day-of-donald-trump-presidency/.

[377] James Bandler et al., "Inside the Fall of the CDC," ProPublica, October 15, 2020, retrieved March 14, 2021, https://www.propublica.org/article/inside-the-fall-of-the-cdc.

How could the authors of the ProPublica article make such an assessment? Part of the answer lies in mistakes that were made in one of the laboratories on the campus of the CDC in Atlanta. But the laboratory mistakes, which I'll explain in a bit, pale in comparison with how the Trump administration took over the CDC's COVID-19 decision-making and public communication. Here are a few examples that shed light on the CDC's fall from grace:[378]

- Senior CDC staff describe waging battles protecting science from the White House as protecting the public from COVID-19.
- White House officials with no public health experience meddled in important CDC meetings on COVID-19, including Trump's daughter Ivanka, Stephen Miller, and "protégés of Jared Kushner, wearing blue suits with red ties and beards."
- There was a loss of faith in CDC director Dr. Robert Redfield.
- Veteran CDC specialists with global reputations were marginalized, silenced, or reassigned. If these top scientists spoke out, they disappeared.
- Trump appropriated the CDC, a public enterprise, and turned it into a propaganda regime.

Several points that should be made at this point in the story. The first has to do with the agency's initial intelligence about news reports of coronavirus cases in Wuhan, China. What did the agency find out, and what did its leading scientists and directors do? The second has to do with the agency's initial messaging to the public and the media about the coronavirus. And the third is Trump's reaction to the CDC announcement and what he did because of the CDC's public statements.

It is during this time that Trump brought the CDC to its knees and removed the agency from the public sphere. The public lost confidence in the CDC. But as important as that loss of confidence is, Trump's

---

[378] Bandler et al., "Fall of the CDC."

decision to take over the messaging of COVID-19 resulted in the most chaotic and disastrous health crisis in United States history.

What follows will probably make you as angry as it did me. The United States could have avoided much of the harm that came about because of the negligence of the president of the United States. Let me explain.

On December 31, 2019, Dr. Anne Schuchat, the CDC's top career scientist, emailed Dr. Jay Butler, later to become the CDC's coronavirus response head. Schuchat asked Butler if any of his colleagues knew anything about the "unknown pneumonia" in Wuhan. According to the ProPublica study, Dr. Dan Jernigan, the flu chief, and his boss, Dr. Nancy Messonnier, met at CDC headquarters in Atlanta. That same day, they learned about twenty-seven cases in China, some of them severe. These patients had difficulty breathing and suffered a buildup of abnormal substances in the lungs. Messonnier immediately realized this could be a SARS virus. She contacted Dr. Martin Cetron, director of the Division of Global Migration and Quarantine at the CDC. While he was with on vacation in New Hampshire, he told those around him about the new virus in China and that he was concerned it could affect the entire world.[379]

Normally Schuchat's team of infectious experts would have been in touch with the CDC's office located within the Chinese CDC in Beijing. But that office no longer existed because of budget cuts going back to the Great Recession of 2008 and, later, Trump's decision to close it down. Remember the CDC had stopped the Ebola epidemic in 2014 when Obama was president, but it now found its global influence waning because of losing as many as three hundred overseas posts.

Robert Redfield, the new director of the CDC, reached out to his close ally in China, according to the ProPublica investigators. The close ally was George Gao, director of China's CDC. Gao was a microbiologist educated at Oxford and Harvard. Redfield hoped he would obtain detailed information about the infections in Wuhan. He didn't. In fact, communications with Gao lessened and eventually ended. Gao was muted by Chinese government officials.

---

[379] Bandler et al., "Fall of the CDC."

The CDC felt an obligation to communicate with the American public. At first they indicated that the public had no reason to panic about the virus detected in China. In the meantime, Trump was told by his intelligence agencies and his national security advisors that the virus in China was serious and would be the most significant national security threat he'd face as president. "What should I do?" Trump asked. Matthew Pottinger told him to stop all flights from China. Trump ordered all flights from China stopped on January 31, 2020. Scientists at the CDC did not see closing borders as helpful because it restricts the flow of medical experts and goods.

Then on February 25, Messonnier, the CDC's director of the National Center for Immunization and Respiratory Diseases, held a press conference in Atlanta about the coronavirus and what steps should Americans take to prevent it. The virus, she said, moves quite rapidly through community spread. As the virus spreads, containment becomes more difficult. The CDC urged American businesses and families to start preparing for a bigger outbreak.

I happened to be watching TV and saw her press conference. At the end, reporters asked her if she was taking any precautions considering the novel virus. "Disruption to everyday life might be severe," Messonnier said, adding that she talked to her children about the issue Tuesday morning. "While I didn't think they are at risk right now, we as a family ought to be preparing for significant disruption to our lives." She had even called her children's school to ask about their plans for online learning.

The stock market and the White House were shocked. One fell and the other screamed. Messonnier was removed from public appearances after her warning about the coronavirus. Unfortunately, instead of listening to Messonnier, the Trump administration silenced her and covered up the actual nature of the virus as early as February 2020.

Trump put Mike Pence in charge of his Coronavirus Task Force, replacing Alex Azar, secretary of health and human services. Trump became the communicator-in-chief. For the next month or so, Trump decided to have daily press conferences and used this forum to play down COVID-19 and sideline the CDC and its scientists. The scientists that he did involve during these TV news conferences were Dr. Anthony Fauci, director of the NIAID, and Dr. Deborah Birx, United States Global AIDS Coordinator. Although Redfield, the director of the CDC, was on the task force, he rarely spoke at these press meetings.

Trump never fully embraced—at least publicly—the pandemic and its effects on the United States. The task force stopped meeting in April and didn't hold a meeting again until June 30. All the while Trump downplayed the disease and spoke only about how well his administration was doing with the virus. He spent most of his time insisting that states open their economies while he played golf.

President Trump, with hands in pockets, visits the CDC on March 6, 2020, in Atlanta. He is joined by Health and Human Services Secretary Alex Azar, left; Dr. Robert Redfield, director of the CDC, speaking; and Dr. Stephen Monroe, associate director of the CDC. And lurking in the background is former Georgia Senator David Perdue. The CDC by this time was being undermined by the Trump administration, and soon the White House took over all communications coming out of the CDC. Source: Public Domain Mark 1.0; no copyright.

BOTCHED TEST KITS

The CDC had the responsibility for developing a COVID-19 test. It developed a coronavirus kit in the Respiratory Viruses Diagnostic Team lab on its Atlanta campus in January 2020, and it was ready for shipment on February 6. The lab that developed the kits learned that the final quality control test suggested the kits were failing 33 percent of the time. However, Stephen Lindstrom, the head of the lab, decided to sign off on the quality control report and ship the kits. A later investigation found that the lab had many quality standard and organizational problems. Laboratory officials were not allowed to make any public comments by the CDC management. By February 6, one hundred or more clinics and public labs across the United States began receiving the kits. Within days labs were reporting that they were getting inconclusive results. The CDC was notified, and their first idea was possible contamination due to quality preparations in the Atlanta lab.

The CDC claimed that one of the chemicals needed for the test got contaminated. None of the test kits that were sent out could be used. It took five weeks for the CDC to correct and produce new test kits. At this point in the pandemic, testing was one of the most important tools for tracking, tracing, and controlling the virus. The United States was unable to take these steps, which were taken in South Korea and Germany. Early in the pandemic, these countries were able to keep the virus under control.

Recall that the first coronavirus case in the United States was identified on January 20, 2020. At that time, the only place in the United States to have a sample tested for COVID-19 was in Atlanta at the CDC headquarters. And for a local clinic to be able to send the samples, they needed to get approval from the CDC. In the first cases detected, the sample was flown to Atlanta, where it was tested. Meanwhile, South Korea had already initiated a testing and tracking program, which led it to control the virus at an early stage.[380]

As described in Chapter 11, Donald Trump failed as a leader to respond to the COVID-19 pandemic. He was unable to face reality and tell the American people the truth. His administration interfered with the scientific community. Scientists were dismissed and their ideas, which would have helped Americans deal with the virus, were ignored or compromised.

---

[380] Katherine Faulders, Matthew Mosk, and John Santucci, "Coronavirus Testing: What Top Officials Say Went Wrong," ABC News, July 29, 2020, retrieved March 14, 2021, https://abcnews.go.com/Health/coronavirus-testing-top-officials-wrong/story?id=71973919.

THE DEVELOPMENT OF SARS-COV-2 VACCINES

Viruses are tiny bits of genetic material inside a protein shell. They are able to make their way into a cell of an organism and take over the cell's machinery in order to replicate themselves. SARS-CoV-2 is an RNA molecule that Chinese scientists had analyzed and publicly reported the genetic sequence of on January 9, 2020. With this information available, scientists worked to find treatments and vaccines that would block the ability of the virus to hook on to human cells.[381]

SARS-CoV-2 vaccines were developed so rapidly in 2020 because of decades of research, developmental, and clinical work by federally funded research scientists at NIH and at research labs at universities around the country, as well as with collaboration with scientists in other countries, especially China. The groundwork for the Moderna, Pfizer-BioNTech, and Johnson & Johnson/Janssen vaccines was laid out previously and was ready to implement.[382]

Most of the development of vaccines for SARS-CoV-2 has been in North America, with 36 (46%) developers as compared to 14 (18%) in China, 14 (18%) in Asia and Australia, and 14 (18%) in Europe.[383]

According to an article in *Nature Reviews*, the response to global vaccine development has been unprecedented. Normally vaccines take between two and ten years to be developed and approved for use on humans. However, the timeline for COVID-19 vaccines has been reduced to months.

In a *Scientific American* article, Arthur Allen describes how pioneering work by several scientists and their lab associates led to what are called mRNA vaccines. According to the CDC, mRNA vaccines are a new type of vaccine to protect against infectious diseases.[384] These

---

[381] Walter Isaacson, *Code Breaker: Jennifer Doudna, Gene Editing, and the Future of the Human Race* (New York: Simon & Schuster, 2021), 403–404.
[382] Arthur Allen, "For Billion-Dollar COVID Vaccines, Basic Government-Funded Science Laid the Groundwork," *Scientific American*, November 18, 2020, retrieved May 2, 2021, https://www.scientificamerican.com/article/for-billion-dollar-covid-vaccines-basic-government-funded-science-laid-the-groundwork/.
[383] Tung Thanh Le et al., "The COVID-19 Vaccine Development Landscape," *Nature Reviews Drug Discovery*, April 2020, retrieved May 2, 2021, https://www.researchgate.net/profile/Tung-Le-10/publication/340535627_The_COVID-19_vaccine_development_landscape/links/5ead65c5a6fdcc7050a1c089/The-COVID-19-vaccine-development-landscape.pdf.
[384] Allen, "For Billion-Dollar COVID Vaccines."

mRNA vaccines teach our cells how to make a protein that triggers an immune response inside our bodies.

Scientists at the NIH pioneered the groundbreaking research that led to the development of multiple SARS-CoV-2 vaccines. One of the earliest pioneering researchers is Dr. Kati Karikó, a Hungarian biochemist and senior vice president with BioNTech who specializes in RNA mechanisms. She and American immunologist Drew Weissman, Pearlman School of Medicine at the University of Pennsylvania, hold the patents for the technology enabling the modification of RNA. This discovery has been licensed by BioNTech and Moderna to develop their COVID-19 vaccines.[385] Karikó and Weissman were awarded the Rosenstiel Award for Distinguished Work in Basic Medical Research by Brandeis University in January 2021.[386]

Another of the early pioneers was Dr. Barney Graham, deputy director of the Vaccine Research Center and the chief of the Viral Pathogenesis Laboratory at the NIH. Graham and his colleague Jason McLellan, along with Chinese scientists, developed in 2013 the "bioengineered protein" that led the way to designing vaccines against emerging pandemic viruses. Graham's NIH lab began working with Moderna in 2017 to design rapid manufacturing systems. During the COVID-19 outbreak in China, the Moderna/Graham group switched goals to work on the novel virus. They produced a vaccine in six weeks and started a 30,000-volunteer late-stage trial. It showed 95 percent effectiveness.[387] My wife and I received the first of two Moderna vaccine shots in early January 2021 and the second in early February, plus a Moderna booster in August 2021.

After Joe Biden was inaugurated, vaccine distribution of SARS-CoV-2 exceeded 3 million people (about the population of Arkansas) per day, and within one hundred days, more than 200 million people were vaccinated in the United States. However, many developing countries still need help, and some developed countries are still experiencing

---

[385] Gina Kolata, "Kati Kariko Helped Shield the World from the Coronavirus," New York Times, April 8, 2021, retrieved November 28, 2021, https://www.nytimes.com/2021/04/08/health/coronavirus-mrna-kariko.html.
[386] Lawrence Goodman, "Rosenstiel Award Given to Pioneering Scientists behind COVID-19 Vaccines," BrandeisNOW, January 21, 2021, retrieved November 28, 2021, https://www.brandeis.edu/now/2021/january/rosenstiel-covid-vaccine.html.
[387] Allen, "For Billion-Dollar COVID Vaccines."

coronavirus outbreaks. Now is the time for a lend-lease or patent-free distribution of the vaccine to any country that needs assistance. The virus needs to be mitigated globally, not just locally. Biden announced at the 2021 G7 summit in the UK that the United States would begin donating vaccines to poorer countries, starting with 500 million doses. Other countries have promised a total of 500 million doses.

Another fundamental problem is the growing anti-vaccination movement. This movement is especially troublesome when the world is trying to manage, control, and rid the Earth of the virus, although that is very unlikely. Fauci thinks that herd immunity will not be reached primarily because of anti-vaxxers. Vaccine hesitancy has been around for decades. Many people refuse to let their children be vaccinated against any contagious disease. Others believe that vaccines cause autism in children. In the United States, some groups are filing lawsuits against companies and organizations that require COVID-19 vaccinations and making themselves available to individuals who wish to refuse the vaccination. They will be happy to file a lawsuit for you.

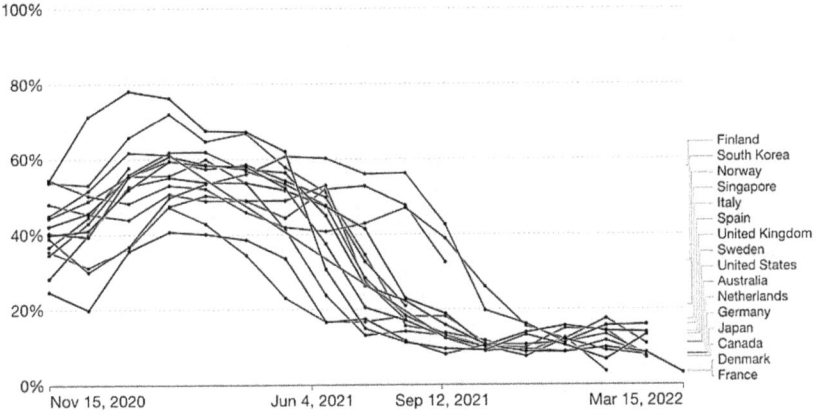

Figure 13. Share of survey respondents who have not received a COVID-19 vaccine and who agree with the statement: "If a COVID-19 vaccine were made available to me this week, I would definitely get it." Source: Our World in Data, CC BY 4.0.

The WHO views vaccine hesitancy as one of the top ten global health threats. In the United States, a recent poll indicated that one in four Americans will refuse the COVID-19 vaccine. Leading the list of anti-vaxxers are Republican men, 49 percent of whom say they will refuse the vaccine. As of fall 2020, Georgia had the lowest percentage of adults and children over twelve vaccinated against COVID-19. Figure 13 shows that even after two years of the pandemic, only 20% of those who are unvaccinated would be willing to be vaccinated. And anti-vaccination is not just a problem in the United States, as shown in the graph.[388]

A connection exists between anti-maskers and anti-lockdown protestors and the anti-vax movement. The anti-masker and anti-lockdown groups include QAnon conspirators as well as ordinary people who don't like being told what to do. QAnon is a far-right conspiracy theory based on false claims made by an internet individual known as "Q." Followers believe that a cannibalistic cabal has conspired against former President Donald Trump. Followers of this cult claim their freedom is being curbed. And there are some anti-maskers who don't believe their children should have to wear masks while at school. However, in some states, governors have lifted mask mandates. You guessed it: Florida, Georgia, and Texas led the way.

The history of anti-vaccinations reveals a thriving movement. Edna Bonhomme, a historian of science and writer who lives in Berlin, writes that in Germany, for instance, anti-science sentiment, right-wing politics, and racism have been entwined since before Jews were accused of spreading the bubonic plague in the fourteenth century.[389] She concludes that anti-science sentiments are tangled with racial prejudice.

Blaming ethnic minorities for viruses and other diseases has also been part of America's racist and anti-science movement. It's been a part of American history, including blaming Irish Catholic immigrants for the 1882 cholera outbreak in New York, quarantining San Francisco's Chinatown in 1876 for smallpox and disease, and screening at Ellis Island in the nineteenth and early twentieth centuries to prohibit "physically inferior" immigrants. In our time, Donald Trump has cast Central American immigrants as disease carriers. And calling COVID-19 the

---

[388] View this chart at https://ourworldindata.org/grapher/covid-vaccine-willingness.
[389] Edna Bonhomme, "Germany's Anti-Vaccination History Is Riddled with Anti-Semitism," *The Atlantic*, May 2, 2021, retrieved May 3, 2021, https://www.theatlantic.com/health/archive/2021/05/anti-vaccination-germany-anti-semitism/618777/.

"China virus" has stigmatized the virus and led to some people blaming Chinese Americans for the pandemic.[390]

Underlying refusals to be vaccinated are conspiracy theories. As mentioned, some claim that vaccines cause autism. No scientific evidence supports this concern. For others, anti-scientific conspiracy theory fosters a disregard for the work of scientists in preventing disease. A distrust of science is also a factor. In the age of Trump, truthfulness is in short supply. Fake news, alternative facts, and distortions of reality impact people's beliefs in facts, reasoning, and science. Millions of people refuse vaccinations because of their denial and refusal to know the science. Naomi Oreskes, in her book *Why Trust Science?*, suggests science confront a public crisis of trust. Suspicion and motivation of scientific theories are abundant but not new.

To remove the threat of the coronavirus, we must prevent the virus from spreading. If people think they won't get the virus or they simply don't believe in putting anything into their bodies, then the virus will be able to spread. There have been at least ten variants of SARS-CoV-2. If the virus is left to spread, new variants are sure to evolve, as we've seen with the Delta and Omicron variants. But if more people get vaccinated, we have a strong possibility of containing SARS-CoV-2.

SCHOOL IN THE AGE OF A GLOBAL PANDEMIC

As soon as the coronavirus was considered a global health emergency, schools across the world closed their doors to face-to-face learning. At the time schools closed their doors, the virus was spreading rapidly. The nature of the virus was understood, but governments hesitated. Even the CDC hesitated in explaining how people could protect themselves from catching the virus. It was a wise decision to close schools, yet mixed messaging created problems for local school districts, often pitting parents against school officials.

The decision to close schools to face-to-face learning led to the question of when should schools open? How can we open them

---

[390] Catherine E. Shoichet, "What Historians Hear When Trump Calls Coronavirus 'Chinese' and 'Foreign,'" CNN, March 17, 2020, retrieved May 3, 2021, https://www.cnn.com/2020/03/12/us/disease-outbreaks-xenophobia-history/index.html.

safely? When schools closed, all teaching and learning was moved to online frameworks. Virtual learning led to a host of problems, including the lack of availability of computers in families in low socio-economic communities, lack of access to reliable networks, and lack of instruction for teachers to learn how to use online resources, plus the effects of learning at home on students and parents. Online learning pushed teachers and students to use multiple technologies, including email, websites, Zoom, and other video services. Many were not prepared.

With respect to school, I was concerned about safety as well the effects of online learning. How could schools manage a safe environment, considering the community spread of the coronavirus? Who would benefit from online learning? Who wouldn't?

For example, in Georgia where I live, more than 360,000 college and university students are enrolled across the state. I used coronavirus data that Ed Johnson compiled using the Georgia Department of Public Health statistics to answer questions about the opening of universities. Johnson is a fellow resident of Georgia and an advocate for public education who published a daily newsletter focusing on public education in Atlanta. He also has been tracking COVID-19 since early March 2020 and publishing his findings on his newsletter. I used his research findings on my blog, and you'll find some of his data in Chapters 10 and 12.

Early in the pandemic, not much was known about the effect of bringing students back to their respective schools. Even now, the safety of students in school is an open question. The question can be answered if the primary consideration is safety, health, and welfare of students and teachers, as well the families of each group.

In the summer of 2021, Fauci supported sending kids back to school, but only if the COVID-19 rate positivity rate is 5 percent or less than 5 per 100,000 population. This is referred to as the green zone. Yellow zones have positivity rates between 5% and 10%. Red zones have positivity rates above 10%. In December 2020, there were only four states in the green zone, meaning that the positivity rate was less than 5%. More than half the states have a positivity rate of more than 10%. Fauci says that to open schools in the yellow and red zones, we've got to lower the positivity rates in the community of these schools. As more people get vaccinated, COVID-19 positivity rates will go down.[391]

In the initial stages of the pandemic, not much research was made available to help school and university officials make decisions on whether to open schools and under what conditions. That omission is beginning to change in late 2021.

However, some medical experts have raised questions about the methodology used in some studies that might become influential in directing schools to open or not. In Chapter 12, several posts raise questions about the relationship between community spread of the virus and the spread in schools. Little data exist on the spread of the virus in schools. Most states provide data on coronavirus cases for each county. I used this type of data to raise questions about returning students to school.

Based on data from MCH Strategic Data, 13,597 of 14,944 US school districts provided school reopening plans for fall 2020. Of those districts, 24% were completely online, 51% were using a hybrid model, and 17% were fully open for in-person instruction. Slightly more than half had students participating in school sports programs. Most school districts required students to wear masks, but on further inspection of the data, only 7% required middle and high school students to wear masks, and only 2% of high schools required masks.[392]

A review of some research on school opening and SARS-CoV-2 infection rates was reported by CDC researchers. The findings reported in the study are of the authors and not the CDC. Crowded conditions in adult living environments or meatpacking facilities are ripe for spreading COVID-19. Schools also risk the possibility of spreading SARS-CoV-2, though one study in North Carolina that involved 90,000 students

---

[391] Kristina Fiore, "Fauci: Here's How Schools Can Safely Reopen," *Medical News*, August 13, 2020, retrieved April 5, 2022, https://www.medpagetoday.com/infectiousdisease/covid19/88065.
[392] MCH Strategic Data, retrieved March 16, 2021, https://www.mchdata.com/.

and staff for a nine-week period found that within-school transmissions were rare (32 infections in schools, whereas 773 community-acquired infections).

However, Stephen Friedman, MD, MPH, and adjunct professor, Department of Medicine, Rutgers University, commented that the infection rates reported for students were limited to the local school data dashboard rather than systematic testing of students. He also noted that comparing students to community spread data was comparing students to adults.[393] School-related activities have increased the risk of SARS-CoV-2 infection, especially in after-school sports programs. One example of how contact sports can lead to infection was a study of a high school wrestling tournament. Among 130 tournament participants, 38 (30 percent) had a lab-confirmed SARS-CoV-2 infection.[394] Only 50 percent of the participants were tested. Secondary transmission was identified through contact tracing in households and in school (classrooms and athletics). Some states banned after-school sports. However, in Georgia, where I live, there is little evidence of schools reducing after-school activities.

The researchers concluded that schools need to take into account community spread and ensure safe environments for students during and after school. Masks, social distancing, and handwashing are essential and should be required. However, in some school districts, parent groups are filing lawsuits opposing mask wearing for students.

Stephanie Jones, distinguished teaching professor in the Department of Educational Theory and Practice at the University of Georgia, expressed a concern I share that too few schools were mandating masks and social distancing to provide safe learning environments, especially for students in grades K–6. Children this age could not be vaccinated until fall 2021 and were very susceptible to being infected with the Delta variant of COVID-19 before that point.[395]

---

[393] Margaret A. Honein, Lisa C. Barrios, and John T. Brooks, "In-Person Education and the Spread of SARS-COV-2 Infection," *JAMA*, March 2, 2021, retrieved February 12, 2022, https://jamanetwork.com/journals/jama/fullarticle/2775875.
[394] Honein et al., "In-Person Education."
[395] Stephani Jones, "We Must Protect Students from Storms and Pandemics," *Atlanta Journal-Constitution*, August 28, 2021, retrieved September 10, 2021, https://www.ajc.com/education/get-schooled-blog/uga-professor-we-must-protect-students-from-storms-and-pandemics/KFF7LLXXA5F2JISDTEPKZTPFNU/.

She wondered what students would think about the fact that we knew about the seriousness of the pandemic. Would they wonder why didn't we go out of our way to provide the protection they needed? As she suggested, we've put teachers and students in the "center of a political and ideological battlefield where children's and youth's best interests are not being prioritized." She continues, "Maybe now, in the quiet after the storm, we can reflect on the dangerous position we forced our young people and teachers into as they waited out our tornado warnings." [396]

In 2022 we find schools in a difficult situation because of the rapid spread of the Omicron variant of COVID-19. Positivity rates are beyond 20 percent in the United States, suggesting that sending kids into schools should only be done with extreme caution. In some school districts, teachers have gone on strike. But in most districts around the country, teachers have little say about whether schools should open for face-to-face instruction or go online.

The CDC's recommendations in early fall 2021 were stated as essential elements of safe K–12 school in-person instruction. They are universal and call for the use of masks, physical separation (six feet), handwashing and respiratory etiquette, cleaning facilities, and contact tracing in combination with isolation and quarantine. These were used successfully during the 1918 flu pandemic, by the way.

Throughout the pandemic, a disconnect existed between CDC guidance for operational strategies for K–12 schools and local and state government COVID-19 guidelines. For instance, the CDC recommended mask wearing and physical separation in schools, while some governors, as noted above, lifted mask mandates. This disconnect is a problem. Some parents continue to say they do not want their children vaccinated. Some parents are not sure what the long-term effect of mRNA vaccines will have on children's brain development, for instance. Other parents are committed anti-vaxxers and won't allow their children to be jabbed.

If the virus is in circulation, then unvaccinated children, teens, and adults can be infected and can pass the infection on to others.

---

[396] Jones, "Protect Students."

PREVIEW

Ahead are seventeen blog posts that I wrote about the SARS-CoV-2 pandemic. In Chapter 10, the nature of the pandemic is explored. What are the facts about SARS-CoV-2? What can we learn about the pandemic we are living through from previous pandemics, especially the 1918 flu pandemic? The United States has registered the greatest number of cases and deaths in the world caused by SARS-CoV-2. How can this knowledge be used to prepare for future pandemics, which are sure to happen?

Chapter 11 includes several posts that show how Donald Trump failed to lead the nation at a time when leadership would have been the difference between failure and success, life and death. Throughout his presidency, Trump ignored the science and scientists that were all around him and instead played down the virus to the detriment of all Americans. More than 800,000 people (about two-thirds the population of Maine) have died, most of whom would not be dead if Trump had done his job.

Chapter 12 explores schooling in the age of SARS-CoV-2. COVID-19 has presented unique problems for educators, parents, and students. Schools operated for months entirely online, with many schools continuing to teach online to this day. Many questions are still unanswered about how safe it is to return all students to school for face-to-face learning.

CHAPTER 10:
SARS-COV-2

10.1. BLOG POST, 3 MARCH 2020: IS THE US PREPARED FOR COVID-19?

Two days ago, I was in a local computer store. I go there often, so the employees recognize me. A young man assisted me with my smartphone. But while we talked, the subject of the coronavirus outbreak came up. He said he was concerned because he needed to work. If he was sick and stayed home, he wouldn't be paid. He also said that he didn't have health insurance. I realized that he was scared not only about getting the coronavirus, but also about what would happen to him and his family if they were to get sick.

More than 27 million Americans (8.5 percent of the population) do not have health coverage. In addition, only eleven states and Washington, DC, provide sick leave pay. In this case, all businesses in sick leave states provide paid leave for sick employees.

THE UNINSURED

Prior to the Affordable Care Act, about 44 million Americans were without health coverage. Because of the Affordable Care Act, the number of uninsured dropped to 27.8 million in 2018 and rose slightly to 28.9 million in 2019. The uninsured are typically non-elderly. They are individuals and families with incomes below the poverty level. They are non-Hispanic whites (41%), but people of color make up 43% of the non-elderly population and account for half of the uninsured. Coronavirus can infect anyone. But seeking adequate care is dependent on a range of factors. Leading the list is not having health coverage.

PAID SICK LEAVE

Does paid sick leave affect communicable diseases such as influenza? The *Washington Post* reported on the research by Stefan Pichler and Nicolas Robert Ziebarth, who looked at the pros and cons of sick leave schemes. Their study showed how paid sick leave has affected the spread of diseases, namely the flu. They used data from Google Flu and influenza-like illnesses (ILI rate). Using this data, they showed ILI rates decreased in cities and states that mandated sick pay by about 5 percent. Moreover, they found that during a flu wave, the sick leave policy reduced the flu rate by up to 40 percent. They report that in the two years before the sick leave mandate, ILI rate in the cities with a mandated sick pay (the treatment group) was comparable to the ILI rate in cities with no sick pay (the control group). After the introduction of sick pay, the ILI rate decreased significantly for the treatment group.[397]

UNIVERSAL HEALTH CARE

The US is one of only a few countries that does not provide universal health care. The US also has the most incompetent president and vice president in the world. Each of these men has a disdain for science. Trump and Pence lack the leadership to handle the COVID-19 outbreak. However, the US has a strong research-based medical community. The CDC and NIH, if left to their own competence, are able deal with this global threat. However, the Trump administration has impaired the work of professionals in these government health agencies.

In the meantime, the best that the American public can do is:

- Do not listen to anything Donald Trump says about diseases, especially the flu or coronavirus. He is not competent to lead a scientific effort to solve the coronavirus outbreak.

---

[397] Stefan Pichler and Nicolas Robert Ziebarth, "The Pros and Cons of Sick Pay," *VoxEU*, May 12, 2018, retrieved February 25, 2021, https://voxeu.org/article/pros-and-cons-sick-pay.

- The same goes for the vice president.
- Do listen to reports from professionals who work at the CDC.
- Get a flu shot. If you have not already, wash your hands. And don't touch your face.

10.2. BLOG POST, 1 APRIL 2020: SOCIAL DISTANCING LESSONS FROM THE 1918 GREAT INFLUENZA

Americans have mixed views about social distancing. Yet evidence shows social separation is an effective nonpharmaceutical measure taken to prevent the spread of a contagious disease, such as COVID-19. Social distancing means keeping your distance from other people and reducing the number of times you might encounter other people.

Infectious diseases spread in a typical pattern approximating a bell-shaped curve. Right now, the US is in the "acceleration" phase of the COVID-19 pandemic. We haven't reached the peak. Depending on where you live, the nature of this curve will depend upon conditions on the ground. For example, if no intervention is undertaken, then the height of the curve will likely be much higher than in locations that implement social separation. Some people think letting the disease run its course is an option they prefer. This approach is called herd immunity. Herd immunity is based on immunity after a high proportion of individuals either become infected or vaccinated. The president of the United States, up to a day or so ago, wanted to send people back to normal life on Easter Sunday. Perhaps he was intending a preference for herd immunity. Experts on the task convinced him not to go ahead with this policy or he would face a disaster.

NONPHARMACEUTICAL MEASURES

Since no medicines or vaccines are available yet for the coronavirus, nonpharmaceutical public health intervention measures are the only way to mitigate the risk and impact of this infectious disease. Although not all states have adopted the same measures, most have implemented some form of social distancing. As shown in the graph below, an intervention of social separation would "flatten the curve" of the pandemic outbreak. If the curve is not flattened, health care is threatened, and hospitals face a severe disruption. We are witnessing horrific scenes in New York hospitals because of the influx of COVID-19 patients.

WHERE'S THE EVIDENCE THAT SOCIAL DISTANCING WORKS?

Does social distancing influence the spread of an infectious disease? Research supports the use of social separation. One source of evidence is research that was done to find out what happened when US cities used social distancing to mitigate the effects of the 1918 flu pandemic. By the end of the pandemic, between 50 and 100 million people were dead worldwide, including more than 500,000 Americans.

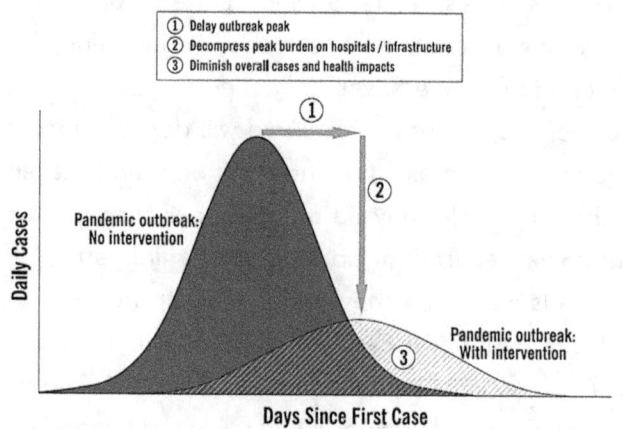

Figure 14. Pandemic influenza or Covid-19 graph of no intervention compared to intervention. Source: CDC

A study published in *The Journal of the American Medical Association* examined the effect of social distancing used during the 1918–1919 influenza pandemic. No computers or online databases were available in 1918, but paper documents were kept by municipalities during this period. The researchers used public health documents and the type of nonpharmaceutical interventions implemented around the country including school closures, cancellation of public gatherings, and isolation and quarantine.[398]

---

[398] Howard Markel et al., "Nonpharmaceutical Interventions Implemented by US Cities During the 1918–1919 Influenza Pandemic," JAMA 298, no. 6 (2007): 644–654, https://doi.org/10.1001/jama.298.6.644.

They looked at the weekly "excess death rate" (EDR)—time from the activation of nonpharmaceutical interventions to the first peak EDR, the first peak weekly EDR, and cumulative EDR during the entire twenty-four-week study period. Mitigation interventions for forty-three cities in the continental United States were studies from September 8, 1918, through February 22, 1919.

They found 115,340 excess pneumonia and influenza deaths in the forty-three cities for the twenty-four-week period. Every city adopted at least one of the three major nonpharmaceutical interventions:

- School closure
- Public gathering ban
- Isolation and quarantine

School closures and public gathering bans were the most often used combination by cities. Using a minimum of four weeks (range was one to ten weeks) was significantly associated with reductions in weekly EDRs. Cities that implemented these mitigations earlier had lower peak mortalities and lower total mortality. According to the authors of the study, "These findings demonstrate a strong association between early, sustained, and layered application of nonpharmaceutical interventions and consequences of the 1918 influenza pandemic in the US."[399]

You've heard Dr. Deborah Birx and Dr. Anthony Fauci tell Americans that we need to flatten the curve. What this study of the 1918 pandemic found was that the curve can be flattened if communities practice social separation. However, in 1918, it took several months to flatten the curve. To mitigate the virus, social distancing can work, but it must be implemented over a longer time than the White House Coronavirus Task Force would like to admit.

The most effective measure appears to be isolation and quarantine, as used in New York City. From the date of the first case detected in New York September 8, 1918, it took until December 1 for the curve to flatten.

---

[399] Markel, "Nonpharmaceutical Interventions."

It took much longer for Denver to flatten the curve. They implemented school closures and banned public gatherings. However, in mid-November, they relaxed these methods, and the number of cases increased, resulting in a second peak. After they took kids out of school for a second time and implemented isolation and quarantine, the curve was again flattened.

The lessons from the 1918 flu epidemic are clear. Nonpharmaceutical methods, including keeping students out of school, banning public gatherings, and isolation and quarantine are effective. They can mitigate the spread of a virus.

Masks were not as effective during the 1918 flu because most masks were homemade and not effective in preventing the spread of droplets or protecting the user from others' droplets.

10.3. BLOG POST, 22 APRIL 2020: CORONAVIRUS DAILY STATUS REPORTS

Ed Johnson, a public school advocate in Atlanta, explains that the Georgia Department of Public Health (GADPH) offers COVID-19 updates on its website twice daily, one update around noon and the other around early evening. Johnson's presentation is meant to supplement the latest or a recent GADPH COVID-19 noon update.

If you live in Georgia, his reports are one of the most informative and important sources of information about the status of coronavirus in the state. In these daily reports, he provides several graphical summaries of COVID-19 in Georgia. His reports include pareto charts, control charts, and prediction charts.

COVID-19 PARETO CHART

A pareto chart (Figure 15) is a combination bar graph and a line graph. Individual values (such as number of infections in a county) are represented in descending order by bars, and the cumulative total is represented by the line. The purpose of the chart is to highlight the most important among many cases. The pareto chart in Figure 15 is helpful in identifying areas in the state that share 80% of the cases while making up only 20% (32) of the 160 counties in Georgia. Note the seven vertical lines on the left of the horizontal axis. These seven counties represent 52% of the COVID-19 cases in the state. Five of the counties are in the metro Atlanta area, while two are more rural. I have lived in three of them: DeKalb County, Fulton County, and Cobb County.

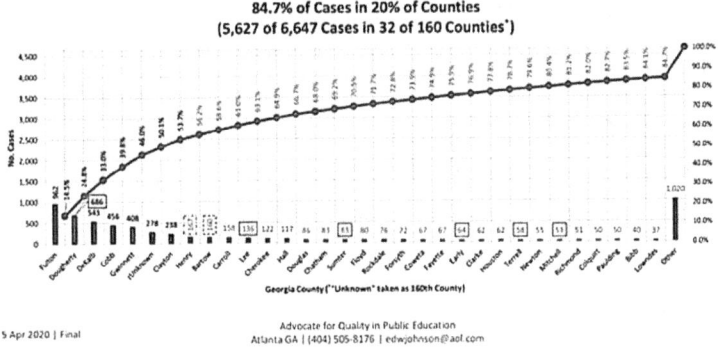

Figure 15. Pareto chart of confirmed coronavirus cases in Georgia. Source: Ed Johnson; used with permission.

COVID-19 CONTROL CHART

A control chart is a graph used to study how a process (infection in this case) either changes over time or compares from one area to another. In the control chart in Figure 16, Georgia counties are plotted on the horizontal, and number of infections per 10,000 people are plotted on the vertical. The line in the center of the graph is the average of infections and the two dashed lines are the upper control limit and the lower control limit. Notice that some of the points fall outside the two horizontal dashed lines, but most are within the control lines. Let's consider these points of departure as unusual. As Johnson states within the notes of the chart, the more distant a county's number of cases or deaths (refer to a death chart) from the upper limit of 14.87 cases, the more unusual its rate. Which county's rate is most unusual? How about your county? Why?

We have a severe problem in the United States. The president is supporting and riling up Americans who want their governors and local officials to open their states for business. We know people are hurting. People have lost jobs. They've lost their health insurance in some cases. However, they could lose their lives and put other people at risk if they don't consider the implications of their actions. Coronavirus is a deadly virus. COVID-19 has already killed more than 2.5 million people (about twice the population of Hawaii) around the world and more than 250,000 people in the United States. We need to tread carefully. Breaking the six-foot barrier and discarding facial masks are sure to cause a resurgence of the virus. We know from the 1918 flu epidemic that when mitigation measures were relaxed, the virus came roaring back. I know it is a tough time for all of us. But for the health of kids, of your family and friends, your coworkers, and others that you meet every day, play it safe. And listen and search for the facts about the coronavirus.

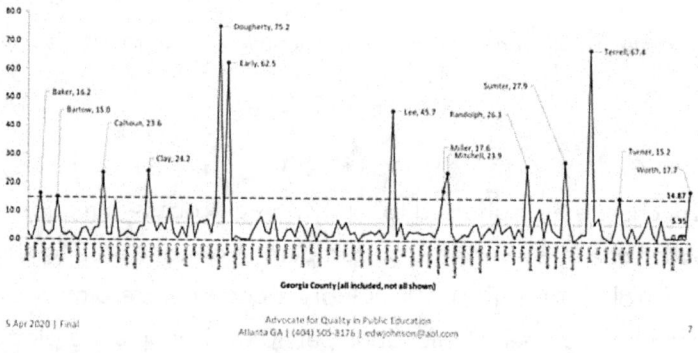

Figure 16. Control chart of coronavirus cases per 10,000 persons for Georgia. Source: Ed Johnson; used with permission.

10.4. BLOG POST, 22 APRIL 2020: CONTACT TRACING

According to the CDC, contact tracing is part of the process of supporting patients with suspected or confirmed infection. Public health staff work with patients to help them recall everyone they have had close contact within a brief time (a week or two). Staff or hired workers then contact the exposed individuals.

The identity of the patient is kept confidential. Contacts are provided with information to monitor themselves for illness and to let them know that they could infect others. Contacts are asked to stay home and maintain social distance from anyone for fourteen days. The CDC recommended checking your temperature twice a day and watch for coughing and shortness of breath. If so, you should be evaluated by medical staff and tested.

CONTROLLING THE SPREAD

Contact tracing is one way we can control the spread of coronavirus. However, getting the results quickly, in a day or two, is necessary to carry out a robust COVID-19 contact tracing program, which has been shown to control the spread of the virus. It requires a lot of people to implement and carry out a contact tracing program. Unfortunately, the Trump administration has failed us in this regard. They announced today that no new funds will be allocated for testing and contact tracing. This is one more part of the national coronavirus failure. Trump thinks that more testing makes him look bad, even if more people are getting infected and more are dying.

Contact tracing has been shown to work in other countries. South Korea implemented an effective contact tracing program soon after the coronavirus began infecting people. However, contact tracing, which many states have begun, is having serious problems. The underlying problem is lack of cooperation. If you are called by the state's health department or designated provider, will you pick up the phone? And if you do, will you answer the interviewers' questions about COVID-19? When they call, they know that you are infected or met someone with COVID-19. They want to know how you are feeling. Do you have any of the symptoms associated with COVID-19? But they also want to know who you have been in contact with recently. They will ask for information on these people, and then they will call them and ask them to get tested. The process continues trying to identify those who might be infected followed by testing and quarantine.

Massachusetts launched a contact tracing effort to contain the coronavirus. As of today, Massachusetts is one of the few states in the country conducting widespread contact tracing, according to Massachusetts Governor Charlie Baker. According to chief strategist and cofounder of Partners in Health Dr. Paul Farmer, the goal of contact tracing is to stop, not just slow, the spread of the virus in Massachusetts.

Chief medical officer and associate professor with the Division of Global Health Equity at the Brigham and Women's Hospital and the

Department of Global Health and Social Medicine at Harvard Medical School Dr. Joia Mukherjee helped organize similar projects to fight Ebola in West Africa and cholera in Haiti. She argues that we must go on the offensive against the virus, otherwise "we're going to get creamed." Instead, "Let's use tools that can reach into that silent epidemic and start to cut that off."[400]

The contact tracing program in Massachusetts hired 2,000 contact tracers and then provided training. However, over the past three months, about half of these folks were laid off. Problems developed between Partners in Health, an international health care company, and local community agencies. Some local health agencies said that it was taking too long for Partners in Health to contact people who were initially infected. Trying to identify people who met the initially infected persons was even more difficult. And the purpose of contact tracing is getting to those people who were near the infected and get them tested. Without this contact happening, stopping the spread is difficult.

In his Twitter feed, Dr. Anthony Fauci explains what is not working with contact tracing. He points out that many people simply do not know they are infected. In fact, when I visited my doctor two days ago, she said that most people who come into her office and test positive for COVID-19 are asymptomatic. And that is a big problem with contact tracing. It is a big problem in trying to rein in the spread of the virus.

In an article in Axios, Bryan Walsh explains that contact tracing is the best tool to stem the spread of the virus.[401] And according to public health standards, each state should have at least thirty contact tracers per 100,000 people. According to Walsh's research, only seven states have reached this capacity. And many states are now experiencing their biggest surges in infections. They are unable to keep up with additional contact tracers. Walsh points out that the US would need 100,000 contact tracers. Right now, there are about 28,000.

---

[400] Martha Bebinger, "COVID-19 Contact Tracing Has Launched in Mass. Here's How the Effort Is Going So Far," WBUR, April 18, 2020, retrieved February 25, 2021, https://www.wbur.org/commonhealth/2020/04/18/contact-tracing-massachusetts-covid19-coronavirus.

[401] Bryan Walsh, "Coronavirus Contact Tracing Efforts Are Understaffed, Underfunded—and Aren't Working," Axios, June 27, 2020, https://www.axios.com/coronavirus-contact-tracing-isnt-working-0d8ec92c-ec1c-4b46-a736-844649b760dd.html.

10.5. BLOG POST, 7 JULY 2020: FACE MASKS FOR HEALTH

Wearing a face mask is the most effective way to protect others and yourself from being infected by COVID-19. In this post I'll discuss how face masks are not only a crucial health standard, but their use is also supported by research.

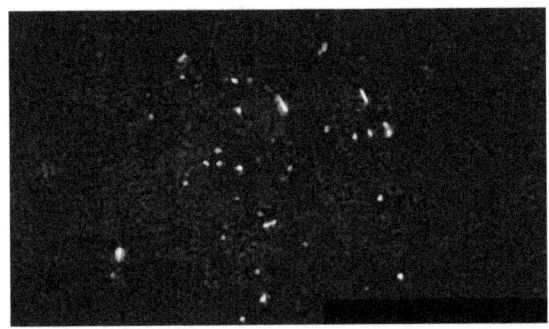

Scientists, using laser light, have been able to show droplets expelled while talking. In the case shown here, the speaker says: "Stay Healthy." If droplets come from a person with COVID-19 or any virus, they can be inhaled by others close to the speaker, possibly spreading the disease. Source: National Institutes of Health, CDC.

Using laser light scattering, researchers from the NIH have been able to illuminate droplets of saliva of a person talking and without a mask. When a mask is worn, the droplets of saliva nearly disappear. Although tiny particles can be seen in the laser light show, cloth masks are effective in reducing the spread of these smaller particles. The science of face masks shows how wearing them reduces the spread of coronavirus.[402]

Dr. Anthony Fauci, director of the NIAID, says that not wearing a face mask increases the risk of the virus being transmitted. He also says that not wearing a mask is irresponsible. We know now that wearing a face mask not only protects others from being infected, but also protects the mask wearer as well.

The health of Americans is at risk. The COVID-19 virus has not been controlled in the United States. In early March 15,000 cases of COVID-19 were reported each day. By early July 2020, nearly 60,000 new cases were being reported. The virus is spreading faster than it did

---

[402] Jeremy Howard, "Masks Help Stop the Spread of Coronavirus—the Science Is Simple and I'm One of 100 Experts Urging Governors to Require Public Mask-Wearing," *The Conversation*, May 25, 2021, https://theconversation.com/masks-help-stop-the-spread-of-coronavirus-the-science-is-simple-and-im-one-of-100-experts-urging-governors-to-require-public-mask-wearing-138507.

in the earliest stage of the pandemic. Not only is the virus spreading faster, but those getting infected are younger Americans. In Florida, twenty-one-year-olds are getting sick.

> **Author's Update:** The CDC now recommends that we should wear either N95 or KN95 face masks. Cloth masks do not give the level of protection that these masks do.

10.6. BLOG POST, 19 JULY 2020: DO I HAVE COVID-19?

About 1.1 million people in Georgia have been tested for COVID-19, and 21,000 new cases were reported today. Although the number of positive tests has been about 10 percent, today's results indicated that 16 percent of the tests were positive.[403]

The question for this post is, do I have COVID-19? Am I one of the 10 percent who tested positive? Whether I do or not is something I cannot tell you right now. I will not know my results for about ten days.

IS COVID-19 OUT OF CONTROL?

At the present time, COVID-19 spread is out of control in the US. It is spreading rapidly in the South and the West, and as a result, openings of businesses are being scaled back. More than 70,000 new cases are being reported every day. More than 3.7 million Americans have been infected. More than 140,000 have died. And in many states, especially Florida, Texas, California, South Carolina, and Georgia, the rate of increase is playing havoc with these state's health care systems—again.

Masks are being mandated in some states. And many national-brand companies will not let you in the door to shop without a face covering. In Georgia, Governor Brian Kemp sued Atlanta Mayor Keisha Lance Bottoms to block the city's mask order. At the end of a contentious battle, the governor decided to drop the lawsuit. The governor of Georgia has threatened other mayors for mandating masks. He hesitated to close

---

[403] "Coronavirus in Georgia: Latest Numbers for Sunday, July 19," 11Alive.com, July 19, 2020, retrieved April 15, 2022, https://www.11alive.com/article/news/health/coronavirus/coronavirus-numbers/coronavirus-cases-georgia-july-19-2020/85-6e96f6f4-1d67-4054-87e6-9db7f93e01b2.

the state down and then opened much earlier than other governors did. Even the president thought Kemp opened too early. Believe it or not, Kemp thought opening the state early would earn him sycophant points. Instead he was ridiculed by Trump and other politicians.

GETTING TESTED

The question I raised at the beginning of this post is: do I have COVID-19? Let me explain. About three weeks ago I occasionally had chills. I wondered what was causing them. I have written quite a bit about the COVID-19 pandemic on this blog, and I have followed the recommendations of science, which included wearing a mask, keeping at safe distances from others, washing my hands, and using hand sanitizers frequently. For most of the day, I am at home.

According to the CDC, people with COVID-19 have reported a wide range of symptoms, from mild symptoms to severe illness. Symptoms may appear two to fourteen days after exposure to the virus. These symptoms include fever or chills, cough, shortness of breath or difficulty breathing, fatigue, muscle or body aches, headache, new loss of taste or smell, sore throat, congestion or runny nose, nausea or vomiting, and diarrhea.

The only symptom on the list that applied to me was chills. I had none of the others. I got in touch with my primary care physician. He scheduled a virtual appointment on June 29. At the time of the video visit, I was feeling fine. And he said, "You look good!" He said just to monitor my condition and keep him informed of any further episodes of chills.

The next week, the chills once again appeared. I decided to make a face-to-face visit with him and was all set to see him at his office on July 6. But at about 8:00 a.m. that day, he called to tell me that I should get a COVID-19 test before coming to see him. He suggested two urgent care centers in the area.

I was able to get an appointment with one of the urgent care centers for July 13. I had assumed it would be a COVID-19 testing center, but after I waited for about half an hour, I was told that they didn't do COVID-19 testing at this center. Fortunately I had contacted the Piedmont Urgent Care system and was able to get a virtual appointment

THE TRUMP FILES

for July 20 at 5:45 a.m. I assumed they would follow this online meeting with a face-to-face meeting to get tested. But I had no idea when.

But over the past few days, I kept getting chills, and not only that, but I was also getting tingling in my hands and feet! Tingling can be a sign of nerve damage or a sign of a viral infection. Viral infection? COVID-19, I thought. It also could be a sign of diabetic neuropathy. But I could not get a test. I logged into both sites I identified above and spent hours trying to book a COVID-19 test. No luck. But I still had the virtual appointment on July 20.

I was concerned about the previous night's episode of chills and tingling, so I decided to go a local health care center about one mile from our home in Marietta, Georgia. I had visited their website and then called their office because they advertised that they do COVID-19 testing! But when I listened to their phone recording, they indicated they temporarily were not doing COVID-19 testing because they were out of test kits.

I still went to the clinic. After filling out the necessary paperwork, I was greeted by a nurse who checked all my vitals. I explained what I thought was going on, and when one of center's doctors came in and listened, she said yes, it was diabetic neuropathy that was causing the tingling. But we talked mostly about COVID-19. She said that all the folks that come to her that test positive for COVID show no signs whatsoever. No chills, no fever, no cough. She said, what good does it do to check people's temperature before they get on or off an airplane?

I told her that I had tried to get a COVID-19 test at her clinic. She said, "Would you like a test?" I was shocked. I had spent days trying to get tested to no avail. I quickly said, "Yes!" She then said, "We had several cancellations, and we have a few test kits in stock." I was in luck. A few minutes later, a nurse appeared and gave me a COVID-19 nasal swab test. No long stick on this test. Just a normal swab of both nostrils. It took about ten seconds, and I was off.

But I will not hear from the clinic for about ten days. I would not be a suitable candidate for COVID-19 contact tracing. But I got tested.

In the end, I tested negative.

CHAPTER 11:
TRUMP'S COVID-19 RESPONSE

11.1. BLOG POST, 19 MARCH 2020: THE TRUMP–COVID-19 TIMELINE

The first cases of the coronavirus were diagnosed in Wuhan, China, in November or December 2019. By January 19, 2020, the first case in the United States was diagnosed in Washington state. He was a male in his thirties who had just returned from Wuhan.

By the end of January, there were more than 11,000 cases of COVID-19 in China, and 250 cases in other countries. By the end of February, China reported 79,300 cases, with an additional 6,800 cases in other countries. Numbers were also going up in the US.

During this two-month period, Donald Trump did nothing to address the global spread of the disease. He said things like, "Well, we pretty much shut it down from coming in from China." He added later in February, "The numbers are going to get progressively better." They did not.[404]

THE TRUMP–COVID-19 TIMELINE

The timeline I have put together tracks the real world of the COVID-19 compared to the world of Donald Trump and his administration. The Trump–COVID-19 timeline covers the period from May 2018–January 20, 2021. I've also use quotation marks to highlight Trump's statements about the coronavirus.

---

[404] Linda Qiu and Mikayla Bouchard, "Tracking Trump's Claims on the Threat from Coronavirus," *New York Times*, March 6, 2020, retrieved November 28, 2021, https://www.nytimes.com/2020/03/05/us/politics/trump-coronavirus-fact-check.html.

THE TRUMP FILES

Author's Update: The original Trump–COVID-19 timeline covered the period up to March 19, 2020. To make the timeline complete, I've extended the timeline to Trump's last day in office.

Date	COVID-19 World	Trump's World
5/2018		Trump disbands White House pandemic response team.
7/2019		CDC staff in Chinese disease control center eliminated by Trump.
11/2019	First cases of a coronavirus circulating in Wuhan, China.	Trump's impeachment hearings are underway.
1/7/2020	First novel coronavirus case confirmed by Chinese authorities in Wuhan, China.	Meeting with prime minister of Hellenic Republic.
1/19/2020	First COVID-19 infection in Washington State (male who traveled to Wuhan and returned to US).	Trump at International Golf Club (West Palm Beach). Speech in Austin to Farm Bureau; self-congratulatory; no mention of virus.
1/22/2020	Confirmed cases in China: 547 WHO confirms human-to-human spread of coronavirus.	Trump in Davos, Switzerland: "The virus is totally under control; it is going to be fine."
1/24/2020	Confirmed cases in China: 916	Trump tweet: "It will all work out. China working very hard to contain the Coronavirus. I want to thank President Xi."
1/26/2020	Confirmed cases in China: 2,700	Nothing to report; he was in the White House.
1/28/2020	Confirmed cases in China: 6,000	Trump learns from his national security team that this virus will be the biggest national security threat in his presidency.
1/29/2020	White House Coronavirus Task Force established; led by Alex Azar, director HHS; in February Vice President Pence replaced him as head of task force.	
1/30/2020	6 cases in the United States	Trump rally speech: "We have it very well under control. We have little problem in this country at this moment—five. And those people are all recuperating successfully."

Date	COVID-19 World	Trump's World
1/31/2020	WHO declared coronavirus a public health emergency of international concern. Confirmed cases in China: 8,124; other locations: 113	Barred foreigners traveling from China, but not Americans.
2/2/2020	Confirmed cases in China: 17,200; other locations: 183	Trump on Fox News: "Well, we pretty much shut it down coming in from China."
2/5/2020	CDC shipped test kits to labs; failed; produced unreliable results.	Trump blames lab kits on previous administration—simply not true. They were botched by current CDC lab.
2/10/2020	Confirmed cases in China: 42,300; other locations: 457	Trump rally speech: "Looks by April, you know, in theory, when it gets warmer, the virus miraculously goes away."
2/11/2020	WHO names the disease causing coronavirus infection: COVID-19	
2/19/2020	Confirmed cases in China: 74,500; other locations: 1,109 cases	Trump on the radio: "The numbers are going to get progressively better as we go along."
2/23/2020	WHO announces virus in thirty countries, 78,800 cases (fivefold increase in three weeks).	Trump: "Very much under control. We had twelve; but they have gotten better."
2/25/2020	Cases around the world continue to increase.	Trump blames CNN and MSNBC for panicking markets, Democrats for their open borders, and Obama for slowing down test kits.
2/26/2020	Confirmed cases China: 78,100; other locations: 3,319 cases Dr. Nancy Messonnier holds tele-briefing saying the novel virus with spread in the community and warns of disruption to everyday life may be severe.	Trump says of numbers of cases, "They are going down, not up."
2/27/2020	Confirmed cases in China: 78,500; other locations: 8,200	Trump: "It's going to disappear."
2/29/2020	Confirmed cases in China: 79,300; other locations: 8,800	Trump: "Vaccine will be available very quickly; my administration is acting aggressively; more than anyone."
3/6/2020	Confirmed cases in China: 80,600; other locations: 21,385	Trump: "Anyone that wants a test can get one."
3/7/2020	Confirmed cases in China: 80,700; other locations: 25,200	At a tour of CDC, Trump says, "People are surprised that I understand it; how much I know."

THE TRUMP FILES

Date	COVID-19 World	Trump's World
3/10/2020	WHO reported 119,100 cases in one hundred countries.	Administration still has its head in the sand; claimed it had millions of test kits—not true; said risk for getting the virus was low.
3/11/2020	Confirmed cases in China: 80,900; other locations: 44,900 WHO declares COVID-19 a pandemic.	White House speech: self-congratulation, blame-shifting, misinformation.
3/12/2020	WHO: 142,000 cases; scientists predict up to 215 million Americans will be infected. The virus may have originated from bats or pangolins.	White House staff corrects Trump's misinformation from last night's speech. Trump continues to say, "It's the China or Chinese Virus."
3/13/2020	Confirmed cases in China: 80,900; other locations: 146,960	White House declares a national emergency. European travel ban. Trump claims Google has national website ready for COVID-19 (not true); Drs. Birx and Fauci speak about testing and containment; Trump claims labs are developing kits. Trump: "Don't blame me. I rate myself a ten for what we've done to fight the virus."
3/15/2020	Some states begin to shut down to prevent spread of virus. Forecasts for UK and US from Imperial College COVID-19 Response Team: 510,000 cases in UK; 2.2 million cases in USA now through July 20.	White House briefing: The Google site is not up and it won't be. Trump uses racist taunt, it's the Chinese virus, and blames fake news for Google debacle.
3/18/2020	British researcher says US is behind Italy by two weeks; COVID-19 could be with us until there is a vaccine (1 to 1.5 years). CDC recommends social distancing, groups of no more than ten, close restaurants and bars, assume you have COVID-19.	Trump, although optimistic, is not trustworthy; his history of misinformation and pathological lying is difficult to dismiss in the COVID-19 era. Coronavirus Task Force does not practice what it preaches. Trump in the middle, others shoulder to shoulder. Practice social distancing? Not us. Trump: "I will be having a news conference to discuss news from FDA concerning the Chinese virus!" "I don't take responsibility at all." "There is fake and corrupt news, day and night."

Date	COVID-19 World	Trump's World
3/19/2020	Total confirmed cases globally: 246,833 Total deaths: 9,785	Coronavirus Task Force adopts British coronavirus recommendations: 1. Social distancing 2. Groups of no more than ten 3. Stay in place Trump: "The virus just snuck up on us!" "It's the Chinese virus."
3/30/2020	Total confirmed cases: 503,341 Total deaths: 35,392	Coronavirus Task Force paints grim picture that 100,000–200,000 Americans could die from coronavirus. They convince Trump to extend lockdown thirty days to the end of April.
4/6/2020	US death toll: 22,000	Trump: "I see light at the end of the tunnel."
4/12/2020	Fauci says that US death toll is an underestimate.	On the coronavirus response, Trump says: "I couldn't have done it any better."
4/23/2020		Trump: "So, supposing we hit the body with a tremendous—whether it's ultraviolet or just very powerful light, and then I see the disinfectant where it knocks it out in a minute. One minute. And is there a way we can do something like that, by injection inside or almost a cleaning?"
5/5/2020	US death toll: 80,000	Trump: "Well-run states should not be bailing out poorly run states, using coronavirus as the excuse."
5/29/2020	US death toll: 110,000	"We will be terminating our relationship with the World Health Organization."
6/18/2020	US death toll passes 120,000.	Trump: "It's fading away. It's going to fade away. And it is dying out. The numbers are starting to go down."
7/1/2020	US death toll passes 130,000.	Trump: "I think we're going to be very good with the coronavirus. I think that, at some point, that's going to disappear. I hope."
7/8/2020	CDC rules on return to school.	Trump tweets: "I disagree with @CDCgov on their very tough & expensive guidelines for opening schools. While they want them open, they are asking schools to do very impractical things. I will meet with them!"

Date	COVID-19 World	Trump's World
8/1/2020	Fauci says US has more cases than Europe because it only shut down a fraction of its economy amid the pandemic.	Trump responds to Fauci: "Wrong! We have more cases because we have tested far more than any other country. If we tested less, there would be less cases."
9/10/2020	US approaches 200,000 deaths.	Trump: "If you take out the blue states, we're at a level I don't think anybody in the world would be at!"
10/3/2020	US death toll over 210,000.	Trump taken to Walter Reed Hospital for three-day COVID-19 treatment. The unhinged Trump tells America (after more than 210,000 deaths): "Don't be afraid of COVID. Don't let it control your life."
10/12/2020	New England Journal of Medicine criticizes Trump's COVID-19 response; states see spikes. Global cases top 40 million.	Trump repeats: "It's China's fault. They allowed this to happen."
11/3/2020	Trump loses election, Joe Biden is president-elect.	Trump launches the Big Lie: the election was stolen.
12/8/2020	Cases in US increasing.	Trump holds holiday parties at White House despite warnings by CDC.
12/31/2020	Trump claims the federal government distributed vaccines to the states. Now it is up to them.	Promised 20 million shots by end of December 2020; only about 2 million in arms by month's end.
1/6/2021	US death toll passes 360,000.	Trump incites mob to storm the US Capitol.
1/20/2021	Trump flees to Florida. US total COVID-19 cases: 25.8 million Deaths: 452,000	Joe Biden and Kamala Harris are sworn in as president and vice president of the United States.

Table 4. The Trump–COVID-19 timeline.

11.2. BLOG POST, 23 MARCH 2020: INTERVIEW WITH DR. ANTHONY FAUCI ON THE PANDEMIC

Jon Cohen's (staff writer for *Science*) interview with Dr. Anthony Fauci shows how difficult it is to deal with truth in the daily coronavirus press conferences.

Like many of you, I've tuned into these daily White House Coronavirus Task Force press briefings. I don't know about you, but I'm usually infuriated by Trump. His history of lying and misrepresenting the truth is fed to us on live TV, and unfortunately the media is contributing to this. They, like Trump, watch the ratings.

The only inkling of truth and accurate information occurs when Dr. Anthony Fauci, director of the NIAID, or Dr. Deborah Birx, coordinator for the Coronavirus Task Force, take the podium.

I've wondered how Drs. Fauci and Birx have dealt with being front and center during the worst pandemic that the world has experienced since the great flu pandemic of 1918. In that pandemic, the only approach that stemmed the growth of the virus was social distancing and isolation. We are at the same point in the COVID-19 pandemic. Now, however, we know that wearing a mask is the most effective way to protect ourselves and others from the virus.

Trump's COVID-19 response was too late, and as a result, governors are scrambling to do the right thing and get the medical tools hospitals need. And the right thing is to tell people to stay at home. The federal government needs to provide frontline health care workers with the tools and equipment they need to deal with the surge of patients that are overcrowding our hospitals.

How do these two scientists who interact daily with Trump as members of the Coronavirus Task Force deal with the mixed messages, untruths, and real concerns of the American people?

INTERVIEW WITH DR. ANTHONY FAUCI

I came across this interview with Dr. Anthony Fauci that was conducted yesterday by Jon Cohen and published in *Science*. The interview brings out some of the frustration but also the resolve of Fauci as he deals with Trump's view of this disease. As he said to Jon Cohen, "So, I'm going to keep pushing."

Here is one of the questions that Cohen asked in his interview with Fauci.[405]

---

[405] J. Cohen, "'I'm Going to Keep Pushing.' Anthony Fauci Tries to Make the White House Listen to Facts of the Pandemic," *Science*, March 26, 2020, retrieved February 25, 2021, https://www.science.org/content/article/i-m-going-keep-pushing-anthony-fauci-tries-make-white-house-listen-facts-pandemic.

Q: You stood nearby while President Trump was in the Rose Garden shaking hands with people. You're a doctor. You must have had a reaction like, "Sir, please don't do that."

A: Yes, I say that to the task force. I say that to the staff. We should not be doing that. Not only that—we should be physically separating a bit more on those press conferences. To his credit, the vice president [Mike Pence] is really pushing for physical separation of the task force [during meetings]. He keeps people out of the room—as soon as the room gets like more than ten people or so, it's, "Out, everybody else out, go to a different room." So, regarding the task force, the vice president is making sure that we don't crowd thirty people into the Situation Room, which is always crowded. So, he's adhering to that. The situation on stage [for the press briefings] is a bit more problematic. I keep saying, "Is there any way we can get a virtual press conference?" Thus far, no. But when you're dealing with the White House, sometimes you have to say things one, two, three, four times, and then it happens. So, I'm going to keep pushing.

11.3. BLOG POST, 25 MARCH 2020: WHAT EXPERTS SAY ABOUT TRUMP'S CORONAVIRUS EASTER PLAN

What do experts say about Trump's coronavirus Easter plan? For most of us, Trump's idea of opening large swarths of the country for "business as usual" is a preposterous idea. As Fauci said right after Trump made the claim, "You need to evaluate the feasibility of what you are trying to do. You must think what kind of metrics, what kind of data are you going to look at. Obviously, no one is going to want to tone down things like in New York City."

CORONAVIRUS CLUSTERS IN THE US

Trump is pushing the idea of returning to what it was like in the US in February. He must be blind to what has happened since then and in denial about the current spread of the virus in the country. A link exists between population density and the metrics of the COVID-19 disease. If you look at COVID-19 global cases by the Center for Systems Science and Engineering at Johns Hopkins University, you can investigate how the virus has populated the world. It's in clusters. If you go to their map on their website [406] and expand it, you will see the clusters of infection. Even in states that have just a few dots, many people would be at risk if we suddenly lifted the social distancing and isolation principles.

We also know that one person who is exposed or has been infected can easily infect many others. The evidence is that the infection spreads, especially in families and groups, such as a church choir. Social distancing and isolation are crucial to stop the spread of the virus.

11.4. BLOG POST, 5 APRIL 2020: WHY HAVE WE WAITED TO IMPLEMENT COMMUNITY MITIGATION?

The goal of community mitigation is to slow the spread of a novel influenza. Coupled with the fact that social distancing and other mitigation methods work, why have we waited to implement community mitigation throughout the United States?

Georgia implemented a statewide stay-at-home order on March 31, 2020. Why did Georgia's governor wait so long when the evidence was clear that coronavirus cases were accelerating at separate locations in the state? The state has several hotspots, and they are not only in the metro Atlanta area.

The White House Coronavirus Task Force has been slow to take urgent action, primarily because of Trump. He refuses to embrace personally what experts on the task force recommend. Even today, after the task force recommended that Americans cover their faces with masks of some sort when they go out, all Trump would say was, "Well, I know I won't wear one."

The task force should immediately tell all states to put a stay-in-place order now. The evidence is clear that these mitigation strategies can work.

---

[406] COVID-19 Dashboard, Center for Systems Science and Engineering and Johns Hopkins University, https://gisanddata.maps.arcgis.com/apps/dashboards/bda7594740fd40299423467b48e9ecf6.

STATE ORDERS OF COMMUNITY MITIGATION

Not all states have stay-in-place orders. The states that have resisted are simply keeping people in harm's way. They are all led by Republican governors. The virus is in those states, and unless they use some form of mitigation, the coronavirus will spread.

Alabama has just put into practice a stay-at-home order. But what about other states? Do those states think they are immune to COVID-19? In some states, even those with stay-at-home orders, scattered locations are open.

LESSONS FROM OTHER COUNTRIES

While we waited, other countries were putting into practice a variety of mitigation plans. There are three that I would like to shine a light on, and they are Spain, Italy, and South Korea.

You can check global coronavirus cases at the Center for Systems Science and Engineering at Johns Hopkins University to learn about COVID-19, including the number of confirmed cases, deaths, and recovered cases. Table 5 is a chart displaying coronavirus data on Spain, Italy, South Korea, and the United States as of April 3, 2020.

Country	Confirmed Cases	Deaths	Recovered
Italy	119,827	14,681	19,758
Spain	119,199	11,198	30,513
South Korea	10,062	174	6,021
United States	275,586	7,406	9,707

Table 5. Coronavirus cases by country as of April 3, 2020.

COVID-19 has hit Italy and Spain hard. Ten percent of people with confirmed cases in these two countries died because of COVID-19. Each country ordered stay-at-home mitigation strategies, as well isolation of individuals who tested positive.

Dennis Adams has shared data and graphical analyses that are pertinent to this discussion about mitigation, as well as previous posts on the coronavirus epidemic. Adams, a retired civil engineer living in the Canary Islands, was introduced to me by Jean Sanders, a colleague in Massachusetts.

The first graph I received from Adams is shown in Figure 17. It shows that Spain might be beginning to turn the corner. For the first time since beginning mitigation, the coronavirus cases are starting to lessen. Notice that the actual Spanish data are beginning to depart from the theoretical expected growth. If you look at the smaller graph superimposed on the larger graph, the trend in daily cases is down. This is what we want. This means that Spain's mitigation strategies are getting ahead of the virus.

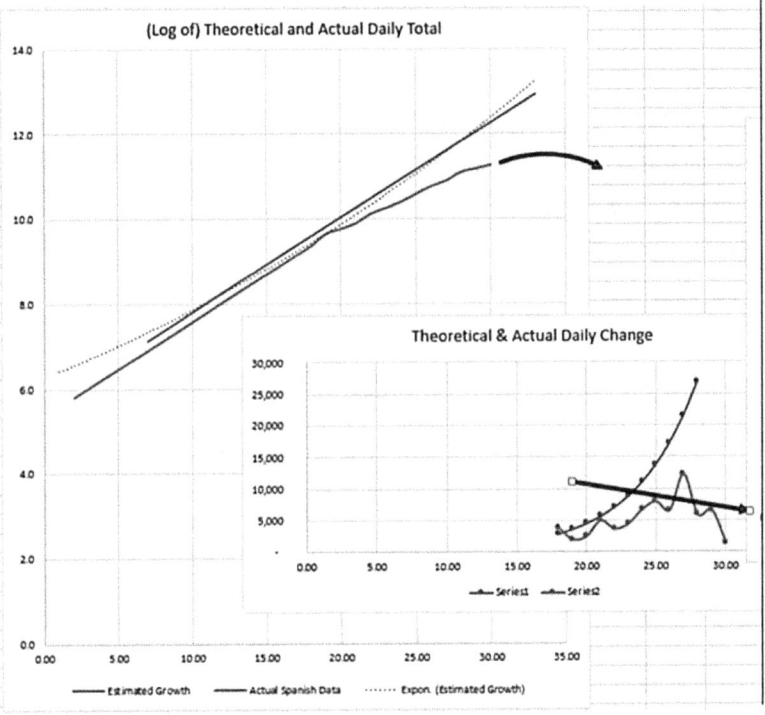

Figure 17. Theoretical and actual daily total of COVID-19 cases in Spain. Source: Dennis Adams; used with permission.

COMPARISONS AMONG FOUR COUNTRIES

The United States should pay attention to the efforts to contain the pandemic in Spain, Italy, and South Korea. The United States has more than 300,000 COVID-19 cases, more than any nation in the world.

First, let's look at this graph (Figure 18) provided by Adams comparing these three countries. South Korea, Italy, and Spain are compared to the theoretical predicted coronavirus cases (identified by an arrow). Italy and Spain are beginning to show progress. According to Spain's prime minister, the current stay-at-home mitigation will be extended until at least April 11. Although evidence shows that the virus spread is slowing, the prime minister said that nothing would change until the curve of the coronavirus pandemic is flattened.[407]

South Korea flattened the curve very soon after diagnosing its COVID-19 cases. You can see in Figure 18 that the line for South Korea is flat and has been for more than twenty days. Korea implemented an extensive contact tracing and testing approach, followed by isolation. According to one report, as soon as the first cases were reported in late January and then surged a few weeks later, the government launched a contact tracing and testing regime to identify and then isolate infected people.

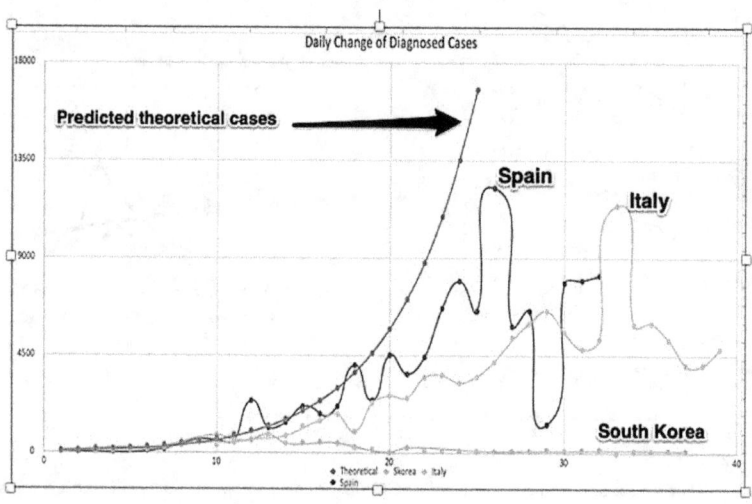

Figure 18. Daily change of diagnosed cases in South Korea, Spain, and Italy. Source: Dennis Adams; used with permission.

South Korea has tested more people per capita than any other country in the world. South Korea had about 10,000 cases (Figure 18) as of April 3, but only a few deaths. Some human rights groups have cautioned that South Korea's disclosure of confidential information to

---

[407] Tim Lister and Isabel Tejera, "Spain's Coronavirus Death Toll Shows Signs of Flattening," CNN, April 4, 2020, retrieved February 24, 2021, https://www.cnn.com/2020/04/04/europe/spain-coronavirus-death-toll-intl/index.html.

do contact tracing is a concern. On the other hand, in one survey, South Korea's public supports the publishing of individuals' movements.

COMMUNITY MITIGATION IN THE UNITED STATES

The first COVID-19 case in the US was reported on January 19, 2020, in the state of Washington. An analysis of the first case was reported in the *New England Journal of Medicine*.[408] Now, seventy-seven days later, the US has 301,902 diagnosed cases of the coronavirus. The implementation of mitigation strategies in the US has been shoddy. The lack of thought and organization at the federal level has put the US in a dangerous situation.

Although the White House has a Coronavirus Task Force with three scientists, it also has Donald Trump. Trump's history on the coronavirus has been careless and continues to be so to this day. The Trump–COVID-19 timeline (Blog Post 11.1) shows how he disregarded and denied the seriousness of the coronavirus for more than seventy days after the first cases were reported in Wuhan, China. Even now, he disrespects the scientific advice from the task force. After they suggested that people use face masks when they go out of their homes, Trump said, "Remember it's optional, and I won't be wearing a face mask."[409]

As a science educator I've been appalled by not only Donald Trump, but also the White House Coronavirus Task Force. Except for the three scientists on the task force, we've not heard from medical doctors, virologists, epidemiologists, or geneticists unless you watched TV or used social media. A lack of a scientific approach dominated our dealing with the pandemic in the United States. It could have been different.

A lot of people in the US don't think the coronavirus is any different from the flu. This belief is simply not true. Eight governors still have not ordered stay-at-home mitigation strategies.

We need to listen to Fauci and his colleagues. We need to seek the truth about the virus from scientists and physicians. Fauci is urging

---
[408] Holshue, "First Case of Novel Coronavirus."
[409] Y. Abutaleb et al., "The US Was Beset by Denial and Dysfunction as the Coronavirus Raged," April 4, 2020, retrieved February 25, 2021, https://www.washingtonpost.com/national-security/2020/04/04/coronavirus-government-dysfunction/.

Americans to work together to mitigate the virus. He commented that the country is "struggling to get the novel virus outbreak under control." He put it this way:

> "So, on the one hand, things are going to get bad, and we need to be prepared for that," Fauci, director of the NIAID, said. "It's going to be shocking to some. It's certainly really disturbing to see that. But that's what's going to happen before it turns around. So just buckle down, continue to mitigate, continue to do the physical separation because we've got to get through this week that's coming up because it is going to be a bad week in the neighborhood."[410]

Even if you don't live in a state that has its citizens staying home except to get food or medicine, you might follow the lead of states that have done this. California was the first state to issue a directive for people to stay at home.

11.5. BLOG POST, 29 MAY 2020: HOW TRUMP LED THE US TO AN ABSOLUTELY CHAOTIC COVID-19 DISASTER

The lack of leadership by the United States government, led by Donald Trump, has put all Americans into a chaotic COVID-19 disaster. As of this writing, more than 102,000 Americans have died from the coronavirus. It keeps rising at a rate of more than 1,000 per day. The country has fallen into an abyss without the kind of leadership that we see in some other countries, such as Germany and New Zealand, each with a woman as leader.

A PROFOUND DANGER

We are also witnessing the aftermath of the murders of two African American men. Ahmaud Arbery was shot to death by three white men

---

[410] Allan Smith, "Fauci: 'We Are Struggling' to Get the Coronavirus Outbreak Under Control," NBC News, April 6, 2020, retrieved February 25, 2021, https://www.nbcnews.com/politics/donald-trump/fauci-we-are-struggling-get-coronavirus-outbreak-under-control-n1177131.

while he was jogging in Brunswick, Georgia, on February 23. George Floyd was murdered by a white police officer in Minneapolis on May 25. Trump has done nothing but issue threats, such as a tweet in which he wrote, "When looting starts, the shooting starts." Twitter blocked it.

Yet Governor Mike DeWine said on May 29 that the protests across Ohio are not only understandable, but they are also appropriate. He even encouraged people to exercise their First Amendment rights. Trump doesn't know how to say things like this. Why? Read on:

> Donald Trump is a profound danger to Americans and to the rest of the world. He will remain a profound danger until he is no longer president, since the dangers clearly result from Trump's serious mental impairments that are untreated and are most likely impervious to treatment.[411]

These are lines from Dr. Brandy X. Lee's book *The Dangerous Case of Donald Trump*. I don't know about you, but every day this man behaves as being unfit for the office he holds, more than anyone before him.

Trump spews erratic, unpredictable, and mostly dangerous ideas. He especially relishes doing so in front of the cameras or by tweeting his nonsense. He has created a chaotic COVID-19 disaster. How does this play out, and what are the ramifications? Are we just to sit by and let him continue lying, breaking the law, and creating chaos? We not only need to speak out. We need to be witnesses to this unacceptable behavior, plus we need to *vote*.

TRUMP'S LIES

Trump is a menace to the American people during the COVID-19 pandemic. At the center of his incompetence is his lying. In an article in *Forbes*, David Markowitz, a professor of language and technology, said that very few of us are prolific liars. He points out that most of us say about one or two little lies a day. Donald Trump, however, lies at a rate

---

[411] Lee, *The Dangerous Case of Donald Trump*, xix.

of more than twenty-three per day. Unbelievably, Dr. Markowitz analyzed more than 18,000 reported Trump lies. He analyzed Trump's lies over time by topic and location. Trump seems to lie about everything from his biography to the Ukraine probe and from campaign rallies to Twitter. Dr. Markowitz concludes his analysis in this way:

> Trump's lies are problematic because they force us to question our institutions and the value of information. Their consequences might also bleed into our everyday meaningful relationships. Our trust in government, media, and other institutions remain quite low, but we still tend to trust one another. What happens when our distrust in government affects our trust in family or friends? When we fail to value truth and instead prioritize alternative facts or self-serving discourse, the fabric that holds our relationships together begins to fray.[412]

CONTRADICTOR OF FACTS AND AGREEMENTS

Before the pandemic, we already knew how Trump would act. Ever since he took office, he has shown his disdain for science, rational thinking, and intelligence. Too many examples of his contempt for these exist to list. However, here are a few that stand out.

He has consistently discredited, blinded, and overridden the intelligence community. Joshua Geltzer, executive director of the Institute for Constitutional Advocacy and Protection at Georgetown Law, and Ryan Goodman, editor in chief of the blog *Just Security*, analyzed Trump's attacks on the intelligence community. They conclude that Trump's demeaning of US government employees is a genuine national security threat. They point out that Trump is better at spreading misinformation than protecting information.[413]

Trump and his cronies have assailed the EPA and have persisted in a wholesale repeal of rules that had been established and were designed

---

[412] Markowitz, "Trump Is Lying More than Ever: Just Look at the Data."
[413] Joshua Geltzer and Ryan Goodman, "The Pattern and Practice of Trump's Assaults on the Intelligence Community," *Just Security*, February 11, 2020, retrieved February 24, 2021, https://www.justsecurity.org/66035/the-pattern-and-practice-of-trumps-assaults-on-the-intelligence-community/.

to protect the American people's environment. They have censored scientists, often silencing them, with the result being the loss of veteran scientists across a wide swath of the EPA and other departments. A former employee and scientist at the EPA, Dr. Elizabeth Southerland, described the nature of Trump's assault. From climate change to drinking water standards, Trump has inflicted severe harm to the nation's efforts to protect the environment.[414]

Trump and his surrogates have aggressively attacked and pulled the US out of important international agreements. The most flagrant is Trump's withdrawal from the Paris Agreement, a climate agreement that all but two nations joined. Trump and his surrogates claimed that the Paris Agreement would undermine the US economy and put the country at a permanent disadvantage. Trump also withdrew the US from the Iran nuclear deal (Joint Comprehensive Plan of Action). Trump said that the Iran deal was a fatally flawed agreement.[415] And today, he announced that the US would be withdrawing from the WHO.[416] These actions, taken together, have endangered citizens around the world.

SCIENCE DENIER

One behavior that Trump has exhibited is his denial of science facts, scientific and medical research, and opinions of medical experts. We call this science denialism.[417]

Although Trump isn't the first to be a science denialist,[418] he's in first place in terms of the number of denials per day. Trump's denial of science has led the United States into an absolutely chaotic disaster. COVID-19 is the latest example of Republican science denialism.[419] In this case, however, that denialism has caused tens of thousands

---

[414] Elizabeth Southerland, "The Trump Administration's Assault on Science and the Environment," The Century Foundation, September 16, 2019, retrieved February 24, 2021, https://tcf.org/content/commentary/remarks-trump-administrations-assault-science-environment/.
[415] Mark Landler, "Trump Abandons Iran Nuclear Deal He Long Scorned," New York Times, May 8, 2018, retrieved February 24, 2021, https://www.nytimes.com/2018/05/08/world/middleeast/trump-iran-nuclear-deal.html.
[416] Brianna Ehley and Alice Miranda Ollstein, "Trump Announces US Withdrawal from the World Health Organization," Politico, May 29, 2020, retrieved February 24, 2021, https://www.politico.com/news/2020/05/29/us-withdrawing-from-who-289799.
[417] David L. Levine, "Science Denialism in the 21st Century," Scientific American, July 19, 2018, retrieved February 24, 2021, https://blogs.scientificamerican.com/observations/science-denialism-in-the-21st-century/.
[418] George W. Bush's presidency undermined climate science and spread misinformation leading to the war in Iraq.
[419] Mooney, The Republican War on Science.

of Americans to die. The poster child of science denialism is Donald Trump, one of the most dangerous persons we must face each day.

PETULANT CHILD

Trump's behavior on May 22, 2020, at the Michigan Ford plant was obnoxious. In front of Ford executives and the people who are the heart of the plant, Trump kept his face bare, spewing droplets as he rejected Ford's policy of mask wearing. He showed us his little mask and claimed he put it on over there, but away from the cameras. Except someone did snap a photo of Trump wearing the mask.

Dana Nessel, Michigan's attorney general, said that Trump threatened the health and safety of her state's residents through his coronavirus response by refusing to wear a mask and supporting those who are protesting Michigan's stay-at-home orders.[420]

Nessel compared the president to a "petulant child" for not wearing a mask while visiting the Ford plant. I think she's correct. There are other words that might describe the petulant Trump. Here are few: perverse, fault-finding, bullying, whiny, mean, pouting, brooding, whining, ungracious, rude, combative, and on and on.

PANDEMIC DEBACLE

Trump is responsible for the awful milestone of 100,000 Americans dying from COVID-19. If he had acted earlier, and if he had consulted his predecessor, he might be staved off tens of thousands of deaths.

He told his followers that the virus would go away with the warm weather. No, it didn't. And he blamed problems with equipment and lab tests on the previous administration. Again, not true. The Obama administration embraced science and insisted that scientists and medical experts lead efforts during a pandemic during his administration. Medical experts have been pushed to the side by Trump, and he refuses to wear a mask, fueling discord in society and creating

---

[420] Alana Wise, "Michigan AG Says She 'Will Not Remain Silent' as Trump Risks Public Health," NPR, May 22, 2020, retrieved February 24, 2021, https://www.npr.org/sections/coronavirus-live-updates/2020/05/22/861373885/michigan-ag-says-she-will-not-remain-silent-as-trump-risks-public-health.

groups of mask wearers and non-wearers. Trump's refusal to wear a mask, as well as his tweets siding with Michigan protestors who opposed Michigan Governor Gretchen Whitmer's stay-at-home order, fueled violence in the state. The anti-lockdown protestors attacked the Michigan State House with an intent to disrupt the government as well as kidnap the governor.[421]

Trump thinks he knows more than physicians who have worked on infectious diseases for decades. He suggested that injecting bleach directly into the body would be like "a cleaning" and would kill the virus.[422] And most recently Trump has claimed he is taking the controversial drug hydroxychloroquine. This is an antimalarial drug that the FDA has warned against its widespread use. Trump said, "What have you got lose?" Well, according to research,[423] the drug is linked to serious and even fatal heart attacks and is not effective in treating COVID-19.

What is Trump's deep research into this and other remedies he suggests? He's heard good things about it!

He's threatened scientists in government departments. He ignored all the work that been done during the Obama administration on preparing for a pandemic. He has walked away from the WHO, a crucial organization that is doing research on global health issues. He's ignored much of what was said by Dr. Anthony Fauci, director of the NIAID. Fauci recommends that we all wear face masks. Trump refuses to wear them.

It is a constant battle with the likes of Donald Trump.

11.6. BLOG POST, 2 OCTOBER 2020: THE SUPER-SPREADER RELEASED FROM HOSPITAL

For eight months Donald J. Trump, aka "the super-spreader," lied about COVID-19. He ignored and dismissed the health advice of the country's

---

[421] Andrew Solender, "Armed Protesters Storm Michigan State House over COVID-19 Lockdown," *Forbes*, May 1, 2020, retrieved February 24, 2021, https://www.forbes.com/sites/andrewsolender/2020/04/30/armed-protesters-storm-michigan-state-house-over-covid-19-lockdown/?sh=236f0cbf69b5.

[422] Matt Flegenheimer, "Trump's Disinfectant Remark Raises a Question about the 'Very Stable Genius,'" *New York Times*, April 26, 2020, retrieved February 24, 2021, https://www.nytimes.com/2020/04/26/us/politics/trump-disinfectant-coronavirus.html.

[423] Center for Drug Evaluation and Research, "FDA Cautions Use of Hydroxychloroquine/Chloroquine for Covid-19 outside of the Hospital Setting or a Clinical Trial Due to Risk of Heart Rhythm Problems," US Food and Drug Administration, retrieved February 11, 2022, https://www.fda.gov/drugs/drug-safety-and-availability/fda-cautions-against-use-hydroxychloroquine-or-chloroquine-covid-19-outside-hospital-setting-or.

top infectious disease experts. He admitted playing down the serious nature of the disease. Meanwhile more than 1 million Americans are infected. Over 210,000 people have died. Now he has the disease. Or so we've been told.

The president of the United State acted recklessly. He put many people at risk by foolishly holding meetings and attending rallies and fundraisers. He also attended the presidential debate knowing he was infected.

SUPER-SPREADER-IN-CHIEF

I believe Trump's behavior has been stupid, foolish, dumb, ludicrous, laughable, half-baked, absurd, pointless, irrelevant—you name it.

Trump's senseless behavior over the entirety of the COVID-19 pandemic has put the country at risk. More specifically, he has caused harm to people in his orbit. Those put in harm includes his Secret Service detail (many of whom have tested positive for COVID-19), his White House staff and employees, and many others who attended his rallies and fundraisers.

The Trump/Barrett super-spreader event in the Rose Garden at the White House, September 26, 2020. Eight persons came down with COVID-19 after this event. Source: Amy Rossetti, CC PDM 1.0.

On September 26, Trump held a gathering in the Rose Garden to announce the nomination of Amy Coney Barrett to the Supreme Court.

Specifically, this was the start of a week in which a string of people who had attended this gathering tested positive for the coronavirus.

In photos of the gathering, Trump and Barrett are standing on a stage looking out at two large arrangements of chairs full of people sitting shoulder-to-shoulder. Days after this meeting, one person after another reported they tested positive for the virus. Those infected included senators, the president of the University of Notre Dame, former New Jersey Governor Chris Christie, and White House officials including Hope Hicks and press secretary Kayleigh McEnany. And of course, the president and first lady.

In other words, Trump may be a COVID-19 super-spreader, or super-spreader-in-chief. Trump could be responsible for tens of people being infected, directly or indirectly. Indeed, evidence exists that his denial of scientific infectious disease advice may have caused between 40,000 and 50,000 deaths.[424]

HOSPITAL AS A SHOW STAGE

Donald Trump was admitted to the Walter Reed National Medical Center. He spent three days in the hospital. He was given multiple drugs, including dexamethasone, a steroid; REGN-COV2, two monoclonal antibodies; remdesivir, an antiviral drug; famotidine, an antacid; vitamin D; melatonin, a sleep hormone; and aspirin. Remdesivir is an experimental drug and has been shown to modestly treat COVID-19 by reducing hospital stays. It's also the kind of treatment not available to the general population.

However, Trump has used this experience to turn COVID-19 into a television dramedy, and all the major media outlets fell for it hook, line, and sinker. It appeared to me that this entire episode was planned to create photo ops for use in the next month's election.

I don't believe what he says while he's hospitalized. He's turning the hospital into a show stage. Trump has not taken responsibility for

---

[424] Apoorva Mandavilli and Tracey Tully, "White House Is Not Tracing Contacts for 'Super-Spreader' Rose Garden Event," *New York Times*, October 5, 2020, retrieved February 25, 2021, https://www.nytimes.com/2020/10/05/health/contact-tracing-white-house.html.

contracting the disease. He deliberately put those near him in harm's way. Fear was instilled in those who worked in the White House and extended to the public sphere, especially while speaking to reporters. He spewed this message and the virus at his rallies. And he went on television to try to embarrass and threaten people. Indeed, he may have spread the disease to innocents that attended a fundraiser at his golf course in New Jersey.

In my view, the hospital visit was nothing more than a plan for Trump to gain an upper hand with the way he has dealt with the COVID-19 pandemic. On Wednesday his closest advisor, Hope Hicks, showed signs of being COVID sick. Trump knew she was sick. She went home having tested positive. After being on an airplane with Hicks, he attended two events with hundreds of people, most of whom were not wearing masks.

During this time, he was showing signs that he was sick with the virus. Remember, this man refused a mask. Trump never said that people should wear facial coverings. He had the nerve to engage with people in close quarters without wearing a mask. He never encouraged people around him to wear a mask. What's the big deal? Well, the big deal is that the top infectious disease doctor in the federal government said he would trust using a face mask more than any experimental vaccine. Wearing a mask is a proven nonpharmaceutical treatment against the virus.

A SICK MAN

In short, Trump is a sick man. Now he's sick with COVID-19. Donald Trump has been a nightmare for over three years. For the past 240 days, he has refused to lead the nation out of this pandemic. Instead, he has pushed the country into the worst health crisis in over a hundred years. His actions have been criminal and evil. While thousands of people were getting sick daily, Trump was telling us that things were going great with the virus.

He urged people to take hydroxychloroquine. He said he was taking the drug. Dr. Anthony Fauci, the leading scientist on the White House Coronavirus Task Force, said the drug was not effective against the virus.

Then Trump recommended "injecting bleach" to kill the virus. As he said, it would act as "almost a cleaning." He made this comment at a Coronavirus Task Force news conference on April 23, 2020. Over the next few days, companies that manufactured disinfectants and bleach had to message that people should not inject or drink these liquids. Really.

CHAPTER 12:
SCHOOL IN THE AGE OF COVID-19

12.1. BLOG POST, 28 JUNE 2020: IS IT REASONABLE FOR COLLEGES TO OFFER FACE-TO-FACE CLASSES?

I am emeritus professor of science education at GSU. When I began my thirty-three-year career at GSU in 1969, the enrollment was about 10,000 students. Now the enrollment at GSU is more than 55,000. GSU has multiple smaller campuses and the main campus in downtown Atlanta.

GSU is one of twenty-six public institutions of higher education in the state. Although this article is not specific about what and how GSU should or will carry out its mission to offer undergraduate and graduate programs, it will be used as a case for the other twenty-five University System of Georgia (USG) institutions.

THE CASE ON MAY 4

On May 4, 2020, I raised this question: Are Georgia's college and university counties safe places to open this fall? My summary to this question was this:

> At the top of the post, I said that the question of opening campuses in Georgia would be complicated. Table 6 is data for the twenty-six Georgia colleges and universities. The data show that most colleges or universities will have to consider the status of COVID-19 cases existing in their respective locations. A number

of variables need to be considered. How many people in college locations have been infected? Are the number of cases increasing, level, or decreasing? What is the trend of cases and deaths in each of these locations?

Institution	Enrollment Fall 2019	COVID-19 Cases	Cases per 100K	Total Deaths	Hospitalizations	County
Augusta University	9,274	416	205	16	120	Richmond
Georgia Institute of Technology	36,489	2927	266	122	547	Fulton
Georgia State University—Main Campus Atlanta	29,662	2927	266	122	547	Fulton
Georgia State University-Perimeter	26,996	2256	284	129	557	Dekalb
Georgia State University -Newton	1260	215	191	8	36	Newton
University of Georgia	38,920	156	120	13	30	Clarke
Georgia Southern	26,054	42	52	2	9	Bulloch
Kennesaw State	37,807	1749	221	96	482	Cobb
University of West Georgia	13,238	383	318	14	72	Carroll
Valdosta State	11,270	158	134	4	28	Loundes
Albany State	6,122	1534	1706	124	314	Dougherty
Clayton State	6,879	777	254	33	138	Clayton
Columbus State	7,877	320	166	7	58	Muscogee
Fort Valley State	2.624	56	204	2	15	Peach
Georgia College & State University	7,031	318	209	11	91	Bibb
Georgia Southwestern	2,950	327	1091	20	46	Lee
Middle Georgia State University	8,066	318	209	11	91	Bibb
Savannah State	3,688	230	78	9	55	Chattam
University of North Georgia	19,748	1694	820	22	216	Hall
Abraham Baldwin Agricultural College	3,927	126	308	5	35	Tift
Atlanta Metropolitan State	1,844	2927	266	122	547	Fulton
College of Coastal Georgia	3,535	59	375	6	4	Glynn
Dalton State	4,964	118	112	4	15	Whitfield
East Georgia State	2,741	21	92	0	4	Emanuel
Georgia Gwinnett College	12,831	1933	199	58	415	Gwinnett
Georgia Highlands College	6,168	145	145	11	36	Floyd
Gordon State College	3,495	512	213	13	60	Lamar
South Georgia State College	2,345	129	359	11	37	Ware
USG Totals	333,507	28,331		1,175	5,388	

Table 6. COVID-19 Cases, Deaths & Hospitalizations in the county locations of the University System of Georgia colleges & universities, June 28, 2020.

Other questions need to be considered. How many students will return to these campuses? For example, University of Georgia's campus is 767 acres (about the area of Central Park in New York City), whereas GSU's main campus has only 110 acres, with additional acreage on five additional campuses in Alpharetta, Clarkston, Decatur, Dunwoody, and Newton. Can these two institutions provide a safe learning environment and prevent the spread of the virus? Naturally, every campus in the USG will have to do the same.

It seems to me that we need to consider these data. Only today, the CDC released information that was daunting. An internal government report projected about 200,000 new cases each day by the end of the month. The report, from the *New York Times*, provides details about the virus's spread throughout the country. Of particular concern to me was the status of Georgia, as shown in the report.

THE CASE ON JUNE 28

Today, the number of new cases of coronavirus in Georgia is rising, not falling. Yet in less than two months, USG students will be returning to twenty-six different campuses in the state. More than 360,000 students (about half the population of Wyoming) will be returning. But these numbers are only the state's public universities. It does not include the thirty-one private universities, enrolling 61,895.

On the next page is a control chart (Figure 19) prepared by Ed Johnson. In this chart, you will note that for all of April, May, and June, cases in Georgia were within expected results shown between the dashed lines. Then, between June 9 and today, something is happening that has not occurred in the last three months. The number of COVID-19 cases are outside expected results.

So now, on June 28, we can report that the data show that there is a trend in which COVID-19 cases are spreading and increasing in the state. Although you can't identify specific counties by examining this chart, you can see that we have a problem. Since the state government "opened" in Georgia, the virus has been spreading. If this trend continues and we bring more than 360,000 students (about half the population of Vermont) back to campuses around the state, we need to raise a red flag.

Georgia Counties COVID-19 New Cases with
5 Prior Days Moving Average **and** 7 Prior Days Moving Average

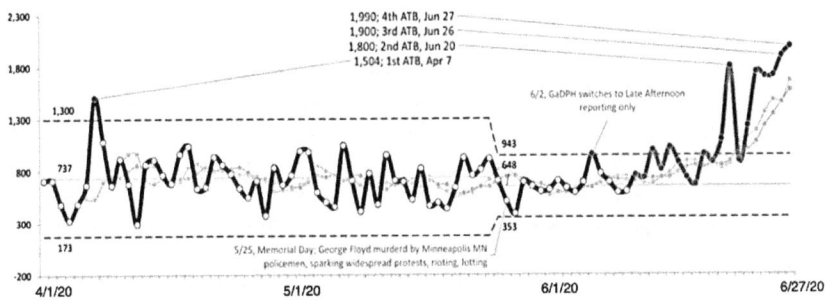

Figure 19. Control chart of covid cases in Georgia, April 1–June 27, 2020. Source: Ed Johnson, Advocate for Quality Public Education; used with permission.

It might not be reasonable to begin face-to-face teaching on our college campuses. How can we ensure that the infection caused by COVID-19 will not be brought to the more than fifty-seven campuses around the state? Can safe environments in classroom and dormitories be ensured? How will faculty, staff, and students be protected?

12.2. BLOG POST, 10 JULY 2020: OPENING SCHOOL?

Will schools reopen?

According to some, "There is absolutely no way this country is presently ready to thrust millions of children back into the close-quarters reality of school."[425]

According to others, there will be pressure put on governors and everybody else to open schools. Trump also said that the CDC guidelines for the reopening of school were too tough and should be changed without offering any suggestions. His sidekick, Mike Pence, claimed that the CDC will be changing their guidelines next week because of what Trump said.

---

[425] William Rivers Pitt, "If Schools Reopen This Fall, More People Will Likely Die. Full Stop," Truthout, July 8, 2020, retrieved February 25, 2021, https://truthout.org/articles/if-schools-reopen-this-fall-more-people-will-likely-die-full-stop/.

Now, this is authoritarianism in action.

So, is William Rivers Pitt's comment (quoted above) and full article closer to the reality of school? Pitt is an author, editor at Truthout, and activist. Or does the White House gang, who haven't stepped foot in a school in a long time, have secret knowledge about schools that they are keeping from us? Will schools reopen?

SAFETY FIRST

Pitt poses a compelling argument for not opening schools. We must keep in mind that there are more than 50 million students (about twice the population of Texas) enrolled in America's public schools. They are taught by more than 3 million professional public school teachers. At the present time, the spread of the coronavirus is at its highest rate of increase since the pandemic ravaged the United States.[426]

Some people in leadership positions simply do not care what happens to these students and teachers who will face each other and the virus every day they step foot into a school.

My guess is that they have little to no knowledge of what the life of a student or teacher is in one day of school. The well-being of the students must be most significant and important factor for students to enter school buildings.

TEACHERS NEED TO KNOW

If you are a teacher, no matter your age, you will wonder what accommodations will be made to keep you and your students safe. Teachers have many questions, and the answers are in short supply. Whether you teach primary or secondary students, you will encounter many people. COVID-19 carriers don't necessarily show any symptoms. If you meet students who have the virus and then return home each day, will your family get sick? If you are a student, you'll meet many fellow students and adults. You'll return home in the afternoon. Will you carry the virus on your coattails?

---

[426] Pitt, "If Schools Reopen This Fall."

Not all students have the same health conditions when they enter a school. Some have autoimmune diseases, such as rheumatoid arthritis, inflammatory bowel disease, Type I diabetes, mellitus, or Guillain-Barre syndrome. Some kids enter school from places where the home environment is unstable because of homelessness, parents having to change jobs, and moving. And even for children who are healthy, we all should realize that crowded spaces are the most dangerous places to be if COVID-19 is spreading.

Classrooms need to be reconfigured and students' schedules should be arranged so only half of the population of students comes to class. They can be at home or in special locations in school for special kinds of activities and programs. Why keep schools the same, and why continue to use the same model of learning?

How will your school district keep every classroom and space in the school clean and disinfected? How will all touched services be cleaned between classes? Will the students be responsible for cleaning desks and chairs before class? Does the district have the funding available to keep schools safe?

Has the government budgeted for transportation costs associated with the COVID-19 pandemic? For instance, large school buses can hold three per seat, meaning seventy-two children on a bus. Obviously, this number should not be allowed because of social distancing. If schools reduce bus passengers by 50 percent to achieve social distancing, will the district be able to transport all of its students to school?

SCHOOLING IN THE PANDEMIC

The COVID-19 pandemic is causing migraine headaches for departments of education, school boards, and high-level administrators as they think about schools reopening. Oh, and the parents of the millions of students and their teachers are wondering what part they'll play in pandemic schooling.

The mayor of New York City said that students might come back in the fall, but only for one to three days a week. Imagine a high school with more than half the students absent each day. What possibilities are there for secondary schools? Courses that only meet twice a week. More flexible scheduling for teachers. Collaborative studies using online protocols. More emphasis on student-developed curriculum. Emphasis on lifelong learning. There are lots of ideas that can and will emerge.

We cannot return to normal yet. We need to create new ways of organizing school. School purpose should begin with the needs of children, not the needs of college and career readiness, which benefit some individuals, groups, and companies.

12.3. BLOG POST, 7 AUGUST 2020: SHOULD STUDENTS WEAR MASKS AT SCHOOL?

The question in this post is, should students wear masks at school? But the underlying question is, should schools open for students to return to face-to-face classes?

Of course, everyone should wear a mask when out in public, especially in a crowded space such as a school. I was a high school teacher and a college for professor for forty years. If I were still teaching, I would join with likeminded colleagues and support online teaching until we get a handle on the coronavirus pandemic.

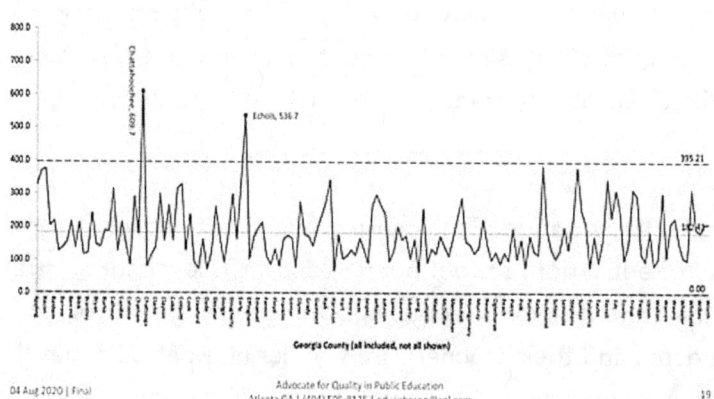

Figure 20. Control chart of number of COVID-19 cases per 10,000 persons in Georgia counties. Note that there are only two points above the upper control limit line. Source: Ed Johnson, Advocate for Quality Education, COVID-19 Daily Status Report as of August 4; used with permission.

THE COVID-19 SURGE IN GEORGIA

Folks like to use the term "COVID-19 hotspots" for areas where the virus is surging. And some places, especially in the Southeast and the West, show cases are spiking. However, if we take a careful look at a state such as Georgia, we might want to think about hot spots in different terms. Ed Johnson has been analyzing coronavirus data for months. He publishes a report each day about the virus's spread in Georgia. He uses process behavior charts that enable him to distinguish between uncommon or unusual rates of spread versus common or usual rates of spread. As of yesterday, only two of Georgia's 159 counties have reached unusual levels and speed of spread.

What about the other 157 counties? Johnson reports that any one county's rate is no longer significantly different from any other county's spread. He puts it this way:

> The whole state of Georgia has now "caught fire," as regards confirmed COVID-19 cases per 10,000 persons. Accordingly, it is now pointless to talk about hotspots and such in this regard. Another aspect of COVID-19's level of spread and speed of spread to consider, but goes unaddressed here, is regarding confirmed COVID-19 cases per unit of land area, say, per ten square miles.[427]

Johnson makes another assertion that is important as the state of Georgia (and other states as well) makes plans to open schools to face-to-face or online learning. The question that administrators and teachers, as well as other officials, need to consider and answer: Are schools safe places for students to interact with each other and their teachers? The fact that Johnson makes clear is that not only is COVID-19 spreading in all counties, but the rate of spread is also accelerating. Figure 21 shows the stark reality of the status of COVID-19 in Georgia. Earlier this year I questioned whether Georgia's

---
[427] Ed Johnson, COVID-19 Data Analysis, 2020.

governor was out his mind opening for business. The data suggest he was.

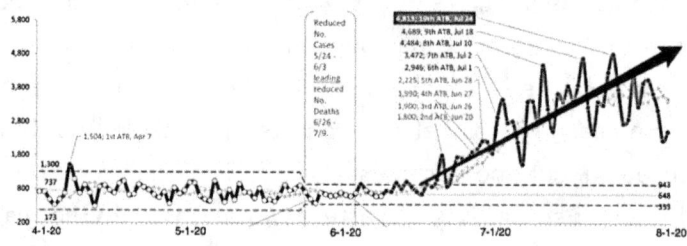

Figure 21. Control chart of Georgia counties' moving average of new cases, April 1–August 3, 2020. Source: Ed Johnson, Advocate for Quality Education, COVID-19 Daily Status Report as of August 4; used with permission.

LET'S USE SOUND SCIENCE

Given the data shown in Figures 20 and 21, the answer should be obvious. But it's not that simple. The CDC has said that sending kids back to school poses low risks to school-aged children. However, in that same statement, the CDC tells us that only in areas with low community transmission is the risk low. Not only is the transmission of the virus high across Georgia, but we do not know how susceptible children and teens are to this virus. Each day we hear of new cases of children getting the virus. The first death of a child in Georgia was reported this week.

Earlier this week, Paulding County High School (Georgia) suspended and then reversed its suspension of a student who posted photos of a crowded school hallway. The student, Hannah Watters, was concerned that the CDC guidelines for school openings were not being followed. She said that her actions were "good and necessary trouble."[428] Her photos showed not only a crowded hallway, but most students weren't wearing face coverings.

The CDC recommends face coverings for students. Most students

---

[428] CNN, "Georgia Student Suspended after Posting a Photo of a Crowded School Hallway Says It Was 'Good and Necessary Trouble,'" Channel3000.com, August 7, 2020, retrieved April 5, 2022, https://www.channel3000.com /georgia-student-suspended-after-posting-a-photo-of-a-crowded-school-hallway-says-it-was-good-and-necessary-trouble/.

were not wearing masks in the photos posted on Twitter by Watters. These lapses are a severe problem. Of all the mitigation strategies that we have against the virus, covering your face is the most effective. Face coverings protect you and others from respiratory droplets that are projected from sneezing, coughing, or talking.

AEROSOLS

Finally, the WHO acknowledged that there is mounting scientific evidence of aerosol transmission of COVID-19, especially indoors. Of particular concern is that some studies have shown that viruses are released during exhalation, talking, and coughing. They are expelled in microdroplets that are small enough to remain aloft at distances of three to six feet from an infected individual.

Crowded indoor spaces are perfect environments for coronavirus spread. Jose-Luis Jimenez, a professor at the University of Colorado, Boulder, has studied aerosol transmission of small particles that can suspend in air for quite some time.

There are studies that show that COVID-19 is transmitted via the airborne route. One research study analyzed the effect of wearing or not wearing face coverings. The researchers found that using face coverings reduced infection by over 78,000 in Italy from April 6 to May 9 and over 66,000 in New York City from April 17 to May 9. They also have found that social distancing by itself is insufficient as a protective measure.[429] The research is summarized in this way:

> We conclude that wearing of face masks in public corresponds to the most effective means to prevent interhuman transmission, and this inexpensive practice, in conjunction with simultaneous social separation, quarantine, and contact tracing, represents the fighting opportunity to stop the COVID-19 pandemic. Our work also highlights the fact that sound science

---

[429] Renyi Zhang et al., "Identifying Airborne Transmission as the Dominant Route for the Spread of COVID-19," Proceedings of the National Academy of Sciences of the United States of America, June 30, 2020, https://pubmed.ncbi.nlm.nih.gov/32527856/.

is essential in decision-making for the current and future public health pandemics.[430]

Given the data presented in this post, the evidence supports not opening schools yet. Until we get the rate of spread down and keep it there, we have no business sending kids into crowded school buildings. And when and if we do, they all should be required to wear face coverings.

---

[430] Zhang et al., "Identifying Airborne Transmission."

PART VI: DEPARTURE

> President Trump's attempt to overturn the will of the American voters was the most destructive act of his time in office.
>
> —Freedom House

INTRODUCTION

IN NORMAL TIMES, THE OUTGOING PRESIDENT INVITES THE newly elected president to the White House for a social visit soon after the election. Indeed, the morning of the inauguration, the president-elect and spouse usually have tea with the sitting president. In early 2021, we were not in normal times. There was no social visit, nor was tea offered to the incoming president on January 20. In the past, a peaceful transfer of power took place in which the president attended the inauguration of his successor. Trump's attendance didn't happen in 2021. Instead, Donald Trump took a ride on the Marine One helicopter to Joint Base Andrews, where he boarded Air Force One for a final flight to Florida. This was Trump's last day as president. However, we must go back in time to understand what preceded Trump's departure from the nation's capital.

As soon as it was announced that Joe Biden won the election to become the forty-sixth president of the United States, Trump went into overdrive to dispute the result and announced that he won the election by a landslide. His claim is that the election was stolen from him. As we know now, it was Donald Trump who crossed a line to try and steal the election in a well-orchestrated conspiracy organized by people close to him who wore suits. Thus, the Big Lie propelled Trump and his minions to contest the election in the courts, including the Supreme Court, and in the Congress, turning the Capitol building into a war zone. Hordes of manipulated Trump supporters charged the Capitol, resulting in a violent attack not only on the police and congressional members and their families and their staff, but also on the very nature of America's democracy.

According to Lawrence Tribe, a Harvard University constitutional law expert, sedition charges against Trump became more likely after the attack on the Capitol. If that were to happen, then Trump could potentially be sentenced to twenty years in prison. Sedition is an act of trying to prevent the government from functioning.

In many Oval Office meetings, Trump tried to convince Vice President Mike Pence to reject the Electoral College votes and send the results back to the states to change the votes in Trump's favor. Pence pursued Trump's request but was told by former Vice President Dan Quayle not to consider it because he lacked the authority to reject the electoral count. Trump had also called Georgia Secretary of State Brad Raffensperger to find additional votes that would result in him winning the Georgia election. Raffensperger told Trump he wouldn't do that. He also told Trump that his numbers were wrong. The Fulton County, Georgia, attorney general has filed criminal charges against Donald Trump for his efforts to try and overturn the Georgia election.

THE BIG LIE

The Big Lie is an authoritarian tactic that Trump forecast well ahead of the 2020 election. He announced that if he lost the election, then it was stolen. Even if there is evidence to the contrary, the authoritarian tactic is to double down and keep repeating the mantra of the Big Lie. Trump constantly repeats he was the winner of the 2020 election. According to some scholars, the Big Lie is a propaganda tool often associated with Nazi Germany. Trump is an expert in lying. In the case of the Big Lie, he repeats it often and refuses to say that it is a lie. People then begin to think that the Big Lie is the truth. Conspiracy theorists' minds cannot be changed with evidence or rational thinking. Those people that hold the Big Lie as truth believe that they are thinking rationally.

Trump and most Republicans believe that massive fraud took place during the 2020 election. Most Republicans still believe that Trump won the election.

The Big Lie conspiracy theory was the fundamental cause of the insurrection and an attempt to seditiously change the outcome of the election on January 6, 2021. For two months, Trump filed more than sixty-two lawsuits in state and federal courts seeking to overturn the election results. Sixty-one failed. The one lawsuit they won was a ruling that voters had three days after the election to provide proper ID and "cure" their ballots. One lawsuit even tried to get a federal judge in Texas to rule that Pence had the conditional power to decide which states' Electoral College votes counted. The Trump-appointed judge dismissed the lawsuit.

The Big Lie rules Republican politics even with Trump out of the White House. Trump's Big Lie is a propaganda technique that uses a gross distortion of the truth to claim that elections in some states were fraught with election fraud.

The Big Lie was to undermine the election process in the United States and convince the American people that something needed to be done to change the outcome of the election. In Trump's mind, he couldn't have lost the election unless it was stolen from him. Trump made it clear he wouldn't accept defeat, nor would be concede that he'd lost the election.

TRUMP'S LEGACY

Some historians of American history asked themselves if Donald Trump would ever go. They wondered if he would try to find a way to stay in office regardless of the outcome. One historian who speculated about this problem is Lawrence Douglas, the James T. Grosfeld Professor of Law, Jurisprudence, and Social Thought at Amherst College. In his book *Will He Go?: Trump and Looming Election Meltdown in 2020*, he asked, what would it look like if an American president behaved badly and refused to accept the results of the election?

Dr. Douglas's prediction was based on evidence that was available to those of us who watched Trump debate Hillary Clinton in 2016. At the end of one of the debates, Trump was asked if he would accept the outcome of the election. He said, "We'll wait and see." This became a major topic of discussion on cable television for weeks following the debate. The outcome of the 2020 election was in Joe Biden's favor, and to this day Trump has not conceded and claims the election was stolen.

Donald Trump used every resource available to him to change the outcome of the 2020 election. In addition to the sixty-two lawsuits he filed, he also directly appealed to state legislators, governors, the secretary of state of Georgia, and the US Justice Department, and he led a group of allies who worked furiously and secretly to change the outcome of the election.

Douglas writes that because Trump was a weak authoritarian, he would be unable to control the outcome of an election. He said: "Most authoritarians gather and consolidate power by building strong alliances with a nation's coercive apparatus—the military, the intelligence services, and the justice community. Trump has done none of this."[431]

Trump spent four years deriding the military and disparaging the intelligence services. Although he had Attorney General William Barr in his corner, the rank-and-file lawyers of the Justice Department considered Trump despicable.[432]

In the 2020 election, Trump acted like many of the authoritarians he admired, including Vladimir Putin (Russia), Recep Tayyip Erdoğan (Turkey), and Victor Orbán (Hungary). He used strongarm tactics at rallies, with the last rally of his term on January 6 leading to the storming of the US Capitol Building. Even though the mob attacked Congress, disrupting the reading of the state electoral votes, Congress reconvened later that evening and completed its task. Mike Pence announced that Joe Biden won the election and was the forty-sixth president of the United States.

---

[431] Lawrence Douglas, *Will He Go? Trump and the Looming Election Meltdown in 2020* (New York: Twelve, 2020), 15.
[432] Douglas, *Will He Go?*

In an article in the *Washington Post*, Joanne B. Freeman questions whether the January 6 siege of the Capitol failed.[433] Freeman is a professor who specializes in the politics and political culture of the Revolutionary and Early National periods of American history. In this article, she states that the insurgency did not fail. I agree with her when she says that "our government is still under attack. The offense is quieter but no less menacing, eroding the government from within."[434]

It's become clear from reports coming out of the House of Representatives Select Committee to Investigate the January 6 Attack on the United States Capitol[435] that there was a group of Trump allies that conspired to overthrow the will of the people by stealing the 2020 election by any means.

We now know that a group of American citizens who either worked in the White House or the Justice Department, or were current or former members of Donald Trump's administration, engaged in a prolonged effort to overturn the 2020 election. These were men and women, many with law degrees, and some of whom were elected officials or appointed to government positions as advisors or lawyers to former President Trump. I believe there is evidence in reports from the House Select Committee investigating the January 6 storming of the US Capitol that this group worked for months to figure out ways to overturn the 2020 presidential election.

One group operated in and from the White House, while another group set up shop in Washington's Willard Hotel, where they secured rooms to set up a command center before and after the January 6 attack on Congress. The group in the White House answered to Trump and his chief of staff, Mark Meadows. The group at the Willard Hotel answered to Trump's personal lawyer, Rudy Giuliani, and former political advisor Stephen K. Bannon. From each of these locations, these people, all answering to Trump, worked the phones and held video conferences

---

[433] Joanne Freeman, "Jan. 6 Crossed a Line. We Need to Say So before It's Too Late for Democracy," *Washington Post*, December 10, 2021, retrieved January 12, 2022, https://www.washingtonpost.com/outlook/2021/12/10/january-6-congress-line/.
[434] Freeman, "Jan. 6 Crossed a Line."
[435] Select Committee to Investigate the January 6th Attack on the United States Capitol, retrieved February 11, 2022, https://january6th.house.gov/.

and group meetings with the intent of convincing each other and those they contacted that the election was stolen.

Even with this knowledge, the Senate has refused to discuss the January 6 siege. In fact, listening to some Republicans in both the House and Senate, that day in January was nothing to get upset about. In her research, Freeman says that this is dangerous. She put it this way: "The nation suffered a deliberate attempt to violently overturn a free and fair election, with little pushback, an astonishing lapse that invites more of the same."[436]

Unfortunately, only the House of Representatives launched an investigation to report the facts, circumstances, and causes related to the January 6, 2021, domestic terrorist attack on the United State Capitol Complex. The FBI announced in January 2022 that it set up a domestic terrorist unit because of the attack. But it's Congress that has the responsibility to show the American people that it is willing to investigate and be accountable for any wrongdoing among its ranks. Failure to do this will further downgrade democracy.

Freeman believes that investigations have power because the public needs to know what happened, and perhaps more important, they need to see that Congress is willing to take the matter in hand. Without doing this, the American public will not see Congress as a functioning institution but one that is not willing to be accountable.[437]

The departure of Donald J. Trump from the presidency was welcomed by millions of Americans. His departure personified the sustained work by activists in many states who brought to the ballot boxes people who hadn't voted before. Joe Biden's victory and Donald Trump's defeat were the result of African American leaders, activists, and ordinary American citizens who believed the words of John Lewis when he said that "the vote is the most powerful nonviolent tool we have." After the big departure, Republicans around the country have taken up arms to fight the success of Black Americans by changing state voting laws, making it harder for Black people, Native Americans, and people of

---

[436] Freeman, "Jan. 6 Crossed a Line."
[437] Freeman, "Jan. 6 Crossed a Line."

color to vote. Republicans have also written laws that ban the teaching of critical race theory and indeed any conversations about race in schools. Conversations about race in schools and communities are fundamental for people to learn about racial justice. These conversations might be uncomfortable, but one might consider these growing pains that enable students to learn new ideas, in this case about tolerance and relationships.

As much as Republicans think that they can rule by accepting the Big Lie, it is up to citizens who believe in the truth to rise and speak out against the cowardly actions in many state legislatures. Trump lost the 2020 election because of his failed leadership and nonstop lying. The Republican state legislators and their colleagues in the House and Senate will be subject to the same kind of scrutiny that was applied to Donald Trump during his one term in office. We cannot sit by silently and do nothing to resist these politicians who have continued the road that Trump paved, which was to undermine democratic norms. We cannot put in the rearview mirror the day when Donald Trump instigated an attack on the halls of Congress where laws are made. January 6, 2021, is another day of infamy.

And finally, it will be crucial for America's democracy to sustain itself by holding Donald Trump and his allies accountable for their attempted overthrow of the United States government. Anything less will leave the country vulnerable not only to Trump, but to others who are willing to accept Trump's lies and scandals.

Trump's subversive actions underscore the nature of his departure. He could be charged with accessory to murder or the federal sedition statute that applies to anyone who incites, assists, or engages in any rebellion or insurrection against the authority of the United States. It is becoming increasingly more evident that many people will be charged with sedition. At the end of one year of investigations by the Justice Department, eleven men were charged with seditious conspiracy and other offenses related to the US Capitol breach. A federal grand jury in the District of Columbia returned the indictments on January 13, 2022. These were the first indictments charging seditious conspiracy.

I believe that seditious conspiracy charges will spread not only to others who stormed the Capitol, but those that conspired to interfere with Congress. Sedition conspiracy occurs when two or more people in the United States conspire to overthrow, put down, or destroy by force the US government or prevent the execution of any law. Sedition is also any act that prevents, hinders, or delays by force the execution of any law of the United States.[438] The Justice Department is responsible for investigating not only the mobs of people who attacked the Capitol by force, but also those who may have instigated or participated in planning activities to prevent the Congress from confirming the election of Joe Biden as president.

Not to do so will invite these episodes to happen again and perhaps result in an overthrow of the will of the people.

---

[438] *18 US Code § 2384 – Seditious Conspiracy*, Legal Information Institute, 1992, retrieved April 6, 2022, https://www.law.cornell.edu/uscode/text/18/2384.

CHAPTER 13:
POLITICAL VIOLENCE

13.1. BLOG POST, 5 NOVEMBER 2020: A BLUE WAVE WASHES OUT TRUMP

A blue wave occurred in the 2020 presidential election. However, it didn't happen as many people expected. For assorted reasons, Donald Trump created the blue wave because of his failed response to the COVID-19 pandemic. His failure to act decisively and use the science that was available to him created a fracture among the American people. Trump flaunted his superiority over scientific advice on TV, in the White House, and during his rallies, which according to some reports led to at least seven hundred deaths among people who attended. He refused to wear a mask. He continued to shake hands. Trump ignored the concept of social distancing. And, as Dr. Fauci predicted, Trump would get COVID-19. Trump used this to mock the country and highlight his disdain for truth and empathy.

But all this cost him the election. He claimed years ago that the election was going to be rigged. He told his crowds around the country that vote by mail would be fraudulent, and he thereby encouraged his followers not to use the mail-in vote. Citizens of the US knew they could vote by mail. And they did, and it helped elect Joe Biden and Kamala Harris.

This situation is how the blue wave wiped out Trump's lead after Donald Trump thought he was the winner. While the early returns in key states showed that Trump was leading Joe Biden, fortunes changed overnight and over the next two days. The votes by people who had voted by mail were not counted until the polls closed, and most of the people who voted by mail were Democrats. They voted for Joe Biden. In four states Trump's lead vanished as the blue wave washed out the edge that Trump had over Biden. Trump led at 11:00 p.m. as follows: Wisconsin by 4.1%, Michigan by 8.4%, Pennsylvania by 13.8%, and Georgia by 2.6%. With these results in, Trump announced that no more votes should be counted and that he should be announced the winner. That announcement didn't happen. He lacked that power to stop the vote, and he wasn't the one who called the election.

By the morning of November 4, Wisconsin and Michigan flipped to Biden. At this time, Biden had secure leads in Nevada and Arizona, and if these four states stayed in the Biden column, he would win the presidency. As the day went on, Trump's lead in Pennsylvania and Georgia was slipping. On November 5, it appeared that Biden might win Pennsylvania and even Georgia. Trump began to claim that these elections were being stolen and demanded that all votes be recounted. They were, and in Georgia the votes were counted three times. By the evening of November 5, Trump's lead had evaporated in Georgia and nearly dried up in Pennsylvania. On November 6, Georgia and Pennsylvania flipped blue. On November 7, Joe Biden was declared the winner of the presidential race. The second blue wave pounded the shores around Mar-a-Lago.

GEORGIA BLUE

Equally impressive as the defeat of Trump is what has happened in Georgia. Stacey Abrams has spent most of the last four years building a network of organizations that highlighted voter suppression and through this work registered hundreds of thousands of new voters. Many people believe that her organization Fair Fight was one of the reasons Georgia is now a blue state and Joe Biden won the state.

The blue wave came after the polls had closed. Mail-in ballots could not be processed until November 3, election day. It takes time to process paper ballots. Each state has its own procedures for processing mail-in ballots. Several people, usually three to four, are involved to approve each absentee ballot. In Georgia this blue wave of votes took several days after the election to come to state election officials. Joe Biden overcame a big deficit and right now is leading Trump by more than 7,000 votes.

Jon Ossoff forced a runoff election for US Senate against incumbent David Perdue. Georgia requires that a candidate must get at least 50 percent of the vote. Right now, Perdue leads Ossoff 49.8% to 47.9%.

The blue wave also has gained momentum in the second senate election in Georgia. Since no one got more than 50 percent of the vote, a runoff between Democrat Raphael Warnock and Republican Kelly Loeffler will also take place. Warnock got 32.9% and Loeffler got 25.9% of the vote.[439]

This will be an unprecedented election. If the Democrats can win both races, the US Senate will be controlled by them because with a 50–50 Senate, Vice President-Elect Harris will be the deciding vote.

13.2. BLOG POST, 8 DECEMBER 2020: TRUMP'S ATTEMPTED COUP

Donald Trump is engaged in a process to steal the 2020 election. And most of his party approves or remains silent. Senator Kelly Loeffler spoke to this issue in a recent debate. She is being challenged by Raphael Warnock in one of two US Senate races in Georgia. In a televised debate, she was asked if Donald Trump lost the election, yes or no? She said neither and told us that Donald Trump has every right to challenge the vote and to make sure every vote counts. Loeffler is a perfect example of how Trump gets away with his charade. In Georgia, each vote for president was counted three times. The outcome was the same. Joe Biden won by more than 8,000 votes.

Trump is using tactics that are typically used in authoritarian and dictatorial regimes. Anyone that opposes the "Trump regime" is an enemy and will be treated as such, as if a war had been declared.

---

[439] Michelle Bocanegra, "Republican Loeffler, Democrat Warnock Head to Georgia Senate Runoff," Politico, November 3, 2020, retrieved April 15, 2022, https://www.politico.com/news/2020/11/03/georgia-senate-special-election-results-2020-433902.

Last Saturday Trump called Georgia Governor Brian Kemp. Kemp has been a huge supporter of Trump. He led the way to open the Georgia economy well before other states because he thought it would please his boss in Washington. However, as soon as Kemp did so, Trump said he "strongly disagrees" with Kemp's decision and went on to say it was too early to reopen the state. Trump made Kemp a laughingstock of governors in the media.

In a phone call[440] with Kemp on December 5, Trump asked Kemp to call the Georgia legislature together for a special meeting to get elected officials to change the vote and make him the winner. He thought by bringing the representatives of Georgia together, they could defy the will of the people. The will of the people was that sixteen electors will vote for Joe Biden because he won the election. Kemp turned the president down. Trump also asked Republicans in Michigan and Pennsylvania to do the same thing.

COUP

In an article in *The Atlantic*, Zeynep Tufekci explains what's going on with Trump and the Republican Party. She makes it clear but also says that most Americans won't recognize or realize what is going on. At one point in her article, she said:

> The US president is trying to steal the election, and, crucially, his party either tacitly approves or is pretending not to see it. This is a particularly dangerous combination and makes it much more than just typical Trumpian bluster or norm shattering.[441]

According to Tufekci, there is only one word in English that can be used to identify and name what is going on. She says it powerfully with these remarks:

---

[440] Amy Gardner, Colby Itkowitz, and Josh Dawsey, "Trump Calls Georgia Governor to Pressure Him for Help Overturning Biden's Win in the State," *Washington Post*, December 6, 2020, retrieved April 6, 2022, https://www.washingtonpost.com/politics/trump-kemp-call-georgia/2020/12/05/fd8d677c-3721-11eb-8d38-6aea1adb3839_story.html.
[441] Zaynep Tufekci, "'This Must Be Your First,'" *The Atlantic*, December 8, 2020, https://www.theatlantic.com/ideas/archive/2020/12/trumps-farcical-inept-and-deadly-serious-coup-attempt/617309/.

Trump is attempting to stage a *coup*, one that is embedded in a broader and ongoing power grab. And if that's hard to recognize, this might be your first.[442]

Although the coup that is identified here involves other states, lower and higher courts, the Supreme Court, a host of lawyers, and election officials, ground zero for the election of the century is the state of Georgia.

GEORGIA SENATE RACES: AT RISK?

There are two senate elections that will be decided in a runoff election on January 5, 2021. Here are the stakes: If Jon Ossoff and Raphael Warnock win their respective campaigns against David Perdue and Kelly Loeffler, then the Democrats will hold the advantage in the US Senate. If the Democrats win both seats, then the Senate will be fifty Democratic and fifty Republican senators. In the case of a tie vote, all tie votes are decided by the vice president of the United States, who in this case is Kamala Harris, the Democratic vice president-elect.

Trump targeted Republican Governor Brian Kemp, Secretary of State Brad Raffensperger, and Election Chief Gabriel Sterling. His targeting has resulted in death threats to Secretary Raffensperger's family. Gabriel Sterling gave an emotional speech on the steps of the state capitol, saying that Trump and Senators Perdue and Loeffler must stop what they are doing before someone gets hurt or killed.[443]

Loeffler and Perdue have called for the resignation of Brad Raffensperger. All three of them are Republicans. The Senators have not backed off and still hold to their position that he should step down. Raffensperger has been clear that he will not resign. He shouldn't.

More than $490 million has been spent on advertising for the two elections. Trump plans to return to the state and hold another of his rallies of lies. In the last rally that was to support Perdue and Loeffler's

---

[442] Tufekci, "'This Must Be Your First.'"
[443] Susan Fowler, "'Someone's Going to Get Killed': Ga. Official Blasts GOP Silence on Election Threats," NPR, December 2, 2020, https://www.npr.org/sections/biden-transition-updates/2020/12/01/940961602 /someones-going-to-get-killed-ga-official-blasts-gop-silence-on-election-threats.

races against Jon Ossoff and Raphael Warnock, respectively, Trump spent most of the time whining about how the election was stolen from him. Except now he's trying to steal it back. Is that possible? In Trump's world, it is.

SAFE HARBOR

Safe Harbor Day, December 8, is the day when states can "lock" in their Electoral College votes. A *Forbes* article helps us understand the importance of this day. Alison Durkee, the author of the article, says that "under federal law, if states have finalized their election results and resolved 'any controversy or contest' involving the appointment of the electors by six days before the Electoral College meets, those results should be treated as 'conclusive' by Congress when lawmakers count the Electoral College votes and should not be challenged."[444]

Well, that day has come and almost gone. Although not set in stone, the results will be difficult to change. Joe Biden will be the next president.

ELECTORS MEET

On December 12, electors in the fifty American states met and cast their Electoral College votes. State by state revealed the vote, and at the end of the day, Joe Biden received 306 votes and Donald Trump got 232 votes. Even at this time, very few Republicans in Congress have recognized Joe Biden as the next president.

Less than a month is left until the Georgia runoff election for two US Senate seats. Mail-in voting has begun in the state, and more than 1 million mail-in votes have been cast. Early voting begins next week and runs until the end of the month. Election day is January 5.

CONGRESS COUNTS ELECTORAL VOTES

On January 6, lawmakers from the House and Senate will meet in the House Chamber, with the vice president presiding. Donald Trump

---

[444] Alison Durkee, "The 'Safe Harbor' Deadline for Election Results Has Arrived: Here's What That Means for Trump's Lawsuits," *Forbes*, December 8, 2020, retrieved February 11, 2022, https://www.forbes.com/sites/alisondurkee/2020/12/08/the-safe-harbor-deadline-for-election-results-has-arrived-what-that-means-for-trump-lawsuits/.

asked Mike Pence to "act" in stopping the ratification of Joe Biden as the next president of the United States. According to some reports, Trump is confused as to why Pence can't overturn the election results. Yet Trump's attempt to overturn the election has now moved to Mar-a-Lago, where he is spending the holidays. His lead attorney, Rudy Giuliani, is with him, and together they will continue to plot a way to overthrow the election results.

I should also point out that in a recent White House meeting, which according to observers was a shouting match, Trump asked about Michael Flynn's idea of using "military capabilities" to "rerun an election" in swing states.

The tide has turned. However, I heard someone on CNN say it's not over until Joe Biden lifts his hand off the Bible.

On January 6, 2021, a mob of 2,000–2,500 supporters of President Donald Trump stormed the Capitol Building in Washington, DC. Source: Tyler Merbler, CC BY 2.0, via Wikimedia Commons.

13.3. BLOG POST, 6 JANUARY 2021: INCITING INSURRECTION TO OVERTHROW THE UNITED STATES GOVERNMENT

It's been suggested to me that what happened on this day was an act of political violence.[445] Donald Trump caused a violent protest that has resulted in the storming of the US Capitol. Between 2,000 and

---

[445] In an email from Dr. Charles Ault, emeritus professor, Lewis & Clark College, on May 31, 2021.

2,500 people storming the building have driven members of Congress and the vice president into hiding in the Capitol. The protestors, encouraged by Trump, have taken over the Capitol. It's dangerous. And looking at the scene, not only is it dangerous, but I was shocked to see how unprepared law enforcement was to deal this Trump protest and rally. Thousands of people have surrounded the US Capitol, and many have broken into the building and reached the House and Senate chambers.

The House and Senate convened in joint session today for the purpose of opening the 2020 presidential election votes submitted by each state. It's legal for legislators to object to any list of electors from any state. Republican members of Congress—more than one hundred in the House and thirteen in the Senate—have said they will oppose the electoral votes in some states. The members of Congress gathered in the House Chamber around noon on January 6. Envelopes from the states are opened in alphabetical order. If at least one House member and one Senate member raises an objection to a state's election results in writing, then lawmakers take this objection under consideration for two hours with the House and Senate debating separately. Senator Ted Cruz (R-TX) and Representative Paul Gosar (R-AZ) led the challenge against the Arizona electors. They each spoke, explaining why the votes from Arizona should be rejected. Eight senators and fifty representatives joined their objection to overturn the vote. While the chambers were debating separately, all hell broke loose outside the US Capitol.

I happened to be watching the debates on CNN and saw the beginning of the storming of the Capitol building.

I wrote at the time that protestors were breaking through windows and entering the Capitol. Police and protestors were engaged in violent actions around the buildings. One woman was shot in the chest inside the Capitol, putting her in critical condition. She later died.

Inside the House chamber, US Capitol Police drew guns on rioters outside the room. People had entered the Senate chamber, and one person was sitting at the House speaker's desk with his feet up on the desk. Even though protestors have been cleared from the Senate floor and moved to the rotunda, the violence is unprecedented.

Viewing this insurrection is not only frightening, but it raises to a new level the gravity of Donald Trump and his Republican sycophants.[446]

A commentator made a critical point. Last summer, during a Black Lives Matter protest, law enforcement by the thousands were present. Today, right-wing protestors, who were mostly white people called to Washington by Donald Trump, faced little to no police presence compared to the Black Lives Matter protest in June 2020.

13.4. BLOG POST, 6 JANUARY 2021: A DATE THAT WILL LIVE IN INFAMY

After the Japanese attack on Pearl Harbor on December 6, 1941, President Franklin Roosevelt at a joint session of Congress gave his famous "infamy" speech. On that date, President Roosevelt appealed to Americans' patriotism. Roosevelt knew that most Americans did not want to be drawn into the war in Europe. Japan's attack on Pearl Harbor changed everything. He acted quickly and briefly told Americans about the attack. He said this will be "a date which will live in infamy."

Today, January 6, the US Capitol was attacked by hundreds of American terrorists, right-wing hate groups, and individuals who thought they were patriotic in attacking the very center of the government of the United States. On this date, which will also live in infamy, the United States was attacked by violent right-wing men and women, who were acting on orders from the president of the United States. They were not patriots. They were violent criminals.

January 6 is one of the most important days in American history. This is the day when the Congress meets every four years to read formally the results of the Electoral College, leading to the inauguration of the next president. In future years, this day will be remembered as

---

[446] Andrew Clyde, a Republican representative from Georgia, said the people who broke into the US Capitol on January 6 were docile as tourists and no insurrection occurred on that day. Other Republicans, including Mitch McConnell and Kevin McCarthy, are now downplaying the mob attack on the Capitol.

the only day in United States history when a violent insurrection and mob rule overtook the US Capitol.

It's now the responsibility of the members of Congress, who have come out of hiding from their secure locations, to resume the Electoral College session.

Beyond this night, it will also be the responsibility of Congress to investigate the president and determine whether Trump should be charged with inciting mob rule and a riot. Several laws should be considered in bringing Trump to trial.

Trump can be charged with rebellion and insurrection if he assisted or engaged in any actions against the authority of the United States. If found guilty, he would be fined or imprisoned for not more than ten years, and he would be incapable of holding any office under the United States.

A second crime that Trump might have committed is seditious (subversive) conspiracy. The law is if two or more persons in the United States conspire to overthrow or destroy by force the government of the United States or by force to seize, take, or possess any property of the United States, they shall each be fined or imprisoned not more than twenty years or both.

13.5. BLOG POST, 6 JANUARY 2021: TRUMP CAUSES VIOLENT INSURRECTION AND WATCHES IT ON TV

This was one of the most frightening days I have witnessed during Donald Trump's presidency. The president of the United States caused a violent insurrection on the grounds of the Capitol. It is a stunning scene. Insurrectionists broke into Nancy Pelosi's office and were photographed sitting at the speaker's chair. One insurgent left a note on a manilla folder with the words, "We will not back down."

Trump has refused to step in and put out a message telling the rioters to cease and go home. Instead, he's asked them to be peaceful. Reports inform that the president was delighted while watching mobs of people attack police and storm the US Capitol in an attempt to capture congressional representatives, senators, and especially Vice President Mike Pence and Speaker Nancy Pelosi.

This was the day Congress was to certify the election of Joe Biden as president of the United States. Trump held a rally on Capitol grounds and encouraged mobs of right-wing hate groups, which were in the large crowd, to make sure that they take back the country. For weeks I read on social media that groups such as the Proud Boys and other hate groups would be in DC for the protest. They were coming to cause trouble and to stir others up. Other groups include Stop the Steal/Wild Protest, Women for America First, Eighty Percent Coalition, and Operation Occupy the Capitol. The chatter on the social media of these right-wing groups has come to fruition today. Members of these groups are only interested in inciting and participating in violence.

Donald Trump's words have stoked the flames of this violence, destructiveness, disorder, and turbulence.

What I am observing on live TV and social media is the nightmare of an authoritarian. I've described in this blog that Trump has been a dictator wannabe. It's not surprising that his term in office is ending with his hate-group followers storming the Capitol.

I believe that Mike Pence could assemble on Zoom a quorum of cabinet secretaries and enact the Twenty-Fifth Amendment. The amendment states that if the president becomes unable to do his job, the vice president becomes the president. The amendment makes it clear that if the president is unable to discharge his powers and duties, the vice president takes over.

But his behavior right now is outrageous and dangerous. In a video clip, he told the rioters just to go home. But he also repeated the unsubstantiated claim that he won the election. This is the fuel that he pours on to these hate groups.

13.6. BLOG POST, 14 FEBRUARY 2021: THE FRAGILITY OF LIBERAL DEMOCRACY

In March 1981, I was a passenger on a Soviet Aeroflot aircraft on a Washington, DC–Moscow route. A blizzard in Moscow diverted the plane to Leningrad, where we sat off the runway for two hours. Losing patience, the pilot took off for Moscow, where we landed at the Sheremetyevo International Airport at about 2:00 p.m. local time. By 4:00 p.m. I was walking on Red Square, amazed by St. Basil's Cathedral; GUM, Moscow's largest department store; and the walls of the Kremlin. This was the first time I had been out of the country.

The USSR consisted of multiple Soviet republics, three of which I would eventually visit. But more importantly for this discussion, the USSR was a one-party state governed by the Communist Party. It was an illiberal one-party state founded by Lenin in 1917.[447]

The ruling party controlled everything from industry and jobs to the government. The only quality that was important was loyalty to the principles of the Communist Party. Keep in mind, however, that an illiberal state can exist with competing political parties. There are many examples of this in the world right now. Historian and author Anne Applebaum calls this type of governing "soft dictatorship." She identifies the following countries as examples of "soft dictatorship": Russia, the Philippines, Poland, and Hungary.

Loyalty was a key priority that Donald Trump expected from anyone working for him. Only seven days after he became president, Trump invited James Comey, director of the FBI, to a one-on-one dinner in the White House. Trump asked in a demanding manner for Comey's loyalty. Comey said that he could only be loyal to the Constitution. Trump was furious, and later in the spring, Comey was fired.[448]

During the time that I was directly involved with Russia, Ukraine, and Soviet Georgia, the one-party illiberal state gave way to forms of democratization. The first two times I was in Tbilisi, Georgia, for meetings with Georgian psychologists and educators, some of my colleagues from America were invited to the home of an artist by the name of Victor. His house was alive. The walls of his apartment were covered with copies of frescoes of his own art. There was intense energy in the room, and in this environment Americans and Georgians came together to bond and share ideas about life.

---

[447] Applebaum, *Twilight of Democracy*.
[448] Schmidt, "Trump Demanded Loyalty."

During my visits to Tbilisi, I became close to the principal of a school and her family. Her son George was fifteen years old. He and I got along very well. He was the first fifteen-year-old to ask me about existential psychology and the unconscious mind. Over the next three years we spoke together at family dinners and explored a lot of topics. But one of his curiosities about America was surfing. Did my wife and I know anything about surfing? We did, in fact, and we shared what we knew.

When the first delegation of Soviet educators came to Atlanta for two weeks of meetings and conferences, they asked me if I would take them to the Martin Luther King Jr. Center for Social Change. We spent the good part of a day at the center.

The experiences we had in Russia were collaborative in nature. We not only met in small groups within institutions and schools, we also were invited into Russian homes and apartments to enjoy more personal times with families.

Russian teacher Sergey Tolstikov explained that small group collaboration was not only possible between Americans and Russians but was essential. He wrote in an email that:

> In fact, Global Thinking Project work created a new, unheard and unseen until then, international cooperation on a school level while giving the students and teachers of our countries a unique chance to work on serious global ecological problems at local levels.[449]

A FLEDGING LIBERAL DEMOCRACY

The fledging liberal democracy that developed in Russia was an asset for the people who we worked with at schools, universities, and research institutes, as well as parents and students. From the late 1980s through the 1990s, hundreds of Americans and Russians visited each other's countries, working and living together in schools and homes.

---

[449] Sergey Tolstikov (private English and Russian tutor, former teacher Moscow School 710, and editor at *Foreign Languages School Journal*), email interview with the author, September 13, 2021.

Yet we have to say that liberal democracy is fragile. Once Putin became president, the country began to slide back into a form of soft dictatorship. Russia is a multiparty state, but Putin has been able to gather elites and wealthy industrialists, a state media, and courts that carry out the government's wishes. Applebaum says that in countries with soft dictatorships (like Russia, Poland, etc.), sycophants understand their role, which is to defend the leaders, however great their corruption or dishonest their statements, and however disastrous their impact on ordinary people and institutions.[450]

AMERICAN SOFT DICTATORSHIP

Donald Trump was on his way to establish a soft dictatorship in the United States. Soft dictators need to be able to control elections. They want to give the appearance of running a government that is "democratically" elected. Trump was unable to control the election, so his only recourse was to claim that it was stolen from him.

Interestingly, one of the tactics used by these would-be dictators is to rig elections. They rig elections by buying votes. They use fear and intimidation to force people to vote for them, as well as stealing and stuffing ballot boxes.

Donald Trump used a slightly different strategy, with the outcome being the same as if the United States had already become a soft dictatorship. First, he claimed that the election would be rigged in favor of his opponent. He then claimed the other side rigged local elections by stealing ballots or manipulating electronic voting computers to change votes away from him and to his competitor, Joe Biden. He also went around the country claiming that he won the election with his Big Lie. The Big Lie was gross propaganda claiming that the election was stolen, and Trump and his minions pushed it with the phrase "Stop the Steal."

TRUMP'S THOUSANDS

With ease, Trump brought thousands of Americans to Washington, DC, on January 6, 2021, the day Congress would be carrying out its duty

---

[450] Tolstikov interview.

to read the results of each state's Electoral College results. The results had been certified a month earlier by each state. Trump insisted that Vice President Mike Pence could change the outcome by sending the results back to each state and ordering the states to change the votes.

This is not farfetched. Recall that Trump called Brad Raffensperger, Georgia's secretary of state, to ask him to find enough votes to change the outcome of the election. By this time, the state of Georgia had counted the presidential vote three times. There was no difference in the results after each count. Now the Fulton County district attorney has opened a criminal case investigating whether Trump broke any election laws in Georgia.

I would not define Trump's move to a dictatorship as soft. He incited an insurrection of hundreds of right-wing individuals who stormed the US Capitol eager to find and kill anyone who was part of the government that was denying Trump the presidency. They came within inches of capturing legislators and were close to the vice president and his family. The mob had constructed a noose and were going to hang Mike Pence. They were also looking for Speaker of the House Nancy Pelosi. They wanted to kill her.

Indeed, a man from Georgia was arrested who texted friends and relatives, "Thinking about heading over to Pelosi (C—'s) speech and putting a bullet in her noggin on live TV." He added, "I'm gonna run that Pelosi over while she chews on her gums….Dead B— Walking."[451] He's facing federal charges. He missed the rally because of truck problems but was in a DC hotel, where he was arrested after a friend of his forwarded screenshots of his messages to the FBI. They tracked him to a Holiday Inn close to the Capitol. He was sentenced to 28 months in prison.

DEMOCRACIES ARE FRAGILE

The United States came the closest it has come to having its Capitol overrun by insurgents. Two previous events come to mind: the War of

---

[451] Ryan King, "Man Who Threatened to Shoot Pelosi in the Head Sentenced to 28 Months in Prison," *Washington Examiner*, December 15, 2021, retrieved April 6, 2022, https://www.washingtonexaminer.com/man-who-threatened-to-shoot-pelosi-in-the-head-sentenced-to-28-months-in-prison.

1812, in which the British burned the Capitol, and the Civil War, when the Confederate Army came close to capturing Washington, DC.

Donald Trump was impeached for a second time because he incited people to attack the United States government, of which he was president. He did nothing to stop the attack. This has been documented by phone calls and text notes of people who overheard a call between Donald Trump and Kevin McCarthy, leader of the Republican minority in the House. The impeachment trial proved the democratic manager's case that Trump incited a mob to attack the Capitol with the intent of securing the halls of Congress and preventing the final certification of Joe Biden as president-elect.

Donald Trump came close to carrying out his wish to overthrow the will and vote of the people by using strongarm dictatorial tactics. Trump had his army of right-wing mobsters, many of whom have been arrested and will face the federal justice system.

Trump lost. He was, in my mind, convicted and found guilty by 57 percent of the Senate. And in the end, millions of American voters will agree that Trump is guilty of insurrection and sedition and will never hold a public office again.

But we need to face some facts. Two-thirds of elected members of the Republican caucus of the US Congress have not accepted that Joe Biden won the election. They still believe the election was stolen from Donald Trump. And now members of Congress are using conspiracy theories to explain the nature of the assault on the Capitol, further weakening the Congress's ability to seek the truth about the near overthrow of the government. Even now, there are reports that some white supremacists are planning to blow up the Capitol on the night when Joe Biden gives the presidential State of the Union address. Democracies are fragile.

13.7. BLOG POST, 14 FEBRUARY 2021: TRUMP'S SECOND IMPEACHMENT TRIAL

The US Senate voted today on the impeachment trial of former president Donald Trump. Fifty-seven senators voted guilty when asked for their vote. This was a historic rebuke. Fifty-seven percent of the elected senators found Trump guilty. Keep in mind that the article of impeachment was a bipartisan effort in the House of Representatives. This was the most bipartisan support for impeachment in the history of the Senate.

Trump was only acquitted because the Senate requires 67 percent of Senators to vote guilty, which would have meant ten more Republicans were needed to find him guilty. But those Republicans hid behind a false wall. A wall that was invisible. It is constitutional to impeach a government official who is out of office. Donald Trump is a former government official. The Senate voted in the affirmative that the impeachment was constitutional. The trial could go forward. The Republicans hung their hat on this question, but they have risked their professional integrity by not voting on the evidence.

The evidence was overwhelming. The videos, text messages, timelines proven by time-stamped videos, and phone records formed a solid case proving Trump's guilt in inciting a riot on the US Capitol.

WELL, KEVIN...

Just as Trump's phone call to the president of Ukraine in 2019 led to his first impeachment, his phone calls to senators while the attack was going on shows that Trump's state of mind was clear. He was supportive of the Capitol rioters. Kevin McCarthy, leader of the Republican minority in the House, called Trump to beg the president to call off the mob, knowing the rioters were Trump's supporters. Trump said to McCarthy, "Well, Kevin, I guess these people are more upset about the election than you are." The phone call was reduced to a shouting match. This, mind you, was just at the beginning of the assault on the nation's Capitol. Another Republican confirmed the exchange between Trump and McCarthy, Representative Jaime Herrera Beutler, (R-WA). Beutler said in an interview with CNN that Trump's mind was clear, that he either didn't care what was going on at the Capitol or he really wanted it to happen.

This and other testimony by a Republican representative and a Democratic senator proved that Trump had no intention of protecting any of the elected representatives of government. This was a dereliction of duty, which also meant that Trump supported the insurrection.

The forty-three Republicans who voted to clear Trump must wonder now what they did. Why did they vote to acquit when some had spoken publicly that Trump handled the Capitol insurrection? Others were in shock when listening to and watching the House Managers present their case, including harrowing video of the despicable assault on the Capitol. Yet these Republican senators refused to cast their vote on the basis on the evidence presented in the trial. They made a partisan decision to vote no. They were fearful of being attacked by Donald Trump. Some of them, I think, will simply run.

GUILTY BY THE MILLIONS

Senator Mitch McConnell is the head of the Republican conference in the Senate. However, I believe he shed any form of leadership based on the speech he made to explain away his vote for acquittal. If you listen to the first half of McConnell's speech, you must scratch your head and wonder why this senator did not vote to find Trump guilty. He's using a legal argument to claim that the Constitution does not say ex-officials can be impeached. However, he is the one interpreting the Second Amendment. Many legal scholars would disagree with McConnell. They would claim that an ex-president is subject to impeachment and trial. An ex-president can be found guilty.[452]

So McConnell gave his Republican conference partisan cowards an excuse not to convict. Not on the evidence. No, on McConnell's interpretation. The problem here is that McConnell is not the supreme head of anything but a senator in the Senate minority.

I noted that Senators Ted Cruz (R-TX) and Josh Hawley (R-MO) voted to acquit. They led the insurrection in the Senate. They spoke in favor of Trump's Big Lie. To them, the election was stolen. And months after Trump was gone from DC, these two still spout the conspiracy of the "stolen election."

---

[452] Cameron Peters, "Mitch McConnell's Speech Shows He's Willing to Condemn Trump—but Not When It Matters," *Vox*, February 13, 2021, retrieved April 6, 2022, https://www.vox.com/2021/2/13/22282034/mitch-mcconnells-speech-trump-acquittal-impeachment.

They gave concurrent speeches which indirectly added fuel to those getting ready to follow Trump's orders to attack the halls of Congress. They each supported the rioters. In fact, Senator Hawley, on his way into his senate office on the morning of January 6, 2021, gave a fist pump to the people gathering for the speeches by Trump and his sycophants. Later, those people would become part of the mob that attacked his office in the nation's capital. Calls for Senators Cruz and Hawley to resign were made. That didn't happen.

Trump may not have been convicted by the one-hundred-member US Senate, but he will be found guilty by more than 100 million Americans.

EPILOGUE

DONALD J. TRUMP IS THE MAIN CHARACTER IN *THE TRUMP Files*. I portrayed him as a seditious, untruthful, and dangerous president of the United States. However, it is the totality of Trump's administration that impaired not only democracy and human rights, but also science and public health.

Although he's out of office, he and his allies continue to besiege America with the Big Lie. Trump presented no evidence that the election was anything except the most secure in American history.

Instead, Trump hired dozens of lawyers who went around the country filing lawsuits claiming fraud in the 2020 election while Trump called foul from the Oval Office. US District Judge Linda Parker, in Detroit, sanctioned several pro-Trump lawyers after dismissing their Michigan suit in December 2020.

In her 2021 written ruling Judge Parker said, "This lawsuit represents a historic and profound abuse of the judicial process, and the case was never about fraud—it was about undermining the People's faith in our democracy and debasing the judicial process to do so." Parker said that these pro-Trump lawyers "have scorned their oath, flouted rules, and attempted to undermine the integrity of the judiciary along the way." According to the judge, they presented nothing but speculation and conjecture, never any evidence of fraud. She recommended that their licenses to practice law should be revoked.[453]

Most presidents when they leave office remain out of the spotlight and refrain from interfering or even commenting on the actions of

---

[453] *King, et al., v Whitmer, et al.*, Civil Case N. 20-13134 (Eastern District of Michigan), https://www.michigan.gov/documents/ag/172_opinion__order_King_733786_7.pdf.

the new president. Donald Trump can't stay away and can't keep his mouth shut. He's acting as if he in charge of something. He's not in charge of the White House, the Oval Office, or the executive branch. He's in charge of nothing except Republican cowards who are afraid of his rage.

What's to become of Donald Trump? A 2021 Pew Research Center poll showed that two-thirds of Republicans want Trump to remain a major political figure, but only 44 percent of Republicans support Trump over the Republican Party.[454] A Quinnipiac University poll showed that 55 percent of Americans do not think Trump should be allowed to hold office in the future. More than half of Americans (including Republicans) think Trump is at least partially responsible for the January 6 attacks on the Capitol.[455]

Yet Trump is lurking in the alleyways of corruption. Trump and his army of sycophants numbering 136 in the House and 43 to 46 in the Senate, depending on the day, continue to deny the truth of the 2020 election. This is a serious right-wing show of force designed to make it possible for Republicans to continue the Big Lie and let others know that what happened in the 2020 election could very possibly continue forward in future elections.

Since Joe Biden took office, the Republicans are pressing at all corners of government, state and federal, to destabilize democracy by inflicting damage on future elections rules, passing legislation that bans protests and forcing election officials into corners for fear of being charged with election process crimes. The Republican Party has become an "authoritarian party" that already has had a tyrant or demagogue at the head of the table. The four years of Trump as president was a practice run for a Republican autocracy.

We are living in a period when one political party has become an authoritarian party and has enacted laws across the country that will enable them to change election results in their own favor. I agree with

---

[454] Amina Dunn, "Two-Thirds of Republicans Want Trump to Retain Major Political Role; 44% Want Him to Run Again in 2024," Pew Research Center, October 18, 2021, retrieved December 2, 2021, https://www.pewresearch.org/fact-tank/2021/10/06/two-thirds-of-republicans-want-trump-to-retain-major-political-role-44-want-him-to-run-again-in-2024/.
[455] Poll results, Quinnipiac University Poll, retrieved December 2, 2021, https://poll.qu.edu/poll-results/.

William Rivers Pitt that Republicans are the greatest threat to American democracy.[456]

The Trump Files has not come to an end. This is not the end of the story. Donald Trump and his administration left a trail of destruction and serious problems that will have to be dealt with by all of us in the years ahead. He and members of his administration have not been held accountable for trying to overthrow the will of the people.

The following are areas of concern that emerged from The Trump Files and that I want to highlight. If we want the country to move forward as a democracy, we will have to be relentless and deliberate in dealing with these circumstances. We are obligated to do so.

THE BIG LIE

The first area of concern is Trump's Big Lie (*Magnum Mendacium*). It is the most atrocious and deplorable conspiracy perpetuated by Donald Trump. The Big Lie is a propaganda tool used by demagogues such as Hitler, Mussolini, and Stalin for political purposes. It is a gross distortion and misrepresentation of the truth. Donald Trump used the Big Lie to try to discredit the results of the 2020 presidential election and claim that he won the election in a landslide. According to Trump and his sycophants, the election was stolen by Democrats who directed widescale voter fraud. The Big Lie has infected millions of Americans and thousands of elected officials. The danger for American democracy is that Republicans are embracing Trump's conspiracies and using them to change the most fundamental right in a democracy: the right to vote. And it isn't about the right to vote; it's how the votes are counted and by whom.

The Big Lie has exacerbated the extreme polarization that has developed in America over the past forty years. Levitsky and Ziblatt in their book *How Democracies Die* explain that extreme polarization weakens through existential conflict over race and culture. They suggest that

---

[456] William Rivers Pitt, "20 Years After 9/11, Republicans Are the Greatest Threat to the United States," Truthout, September 11, 2021, retrieved September 11, 2021, https://truthout.org/articles/20-years-after-9-11-republicans-are-the-greatest-threat-to-the-united-states/.

America's efforts to achieve racial equality in an increasingly diverse society has fueled an "insidious reaction and intensifying polarization." Their concern raises the alarm that we already elected a demagogue and have weakened the guardrails of democracy.[457]

SAFEGUARDING AMERICAN DEMOCRACY

The Mueller team of investigators spent two years delving into the electoral intervention of the 2016 campaign. Although it was found that Russia did target the election, Russia was aided in this subversion by an assortment of Trump senior advisors and assistants, and even members of his family. Although common knowledge of the Mueller report is that no collusion existed between Russia and Trump's campaign, if you carefully read the Mueller report, many of Trump's associates did collude with Russia. At the same time, the US government failed to reveal that meddling in elections has been an important component of the United States' foreign policy. The US has meddled in more than twice as many elections in other countries than has Russia. We know that the target in 2016 was to damage Hillary Clinton's campaign and aid in the election of Donald Trump.

However, the intervention in the 2016 election doesn't compare to what Donald Trump and his allies carried out as soon as it was announced that Joe Biden was elected president. Donald Trump and the Republicans have led an audacious and violent intervention against America's electoral system. It's very clear that interventions in elections can be covert or overt. Some can be military interventions. In the 2020 American election, the intervention was conniving and brutal. And it wasn't led by a foreign power, it was coordinated by an American president and his advisors. And it began long before the 2020 election, when Donald Trump bribed the president of Ukraine to find dirt on President Biden and his son. Trump was impeached for this act of bribery.

American democracy is under assault from within its borders. In a recent testimony by the US intelligence community to the House and

---

[457] Steven Levitsky and Daniel Ziblatt, *How Democracies Die* (New York: Penguin Books, 2019).

Senate intelligence committees, it was suggested that limits of national security institutions are limited in protecting the country from domestic efforts to undermine its own democracy. Every American witnessed the assault on the US Capitol on January 6, 2021, and the attempted but failed coup by the president of the United States. This kind of coup has never happened in American history. Other countries are questioning America's ability to maintain a liberal democracy. We came remarkably close to becoming victims of an authoritarian president with hundreds of political allies and becoming a one-party state. Applebaum warns us of the "seductive lure" of authoritarianism. She says that "the one-party state was not merely undemocratic; it was also anticompetitive" and perks went to those who were most loyal.[458] These were rules that appealed to Donald Trump. Although Donald Trump was defeated in 2020, he still commands the loyalty of politicians who supported him while in office.

Carrie Cordero, former national security lawyer at the Department of Justice and Office of the Director of National Intelligence and now senior fellow at the Center for a New American Security, provides three prescriptions to address the current national security threat. First is to affirm commitment to the rule of law. The second is diffuse political polarization and realize that domestic and foreign actors make use of computer hacking and social media to exploit the divisions that exist in American society. This was a successful strategy for the Trump campaign, thanks to the Russian hacking of Democratic Party computers. The third is to strengthen the country's national security institutions within the bounds of the law.[459]

The Republican effort to change election procedures is the most serious challenge to American democracy. No country can have a democratic form of government without regular, free, and fair elections. Every adult citizen must have the right to vote and possess basic civil liberties, such as freedom of speech and association. Our democracy

---

[458] Applebaum, *Twilight of Democracy*.
[459] Carrie Cordero, "Enemies Foreign and Domestic," Center for a New American Security, April 29, 2021, https://www.cnas.org/publications/commentary/enemies-foreign-and-domestic.

was threatened by failing the first test, which was to prevent an established political party from bringing an extremist into the mainstream, as the Republicans did in 2016 in nominating Donald Trump for the office of president in 2020.[460]

Although the For the People Act[461] was rejected by the US Senate, it was revised and combined with the John Lewis Voting Rights Advancement Act. The combined bill would have restored the basic tenants of the 1965 Voting Rights Bill and regulated state elections to include vote by mail for all citizens and to establish a national holiday for the November election. Unfortunately, because Republicans blocked the vote with a filibuster, the acts fell by the wayside, to the disappointment of forty-eight Democrats. One of the arguments that Republicans make is that only the states have the right to regulate elections. That's true, except the Congress has the right to alter election rules for the states, as revealed in the Constitution of the United States, which says:

> The Times, Places and Manner of holding Elections for Senators and Representatives, shall be prescribed in each State by the Legislature thereof; but the Congress may at any time by Law make or alter such Regulations, except as to the Place of Chusing Senators.[462]

The 1965 Voting Rights Act is the prime example of how Congress can alter state election rules. With the wave of Republican voter repression and suppression in nearly half of the states, it's imperative that the Congress pass laws that ensure vote by mail is legal in all states and that voting is made easier, not more difficult, for people to exercise their right to vote.

---

[460] Levitsky and Ziblatt, *How Democracies Die.*
[461] The For the People Act would expand and protect the fundamental right to vote by modernizing registration, restoring the Voting Rights Act of 1965, restoring voting rights to people with prior convictions, strengthening mail voting, instituting nationwide early voting, reducing unreasonable wait time at the polls, and protecting against deceptive practices. Wendy R. Wiser, Daniel I. Weiner, and Dominique Erney, "Congress Must Pass the 'For the People Act,'" Brenham Center for Justice, March 18, 2021, https://www.brennancenter.org/our-work/policy-solutions/congress-must-pass-people-act.
[462] US Const. art 1, § 4.

SEDITION FOR AN ATTEMPTED COUP

Donald Trump and his co-conspirators need to be held responsible for the political violence that they executed. Federal investigators are looking into Donald Trump's role in inciting the attack on the US Capitol on January 6, 2021. Trump was held responsible for the insurrection, as stated in the impeachment documents filed in January 2021. Although he was acquitted by the Senate, fifty-seven United States senators found that Trump was guilty and responsible for the insurrection. According to Michael Sherwin, a former acting US attorney for the District of Columbia, Trump is being investigated for the January 6 attack. Six people died and hundreds were injured during the attack. Charging Trump with sedition is on the table, according to federal investigators.

The House of Representatives approved a bipartisan deal on a panel to investigate the January 6 attack on the Capitol. Legislation supported to set up a 9/11-style commission to find the facts and circumstances of the attack as well as the influencing factors that may have provoked the attack. The Senate turned it down. However, the House of Representatives has appointed a select committee made up of Republicans and Democrats to investigate the January 6 attack. The goal of the panel is to find the truth about the insurrection and attack on Congress.

New details have emerged to suggest that senior Trump aides knew that the January 6 rally would be chaotic. Trump sent out tweets inviting supporters to DC to a rally which would be "wild."[463] We also know other legal and political actors (Giuliani, Eastman, and Bannon) set up a war room at the historic Willard Hotel in Washington. They were plotting to undermine American democracy by trying to pull off a "soft coup" to keep Trump in office.[464]

In my view, based on the research presented in this book, Donald Trump and some of his allies should be held accountable for the violent attempt of the overthrow of the government of the United States.

---

[463] Joshua Sapien and Joaquin Kaplan, "New Details Suggest Senior Trump Aides Knew Jan. 6 Rally Could Get Chaotic," ProPublica, June 25, 2021, retrieved November 30, 2021, https://www.propublica.org/article/new-details-suggest-senior-trump-aides-knew-jan-6-rally-could-get-chaotic.

[464] L. E. Smith, "Before Jan. 6, Trump's Allies Chose a Citadel of Democracy for Their War Room," Washington Post, November 2, 2021, retrieved November 30, 2021, https://www.washingtonpost.com/outlook/2021/11/02/before-january-6-trumps-allies-chose-citadel-democracy-their-war-room/.

LAWSUITS

For Donald Trump, there is a storm brewing in New York and Georgia. Criminal investigations have been opened in these two states. Donald Trump and some of his associates face lawsuits that will be prosecuted in the coming months and years.

RACKETEERING

As a Georgia citizen, I was incensed by Trump's attempt to change the will of the voters in the 2020 election. Fani Willis, Fulton County district attorney in Georgia's largest county, has opened a case against Donald Trump and others associated with Trump. The district attorney is looking into the call that Trump made to Secretary of State Brad Raffensperger in which Trump urged him to "find" votes.

According to a letter to several Georgia officials, Willis requested that the officials preserve documents related to "an investigation into attempts to influence" the state's 2020 presidential election.[465] Willis said that the DA's office will look at the solicitation of election fraud, the making of false statements to state and local government bodies, conspiracy, racketeering, violation of oath of office, and any involvement in violence or threats related to the election's administration. Willis has called a special grand jury to further the Trump investigation.

FINANCIAL AND TAX FRAUD

New York Attorney General Letitia James is looking into the dealings of the Trump Organization. The attorney general's office has found significant evidence that the Trump Organization misrepresented the value of its assets for loan and tax benefits for at least six properties. Trump's family business, according to James, has been repeatedly misrepresenting values.[466] The New York civil investigation is running

---

[465] Fulton County District Attorney's Office, "The Fulton County District Attorney's Letter," *New York Times*, February 10, 2021, retrieved April 15, 2022, https://www.nytimes.com/interactive/2021/02/10/us/politics/letters-to-georgia-officials-from-fulton-district-attorney.html.

[466] Jonah E. Bromwich, Ben Protess, and William K. Rashbaum, "N.Y. Attorney General Outlines Pattern of Possible Fraud at Trump Business," *New York Times*, January 19, 2022, retrieved April 6, 2022, https://www.nytimes.com/2022/01/18/nyregion/trump-organization-fraud-letitia-james.html.

alongside a separate criminal investigation led by Manhattan District Attorney Alvin Bragg.

On July 1, 2021, the Trump Organization's financial chief pleaded not guilty to a sweeping tax fraud. Although Trump himself was not charged, he's the head of the organization that has been charged with tax fraud.

SEXUAL ASSAULT CHARGES

Trump also faces several lawsuits brought on by women who have accused Trump of defamation based on sexual assault charges.

Author and journalist E. Jean Carroll filed a defamation lawsuit against Trump after he denied her accusation that he raped her in a Manhattan department store in the mid-1990s. Trump accused her of lying to sell her new book.[467]

SCIENTIFIC SKEPTICISM

Anti-science (scientific skepticism) is a distinction of the Trump administration. In fact, when the Biden transition team delved into Trump's climate change and EPA rollbacks, they were shocked to find how much damage had been inflicted on science. They found deep budget cuts, wide staff loses, and systematic elimination of climate programs.[468]

Anti-science is the dismissal of mainstream scientific and medical views and their replacement with unproven or misleading theories. Anti-science advocates typically target prominent scientists, such as Rachel Carson, James Hansen, or Anthony Fauci. The verbal attacks on Fauci carried out by members of the House and Senate sow discord among the American public. Fauci has received death threats, and his family has been threatened as well. Senator Rand Paul, in my opinion one of Fauci's chief accusers, might be responsible for some of these threats to the Fauci family.

---

[467] E. Jean Carroll, *What Do We Need Men For?: A Modest Proposal* (New York: St. Martin's Press, 2019).
[468] Adam Aton, "Biden Climate Team Says It Underestimated Trump's Damage," *Scientific American*, January 6, 2021, retrieved April 3, 2021, https://www.scientificamerican.com/article/biden-climate-team-says-it-underestimated-trumps-damage/.

According to Peter J. Hotez, anti-science has caused mass deaths in the COVID-19 pandemic. He says that the Trump White House began dispensing misinformation about the pandemic early in 2020.[469]

Anti-science sentiment is a major force directing people's behavior and beliefs not only in science and medicine, but in many aspects of life. It's a global phenomenon and is leading to the unwarranted deaths of thousands of people. For example, ignoring the COVID-19 advice from the CDC caused the virus to spread among the unvaccinated populations in every country. Hotez reports that according to multiple polls, Republicans—specifically white male Republicans—are the most vaccine-resistant group in America. Also, Republican governors have defied mask and social distancing protocols by lifting these restrictions much earlier than advised by the CDC. And in a recent poll, many people ages eighteen to twenty-four have indicated that they will not be vaccinated because they think they are immune to the virus.

SARS-COV-2 PANDEMIC

Although there are no legal issues at this time associated with Trump's behavior during the pandemic, I wrote earlier in the book that he created an absolutely chaotic COVID-19 disaster. Trump should be held liable for his irresponsible response to the virus. He knew that the virus was a serious threat to the country, yet he spent most of his time downplaying the seriousness of the disease and disregarding scientific warnings. He offered advice that bordered on criminal behavior, promoting hydroxychloroquine and bleach against medical advice.

Trump failed to unify the country to deal with the COVID-19 pandemic. Instead, he sowed division amongst the states and blamed individual governors instead of coming to their aid. Trump's COVID-19 response coordinator, Dr. Deborah Birx, said that thousands of people died needlessly during the pandemic. She said that 100,000 people died

---

[469] Peter J. Hotez, "The Antiscience Movement Is Escalating, Going Global and Killing Thousands," *Scientific American*, March 29, 2021, https://www.scientificamerican.com/article/the-antiscience-movement-is-escalating-going-global-and-killing-thousands/.

from the first surge, but additional deaths could have been prevented.[470] Other scientists said that Trump and his White House advisors pressured them to change scientific reports to reflect the administration's spin on the pandemic rather than level with the American people.[471]

The virus has not been contained. Mutations of viruses are common and neither new nor unexpected. In the case of coronavirus, different versions have emerged in various parts of the world. The Alpha variant appeared in the UK in the fall of 2020. Other variants have appeared in Brazil (Gamma), South Africa (Beta), the UK and India (Delta), and southern African nations (Omicron).

The Delta variant was first detected in the UK and India in April and May 2021. Delta is highly infectious and caused waves of infections in those countries. In India, confirmed cases exceeded 400,000 per day. Unvaccinated people who contract the virus are more likely to end up in a hospital. The Delta variant infected thousands of people in United States, with more than 150,000 infections per day in late 2021. But the Omicron variant has spread throughout the world and by early 2022 had infected millions of people on a daily basis. The Omicron spike in infections is more than two times greater than the Delta spike in 2021.

If there are people who are not vaccinated, the virus will continue to spread and new variants will evolve. COVID-19 will be a health threat until it is contained, and containment will not happen until a large part of the Earth's population is immune. My personal physician told me that Omicron might be a blessing in disguise. Although it is spreading rapidly and infecting a lot of people, it is not as severe as the Delta variant. More people will be infected, but most won't get very ill, and this will mean that large numbers of people will develop some type of immunity to the virus.

Many of the nonpharmaceutical mitigations need to be used by vaccinated as well as unvaccinated people. Wearing masks and social distancing

---

[470] Sheryl Gay Stolberg, "Covid-19: Birx Lashes Trump's Pandemic Response and Says Deaths Could Have Been 'Decreased Substantially,'" *New York Times*, June 11, 2021, retrieved April 6, 2022, https://www.nytimes.com/live/2021/03/28/world/covid-vaccine-coronavirus-cases.
[471] Stolberg, "Covid-19."

are still two effective mitigation strategies that we should continue to use. Bringing unvaccinated children to school will potentially lead to unnecessary deaths and illness unless mitigation methods are used by all students, teachers, and staff. Let's be clear: all teachers and staff must be vaccinated, and students need to wear masks and social distance.[472]

EXISTENTIAL THREATS: CLIMATE CHANGE AND NUCLEAR WAR

Climate change and nuclear war are existential threats facing the world that cannot be ignored by politicians and citizens. Depending upon which party has control in the House and the Senate, climate change will either be dealt with or not. This is a dangerous situation. Climate change is real. All the research suggests that a hotter planet will make many areas of the Earth uninhabitable in the next fifty to one hundred years. Regardless of political party, climate change needs to be at the top of America's policy decisions.

The Biden administration is making climate change a central aspect of its governing strategy. Director of National Intelligence Avril Haines says that climate change will be at the center of US foreign policy. She urges attention to rising sea levels, droughts, crop failures, fires, diseases, and more frequent severe weather.[473] The challenge here is finding a way to overcome the polarization of political actors who will bring harm to the nation if they let their party rule rather than take what we know is the correct path to follow.

The Earth is getting hotter with each passing year. In June 2021, astounding heat waves broke all-time records across the Pacific Northwest and western Canada.

For example, the average temperature in Portland, Oregon, during the heatwave was 112 degrees Fahrenheit, more than 6 degrees higher than previous records. In some locations in western Canada, temperatures

---

[472] Robert Bollinger and Stuart Ray, "New Variants of Coronavirus: What You Should Know," Johns Hopkins Medicine, February 22, 2021, retrieved April 3, 2021, https://www.hopkinsmedicine.org/health/conditions-and-diseases/coronavirus/a-new-strain-of-coronavirus-what-you-should-know.
[473] Glenn Thrush and Julian E. Barnes, "Biden's Intelligence Director Vows to Put Climate at 'Center' of Foreign Policy," New York Times, May 4, 2021, retrieved May 7, 2021, https://www.nytimes.com/live/2021/04/22/us/biden-earth-day-climate-summit#bidens-intelligence-director-tells-world-leaders-climate-is-now-at-the-center-of-us-foreign-policy.

surpassed 120 degrees Fahrenheit. Nearly one-third of Americans experienced a weather disaster in the summer of 2021. Hurricanes and fires have devastated hundreds of communities and especially left marginalized people to suffer. We have to become a climate-conscious species.

The United States and other countries that developed nuclear weapons have refused to sign on with the United Nations Treaty on the Prohibition of Nuclear Weapons, which was adopted in 2017.[474] Although they refuse to sign on, they have a moral obligation to use diplomacy to rid the world of nuclear weapons. This must be a goal; otherwise, we might wonder why we have turned the planet Earth into a nuclear time bomb.

Climate change and nuclear threats reflect a deep psychological illness that has led to the normalization of behavior that has put the entire living world in danger of extinction. These are examples of an existential malignant normality. These two threats are here now. We must deal with them.

Robert Jay Lifton writes[475] that two events in recent decades provide some hope that we can avoid extinction. The first event was when International Physicians for the Prevention of Nuclear War was awarded the Nobel Peace Prize in 1985. Delegates from sixty countries were in attendance when the Nobel Prize was awarded. The second event was the Paris Agreement on climate change in 2015, when approximately two hundred countries signed on to the plan. And I would add a third. Even with the world dealing with a pandemic, nearly two hundred countries participated in COP26 in November 2021 in Glasgow. Lifton believes that these events are a step forward in which humankind uses its mental assets on behalf of all species on the earth. To sustain our habitat and civilization will require action. I believe this is possible. It will require a level of collaboration and cooperation that exists in the human species, and there are many examples from which to draw.

---

[474] ICAN: https://www.icanw.org/.
[475] Robert J. Lifton, *The Climate Swerve: Reflections on Mind, Hope, and Survival* (New York: The New Press, 2017).

FINAL WORDS

The Trump Files reveals the wide range of harm brought on American democracy, human rights, science, and public health by Donald Trump and his administration.

Unfortunately Donald Trump is advancing the Big Lie with support from a large group of sycophants in the United States Congress and millions of followers from around the country. Imagine it is 2024, and at the RNC, Donald Trump becomes the party's nominee for president again for the third time.

Recall that Lawrence Douglas wondered if Trump would leave the White House no matter what the outcome of 2020 election. Douglas asked, "Will he go?"[476]

Now the question is: Will he run? According to many journalists and political scientists, the likelihood is that Trump desires to run again. That Trump could be elected president again and return to the White House will in my opinion be the third existential threat facing the world.

I'll be eighty-four when the 2024 election comes around, and I'll be casting my ballot by mail come hell or high water. The Republicans in Georgia have gone out of their way to make it harder to vote. But those of us who care about free and fair elections will be out in droves. Look out for us.

As Congressman John Lewis reminded us: "The vote is precious. It is almost sacred. It is the most powerful nonviolent tool we have in a democracy."[477]

---

[476] Douglas, *Will He Go?*
[477] Public Broadcasting Service, "Rep. John Lewis: 'Your Vote Is Precious, Almost Sacred,'" PBS News Hour, September 6, 2012, retrieved April 6, 2022, https://www.pbs.org/newshour/show/rep-john-lewis-your-vote-is-precious-almost-sacred.

FURTHER READING

Acho, Emmanuel. *Uncomfortable Conversations with a Black Man.* New York: Flatiron Books, 2020.

Applebaum, Anne. *Twilight of Democracy: The Seductive Lure of the Authoritarian State.* Toronto: Signal, 2020.

Ault, Charles R. Jr. *Challenging Science Standards: A Skeptical Critique of the Quest for Unity.* Lanham: Rowman & Littlefield, 2015.

———. *Beyond Science Standards.* Lanham: Rowman & Littlefield, 2021.

Barry, John M. *The Great Influenza: The Story of the Deadliest Pandemic in History.* New York: Penguin Books, 2004.

Bauer, Bob, and Jack Goldsmith. *After Trump: Reconstructing the Presidency.* Washington, DC: Lawfare Press, 2020.

Blight, David W. *Frederick Douglass: Prophet of Freedom.* New York: Simon & Schuster, 2018.

Bonneuil, Christophe, and Jean-Baptiste Freessoz. *The Shock of the Anthropocene: The Earth, History and Us.* New York: Verso, 2017.

Bowen, Mark. *Censoring Science: Inside the Political Attack on Dr. James Hansen and the Truth of Global Warming.* New York: Dutton, 2008.

Bronowski, Jacob. *Science and Human Values.* New York: Harper & Row, 1972.

Carson, Clayborne. *The Autobiography of Martin Luther King, Jr.* New York: Grand Central Publishing, 1998.

Carson, Rachel. *Silent Spring.* London: Hamish Hamilton, 1962.

Cohen, Michael. *Disloyal, a Memoir: The True Story of the Former Personal Attorney to President Donald J. Trump.* New York: Skyhorse Publishing, 2020.

Dáte, S. V. *The Useful Idiot: How Donald Trump Killed the Republican Party with Racism and the Rest of Us with Coronavirus.* Sounion Books, 2020.

Davis, Mike. *The Monster Enters: COVID-19, Avian Flu, and the Plagues of Capitalism*. New York: OR Books, 2020.

Dean, John W., and Bob Altemeyer. *Authoritarian Nightmare: Trump and His Followers*. Brooklyn: Melville House, 2020.

Douglas, Lawrence. *Will He Go?: Trump and the Looming Election Meltdown in 2020*. New York: Twelve, 2020.

Finn, Peter. *The Mueller Report: The Washington Post*. New York: Scribner, 2019.

Graham, Loren. *Lonely Ideas: Can Russia Compete?* Cambridge, MA: The MIT Press, 2013.

Guerrero, Jean. *Hatemonger: Stephen Miller, Donald Trump, and the White Nationalist Agenda*. New York: HarperCollins, 2020.

Hill, Fiona. *There Is Nothing for You Here: Finding Opportunity in the Twenty-First Century*. New York: HarperCollins, 2021.

——— and Clifford G. Gaddy. *Mr. Putin: Operative in the Kremlin*. Washington, DC: Brookings Institution Press, 2013.

Hochschild, Arlie Russell. *Strangers in Their Own Land: Anger and Mourning on the American Right*. New York: The New Press, 2016.

Johnson, Hannibal B. *Black Wall Street: From Riot to Renaissance in Tulsa's Historic Greenwood District*. Fort Worth: Eakin Press, 2007.

Kessler, Glenn, Salvador Rizzo, and Meg Kelly. *Donald Trump and His Assault on Truth: The President's Falsehoods, Misleading Claims and Flat-Out Lies*. New York: Scribner, 2020.

Lakoff, George. *Moral Politics: How Liberals and Conservatives Think*. Chicago: The University of Chicago Press, 2016.

Lazarus, Richard. *The Rule of Five: Making Climate History at the Supreme Court*. Cambridge, MA: The Belknap Press, 2020.

Lee, Bandy X. *Trump's Mind, America's Soul*. New York: World Mental Health Coalition, Inc., 2020.

———, ed. *The Dangerous Case of Donald Trump: 27 Psychiatrists and Mental Health Experts Assess a President*. New York: St. Martin's Press, 2017.

Leonning, Carol, and Philip Rucker. *I Alone Can Fix It: Donald Trump's Final Year*. New York: Penguin Press, 2021.

Levin, Dov H. *Meddling in the Ballot Box: The Causes and Effects of Partisan Electoral Interventions*. New York: Oxford University Press, 2020.

Levitsky, Stephen, and Daniel Ziblatt. *How Democracies Die*. Penguin Books, 2019.

Lifton, Robert Jay. *Climate Swerve: Reflection on Mind, Hope and Survival*. New York: The New Press, 2017.

Lozada, Carolos. *What Were We Thinking: A Brief Intellectual History of the Trump Era*. New York: Simon & Schuster Paperbacks, 2020.

Lytle, Mark H. *The Gentle Subversive: Rachel Carson, Silent Spring, and the Rise of the Environmental Movement*. Oxford: Oxford University, 2007.

MacLean, Nancy. *Democracy in Chains: The Deep History of the Radical Right's Stealth Plan for America*. New York: Viking, 2017.

Markowitz, Gerald, and David Rosner. *Deceit and Denial: The Deadly Politics of Industrial Pollution*. Berkeley: University of California Press, 2013.

———. *Lead Wars: The Politics of Science and the Fate of America's Children*. Berkeley: University of California Press, 2013.

Mooney, Chris. *The Republican War on Science*. New York: Basic Books, 2005.

——— and Sheril Kirshenbaum. *Unscientific America: How Scientific Literacy Threatens Our Future*. New York: Basic Books, 2009.

Oreskes, Naomi. *Why Trust Science?* Princeton: Princeton University Press, 2019.

——— and Erik M. Conway. *Merchants of Doubt: How a Handful of Scientists Obscured the Truth on Issues from Tobacco Smoke to Global Warming*. New York: Bloomsbury Press, 2010.

Otto, Shawn. *The War on Science: Who's Waging It, Why It Matters, and What We Can Do About It*. Minneapolis: Milkweed Editions, 2016.

Packer, George. *Last Best Hope: America in Crisis and Renewal*. New York: Farrar, Straus and Giroux, 2021.

Proenza-Coles, Christina. *American Founders: How People of African*

Descent Established Freedom in the New World. Montgomery: NewSouth Books, 2019.

Quammen, David. *Spillover: Animal Infections and the Next Human Pandemic*. New York: W. W. Norton & Company, 2012.

Rabb, Katherine A. *Censoring Science: A Stem Cell Story*. New York: National Coalition Against Censorship, 2008.

Ray, Sarah Jaquette. *A Field Guide to Climate Anxiety*. Oakland: University of California Press, 2020.

Rosenthal, Lawrence. *Empire of Resentment: Populism's Toxic Embrace of Nationalism*. New York: The New Press, 2020.

Schmidt, Michael S. *Donald Trump v. the United States: Inside the Struggle to Stop a President*. New York: Random House, 2020.

Slavitt, Andy. *Preventable: The Inside Story of How Leadership Failures, Politics, and Selfishness Doomed the US Coronavirus Response*. New York: St. Martin's Press, 2021.

Trump, Mary L. *Too Much and Never Enough: How My Family Created the World's Most Dangerous Man*. New York: Simon & Schuster, 2020.

———. *The Reckoning: America's Trauma and Finding a Way to Heal*. New York: St. Martin's Publishing Group, 2021.

US Global Change Research Program. *The Climate Report: The Climate Assessment—Impacts, Risks, and Adaptation in the United States*. Brooklyn: Melville House, 2018.

Vindman, Alexander. *Here, Right Matters: An American Story*. New York: HarperCollins, 2021.

Wallace-Wells, David. *The Uninhabitable Earth: Life After Warming*. New York: Tim Duggan Books, 2019.

Woodward, Bob. *Rage*. New York: Simon & Schuster, 2019.

——— and Robert Costa. *Peril*. New York: Simon & Schuster, 2021.

Wright, Lawrence. *The Plague Year: America in the Time of COVID*. New York: Knopf, 2021.

ACKNOWLEDGMENTS

This is a book that I didn't think I would write. Although my contributions to the field of science, science education, and global collaboration go back some years, other areas—such as writing about politics, democracy, voting rights, impeachment, and government—not so much.

So to write this book, I sought the support and advice from people in different parts of the world, as well as the scholarship and research produced by government agencies, historians, journalists, political scientists, philosophers, psychologists, and scientists. I amassed books, expanded my Kindle library, and filled binders and folders with articles and notes I made of their work. Many people contributed to this book. Without their tireless work, which was published in journals, magazines, books, and online, I wouldn't have been able to document my ideas. I have used footnotes to chronicle their literature, research, and findings. You will also find a selection of readings at the end of the book that identify many of the scholars and journalists whose work I studied and recommend to you. I thank all these individuals and take any blame if I didn't represent their ideas accurately and thoughtfully.

The content of the book depicts a malignant character who corroded the nature of American society and continues to do so. Many journalists and scholars in a wide range of fields described and answered questions such as how we got here and what were we thinking. Many people have helped me to try to answer these and similar questions. Following is my appreciation telling how and what they did to help me produce this book.

The first person who was aware of me writing this book was my wife, Mary-Alice Hassard. She insisted I write the book after witnessing my nightly temper tantrums caused by Trump and his minions. She also was the first person to read my initial manuscript. She encouraged me from the start, and the book never would have been completed without her help. We have been involved in each other's work from the day we met in Portland, Oregon, in 1984. In 1986, she joined me to travel with the Association for Humanistic Psychology (AHP) and Global Thinking Project (GTP) delegations to Russia to work with Russian colleagues, students, and families. She is an experienced teacher and educator, publishing consultant, and business owner. In 1987 one of our Russian colleagues in the Foreign Relations Department of the Russian Academy of Education said that Mary-Alice may have been one of the first Americans to teach Russian children. Your love and support is all I need.

Nearly a decade ago I discovered Charles "Kip" Ault's science education research. I based several blog posts on his research, especially in the areas of paleontology and the nature of science. In 2020, he shared chapters of his manuscript from his latest book, *Beyond Science Standards*, which was sequel to his 2015 book, *Challenging Science Standards*. A few weeks later, he wrote and asked me if I would write the foreword to his new book. It was an honor to write it and to be part of his book.

I mentioned to Kip that I was working on *The Trump Files* and was thinking about self-publishing. He had read some of the early chapters of the book and was extremely encouraging. He suggested that I consider Indigo: Editing, Design, and More, a company in Beaverton, Oregon, that provides support for independent authors. He gave me the name of an editor at Indigo, Kristen Hall-Geisler, who edited his books. He doesn't realize how important this introduction to Kristen meant to me. She is not only a professional editor, but also an author of *Take the Wheel: A Woman's Guide to Buying a Car Her Own Damn Self* and *Lightning in a Throttle: Three Early Electric Vehicle Victories*. She asked for a sample of my manuscript and after reading it said she would be happy to work with me. From a reader's review through line editing, proofreading, and Zoom meetups, she has advised me through the editing process and into the design process. I am indebted to her for giving me the professional council and personal advice that I needed to complete this work. Without her, it wouldn't have happened. Thank you, Kristen.

The completion of my book would have been impossible without the professional work of Jenny Kimura, who designed the cover and interior; Vinnie Kinsella, who prepared it for e-book conversion; Sarah Currin and Bailey Potter, who proofread the manuscript; and Kento Ikeda, who provided indexing.

And one more shout-out to Kip Ault. While I was working on the editing of the book with Kristen, I asked Kip if he would write the foreword to my book. He graciously accepted and for that I am forever grateful.

I wish to thank Paul Hillery, Charles B. Hutchison and Carol Maglio for reading and writing reviews of The Trump Files. Their reviews can be found on my blog at jackhassard.org.

I am grateful I met Paul through our mutual work in citizen diplomacy. He worked for the UN for 29 years, taught literacy at universities in Germany, Saint Petersburg, and Moscow and lectured on the UN in Germany, Russia and Scotland. Paul lives in Karlsruhe, Germany. Paul is a highly regarded in the international community and I am indebted for his support on this book.

Charles B. Hutchison was born in Ghana and now is professor of science education at The University of North Carolina at Charlotte. Charles has lived and studied in Africa, Europe and the U.S. I had the honor to direct his doctoral work at GSU from 1998–2001 and then to follow his work over the past two decades. Charles is an accomplished author and educational researcher, and I am privileged that he reviewed my book.

Carol Maglio is a colleague and friend who my wife and I met at the Round Top Antiques Festival in Texas in 2005. Carol is an antiques business owner and was a pioneer in the telecommunications field in the 1980s and 1990s. She graciously agreed to provide an analysis of my work from the standpoint of a citizen from Texas. Thank you Carol, for your advice and support throughout the project.

Don Peck, a fellow science educator and writing collaborator, read an early draft of the manuscript. He and I met in 1978 in New York City where we became members of a small writing team to write an elementary science textbook series. He is an author and recently published *Mineral Identification: A Practical Guide for the Amateur Mineralogist*. He taught high school chemistry, earth science, geology, and physics, and he directed an elementary science teacher education program at Fairleigh Dickinson University after being a science education administrator in New Jersey. His feedback on the early parts of the book were crucial in pushing me further. Thank you, Don, for supporting me throughout this project.

I want to thank Michael Dias, professor of biology education at Kennesaw State University, for encouraging me, giving me advice, and reading the first edition of the manuscript. Michael is one of my former doctoral students at Georgia State University. He is a research professor and coauthor of *The Art of Teaching Science* and *Science Teacher Educators as K–12 Teachers: Practicing What We Teach*, as well as author of numerous peer-reviewed science education research papers. We've known each other for more than thirty years, and his support was important to me.

Jennie Springer, PhD, former principal of Dunwoody High School and associate superintendent of instruction of the DeKalb County School District in Georgia, was instrumental in the emergence of the GTP and the exchange of American and Russian teachers and students. She was a participant in the first educator exchange in 1987 of our work with the Soviet Union. She and her Russian counterpart, Vadim Zhukov, director of Moscow School 710, agreed to support an exchange of fifteen students in 1989. This laid the groundwork for future exchanges, which were funded by the United States Information Agency. Dr. Springer did her doctoral research on the nature and philosophy of global thinking, which was one of the foundational studies in the field. Thank you, Jennie for your continued support and encouragement.

To personalize the importance of global collaboration at a time when nationalist devotions are emerging, even in democracies, I interviewed people from four countries who shared their insights and experiences.

There are many people in Russia who I wish to thank for welcoming us to their country, which was the Soviet Union when we first met. For two decades I had the privilege to work with colleagues in their country. The backbone of our collaboration involved many people, and I would like to express my very great appreciation for their inspiration and dedication to our early collaborations: Simeone Vershlovsky, Yuvanali Koulutkin, Galina Manke, Yulia Siroyezhina, Julia Gipperreito, Marina Goryunova, Alexander Orlov, Olga Olenynikova, Ludmila Bolshakova, Nadezhada Feruloyova, Valentina Zalim, Nadya Nevpokoeva, Galina Soukhobskaya, Alexei Matushkin, Vadim Zhudov, Anatoly Karpov, and too many others to list. They worked with us to write initial proposals, open the doors to their schools and institutions, and visit us in America to forge lasting and important ways to show that global collaboration is not only possible but also crucial for our well-being.

I want to offer my deepest thanks to Sergey Tolstikov and Anatoly Zakhlebny, who I have known since 1987. They were key educators in the development and establishment of the GTP in Russia. Sergey, a former teacher at Moscow School 710, education editor, and language consultant, went out of his way to welcome us and take a leading role directing activities of American teachers and students while in Russia. Sergey shared his life and experiences with us and was a crucial leader in the GTP.

Anatoly Zakhlebny introduced us to the Russian science community and supported the work of teachers in his country. He provided us with scientific and ecological educational advice, which were important factors in the success of our collaboration.

In the United States, there were many educators who supported our work by welcoming Russian colleagues into their homes and participating in delegations to Russia for many years. I would like to especially thank Stewart Brewster, Barbara Broadway, Helen Davis, Marcia Eidelman, Marylou Foley, Phil Gang, Cheryl Garner, Tom Greening, Trinna Johnson, Gary Lieber, Bob Maxfield, Dorothea McAlvin, Martha McIlveene, Robert Pike, Wayne Robinson, Lee Sisson, Dennis Springer, Catherine Warfield, Julie Weisberg, and Derek Whordley.

I want to thank Sara Crim, a former science teacher in Walker County, Georgia; GTP exchange teacher; and artist, for sharing her vision and beliefs about the value of having students from different nations live and go to school with each other. Sara led her middle school students on three exchanges to Russia to the cities of Chelyabinsk, Moscow, and St. Petersburg. She is a leader among teachers and contributed to improving relationships between the American and Russian people.

Mathew Searels, a former student at Lafayette Middle School in Lafayette, Georgia, contacted me via LinkedIn and shared his experience of participating in the GTP exchange project in 1998. Thank you, Mathew, for sharing how the GTP influenced your career and the work you are now doing in the world of forestry management.

Gail and Bill Fisher are parents of two students who traveled to Russia as part of the GTP exchange program. Thank you for offering your thoughts and opinions on the value of the exchanges, especially from the point of view of parents who trusted us to take their children to a foreign country.

In 1992 I was invited to Barcelona by Narcís Vives after he visited us in Atlanta. I met Ramon Barlam at his school in Callús on the first trip to Spain, and we have collaborated with each other since. Narcís and Ramon invited more than twenty schools in Spain to join the GTP. They are two of the world's most respected leaders who use the internet to foster global collaboration among student and teachers. To this day, they are involved in important telecommunications projects. Thank you each for becoming a part of my life and for supporting my work on this book. Your contributions are immense.

Roger Cross, a friend, colleague, and prolific Australian writer of science and science education books, wrote an important piece on the nuclear age for this book. Thank you, Roger and Jenny, for your support on this book and for becoming a part of our life.

Diane Ravitch, thank you for giving me permission to republish one of your blog posts. Diane is a historian of education and professor of education research at New York University and a voracious blog writer. Her books on education have been an important and influential part of my research and writing about education over the past twenty years.

Ed Johnson is one of the most compelling advocates for public education in Atlanta. His newsletters have provided me with his insight into how schools should serve students and why public schools are an important determiner of a democratic republic. Ed produced abundant analyses of the COVID-19 pandemic in the form of daily graphs and charts, which were important in telling the story of the virus in Georgia. Thank you, Ed, for sharing your research with me.

Dennis Adams, scientist and engineer from Tenerife Island, shared two important graphs during the early stages of the pandemic, which you will find in Chapter 11. Thank you, Dennis, for your graphs, but also for your advocacy of science and support of this work.

In 1981 the late Dr. Ted Colton asked me to join him on a group trip to the Soviet Union. That trip changed my life and nature of the work I did for the rest of my career at Georgia State University. I am indebted to this man, my dearest friend, who opened me to the Soviet Union and the Russian people.

To all of you mentioned above and to others: thank you for supporting me in the development of this book.

INDEX

#

1619 Project, 23–24
1776 Project, 23
1918 influenza pandemic, 222–224, 251, 256–258, 260

A

Abrams, Stacey, 41, 85, 87, 114, 310
Academy of Pedagogical Sciences (USSR), 12, 34, 35
Adams, Dennis, 276–278
AES Corporation, 178
Affordable Care Act (2010), 58, 253–254
After Trump, 70
air pollution, 145–147, 155–156, 161–162, 167–168, 172
Allen, Arthur, 243
Alliance for Climate Education, 191
alt-right, 65–67
Ameren Corporation, 178
American Conservation Coalition, 191
American Electrical Power, 178
American Federation of Government Employees, 154
American Legislative Exchange Council (ALEC), 41–42
Amherst College, 303
Amnesty International, 91
Anderson, Carol, 96
Anthropocene, 175–177, 203
anti-Asian violence, 236
anti-mask movement, 246, 275, 279, 284–285, 288

anti-vaccine movement, 245–247, 251, 337
APA Dictionary of Psychology, 61
Applebaum, Anne, 39, 320–322, 332
Arbery, Ahmaud, 280–281
Arrhenius, Svante, 198
Art of Teaching Science, The, 3, 5
Association for Humanistic Psychology (AHP), 3, 10, 103
asylum, 43, 89, 105–107
Atkinson, Michael, 136
Atlanta Journal-Constitution, 114
Atlantic, The, 69, 108, 312–313
Ault, Charles "Kip," xi–xv, 6, 201
Australia
  bushfires in, 183–184
  nuclear tests in, 205–207
Axios, 262
Azar, Alex, 240–241, 268

B

Bachman, Michele, 32
Backer, Benji, 191
Bakaj, Andrew, 136–137
Baker, Charlie, 261
Ball, Alice Augusta, 198
Bannon, Steve, 31–32, 39, 86, 305, 334
Barber, William J., II, 49–51, 110
Barlam, Ramon, 216–217
Barr, William, 124–128, 137–138, 304
Barrett, Amy Coney, 286–287
Barrett, Vic, 191
Barry, John, 223–224
Bauer, Bob, 70

Bears Ears National Monument, 151
Bell, Derrick, 24–25
Berkeley Center for Right-Wing Studies, 31
Berkshire Hathaway, 178
Bernhardt, David, 151, 163
Beutler, Jaime Herrera, 325
Beyond Belief, 206
Beyond Science Standards, xv, 201
Biden, Hunter, 121, 127, 134, 138
Biden, Joe
    appointees of, 152, 153, 156, 339
    COVID-19 and, 232, 244–245
    Donald Trump's attempted investigation of, 127, 138–145
    presidential inauguration of, 1, 301
    voting rights and, 100
"Big Lie," 41, 95–100, 302–303, 307, 322, 326, 329–331
BioNTech, 243–244
birtherism, 72–73
Birx, Deborah, 241, 257, 270, 273, 337–338
Black Lives Matter, 23, 85, 94, 317
bleach, 147, 289
Blitzer, Jonathan, 32–33
Blow, Charles, 86–88
Bolsonaro, Jair, 217
Bolton, John, 47–48
Bonhomme, Edna, 246
Bonneuil, Christophe, 176–177
Boortz, Neal, 21
border wall, 88–91
Boston University, 2
Bottoms, Keisha Lance, 264
Bowen, Mark, 199
BP, 177
Bragg, Alvin, 336
Brandeis University, 244

Breitbart News Network, 31
Brennan Center for Justice, 43, 96–97
Brooks, Mo, 33
Burr, Richard, 137
Bush, George H. W., 14, 201
Bush, George W., 56, 129, 143–144, 170, 200
Bush, Vannevar, 142
Bush v. Gore, 129, 170
Butler, Jay, 239

C

Cain, Herman, 70
CalFire, 185
California Department of Forestry and Fire Protection, 185
Camp Fire (2018), 184
Campaign for Nuclear Disarmament (CND), 206
Cannon, Park, 41
Caputo, Michael, 152–153
Carnegie Institution of Washington, 141
Carroll, E. Jean, 336
Carson, Rachel, 198, 336
Carter, Jimmy, 169
Catalan independence movement, 217
Catalyst, 164
censorship of science, 140, 145, 159–160, 198–200
Center for Climate Science Communication, 165
Center for Science & Democracy, 167
Centers for Disease Control and Prevention (CDC)
    China and, 225, 239, 268
    communication guidelines of, 223

contact tracing and, 260–261
guidance for schools, 251, 271, 293, 298–299
test kits and, 241–242, 269
Trump administration interference in, 145–148, 152–153, 237–241
Cetron, Martin, 238
Charlottesville, Virginia, 66, 110
charter schools, 64
Chauvin, Derek, 92
Chechnya, 38
chemical safety, 162
Chevron, 177
Chicago, 112
child separation. *See* family separation
China
    COVID-19 and, 224–225, 239, 268–270
    COVID-19 vaccine and, 243–244
    Donald Trump blaming COVID-19 on, 236, 270–271
    nuclear weapons and, 210–211
Christie, Chris, 287
Chronicle of Higher Education, 102
Chu, Steven, 144
citizen diplomacy, 3–4, 10–12, 33–37, 102–105
Citizens for Clean Energy, 156
Civil Rights Act (1964), 94
Clean Air Act, 172
Clean Water Act, 171–172
Climate Action Now Act, 180
climate change, 65, 191–203
    conspiracy theories about, 63, 72, 202
    extreme weather events and, 30, 173–190

climate change denial, 65, 186–190, 192–193, 201–203
climate grief, 193–197
Clinton, Bill, 169, 201
Clinton, Hillary, 50
    2016 presidential election and, 62, 129
    hacking of the Clinton campaign, 9, 15, 39, 122–123, 128, 131–133, 160–161
coal, 150–151, 168, 177
Coats, Dan, 47
Cohen, Jon, 272–274
Cohen, Michael, 47–48, 131, 133
Collins, Francis, 228
Comey, James, 74, 76, 123, 130, 133, 161, 320
Communist Party of the Soviet Union, 36, 320
Constitution of the United States, 121, 325–326, 333
    First Amendment of, 112
    Fifteenth Amendment of, 117
    Nineteenth Amendment of, 116–117
    Twenty-Fifth Amendment of, 112, 319
    contact tracing, 250–251, 260–262, 266, 278–279
COP26, 204, 340
Cordero, Carrie, 332
Coronavirus Task Force, 224, 240–241, 268–271, 275, 279
Costa, Robert, 47
Cotton, Tom, 226
COVID-19
    anti-mask movement and, 246, 275, 279, 284–285, 288
    anti-vaccine movement and, 245–247, 251, 337

contact tracing and, 250–251,
    260–262, 266, 278–279
death toll of, 16, 271–272, 276,
    291
Donald Trump contracting,
    285–289
education and, 247–251, 290–
    300, 339
masks and masking, 224,
    250–251, 258, 263–264, 279,
    284–285, 296–300, 338–339
origins of, 226–236
tests and testing of, 148, 265–
    266, 269–272, 278
timeline of, 268–272
Trump rallies and, 69–70, 286–
    288, 309
vaccines for, 243–245
variants of, 247, 250–251, 338
voting and, 114–118
creationism, 26
Crim, Sara, 217–218
critical race theory (CRT), 23–27,
    307
Cromwell, Oliver, 57–58
Cross, Roger, 77–79, 205–207
Crossfire Hurricane (FBI
    investigation), 123
CrowdStrike, 137
Crowfoot, Wade, 187–188
Crutzen, Paul, 176
Cruz, Ted, 63, 316, 326–327
Cuban Missile Crisis, 212
Customs and Border Protection
    (CBP), 90

D
*Dangerous Case of Donald Trump,
The*, 80, 281
dangerousness, 61–62
Davydov, Vasily Vasilovich, 12

de Blasio, Bill, 295–296
Delgado, Richard, 25
Democratic National Convention,
    49–50
deregulation, 140, 149–151, 155–156,
    161–165, 189
DeVos, Betsy, 63–64
DeWine, Mike, 281
Dias, Mike, 235
Domestic Policy Council, 32
Douglas, Lawrence, 303–304, 341
Douglass, Frederick, 25
Dow Chemical, 29
drilling and extraction, 151, 155, 162
Droegemeier, Kelvin, 147, 149
Duda, Andrzej, 39
Duhigg, Charles, 69
Duke, David, 110
Duke Energy, 178
Duke University, 32
Durbin, Dick, 108
Durkee, Alison, 314

E
Eastern Michigan University, 160
Eastman, John, 334
Edel, Anastasia, 94–95
education
    Betsy DeVos and, 63–64
    COVID-19 and, 247–251, 290–
        300, 339
    critical race theory and, 23–27,
        307
Eighty Percent Coalition, 319
Eisenberg, John A., 134–135
Eisenhower, Dwight, 102
El Salvador, 89, 105, 203
Ellis, Michael, 135
Emory University, 96
empathy, 28, 45, 52, 74–77, 220
Environmental Defense Fund, 156

Environmental Integrity Project, 163
Environmental Protection Agency (EPA)
    Supreme Court decisions and, 172
    Trump administration rollbacks and censorship of, 55–57, 144–148, 155–157, 159–160, 161–168, 202
    Trump appointees to, 149–151, 178
Erdoğan, Recep Tayyip, 39
ESALEN, 10
European travel ban, 270
Excel Energy, Inc., 178
ExxonMobil, 177, 178, 193

F

Facebook, 128, 131–132
Fair Fight, 41, 85, 87
Fallout, 205
family separation, 89–90, 107
Farmer, Paul, 261
Fauci, Anthony
    on contract tracing, 262
    on COVID-19 death toll, 270
    on hydroxychloroquine, 288
    on masking, 263, 285
    on the origins of COVID-19, 226
    on physical distancing, 257, 272–274, 279–280
    on reopening schools, 248–249
    threats made against, 148, 336
    on vaccine hesitancy, 245
Federal Bureau of Investigation (FBI)
    January 6th insurrection and, 67, 306, 323
    Russian electoral interference and, 39, 122–123
    targeting of political dissent by, 93–94
    voter suppression and, 106
Federal Emergency Management Agency (FEMA), 147, 180–181
Ferguson, Missouri, 22–23
Field Guide to Climate Anxiety, A, 17, 203–204
Fiorina, Carly, 62
First Energy, 178
Fisher, Bill, 34
Fisher, Gail, 34
Fitzgerald, Brenda, 152
Flint, Michigan, 162
floods and flooding, 30, 163–164, 174–175, 179, 197
Floyd, George, 92–93, 109–110, 280–281
Flynn, Michael, 123, 131, 133, 315
Foley, Marylou, 11
Food and Drug Administration (FDA), 146
For the People Act, 333
Forbes, 160, 281, 314
Ford, Gerald, 149
Ford Motor Company, 284
Fox News, 30, 76, 181, 192, 269
Francis (pope), 79
Franco, Francisco, 217
Frazier, Darnella, 93
"Free America" (Packer), 20–23
Freedom House, 43, 301
Freedom to Learn, 12
Freedom to Vote Act, 97–98
Freeman, Joanne B., 305–306
Fressoz, Jean-Baptiste, 176–177
Frey, Chris, 167
Friday for Future, 191, 196
Friedman, Stephen, 250
Frieler, Katja, 205
Fulton County, Georgia, 5, 302, 323, 335

G

Gaddy, Clifford G., 38
Gang, Phil, 34
Gao, George, 239
Garland, Merrick, 169
Gates, Rick, 39, 131
Geltzer, Joshua, 282
General Dynamics, 90
George Mason University, 165
Georgetown University, 226, 282
Georgia (Caucasus), 38, 320–321
Georgia (United States), 5, 27
    2020–2021 elections and, 5, 41, 87–88, 310–314
    COVID-19 and, 223, 246, 258–260, 275, 290–293, 296–299
    voter suppression and, 41–42, 88, 98–100, 114–115, 341
Georgia Department of Public Health, 248, 258
Georgia State University, 3–5, 12–13, 290–291
Gingrich, Newt, 21, 67–68
Ginsburg, Ruth Bader, 168–172
Giroux, Henry A., 41, 44, 81
Giuliani, Rudy, 127, 135–138, 305, 315, 334
glaciers, 175, 179, 194–195
glasnost, 34
Global Thinking Project (GTP), 4–5, 12–15, 34–37, 104, 205–207, 214–220, 321
Gold Butte National Monument, 151
Goldberg, Jeffrey, 108
Goldman, Gretchen T., 147, 156, 167
Goldsmith, Jack, 70
Gonzalez, Anthony, 70
Goodman, Ryan, 282
Google Flu, 254, 270
Gorbachev, Mikhail, 4, 14, 34–36

Gore, Al, 129, 170
Gorman, Amanda, 18
Gosar, Paul, 316
Graham, Barney, 244
Grande, Ariana, 76
Great Influenza, The, 223–224
"Great Paradox" (Arlie Russell Hochschild), 28–29
Green Party (United States), 62
greenhouse gases, 155–156, 161–162, 172, 189, 199–200
Guatemala, 89, 105, 203
Guerrero, Jean, 33
Gupta, Sanjay, 233

H

Haaland, Deb, 152
Haines, Avril, 339
Haley, Nikki, 72
Hannah-Jones, Nikole, 23
Hannity, Sean, 21, 30
Hansen, James, 198–201, 336
Hansen, Terri, 160
Harlem riots (1964), 92
Harris, Kamala, 1, 313
Hartman, Arthur A., 11
Harvard University, 24, 144, 302
Hatch Act (1939), 154
Hate Monger, 33
Hawley, Josh, 326–327
health insurance, 253–254
heat waves, 178–180, 339–340
Helderman, Rosalind S., 124–125
Hicks, Hope, 288
Hill, Fiona, 38
Hitler, Adolf, 81–82, 112–113, 217
Hitzik, Michael, 233
Hochschild, Arlie Russell, 27–30, 68
Holdren, John, 144–145
Honduras, 89, 105, 203
Hoover, J. Edgar, 93

Hotez, Peter J., 337
Houston, Texas, 174
Huanan Market (Wuhan, China), 225, 230, 234
Hudson, Avon, 206
Hudson, Winson, 24–25
Hudson v. Leake County School Board (1963), 24–25
Hurricane Harvey, 30, 146, 164, 173–175, 197
Hurricane Maria, 85
hurricanes
    climate change and, 173–175, 202–203
    "sharpiegate," 147, 180–183
hydroxychloroquine, 285

I

Immigration and Customs Enforcement (ICE), 90, 93
impeachments
    first impeachment of Donald Trump, 126–127, 129, 134–138
    second impeachment of Donald Trump, 324–327
inaugurations
    of Donald Trump, 1, 54–55, 73
    of Joe Biden, 1, 301
influenza, 1918 pandemic, 222–224, 251, 256–258, 260
Inhofe, James, 150
Institut Cal Gravat, 216
Institute for General and Educational Psychology, 11
Institute of Adult Research and Education, 13, 36
Institute of International Education, 100, 103
Institute of Technology, 167
Intelligence Advanced Research Projects Activity (IARPA), 142
Intergovernmental Panel on Climate Change (IPCC), 192, 196, 198, 205
International Physicians for the Prevention of Nuclear War, 340
Internet Research Agency (IRA), 128
Iran nuclear deal, 147, 283
Italy, COVID-19 response in, 276–278, 299

J

Jackson, Lisa P., 144
Jacobs, Neil, 181–183
James, Letitia, 335
January 6th insurrection, 67, 305–308, 315–319, 322–327, 329, 332, 334
JASON (advisory group), 147
Jernigan, Dan, 239
Jimenez, Jose-Luis, 299
John Hopkins University, 275
John R. Lewis Voting Rights Advancement Act, 98, 100, 333
Johns Hopkins University, 276
Johnson, Ed, 248, 258–260, 297–298
Johnson, Randi, 153–154
Johnson & Johnson/Janssen vaccine, 243
Jones, Stephanie, 250
Journal of the American Medical Association, 256
Juneteenth, 83
"Just America" (Packer), 22–23
Just Security, 282

K

Karikó, Kati, 244
Keeling, Charles David, 200
Kelly, Megan, 62–63
Kemp, Brian, 41, 114, 119, 264–265, 312–313

Kennesaw State University, 235
Khan, Sadiq, 76
Kilimnik, Konstantin, 131
Kim Jong-un, 39, 81, 211
King, Coretta Scott, 106
King, Martin Luther, Jr., 23, 91–92, 93–94, 117
Kings Bay Naval Submarine Base, 208
Koch brothers, 21, 41
Korea, North, 210–213
Korea, South, COVID-19 response in, 242, 261, 276–279
Korean Air Lines Flight 007, 11, 103, 213
K-pop, 84
Kucharev, Anya, 10–11
Kushner, Jared, 78, 238

L

"lab leak" theory (COVID-19), 226–234
Lakoff, George, 51–53, 68, 71, 74–76
Lancet, The, 227
Lati, Marisa, 26
LaTrobe University, 205
Lazaroff, Cynthia, 213–214
Leake County, Mississippi, 24
Lee, Bandy X., 8, 46–47, 281
Leetaru, Kalev, 160
Lenin, Vladamir, 31, 320
Levin, Don H., 122
Levitsky, Steven, 330–331
Lewis, John, 54, 86, 101, 117, 341
Lewis & Clark College, xv
Li Zuocheng, 211
lies and lying, 84–85, 118–119, 180–183, 282
    See also "Big Lie"
Lifton, Robert Jay, 6–7, 61–62, 340

Limbaugh, Rush, 21, 30
Lindstrom, Stephen, 242
Lockheed Martin, 90
Loeffler, Kelly, 119–120, 311, 313
Los Angeles Times, 86, 193–194, 233
Lukashenko, Alexander, 93
Luminant Generation Company, 178

M

Macron, Emmanuel, 79
Macy, Francis Underhill, 3–4, 10
mail-in voting, 114–118, 333
Manafort, Paul, 39, 78, 131, 133
Manchester, England, 76–77
Manhattan Project, 141
Manke, Galena, xii
March for Science, 56–57, 161, 165–166
Margolin, Jamie, 191
Marietta, Georgia, 2
Markowitz, David, 84, 281–282
Maroons, 27
Marston, Hedley, 198, 205–207
masks and masking, 224, 250–251, 258, 263–264, 279, 284–285, 296–300, 338–339
Massachusetts Institute of Technology (MIT), 141
Massachusetts v. EPA, 179
Mattis, Jim, 81
McCain, John, 44–45, 58, 63
McCarthy, Kevin, 21, 324–326
McConnell, Mitch, 21, 59, 106, 111, 168–169, 326
McEnany, Kayleigh, 287
MCH Strategic Data, 249
McLellan, Jason, 244
Meadows, Mark, 305
Meddling in the Ballot Box, 122
Medicaid, 50, 58
Messonnier, Nancy, 239–240, 269

Mexico, 89, 105
Mika, Elizabeth, 80–81
Mikulicz, Johannes von, 224
military spending, 177
Milken Institute Global Conference, 58
Miller, Stephen, 31–33, 39, 86, 238
Miller, Todd, 90–91
Milley, Mark A., 211
Minds on Science, xiii, 3
Moderna vaccine, 243, 244
Mohan, Caroline Teisen, 67–69
Molnar, Daniela Naomi, 194–195
Monroe, Stephen, 241
Montana Environmental Information Center, 156
Mooney, Chris, 143
Moscow School 710, 34–36, 104
Mother Jones, 100
Mr. Putin: Operative in the Kremlin, 38
mRNA vaccines, 243–244
MS-13, 105
Mt. Hood, 194
Mueller, Robert S., 121, 124–126, 130–132
Mueller investigation and report, 124–134, 331
Mukherjee, Joia, 262
Murray, Patty, 152
Muslim ban, 32, 76, 86, 146
Mussolini, Benito, 81
Muzzle Award, 56

N

narcissism, 54, 80
Nation, The, 49
National Aeronautics and Space Administration (NASA), 142, 146–147, 160, 199–200
National Association for the Advancement of Colored People (NAACP), 25, 49
National Hurricane Center, 180–183
National Institute of Allergy and Infectious Diseases (NIAID). See Fauci, Anthony
National Institutes of Health (NIH), 142, 228, 237, 243, 254, 263
National Oceanic and Atmospheric Administration (NOAA), 160, 181–183
National Public Radio (NPR), 66
National Research University Higher School of Economics, 12
National Science Foundation (NSF), 142
National Security Council (NSC), 126–127, 134, 225
National Weather Service, 147, 181–182
Nature Medicine, 226, 228–229
Nature Reviews, 243
Navalny, Alexei, 94–95
Nessel, Dana, 284
Network for Public Education, 64
New Earth, 194–195
New England Journal of Medicine, 141, 225, 272
New Georgia Project (NGP), 87–88
New York Times, 64, 87, 94, 155, 163, 174, 292
Nichols, Monroe, 83
Nixon, Richard, 161, 212–213
Northrop Grumman, 90
nuclear weapons and disarmament, 205–214, 340
"nurturant parent" (Lakoff), 52, 75

O

Oath Keepers, 67

Obama, Barack, 1, 22–23, 73, 101, 144–145, 201
Obama, Michelle, 1, 77
Obergefell v. Hodges, 171
O'Brien, Robert, 221
obstruction of justice, 31, 125, 132–134
Ocala, Florida, 18
Ocasio-Cortez, Alexandria, 108
Occupational Safety and Health Administration (OSHA), 146
Office of Science and Technology Policy (OSTP), 144, 149
Office of Scientific Research and Development (OSRD), 141
Ohio State University, The, 3, 194
Olenynikova, Olga, 35
Omar, Ilhan, 108–109
Onushkin, Victor, 36
Operation Occupy the Capitol, 319
Operation Warp Speed, 147
Oregonian, 112
Oreskes, Naomi, 247
Orlov, Alexander, 11–12
Ossoff, Jon, 41, 87, 119–120, 311, 313–314
Oxford Handbook of Climate Change and Society, The, 192–193
Oyez, 171–172

P

Packer, George, 20–23
paid sick leave, 254
Papadopoulos, George, 131
Paradise, California, 184
Paris Agreement, 72–73, 144–147, 202, 283, 340
Parker, Linda, 328
Partners in Health, 262
Patriot Act, 94
Paul, Rand, 336
Peck, Don, 179
Pelosi, Nancy, 95, 318, 323
Pence, Mike
    COVID-19 and, 240, 268, 274, 293
    January 6th insurrection and, 95, 318–319, 323
    ratification of the 2020 election and, 302–304, 315, 323
People's Climate March, 57
People-to-People Student Ambassador Program, 102
Perdue, David, 108, 119, 241, 313
Perdue, Sunny, 153–154
perestroika, 34
Peril, 47
Petrov, Stanislav, 213
Pew Research Center, 19, 189, 329
Pfizer-BioNTech vaccine, 243
Pichler, Stefan, 254
Pinedo, Richard, 131
Pitt, William Rivers, 293–294, 330
Podesta, John, 160
polarization, 19, 28, 330–331
polymerase chain reaction testing (PCR), 225
Poor People's Campaign, 49
Portland, Oregon, 61, 111–112, 339
Potsdam Institute for Climate Impact Research, 205
Pottinger, Matt, 221, 240
Powell, John A., 68
Pressley, Ayanna S., 108
Prigozhin, Yevgeniy Viktoraovich, 128
Proenza-Coles, Christina, 26–27
Project Plowshare, 209, 212
ProPublica, 107, 174, 237–238
protest, 55–57, 91–95, 109–113
    See also specific protests

Proud Boys, 319
Pruitt, Scott, 57, 59, 147, 149–150, 159, 163–164, 167
Pulitzer Prize, 39, 88, 93
Putin, Vladamir, 4, 15, 37–40, 81, 93, 322
    Donald Trump's admiration for, 48

Q

QAnon (conspiracy theory), 246
Quammen, David, 234–235
Quayle, Dan, 302
Quinnipiac University, 329

R

racial equity, 86–88
racism, 25, 41, 108–111
Raffensperger, Brad, 5, 99, 118–120, 302, 313, 323, 335
Rasmussen, A. L., 226, 228–229
Ravitch, Diane, 25, 109–111
Ray, Sarah Jaquette, 17, 203–204
Raytheon, 90, 141
Reagan, Ronald, 14, 20, 103, 201
"Real America" (Packer), 22
Redfield, Robert, 152–153, 238, 239, 241
Regan, Michael, 155
Rehnquist, William, 96
Reilly, James, 140
Repairers of the Breach, 49
Republican National Convention (RNC), 50
Republican Party (United States)
    anti-vaccine movement and, 337
    voter suppression and, 41–43, 95–100, 306–307, 329–330, 332–333, 341

Rogers, Carl, 12
Röhm, Ernst, 112–113
Roosevelt, Franklin Delano, 110–111, 141, 317
Rosa, John, 160
Rosen, Julia, 193–195
Rosenstein, Rod J., 123–124, 130
Rosenthal, Lawrence, 30–31
Rosenwald, Julius, 24
Ross, Wilbur, 58, 181
Round Top, Texas, 28–29
Rubio, Marco, 63
Russell, Bertrand, 206
Russia
    electoral interferences by, 121–126, 128–133, 331
    experiences in, 3–5, 9–14, 33–37, 321
    nuclear weapons and, 210–211
    Vladimir Putin and, 37–40, 322
Russian Academy of Education, 12
Russian–Ukrainian war, 37–38, 40, 134
Rutgers University, 250

S

Sachs, Jeffrey D., 80, 91
San Juan, Puerto Rico, 85
Sanders, Jean, 276
SARS-CoV-2. *See* COVID-19
Savage, Michael, 30
Save EPA, 150
Schiff, Adam, 136–137
Schmidt, Michael, 135
Schneider, Mercedes, 2
school. *See* education
Schuchat, Anne, 239
Schwartz, Tony, 47
Science, the Endless Frontier, 141
Science Advisor to the President, 147, 149

Science, 272–274
Science as Inquiry, 3
science censorship, 140, 145, 159–160, 198-200
science denialism, 72, 140, 186–190, 283–284, 336–337
    See also anti-mask movement; anti-vaccine movement; climate change denial
Scientific American, 141, 203, 243
Searels, Mathew, 13–14
Sebelius, Kathleen, 144
September 2019 climate strikes, 191–192
Sessions, Jeff, 32, 89, 105–107, 123–124
"Sharpiegate," 147, 180–183
Shelby County v. Holder, 171
Sherwin, Michael, 334
Shock of the Anthropocene, The, 176
Silent Spring, 60
Silent Storm, 205
Sixth Assessment Report (2021), 198
"Smart America" (Packer), 21–22
Snowden, Edward, 94
social distancing, 255–258, 271, 274–275, 299, 338–339
Southerland, Elizabeth, 283
Southern Christian Leadership Conference (SCLC), 94
Southern Company, 178
Southern Poverty Law Center (SPLC), 105–106
Soviet Union
    electoral interferences by, 122
    experiences in, 3–5, 9–14, 33–36, 319–321
    nuclear weapons and, 209, 212–213

Spain, 216–217
    COVID-19 response in, 276–278
Spencer, Richard, 65
Spillover, 234–235
spillover (epidemiology), 226–236
Springer, Jennie, 139, 350
St. Charles, Louisiana, 28–29
Stalin, Joseph, 81
Stanford University, 91–92
stay-at-home orders, 275–276, 278–280, 284–285
Stefancic, Jean, 25
Stein, Jill, 62
Stelter, Brian, 79–80
Sterling, Gabriel, 313
Stevens, John Paul, 172
Stitt, Kevin, 83
Stone, Roger, 131
Stop the Steal, 319
stormtroopers, 111–113
Strangers in Their Own Land, 27–28
"strict father" (Lakoff), 52, 68, 71, 75
Supplemental Nutrition Assistance Program (SNAP), 154
Supreme Court of the United States
    the environment and, 171–172, 179
    Ruth Bader Ginsburg and, 168–172
    voting rights and, 117, 129
sycophant(s), 8, 15, 54, 82, 96, 194, 116, 119, 146, 149, 207, 265, 317, 322, 327, 329, 330, 341
Syria, 58

T

Tbilisi, 320–321
Tea Party, 28, 31
Tennessee Valley Authority, 178
Third Reconstruction, 49

This Is Zero Hour, 191
Three Percenters, 9
Thunberg, Greta, 191, 195–197,
    204–205
TikTok, 84
Tillerson, Rex, 47
Time, 189
Tinker, Barbara, 95
Tlaib, Rashida, 108
Tolstikov, Sergey, 104–105, 321
Toobin, Jeffrey, 126
travel bans
    European travel ban, 270
    Muslim ban, 32, 76, 86, 146
Treaty on the Prohibition of Nuclear
    Weapons, 209
Tribe, Lawrence, 302
Truman, Harry, 141
Trump, Donald
    2020 presidential election and,
        309–310
    COVID-19 case of, 285–289
    early relationship with Russia,
        14–15
    first impeachment of, 126–127,
        134–138
    mental health of, 46–48, 80, 211
    presidential inauguration of, 1,
        54–55, 73
    remarks about COVID-19, 268–
        273, 275, 279, 285, 289
    second impeachment of,
        324–327
    See also lies and lying; *specific
        policies*; *specific Trump
        administration officials*
Trump, Donald, Jr., 78, 123
Trump, Dr. Mary, 44–46, 47
Trump, Fred, 44–46
Trump, Ivanka, 238
Trump Organization, 131, 335–336

Truthout, 160, 293–294
Tufekci, Zeynep, 312–313
Tulsa rally, 82–84
Tulsa World, 83
Twitter
    disinformation accounts,
        127–129, 131
    Donald Trump and, 281
    rogue Twitter accounts, 55–56,
        160–161
tyrants, 80–81

U

Ukraine, 37–38, 40, 121, 126–127,
    134–138, 331
uninsured Americans, 253–254
Union Carbide, 29
Union of Concerned Scientists
    (UCS), 143, 145–147, 154, 156, 164
"Unite the Right" rally, 66
United Nations High Commissioner
    for Refugees (UNHCR), 89, 105
United Nations Intergovernmental
    Panel on Climate Change, 179
United Nations Treaty on the
    Prohibition of Nuclear Weapons,
    339
United States
    COVID-19 death toll, 271–272
    electoral interferences by, 122,
        331
    military spending of, 177
    nuclear weapons and, 207–214
United States Border Protection
    Services, 106
United States Department of
    Agriculture (USDA), 55–56,
    153–154
United States Department of
    Defense, 147
    nuclear weapons and, 210

United States Department of Energy, 144, 146, 155
　nuclear weapons and, 210
United States Department of Health and Human Services, 55–56, 144
United States Department of Homeland Security, 86, 113
United States Department of Justice, 2, 33, 43, 125, 304–308
United States Department of the Interior, 55–56, 151–152
United States Geological Survey (USGS), 140, 146, 155, 160
United States Information Agency (USIA), 36
United States Intelligence Community, 136, 226, 232, 331–332
United States Navy, 146, 208
United States Postal Service, 114–117
universal healthcare, 254–255
University of California, Berkeley, 27, 31, 51, 68
University of California, Davis, 102
University of Georgia, 250
University of Hong Kong, 122
University of Melbourne, 170
University of Notre Dame, 287
University of Oklahoma, 149
University of Pennsylvania, 244
USA Today, 88–89
USSR. *See* Soviet Union

V

vaccines, 243–245
　See also anti-vaccine movement
van der Zwaan, Alex, 131
Vindman, Alexander, 134–135, 138
Vindman, Yevgeny, 134–135, 138
Vives, Narcís, 215

Volkova, Inna, 10–11
von Ward, Paul, 10
voter suppression, 41–43, 50, 95–100, 114–120, 306–307, 329–330, 332–333, 341
Voting Rights Act (1965), 8, 98–99, 117, 333

W

Walensky, Rochelle, 153
Wall, The, 88–89
Walsh, Bryan, 262
Walter Reed National Medical Center, 287
Warnock, Raphael, 41, 87, 98–100, 119–120, 311, 313–314
Warren, Elizabeth, 106
Washington Post, 26, 63, 92, 115, 123, 162, 179, 254, 305–306
Watenpaugh, Keith David, 102–104
water pollution, 155, 161–163
Watters, Hannah, 298–299
Watts riots, 92
Wayback Machine, 159
Weissman, Drew, 243–244
Wheeler, Andrew, 150–151, 156, 167–168
White House Coronavirus Task Force, 224, 240–241, 257, 268–271, 275, 279
White House Science Fairs, 144
White Rage, 96
Whitmer, Gretchen, 285
WHO-Convened Global Study of Origins of SARS-CoV-2, 229–232
Whole Cosmos Catalogue of Science Activities, The, 3
Why Trust Science? 247
WikiLeaks, 39, 122, 160–161
Wild Protest, 319
wildfires, 183–190

Will He Go? 303–304
Willis, Fani T., 120, 335
Wolf, Chad, 112–113
Women for America First, 319
Women on the Run, 89
Women's March, 55
Wood, Lisa Godbey, 208
Woods Hole Research Center, 144
Woodward, Bob, 47, 147, 221
World Health Organization (WHO)
    declarations and reporting on COVID-19, 269–270, 299
    United States withdrawal from, 147, 271, 283
    WHO-Convened Global Study of Origins of SARS-CoV-2, 229–232
Wu Lien-teh, 224
Wuhan, China, 224–239
Wuhan Institute of Virology, 229, 231–233

Ziblatt, Daniel, 330–331
Ziebarth, Nicolas Robert, 254
Zinke, Ryan, 151–152
Zoom, 248
zoonotic transmission, 226–236

X
Xi Jinping, 236

Y
Yanukovych, Viktor, 134
Yates, Sally, 102
Yeltsin, Boris, 4, 37
Yersinia pestis, 224
Youth4Climate, 204
YouTube, 189

Z
Zakhlebny, Anatoly, xii, 219–220
Zapotosky, Matt, 124–125
Zelenskyy, Volodymyr, 126–127, 134–138, 331
Zernike, Kate, 64
Zhudov, Vadim, 35–36

ABOUT THE AUTHOR

Jack Hassard, professor emeritus of science education at Georgia State University, is an internationally known science educator, researcher, and writer. He is the author of more than fifteen books on science, environmental science, and science teaching, including *Minds on Science*, *Environmental Science on the Net: The Global Thinking Project* with Julie Weisberg, *The Art of Teaching Science* with Michael Dias, *Science as Inquiry*, *Science Experiences*, and *The Whole Cosmos Catalog of Science* with Joe Abruscato. For thirty-three years (1969–2003) he was a professor of science education at Georgia State University, where he was also the coordinator of science education. He developed several science teacher education programs, including the design and implementation of Teacher Education Environments for Mathematics and Science (TEEMS), a clinically based master's degree program for mathematics, science, and engineering majors. He directed the doctoral and specialist research of dozens of graduate students. He was a visiting professor at Florida State University, the University of Vermont, and the University of Hawaii. Starting in 1983, he participated in and then coordinated the Association for Humanistic Psychology's exchange program among North American and Soviet/Russian psychologists and educators. He was the co-director of the Global Thinking Project, an internet-based environmental program linking schools at first between Russia and the United States and then among many countries around the world. He has been blogging since 2005 at jackhassard.org. His blog writing served as the foundation for *The Trump Files*, his first venture into political science.

www.ingramcontent.com/pod-product-compliance
Lightning Source LLC
LaVergne TN
LVHW020434070526
838199LV00031B/626/J